The Islands

Other Books

The Great California Deserts
The Sierra
Canal across a Continent
God Bless Our Queer Old Dean
The Strength to Move a Mountain
Yankees of Connecticut
Green Mountains of Vermont
Town Father
Stagecoach North
Father Went to College

A Vanishing America (CONTRIBUTOR)
Bread Loaf Anthology (EDITOR)
Footpath in the Wilderness (EDITOR)

The Islands

W. STORRS LEE

Photographs by the Author

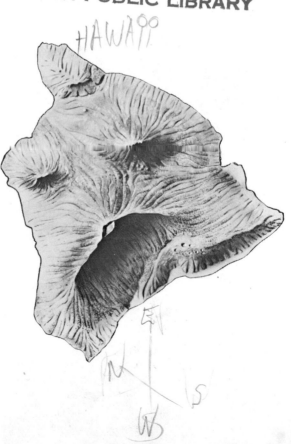

Holt, Rinehart
and Winston

NEW YORK   CHICAGO
SAN FRANCISCO

Designer: Ernst Reichl
85195-0316
Printed in the United States of America

To Jim and Elizabeth Murray

Acknowledgments

For *kokua* in the preparation of this book, I express appreciation particularly to: Miss Lucille K. Berg, Mr. and Mrs. Charles H. Bond, the Reverend B. R. Cleeland, Mrs. Gene Cox, Commander R. M. Robinson, Mr. Douglas L. Jocelyn, Mrs. Jeanne Booth Johnson, Mr. Karl H. Korte, the Reverend Thomas K. Kunichika, Mr. and Mrs. Ralph S. Minor, Dr. Howard Munford, Mr. and Mrs. James M. Murray, Mrs. Emma K. Sharpe, Miss Lois Stewart, Mrs. W. F. Robertson, and my wife Mary Louise; also to the librarians at Bowdoin College, Brunswick, Maine; the University of California, Berkeley, California; the University of Hawaii; and the Maui County libraries at Kahului, Lahaina, and Wailuku.

Contents

The Islands

The Invaders

The story of Hawaii is the chronicle of its invaders. Wave on wave they came, as if each was intent on dislodging a prior beachhead—Polynesians, European explorers, traders from half the marts of the world, Yankee missionaries, Yankee whalers, ranchers, planters, political opportunists, Asian and European field hands by the shipload, generals and admirals scenting out the best spot for a Pacific Gibraltar, fire worshipers bound for the volcanoes, travelers and journalists in search of the exotic, speculators in land, people and promise, legions of warriors en route to Oriental hunting grounds, tourists by the thousands, the tens of thousands, and the hundreds of thousands questing for an enchanted South Seas asylum.

Each invasion left an indelible impression on the Islands; each created a chapter in Hawaii's annals. Once westerners had added the island chain to their maps, there was no letup in the procession of newcomers—*malihinis*, as the natives called them. The only pro-

3

tracted intermission was in the centuries before the coming of Cook, and that was long enough to give the original invaders a chance to settle in and establish a way of life that has not yet been entirely uprooted. It is an affront to those settlers to credit Captain Cook with "discovering" the Sandwich Islands. The Polynesians had done that some fifteen hundred years before, and their exploit was far more glamorous than his.

Back in the early years of the Christian Era when European sailors were still hugging the coasts, fearing to pilot their hulking galleys out of sight of land, the Polynesians were already freely roaming the Pacific, without compass or sextant, in light canoes—twin canoes connected by a deck that could carry fifty passengers or more with a cargo of food and freight.

They set their course by the stars, the prevailing winds, familiar cloud formations, and a sixth sense, logging a hundred miles a day, and voyaging thousands of miles from home bases like the Marquesas Islands and Tahiti. These were the navigators that discovered and colonized the Hawaiian Islands before A.D. 500—perhaps as early as A.D. 200.

Then, as now, they were young islands that had been thrown up from the ocean depths in recurrent volcanic cataclysms, almost as a Creator's afterthought, two thousand miles from the nearest continental shelf. It was an untenanted land, as primeval as any spot on earth, relatively barren, improvident, virginal. The only life it supported was what had accidentally drifted there on the sea, been driven by the winds, or carried in flight.

Though the uplands and valleys were forested and the shores rimmed here and there with greenery, there were vast reaches of barren lava and windswept desert and no animal life except birds, a few insects, and creatures of the sea. It was no Garden of Eden they found.

But the Polynesians had populated scores of similar landfalls in the South Seas. They were past masters at establishing a foothold on such stark shores, and their husbandry was as good as their seamanship. Wherever their colonizing efforts were directed, they took along the makings of future plantations and a domestic menagerie. To Hawaii they brought subsistence essentials like taro, sugar cane, the South American sweet potato, breadfruit, a variety of coconuts, bamboo, gourds, dogs, pigs, fowl—and the rat as a stowaway.

For hundreds of years traffic was maintained between Hawaii and the homeland, and perennially great migrations were conducted over the thousands of ocean miles. Then, possibly in the interest of avoiding overpopulation, the voyaging gradually diminished and ceased altogether. The immigrants were on their own. For at least half a millennium they were independent of their South Sea cousins, completely isolated in the middle of the Pacific.

As generation after generation passed, their ancestors were remembered only in ancient chants and epic genealogies recited by professional bards; even some of the original gods were forgotten, and those still worshiped took on slightly altered names and authority. The unwritten language evolved into a dialect of Polynesian. Old habits and practices changed. In their isolation the islanders multiplied prodigiously. Communities grew into kingdoms. Yet kings and commoners alike remained completely ignorant of the rest of the world, ignorant even of its existence. The Hawaiian Islands were their world.

This was the social order that Captain Cook's chance discovery in 1778 threw into confusion and tumult. After that, waves of new invaders added relentlessly to the disruption. Other peoples had taken twenty thousand years to discard the last vestiges of the Stone Age and adapt themselves to standards of high living; in Hawaii the transition was telescoped into a mere century and a half. Little by little the old Hawaiian culture was abandoned, submerged, or commercialized. Each group of invaders had a go at trying to recast the natives in a foreign image, and all were remarkably successful—both the saints and scoundrels.

With equal success, they tackled the terrain, too, and tried to improve on nature and the efforts of the Hawaiians. They tore out ancient landmarks and created new ones, turned deserts into verdant expanses, converted grass-hut settlements into cities, coral-strewn shore fronts into palmy beaches, mountains into fortresses, wastelands into playgrounds, treacherous bays into harbors, inaccessible island outposts into popular tourist havens less than half a day from the West Coast.

In the process of taking over, they ravaged and they renovated, but they could not destroy the original charm of the place. To that, lens and imprint offer better testimony than expansive prefatory paragraphs. The setting still retains its enchantment, supplying of itself ample reason for the beckoning of so many invaders.

I
Strong Men Bow Themselves

They were as hale a people as lived anywhere on God's green earth—robust, vivacious, virile. By the western world's standards, they were a social contradiction—civilized savages, genteel barbarians; men of violence and of great compassion; an illiterate folk who had demonstrated a high order of intelligence and an aptitude for ingenious invention; macabre warriors who paradoxically loved to deck themselves in wreaths of pretty flowers. Three-quarters of the way through the eighteenth century, the world had fortunately not yet had an opportunity to impose its arbitrary standards upon the inhabitants of the Hawaiian Islands.

These sharp-witted Islanders still used tools of the Stone Age, the like of which more advanced races had abandoned thousands of years before. Yet they were not Stone Age men. Among them were talented craftsmen, canny fighters, excellent husbandmen, sculptors and scholars of a sort, shrewd conservationists, and engineers capable of constructing complex irrigation systems, massive stone temples, and serviceable breakwaters.

They had even dabbled in science. Amateur astronomers could identify over a hundred stars, and navigators plot a course by them far into the Pacific. Botanists had classified the principal trees and plants; geologists could sort out fifty different kinds of rocks; zoologists knew the habits and habitat of the birds and their migratory calendar, had made observations on the breeding and heredity of domesticated dogs and pigs, and had gathered such an ample knowledge of the many species of fish that seasonal bans for their protection had long been in effect.

They had a keen sense of rhythm and an innate fondness for music. They could sculpture from wood or stone awe-inspiring representations of the gods. Their dance was a highly developed art form. Everybody danced—solo, in chorus, in impressive extravaganzas. Though they had never discovered the art of writing, they had mastered the more demanding art of memorizing. They thought nothing of reciting historic annals, genealogy, or poetry by the hour, and, lest any of the learning become lost to time or altered, professional raconteurs acted as its custodians, filed it away in indelible memory, and passed it on by rote from one generation to the next. The Hawaiians were far from uncultivated.

Nor could the state of their civilization be judged by the apparel they wore. Except for the flowers bedecking necks and brows and the exotic head-to-foot tatooing, there was little to judge. The perennial summer discouraged toggery. A loinstrap *malo* was enough for the men; and a short-skirted *pau* sufficient for the women. To shed the rain or fend the night winds, a brief *kihei* of tapa was sometimes thrown over the shoulders, but it was not essential to the wardrobe. For men and women constantly in and out of the water, in and out of the sun, *malo* or *pau* made a sensible garb that remained in perpetual fashion. Children, of course, went naked, and their parents suffered no embarrassment when discovered in similar undress, though a certain modesty called for a free hand to substitute for a leaf in mixed company.

To such a free-living people, taking anything seriously came hard. Perennially they were at war with one another, but even war was accepted more with anticipation than foreboding. They made a game out of it, with the time and playing field often prearranged.

They were as playful a people as ever existed. Amusement came to them as easily as breathing, sleeping, or climbing a coconut tree. They laughed among themselves as though laughter were a language. They sported in the surf, sported on the beach, sported in the hills; they indulged in arduous athletic contests, had a game for every mood and enough nighttime diversions to keep the mountains echoing with revelry from dusk to dawn. They were born mimics, comedians, and practical jokesters. There was always time for play.

Work perhaps was secondary to fun making, but work they did, brutally hard, back-stooping, enervating labor, all by hand. They lived off the land and the sea, and, though both were provident, neither made it easy for them. The land was always rock-strewn, too dry or too wet, and the sea too turbulent. All the necessities for sustenance were there, but seldom handy. Half the task of making use of the bounty seemed to consist of shouldering loads over great distances.

Firewood, grass for thatching, bark for tapa, *lau hala* for mats had to be lugged in. Shore villages were often an hour's tramp from taro, yam, and sweet-potato patches. Giant tree trunks for canoe hulls and poles for house frames grew far up on the mountains and had to be dragged down over impossible terrain. Trails to the uplands and along the shores were worn deep by the tread of porters and calabash carriers.

Always there were home chores, too—the penned dogs and pigs to feed and tend, breadfruit and coconuts to gather, poi to pound, mats to weave, fresh water to be fetched from the hills and sea water for salt making, baking to be done in the outdoor ground oven, wood to be chopped laboriously with a stone ax. Yet none of this was drudgery. The Hawaiian worked with a song and a light heart.

In constructing great public works, the buoyant spirit was even more conspicuous. The village walls, the king's paved highway around an island, the temples, irrigation ditches, fishponds, all these were built *laulima*—with many hands—a cooperative effort in which everyone joined with obstreperous enthusiasm and off-color singing. As in warring, they turned the endeavor into a kind of sport, a bee, a competitive game in which one vied with another at hefting heavier rocks for greater distances, at felling loftier trees, at spading deeper—or at chanting longer and louder.

They were inalterably gregarious. In tamping the site of a ditch or pond with their bare feet, to make the bottom impervious, a thousand mudsplashed, sweating bodies would be packed so closely together that they had to raise their legs in unison, chanting to keep time. Brigades, enlisted to assemble rocks for major construction, stretched for miles; stationed an arm's length apart, heaving boulders one man to the next, the members could collect a small mountain of material in a day. Without wheels, without pack or dray animals, they performed miracles in weight lifting, in rolling and levering massive stones, and in skidding giant logs out of the mountains. The discipline and the exertion toughened and seasoned. They became giants, many of them strapping six-footers and better, with character as solid as the muscle.

Some forty or fifty generations had gone into the molding of Hawaii and Hawaiians. The work, the play, the climate, and the diet manifestly agreed with the descendants of the first Polynesian invaders, for by the 1700's little kingdoms existed on all the major islands and the total population had swelled to a third of a million. Noisy villages dotted the shores everywhere and crowded inland onto the plateaus. Cultivated lands extended deep into the valleys and up the bordering mountain sides, where sheer slopes were ingeniously terraced, the terraces packed with soil lugged up from below, irrigated, and planted to taro, plantains, and sweet potatoes.

The Islands were getting crowded, but the more the merrier. The rich volcanic soil could readily supply the demands of three hundred thousand and many more. Far removed from the chronic diseases of the continents, the Hawaiians were as healthy as they were happy. Their isolation was their boon. Nowhere was there a more contented people.

Poet-historians still recited chants that hinted of lands whence their ancestors had come, but the routes back had long been untraveled, and no one took much stock in the existence of a world outside their own. As much as anything, it was the ignorance of other worlds that kept them contented. They took for granted that theirs was the only way of life.

To be sure, there were shades of contentment, shades of happiness, occasional recognition of stark inequalities in class and in the distribution of Hawaiian largess. Chiefs, who claimed preferential honors and preferential shares, perpetually harassed their inferiors, but that was the way things had always been and always would be. Families who worked the land could never own it, and that bothered them not in the least. The land was common property, indivisible, eternal, like the sky and the seas. Individual ownership of property was beyond their conception.

So long had commoners lived without anything they called their own that they had no realistic sense of acquisition. Contentment had nothing to do with wealth. All they needed for the good life was a few bowls and calabashes, *lau hala* mats for bed and coverings, tapa strips for clothing, a spade, an ax, an assortment of fishhooks, lures, lines, and nets, flowers to pluck, and a thatched roof over their heads. Beyond these, possessions were an incumbrance.

Far from wanting to accumulate belongings, they had discovered that it was almost as blessed to give as to receive; giving things away was an irresistible pleasure, an indulgence, a form of temptation. The lower-class Hawaiian was a compulsive sharer; in presenting a gift, he was merely circulating common property.

Kings and chiefs were no less generous, but their benefactions were of a different cast. They handed out what had been collected in taxes and tribute from the commoners. It was not a product of the donor's personal sweat and toil. And their status required the accumulation of property, symbols of authority like priceless feathered capes, feather leis, and feather-topped ceremonial standards, canoes and cordage, mounds of woven mats and bolts of tapa, an armory of weapons, stacks of carved plates and platters and decorated gourd utensils, a vast piggery, and a storehouse of food.

Even this disparity was accepted by commoners without resentment. Every man knew his place. Under an island king were four major classes: the chiefs of high rank and royal blood—the *alii;* the professionals or specialists—*kahunas,* priests, medical practitioners, councilors, prophets, astronomers, seers, sorcerers, artisans, historians, teachers; the masses—*makaainana,* land laborers, comprising fully 90 per cent of the total; and slaves—*kauwas,* a small group of abominated outcasts whose ancestors from time immemorial had been slaves and whose offspring would continue to be.

The slaves owned nothing; the commoners owned nothing; neither the *kahunas* nor the chiefs actually owned anything. All property in the realm was in the name of the king, from the last square rod of terrain and shore front to the most personal chattel in the hands of a subject. The king alone held the power of life and death. He owned all and ruled all. And Hawaiians would have it no other way. They believed implicitly in the divine right of kings.

"It is probable," quaintly reasoned a philosophic subject who, after spending all his life under the kings, still wanted to account for the way in which the system of rulership had started, "that because it was impossible for all the people to act in concert in the government, in settling the difficulties, lifting the burdens and disentangling the embarrassments of the people from one end of the land to the other, that one was made king, with sole authority to conduct the government and do all its business."

In doing that business, the king usually was a benevolent despot. However, his subjects somewhat inconsistently limited their belief in the doctrine of divine right by insisting that he not be too oppressive or contentious. Every king lived with the uncomfortable knowledge that at least eight unworthy regional monarchs in the history of the Islands had been assassinated or banished by demurring rebels.

The royal duties included conscripting and commanding the armies, deciding all important questions of state, dealing out land grants to the chiefs and dispossessing those who neglected their responsibilities, collecting the annual taxes, consecrating the temples, serving as master of ceremonies at festivals, and, in the absence of any written or unwritten laws, periodically issuing and revoking a flux of taboos on anything from diet to devotions.

The king's person was sacred; everything about him from his glorious scarlet and golden cape of feathers to his very spittle was sacred. No ordinary mortal was permitted to come in contact with any of his personal effects, on pain of death. All his subjects prostrated themselves before him. If so much as the shadow of a commoner fell upon his Highness or his grass palace, the owner of the shadow was immediately impounded for capital punishment. That ancient taboo was at least one way of preserving the monarch from the fate met by the eight unpopular forerunners in office.

Guarded by these security precautions, he could live as convivial a private life as he chose, and the conviviality frequently went to extremes, for his court comprised a harem of royal-blooded wives, a corps of chiefs, relatives, friends, advisers, and assorted hangers-on. A king lived on the fat of the land, attended by a throng of trained servants and guardians—*kahus,* whose duty it was to anticipate his every desire and discomfort: valets, masseurs, fly-wafters, steward, sleep watchman, idol custodian, spittoon porter, even a master of the *pot de chambre.* All ranged within his royal beck and call while he carried on the affairs of state.

High chiefs lived in luxury somewhat less plush, low chiefs in ordinary calabash-oriented luxury, and so on down the scale. For purposes of administration, the king parceled out among the nobility enormous pie-pieces of the kingdom, ranging from a modest slice of a few thousand acres to a generous wedge of a hundred thousand. In order that the parcels might be distributed fairly, each, ideally, extended from sea to mountain heights, incorporating shore front, with access to fishing grounds and salt flats, a section of inland agricultural land with water rights, and above it a stretch of the forest zone for fuel, timber, bark, and—of utmost importance—birds, for feathers of rare color and fluff were the nearest thing to portable currency in the realm. The humpback geography of the Islands lent itself naturally to triangular carving, with the base of the triangle on the beach.

High chiefs subdivided these estates into substantial *ili*—plantations, which were granted to lesser chiefs, and these in turn were cut up into small home plots for the commoners, who paid for the privilege of tenancy whatever the landlord might requisition in produce, labor, fish line, *lau hala* mats, tapa rolls, or bird feathers, receiving in return protection and sustenance during periods of war or shortage. However, nothing about the royal grants, the plantations, or the home sites was permanent. Upon the death of a king, his successor, if he chose, could cancel all grants and start the parceling game all over again, to reward his special favorites and admirers.

Despite the fact that half or two-thirds of the land's produce went in taxes either to the king or a chief, an industrious farmer had little to complain about; the rich soil grew such prolific crops that a surplus was inevitable in a normal season. In the eyes of less diligent villagers, he was *waiwai*—prosperous. A lucky fisherman, steady woodsman, handy builder, or any other earnest laborer could do as well.

From enterprising producers came few murmurs about high tax rates. They regarded the assessments as "tribute," in the elemental sense, rather than tax—a share fully deserved by their superiors. Hawaiians, with their sentimental affection for the king, gave to him, in preference to all others. And the same kind of devotion and respect was often extended to the chiefs. There was an element of joy in bestowing upon them their due.

So firmly fixed was the sentiment that years after the feudal system had broken down and the sovereign was less nervous about having shadows cast upon him, the mass offerings of the commoners were continued under any pretext. "Not a man, woman or child came empty-handed," declared a witness to the ceremony of tribute, attended by a milling throng of thousands, hailing the king's visit to Hilo in 1873. "Some half dropped down on their knees, others passionately and with tears kissed the king's hand, or grasped it convulsively in their own. . . .

"Ancient men, tattooed all over . . . came up bewildered, trembling, almost falling on their knees, hardly daring to raise their eyes. . . . Many of the women presented live fowls tied by their legs, which were deposited, one upon another, till they formed a fainting, palpitating heap in the hot sun. Some of the men brought decorated hogs tied by one leg. . . .

"Hundreds carried nets of sweet potatoes, eggs and taro, artistically arranged. Men staggered along in couples with bamboo between them, supporting clusters of bananas weighing nearly a hundredweight. Others brought yams, cocoanuts, oranges, onions, pumpkins, early pineapples, and even the great delicious fruit of the large passionflower. A few maidens presented the king with bouquets of choice flowers and costly leis of yellow feathers. . . .

"There were fully two tons of taro and sweet potatoes, . . . hundreds of fowls and piles of bananas, eggs and cocoanuts . . . a beautiful sight, all the more so that not one came for anything that he could obtain. It was just the old-time spirit of reverence for the man who typifies rule, blended with the extreme of personal devotion . . . genuine and pathetic in its intensity."

But commoners did not limit their charity to royalty. They tramped long distances for the pleasure of bestowing a gift upon one of their own class; at home they gave with openhandedness to neighbors, relatives, strangers, to anyone who happened to pass by; they gracefully parted with any object a visitor made the mistake of admiring, and no insult was more cutting than a refusal to accept it. Entertainment of each other was equally unsparing. There might be little food on hand to offer, but what there was went unstintingly to the guest. *Mai kakou e pu paakai* (Come and share a little salt with us) was the spirit, always uttered in humility.

Chances were that half the produce left after taxes was given away or shared. Catching a bumper net of fish or dressing a plump pig were occasions for summoning friends to share in the bounty—all of it—in a festive fling, with impromptu dancing and games and free sex play. The generosity fitted neatly into the Island code of economy, for the benefactor of one day well knew that he could be a beneficiary the next.

Simplicity in entertainment, simplicity in shelter, simplicity in diet made the economy practical. Universally the diet was limited to fruit and vegetables like bananas, breadfruit, coconuts, berries, sweet potatoes, and yams, a wide assortment of sea food and sea mosses, occasional morsels of pig and dog—both fattened on vegetables—and poi.

Poi, a product of taro root that had been baked, mashed, and allowed to ferment slightly, was the staff of life, a satisfying meal in itself if there were nothing else on the menu, and, though the consumers were unaware of it, packed with so much nutriment and so many vitamins, healthful minerals, and multiple calories, that it was virtually a tonic as well as a glutenous food. Families could live on poi frugally and salubriously for weeks on end without anything else.

Housing was as unpretentious as the diet, though more careful craftsmanship went into the construction of a grass shack than the frowzy exterior hinted. From a distance, a settlement looked like a helterskelter collection of haystacks, picturesque and untidy. In reality a Hawaiian community was a village of villages, for every householder who minded the king's taboos had a cluster of shelters that was almost a village in itself: the central family structure for lounging, sleeping, and entertaining—the *hale noa;* a cookhouse or open shelter for the ground oven—*imu;* a men's eating house; a women's eating house; a private chapel in which the elder male of the family stored and worshiped his personal gods; a women's workshop for tapa beating and other domestic activities; and the *halau* or "long house," for anything from storage of canoes and fishpoles to hula practice.

In general, family life was complicated by the prohibitions against common use of the same building by men and women for dining and other routine activities. It was unthinkable, for instance, for a husband and wife to eat from the same dish or even share food cooked in the same oven. But many a laggard householder somehow managed to fulfill the taboos without cluttering his yard with outbuildings. Chiefs and *kahunas,* on the other hand, frequently had establishments of a dozen or more huts.

Considering the meager size of the shelters, a full housing complement represented no great extravagance either for chief or commoner. The construction cost nothing but the time, energy, and ingenuity that went into it. Framing poles came from the nearest forest, cord for lashing them together from readily available roots and fibers, and thatch from plots of *pili* grass, cane, ti, or *hala*—whichever happened to grow nearer. With the whole family working at it, a simple hut could be put together in a couple of days and a substantial *hale noa* in a week or two.

However, it took know-how. The frame was a network of notched wall supports, plates, rafters, and purlins, tightly lashed together at joints to withstand the thrusts of the trade winds. An accentuated hip roof, with sloping ends as well as sides, was the most common kind of covering. Woven horizontally into the frame was a screen of cross braces to which the thatch was tied. Where loose rock was handy, the lower part of the house was usually of stone, and in areas subject to flooding, the floor was often built on stilts.

One low door served both as entrance and window. Except in the stilt houses, the dirt surface was the floor, and over it were spread layers of *lau hala* mats to reduce contact with ground moisture in the rainy season, to screen out the larger insects, and to serve as a common sleeping mattress.

Fortunately pests like mosquitoes, fleas, scorpions, and centipedes had not yet found their way to the Islands, so that the tenants and the retinue of pet pigs and dogs could live relatively unmolested. A new grass hut, with its groomed thatch and fresh mats, was comfortable, airy, aromatic and romantic. Decorated with tapa hangings, spears, fishing equipment, and a few calabashes, it was the native symbol of bliss, and, with occasional patching or replacement of the thatch, would stand for years.

But life was not all as romantic as their snuggery. Eighteenth-century Hawaii could have come closer to the idyllic existence for which it later became renowned if the finer virtues of its people had been universally practiced, if excesses had not been allowed to get out of hand, if chiefs had been a little more consistent in showing consideration for the *makaainana*. Even in utopian Hawaii some human beings were less human than others; a few were guilty of a great deal of mischief, which, together with the little mischiefs of the many, amassed into *pilikia*—trouble.

Ambitious kings, discontent with modest realms, again and again made war upon neighboring kingdoms to add to their personal glory and sphere of authority. There were wars of retaliation, wars of retribution, wars of conquest and reconquest, expensive in both lives and property. Overbearing chiefs all too often were oppressive in their demands upon lesser chiefs and commoners. Officious priests, in an effort to propitiate the gods, made inordinate demands in hogs and produce for altar sacrifices, and when these efforts failed, they called for human sacrifices. Sometimes the gods could not be brought to reason until scores of bodies had gone up in hallowed smoke.

Besides such losses to kith and kin, an angered chief was at liberty to strike down any commoner who crossed him. If the offender could break away before the bludgeon fell, the only recourse was escape to the hills. There the fugitive would encounter other outcasts who formed themselves into bands of thieves and robbers to prey upon farmers and wayfarers. But a far sorer affliction to the workers of the soil were the hundreds of high-class robbers who curried favor with a chief, wormed their way into court and lived in style—ultimately at the expense of taxpayers and tribute givers.

There was no protective law, no prescribed standard of conduct, except the taboos, and though the system presumably applied to all classes, its real objective was to keep the commoner in his place. He took the taboo mandate for granted, unquestioningly accepted its validity, conscientiously and naïvely attempted to live within its constraints. It was a religion, as well as the only rule of the land, and it was all that kept the gods in the temples, the kings and chiefs at the helm, and the Hawaiian cosmos pasted together.

In addition to those taboos that protected the *alii* from the shadow of the people and prescribed eating and living habits, others were issued willy-nilly to cover every exigency. There were permanent taboos, seasonal taboos, and temporary taboos. Between February and October, nine days in each month were regularly taboo—set aside as fast days or days of limited activity in honor of various gods, a total of seventy-two days in the year in which all good men presumably worshiped and went hungry—and these did not include the general taboo days which a priest could peremptorily declare to cope with the omens detected by seers and soothsayers.

A taboo involved sanctity as well as prohibition. The king or a high chief was sacred, and therefore no person of lower rank was permitted to stand profanely in his presence; a day declared taboo was sacred, and therefore people were prohibited from general circulation during it, from using their canoes or working their gardens.

There were, of course, degrees of sanctity, and nothing was more taboo than a dead body. When death came, all activity in the environs of the house of mourning came to a standstill until the deceased was buried. In the case of a commoner the taboo period might be limited to a day or two; in the case of a great chief, to a week or longer.

Immediately upon announcement of the demise, a great wailing went up: *"Auwe, au-we!"*—Alas, alas! The baying of the two syllables over and over, hour after hour, contained a mixture of lament, despair, fear, pity, and affection, and, out of respect to near kin or high rank, was accompanied by a dismantling of the scant attire, flagellation, rending of hair, knocking out of teeth, or other disfigurement.

But on the night of burial, the ultimate taboo went into effect. Utter silence was ordered. No person, except those concerned with the obsequies, was allowed abroad; all were confined to their houses; lights were snuffed; canoes beached; even the dogs were muzzled and the chickens shut up to prevent a sound from breaking the silence. In secrecy the body was carried to a remote cave or burial spot, and the place of interment was never revealed. It was taboo.

The gods credited with prescribing the taboos populated the firmament, the earth, the sea, and the underworld in countless legion. Hawaiian arithmetic went only to four hundred thousand, their equivalent of infinity; so they acknowledged allegiance to a minimum of four hundred thousand deities—ancestral gods, fish gods, household gods, gods of war, gods of sports, gods of tapa beating, gods of harvest and the hula, a galaxy of gods identified with various phases of the priesthood and duties of the priests, major gods, minor gods, and demigods, with a myriad of ghosts, spooks, sprites, and elves to fill any theological vacuum.

Over and above the four hundred thousand, every individual had his own, personal god, imaginatively represented in wood or stone—

the abstraction of an animal, fish, bird, insect, plant, or human being; even an odd-shaped piece of lava served the purpose. It was a sort of divine toy and good-luck charm. The shape was unimportant, but the prayers, sacrifices, and frequency of attention directed to it were very important.

Characteristically, the personal gods were excessively jealous, and, if neglected or undernourished, were capable of bringing all manner of evil to the custodian. Given daily attention, a dispensable portion of the morning meal, an occasional fish, a handful of salad, or a dab of poi, the god returned its blessing, protection, and cooperation.

Worshiped by all were four divinities transplanted from southern Polynesia generations earlier and modified in the passage of time to conform to local circumstances. This quartet comprised the sacrosanct headmen, Kane, creator and patron of life and light; Lono, god of agriculture, the harvest, rain, and peace; Ku, the celestial warrior who supervised all earthly military operations and crafts in general; and Kanaloa, the original Polynesian Poseidon, demoted in Hawaii to the nether regions to nourish the departed spirits.

There was, however, a great deal of disagreement and confusion in different parts of the Islands about who was who among the eternals and about the exact responsibilities of each. But regardless of the powers ascribed by worshipers of conflicting persuasions, neither individual nor collective faith in divine authority ever wavered. No god-fearing Hawaiian dared proceed upon any enterprise without first securing assistance from the appropriate deity.

Like all the world's inventors of a pantheon, the Islanders were inclined to order their conception of the heavenly host in terms of familiar earthly society and familiar local geography. Characteristics of the *alii* were freely transferred to the gods. Since it was the privilege of kings and chiefs to be proud, peevish, and overbearing, worshipers conferred like dispositions upon the gods. They, too, possessed all the arrogant, fierce, cruel, unrighteous passions of men, delighting in the sufferings and sacrifices of human victims.

They dwelt above the clouds but also frequented those most fascinating and terrifying regions of Hawaii, the volcanoes. In the fiery cones of the craters, they gathered to amuse themselves, playing games, gamboling, and dancing. They rode the surges of red molten lava in the caldron of Kilauea as *kanakas* rode the surges of surf on the beaches, and they danced the hula to the throbbing music of volcanic furnaces and the crackling of sulphurous flame.

On the island of Hawaii, the divine merrymaking was dominated by Pele, hostess of Kilauea, one of the few females who could hold her own among the overwhelming majority of male immortals and the only deity allowed to put in frequent personal appearances among mankind. She was ill-tempered, sinister, spiteful.

Disguised as a charming princess, a foot-worn traveler, a dissolute hag, she could show up anywhere to test the character of her subjects. The slightest offense brought quick reprisal in the form of a massive lava flow to overwhelm the offender and his locale. Her testy nature was evidenced by the horribly destructive, solidified, black rivers that scarred the island everywhere. No great eruption ever occurred on Hawaii without a confession from someone, after the event, that Pele had all too recently been seen scouting the area.

Of all the divinities, she was perhaps the most difficult to appease. A special contingent of priests was assigned to keep track of her activities, to reconnoiter and maintain communication with her. Thousands of hogs, priceless valuables, and a great many commoners were tossed over the brink of Kilauea Crater into the burning lake in attempts at conciliation, but she was so guileful that even these were not always effective.

Though Kilauea was her headquarters, Pele freely roved over the length and breadth of the Island chain, like the other gods. They had no Olympus; so temples to them were erected on strategic promontories, always with a glorious outlook, on the periphery of the major islands—sprawling, uncovered platforms that resembled ramparts in other parts of the world. There, amidst a gallery of awe-inspiring statues, images, and altars, a corps of priests made sure that their charges were properly victualed and propitiated. The gods voiced their peeves and sources of anger directly to seers, and sacrifices were meted out accordingly.

The temple, or *heiau,* was a very holy place, so taboo that no commoner was permitted to approach it, though kings and high chiefs were welcome and regularly joined the *kahunas* in elaborate feasts provisioned from the divine leftovers.

But the first harvest moon of October brought a respite to the emphasis on routine worship—and all other routine. The priests closed shop; wars ceased; work stopped. It was the *Makahiki* season, the period of the year that Hawaiians lived for—Thanksgiving, Christmas, New Year's, Easter, Fourth of July, and Hallowe'en wrapped together. *Makahiki* lasted four months and more than made up for the tribulations, oppression, and *pilikia* of the other two-thirds of the year. This was the universal vacation, the like of which no other civilization ever invented.

Work was all but taboo. It was the time for games, sports, loafing, pageantry, hula, endless surfing, celebrating—and tax collection. The anteing of revenue came first, and as soon as community assessments were accounted for, the fun began. Harvest god Lono was patron. During the opening days of the festivities, his likeness, a miniature image riding on the mast tip of what looked like a square-rigged sail, complete with yard and billowing white tapa, put in an appearance at the head of an imposing procession. He ruled in gala spirit from then on.

There was considerable regimentation in the scheduling and pro-graming even of those holiday months, with specific events ordered for particular days, but the activity ran the full gamut of amusement. Athletic competition included dashes and distance runs, boxing, wrestling, javelin throwing and juggling, dart tossing, stone bowling, slingshooting, canoe racing, and surf riding. There were also spectator sports, like cock fighting, with serious betting, or war games including hand-to-hand combat with all the make-believe omitted, dagger fights, spear tossing, stone throwing, in which the targets were live and human.

In free time, old and young scrambled en masse up the precipitous slopes of damp hillsides for the thrill of catapulting down on their bare bottoms, gripping between their legs a swatch of ti leaves that were supposed to eliminate some of the abrasion.

That kind of sliding was a sport of commoners. The sport of kings was ripping down rock chutes on the narrow runners of tipsy, low-slung sleds. Royalty past their prime, young princes, chiefs, and courtiers all went down belly-bump, risking their necks in complete abandon, and a few even learned the more dangerous art of shooting down the sheer course standing erect.

For the long, balmy evenings there were group diversions as unsophisticated as "Button-Button," "Hide-the-Thimble," or "Drop-the-Handkerchief," but adult Hawaiians played them with the sophistication, zest and hullabaloo of professional gamblers. They bet their limited worldly belongings and staked their lives on guessing games like *noa*, in which a sliver of wood was slipped surreptitiously under one of five tapa cushions and wagers were made on its hiding place.

They gambled as liberally on a game resembling checkers or draughts, played with colored pebbles on flat stones into which the "squares" had been chiseled. But the ultimate in evening pastime for commoners was *ume*, in which a master of ceremonies, to the accompaniment of lusty chants and rakish dance, singled out male and female partners to leave the circle for an hour of sexual pleasure.

Alii were obliged to exercise appropriate discretion in refraining from such low-class entertainment; so they never indulged in *ume*, but they had their own substitute in *kilu*, a more aristocratic evening sport calling for men and women participants to sit in opposite semicircles and take turns at bowling a lopsided gourd disc toward their targets; for every hit a kiss was exacted, and ten hits netted the same reward as in *ume*.

Neither of these games raised any question of unchastity or impropriety. Sex had not yet been revealed to Hawaiians as sinful. Gratification of appetite for sex was no more indecent than satisfying hunger or thirst or a sense of humor. Marriage was an informality, accomplished by the simple parental ceremony of inviting the prospective bride and groom to recline side by side and pulling a tapa covering over them. Separation came about as easily.

Husbands freely exchanged wives, and wives thought no less of their husbands for being sought after by other women. Incest, homosexuality, and a wide variety of sexual irregularities were practiced without stigma or taboo. Of course, the fatherhood of children was frequently in doubt, but that was of small concern to commoners; childbirth was easy, and children were given away as casually as other personal chattels.

This held true only for the *makaainana*, however. Parentage was of vital concern to the *alii*, for the status of kings, queens, chiefs, and chiefesses depended entirely on their lineage, and professional genealogists spared no research in tracing the eligibility of marriage partners for them and their heirs.

Makahiki was a harvest festival; but it was also a mating season. All the conviviality brought couples together from different villages and invited promiscuity. Community feastings went on for days and nights, uninterrupted except for a turn in the surf, another round of games, a few hours of sleep, and love making.

One whole night was reserved for surfing. Inland villagers joined seaside villagers on the beaches. At intervals along the shores and headlands great bonfires were lighted and kept burning through the night until an entire island was aglow and the breaking sea out to the reef and beyond was bathed in ruddy illumination. Thousands sported within the compass of that glow. Close inshore the women and the toddlers swept in on the rollers, body surfing, gliding along the lip of the breakers as gracefully as nymphs, shouting, hooting their hilarity into the night.

Offshore where the light barely touched the streamers of back-blown spindrift, a hundred yards out, a quarter-mile, a half-mile, bobbed the real water wizards. Lying flat on their fifteen- or twenty-foot boards, they waited for the great rollers to lift and curl, the surge that only experience and instinct could identify, usually the third or fourth in a series. Suddenly, as if on signal, fifty riders would come to life, head their boards shoreward, and paddle like fiends to catch the exact speed of the swell. Those that made it would maneuver to keep slightly forward of the breaking crest and let the thrust sweep board and rider in, sliding downhill all the way.

With shouts of exhilaration, rider after rider would rise to his knees, ease his legs forward to sitting position, or, straightening up, stand erect on the board, one foot forward for balance, and race shoreward, occasionally directing the board into a slide to the right or left by a deft lean to that side or the trail of a foot in the water. There was no Hawaiian thrill to match it.

Surfing was spectacular, but the one most popular spectacle and diversion of *Makahiki* was not the water sport nor the colorful processions nor the war games. It was the dancing—the hula performances, magnificent extravaganzas in which scores or hundreds participated, male and female, old and young, professionals and amateurs.

Hula, as combined music and dance, or as either one alone, was an integral part of most of *Mahahiki* events; it was interspersed in track and field displays of prowess; it was featured in games like *ume;* people danced in the processions, on the beaches, during the luau feasts. Nor were these gawkish, amorphous improvisations. They were rehearsed and memorized routines, a part of the Hawaiian vocabulary.

The Islanders had to give vent to their feelings. Emotions that could not be released in any other way were expressed with hands, arms, feet, legs, hips, torso, in a formalized routine. An appropriate form of dance existed for any occasion—serious and comic hulas; altar dances; ceremonial dances; character dances; routines to illustrate stories; dances to imitate birds, pigs, turtles, dogs, fish; sacred hulas to honor or mollify particular gods; sitting dances, with scarcely more than subtle suggestions of motion, vigorous sporting dances with stamping, leaping, heel twisting, thigh slapping, dipping of knees, clenching of fists, and hip convolutions.

The repertory was endless, and professional choreographers or hula instructors were constantly augmenting it. To celebrate a victory, to consecrate a new temple, to welcome a visiting king, ostentatious programs were prepared with elaborate costuming, mass choral singing, splendid backdrops, and dramatic percussion orchestration. Weeks and months often went into the casting, training, and rehearsals for such programs, and no *Makahiki* was complete without its special extravaganza.

Hula was Polynesian dance, music, poetry, pantomime, drama,

and opera rolled into one. At its best it was an imaginative, graceful, and sincerely artistic blend of all these. Audiences were spellbound by a good performance and equally critical of an inferior one.

But only a Hawaiian would have been carried away by the instrumental quarrel with concord. His kinesthetic sense far surpassed his musical sense. Wind instruments were represented by nose flutes and whistles, strings by the *ukeke*, a crude bow with two or three fiber threads that produced a muted twang when plucked and held to the mouth for resonance. All the other instruments were percussion— gourds, drums, bamboo poles, sticks, stones, whirring tops, and an assortment of rattles. Since few yielded more than two or three notes, instrumental music had little melodic or harmonic significance.

Vocal music was almost as limited, with a range of perhaps five or six notes, but no free melody and nothing like theme development or modulation. The recounting of genealogy or an historical event was normally presented as a solo chant or *oli*, without dance accompaniment and almost entirely in a monotone, while the lighter hula, with dance or instrumental accompaniment, was sung either solo or in chorus. Choral singing was in unison, or with the men singing an octave or a fifth below the women. Nevertheless, a choir of a hundred voices or more, backed up by a full percussion orchestra, could create an impressive musical effect, and when a chorus of dances was added, the total production was a stirring event. The big shows, all staged in an outdoor arena, lavishly decorated with greenery, were the highlight of *Makahiki*.

Four months of pageantry, parading, athletic contests, overeating, surf frolicking, gaming, and general indulgence, with intermittent days for sleeping it off, were enough to make the average Hawaiian forget any grievances against the chiefs and to prepare him for the routine of arduous labor that resumed in February. It was *Makahiki*, more than any other feature of the calendar, that promoted Island contentment and perennial cheer.

The playtime atmosphere of those four months did not end completely with the waning January moon. It carried over into the rest of the year. The surf sport, hula dancing, *ume*, and hill sliding could be entertainment any day, after the demands of the chiefs had been met. Hawaii did not yet offer an eternal holiday, but life was pretty tolerable—as long as the gods did not interfere.

Three-quarters through the eighteenth century the kings still ruled in feathered splendor; the feudal system and the taboo system were unchallenged; interisland pitched battles were being fought with weapons almost as ancient as the cave man's; the four hundred thousand gods were receiving conscientious homage; and against the battle casualties, the toll in human sacrifices, and the inclemency of landlords, the population was still holding its own at about a third of a million.

The American Revolution was going full blast, but not a soul in any of the Hawaiian kingdoms had ever heard of George Washington, or Lexington, or George III, nor, for that matter, of America or Europe or Asia. The Islanders lived unto themselves and had every reason to believe they would continue to indefinitely. Fifteen hundred years before, they had been invaders, but by length of tenancy and priority of tenancy, they had established for all time their claim to Hawaii *nei*.

II

Isles at the Ends of the Earth

Captain James Cook of the Royal British Navy could afford to be nonchalant about the discovery of another island. Though still only in his forties, his reputation was made. He had surveyed the coasts of Newfoundland and Labrador on one side of 'the world and the coasts of New Zealand and eastern Australia on the other. In a succession of well-publicized expeditions, he had circumnavigated the globe, explored the Antarctic Ocean and the New Hebrides, discovered New Caledonia and a considerable roster of lesser islands.

Most of 1777 had been spent combing the South Pacific for more ocean dots; late in the year he weighed anchor off Tahiti and set course for the Arctic on the most important leg of his current mission —finding the elusive Northwest Passage across the top of the Americas. Others had unsuccessfully scouted the east coast in search of a front door to the Passage; with his two ships *Resolution* and *Discovery*, he was going to try for the back door. Locating the Passage would be the crowning glory for the record of any mariner.

The Cook luck still held. Just north of the equator, only a few days from Papeete, he turned up Christmas Island, the largest atoll in the Pacific. It was duly charted, the last known steppingstone in the thousands of miles to the American coast. But the explorer was not yet through making alterations on his mid-Pacific charts. On January 18, 1778, another island loomed up on his course. He headed for it.

Landing on Pacific isles, where natives had never before seen a white man, was old stuff for the captain. Anything could be expected from deferential worship to attempted seizure for a meal. As had happened to him many times before in other places, the ships were soon surrounded by canoes, filled with jabbering, all-but-naked savages, stricken with awe and curiosity. Cook played safe, armed his men, and ordered that the savages be kept at a distance until their disposition could be sized up.

A headman eventually edged up within calling range of the rail, and, in the course of a long exchange, the captain learned that the savages used a dialect of familiar Tahitian, that they were not un friendly, that they were stunned by the magnificence of the great ships, that the land was known as Kauai. An old hand at winning the hearts of savages, Cook enticed the spokesman nearer to the side with a gift of a few nails and scraps of iron.

That did it. Over the centuries the bits of iron, implanted in wood, that drifted ashore on Hawaii, had come to be considered almost as valuable as feathers. No offering could have been more propitious, not even if the same weight had been in gold. Immediately the crews of the *Resolution* and *Discovery* were in business. "The cheapest market I ever saw," declared the skipper of the *Discovery*. "A moderate-sized nail will supply my ship's company very plentifully with excellent pork for the day, and as to the potatoes and taro, they are obtained upon still easier terms, such is these people's avidity for iron."

Decks were soon swarming with traders in a festive *Makahiki* mood, loaded down with everything from coconuts and conches to dogs and dogfish. Cook relaxed and enjoyed the scene, commenting that he had never in his life witnessed such expressions of astonishment as appeared on the faces of the natives as they boarded—eyes darting from object to object, wild looks and gestures, obviously showing that they had never before been visited by Europeans.

He was impressed with their bearing, their manner, and their physique, particularly the dexterity with which they handled canoes and themselves in the water. When the sea was too high for paddlers to beach their canoes, he watched women leap over the gunwales, with babes in their arms, and casually swim through the towering surf as though they were amphibians.

He was impressed with the quaint courtesy of all the natives and accepted in good humor the homage they paid him, flinging themselves to the ground or deck upon his approach and never daring to lift their eyes in his presence. And most of all he was impressed with their apparent sense of honesty, "never once attempting to cheat us, either ashore or alongside the ships."

In turn he made a humane effort to protect them. He was aware that many of his crew were afflicted with venereal diseases, and, sensing the disaster that his seamen could bring to the Islanders in a few hours of liberty, he issued strict orders that no man be given shore leave and no female visitor be permitted on board. "The women," he noted, "would as readily have favored us with their company on board as the men; but I wanted to prevent all connection which might too probably convey an irreparable injury to themselves and through their means to the whole nation."

The order was apparently enforced until heavy weather marooned a trading party overnight on the neighboring island of Niihau. That company took advantage of the hospitality; Cook's worst fears were realized, and the "irreparable injury" was done.

At best the visit of the *Resolution* and *Discovery* was somewhat perfunctory. He could have profitably spent the rest of the winter on Kauai and backtracked to investigate another island which a lookout claimed he had sighted a few leagues to the southeast. But the captain's mind was on the Northwest Passage, and at the end of a fortnight he declined to delay his primary mission any longer.

With the holds bulging yams and taro and the deck cluttered with tethered hogs, he made his farewells and set sail, gratified that he had come across a group of such civilized savages, gratified, too, that only one unfortunate incident had occurred during the stay—the guards had been obliged to shoot a native who had tried to make off with a boathook. But it was as clean a record as one could hope for. The discovery of Kauai and Niihau might not be of any great consequence; yet the supplies they had taken on could well prove to be a salvation on the voyage they hoped to make across the continent of North America.

He marked the islands on his chart, as a matter of routine, officially designating them the Sandwich Islands, in honor of his sponsor, First Lord of the Admiralty, the Earl of Sandwich, and once more pointed toward the Arctic.

Cook, of course, was unsuccessful in his search for a short cut back to England, and, after probing frigid bays, inlets, and river mouths for eight months and exhausting the reserves of Kauai pork, he decided it was advisable to retreat south for the winter, get the barnacles off his bottom, and replenish his supplies before making one last effort to find the Passage. What better refuge could there be than the Sandwich Islands? Moreover, he realized now that his inspection had been cursory, and he had not forgotten that reported shadow of another island to the southeast of Kauai. Located as they were, hundreds of miles from other known landings, those islands might prove quite a find.

Late in the fall of 1778 he was back in Hawaiian waters. Maui, which he had missed previously, loomed up first this time. That was on the morning of November 26th. Later in the day Molokai appeared in the distance. Approaching Maui, Cook observed that vast throngs of people were assembled on the beaches watching the ships in a state of great excitement.

On the afternoon of the 27th, the king of Maui boarded the *Discovery* and presented its captain with a gorgeous red feather cloak. As other islands showed their outlines and the magnitude of his discovery became clear, Cook was aware that he had bestowed a much greater honor upon the Earl of Sandwich than he originally conceived. A few days after the cloak presentation, off the east coast of Maui, the *Resolution* encountered a flotilla of canoes commanded by a potentate who introduced himself as king of the nearby island of Hawaii and explained that he was at war with the king of Maui.

It was *Makahiki* again, and either Ku or Lono must have granted the warriors special dispensation, for peace traditionally prevailed during that season. But Cook was not yet familiar with the Hawaiian calendar. He concluded it would be in his best interests to avoid getting involved in any interisland conflict and to stay afloat until an armistice was declared. In any case, continuous heavy weather prevented a landing. So for six weeks the crews maneuvered their ships around Hawaii in search of a safe harbor, surveying and mapping the coast, studying the winds and channels, and approaching a native village only when a fresh supply of pork and bananas was needed.

But the Islanders, who watched every tack of the ships during those weeks, placed their own interpretation on the strange maneuvers: the gods were putting on a show for their benefit. Those ships were far too enormous to be any man-made craft; they were "floating islands," contrived by a deity, and naturally during the *Makahiki* season of the year the principal passenger aboard would be Lono. The tall mast, cross spar, and square-rigged sail were, after all, merely a majestic representation of the symbol of Lono carried around the Islands every year. And sooner or later, prophesied the priests on the island of Hawaii, the ships would put in at Kealakekua Bay—the Pathway of the Gods.

As the squadron moved in that direction after the weeks of suspense, the king's runners were dispatched around the Big Island with the tidings and a summons to rally for the reception. While bartering for supplies along the coast, the visitors had already made a telling impression on the runners. At every stopping point, the couriers flavored the official message with a little addition of their own, breathlessly exploding, as a native recounted years later: "The men are white; their skin is loose and folding; their heads are angular; fire and smoke issue from their mouths; they have openings in the sides of their bodies into which they thrust their hands and draw out iron, beads, nails and other treasures, and their speech is unintelligible: 'a hikapalale, hikapalale, hioluai, oalaki, walawalaki, waikipoho.'"

Exactly as predicted, the superhumans with loose skin and openings in their sides proceeded along the pathway of the gods into Kealakekua Bay, and the ships dropped anchor offshore from the king's grass palace. John Ledyard, the Yankee Marco Polo of the day, who happened to be part of the ship's company, described the astonishing reception. Thousands upon thousands crowded the beaches and surrounding hills. Trees were alive with people, and the roofs of grass houses sagged under their weight. Here and there, groups of women performed wild dances, leaping and clapping their hands to the accompaniment of shrill chants that could be heard above the pandemonium of the crowd.

The confusion around the ships was even more chaotic. "We were surrounded by so great a number of canoes," he wrote, "that Cook ordered two officers into each top to number them . . . and as they both exceeded 3,000 in their amounts, I shall with safety say there were 2,500, and as there were upon an average six persons at least in each canoe, it will follow that there were at least 15,000 men, women and children in the canoes, besides those that were in floats, swimming without floats, and actually on board and hanging round the outside of the ships."

Captain Cook had to measure up to the challenge of his audience and put on a performance in keeping with its mood of jubilation. As soon as the *Resolution* was moored, he ordered his pinnace over the side, took aboard two high chiefs who appeared to outrank all others, and, attended only by the barge crew, was rowed toward shore through the sea of splashing, vociferating humanity, then heaved onto the shoulders of his bargemen and deferentially conveyed through the surf.

The two chiefs preceded him up the beach, gently waving tall white poles from side to side, as a signal for the people to make room. "Lono is with us. The great Lono is coming," they rumbled. Instantly the throng parted; people covered their faces and prostrated themselves.

Cook had no idea who Lono might be, but there was no mistaking that he was being welcomed with what he admitted was "religious veneration." Then and there he could have halted the proceedings and set the record straight. Carried away by the excitement, however, and apprehensive that the reception might be far less cordial if the mob were told he was an ordinary mortal Englishman, he permitted the adoration to continue.

More chiefs equipped with white taboo poles joined the barge attendants, and together they forced a narrow avenue through the crush. Cook strode down it grandly. At his approach, standing natives in vast waves fell to the ground in obeisance, fell in huddles four and six bodies deep, they were so closely packed. No sooner had he passed than they were struggling to their feet, staring wild-eyed and shouting acclamation. And he had only to turn his head to see the throng go down again in unison, as if there were magic in his glance. Hundreds were trampled.

Fascinated and amused, the captain inconsiderately kept looking behind, so that eventually his admirers stayed down and crawled, and he was treated to the comic spectacle of seeing ten thousand brown bodies pursuing him, groveling on all fours.

The procession headed directly for the great temple, taboo to the commoners. They were obliged to withdraw gradually, and only the high priests, Cook, and a few of his officers, who landed separately, were conducted to the sanctum sanctorum. There, in honor of the visiting god, the priests staged an elaborate ritual, not a word or motion of which the guests of honor could comprehend.

The captain's head was anointed with an unpleasant concoction of coconut oil; in the company of the high priest he was obliged to climb the "rotten scaffolding" of a lofty oracle tower and cling there precariously during a meaningless ceremony below; for over an hour speeches, prayers, and incantations were recited in his behalf; and then he was seated as the grand panjandrum at a sumptuous feast, with a priest to chew his food for him. Never for a moment, insisted Cook's lieutenants, did the captain suspect he was being mistaken for a god; but even if he had, it was too late for him to reveal his identity. It might have proved fatal then and there.

But the expedition commander could not live on veneration. He had serious business to attend to. His ships were in dire need of repair; his water casks were empty; quantities of food supplies had to be obtained; he wanted to complete a survey of the Islands and make some accurate astronomical observations. He was a methodical scientist, as well as mariner; the interests of science came before kowtowing to native caprice.

Accepting the high homage brought him no great personal embarrassment at first. His imposed rank gave him superiority over chiefs and *kahunas* and facilitated his operations. He, too, was taboo. Peremptorily he took over the sacred areas around the temple to use as a shipyard and set up his telescope and other scientific paraphernalia on the *heiau* grounds. The tools and instruments were mysterious enough to identify him and his men more conclusively with the gods and incidentally guarantee freedom from being pestered by prying natives.

Hawaiians competed with one another for the privilege of helping to fill the ship's water casks and were overgenerous in supplying pork, fruit, and vegetables in exchange for a few coveted nails and iron scraps. Most popular man in the ship's company was the blacksmith, who fired up his forge and accommodatingly fashioned spear points and fishhooks to order.

The repairs proceeded more smoothly than an optimistic mate could have hoped, and overtime night work observing the stars paid off handsomely in general mystification. Even ordinary seamen thoroughly enjoyed their stay, for standing orders were soon overlooked and they could have all the women's company they wanted.

The call at Kealakekua would have been a complete success, had it not been for a raging winter storm that swept over the Islands on February 7th. A few misunderstandings had been patched up; Cook had been decked in priceless feathered capes; hulls and rigging had been repaired, the commissary victualed, and the ships given a send-off with appropriate fanfare. But before the island was cleared, the tempest came on—"a wind in irregular and most terrible gusts, such as we had never seen."

On the eighth the violence turned into an erratic hurricane. Before nightfall the sails of the *Discovery* were split and the foremast of the *Resolution* had given way. The crews of both ships were at the pumps. There was no choice. Back to Kealakekua, ordered Cook. And even then, the wind was so contrary that the retreat took three days.

Before nightfall on the eleventh, the ships were again in their old berths in Kealakekua Bay. But where they had been welcomed by the shouts of thousands a month before, they now had "the mortification not to see a single canoe, and hardly any inhabitants in the towns." The Lono concept was wearing off. Surely a god ought to be more resolute about his comings and goings, ought to be on friendlier relations with the elements.

The damaged mast was laboriously floated ashore for repairs, and the astronomical instruments again set up for effect. But there was no cooperation from the Hawaiians. Their surly looks, their display of the daggers which the ship's blacksmith had so considerately hammered out only a few days before, the extortionate prices demanded for pigs and potatoes, the increase in petty larceny revealed all too clearly the changed temper. Altercation followed altercation.

On the fourteenth the morning watch reported that the *Discovery*'s cutter was missing. This was too much for Cook. He could not spare the cutter and, taking charge himself, landed with a squad of armed marines. The melee that followed was inevitable. An hour later four of the marines were dead, a score of chiefs and commoners were dead, and Cook was dead.

Toward the end the captain failed to live up to the Lono role. He winced and cried out when his arm was painfully seized by an angered chief. Instantly the protective spell was broken. "He groans; he is not a god," chorused the astonished witnesses. A blow and a ṣtab in the back a moment later proved how mortal he was.

But even then the native morticians took no chances on his identity. His body was given the sanctimonious treatment of deceased royalty, the flesh baked off the bones and the bones divided among the *alii* for orthodox disposal.

In the series of frays that followed Cook's death, many more natives were killed and half the town burned. Later in the week tempers cooled long enough to permit the removal of the mast and the astronomical equipment, and the collection of most of the captain's bones. Captain Charles Clerke took over the command of the expedition, and on February 22nd the *Discovery* and *Resolution* weighed anchor to resume the quest for the Northwest Passage. The ships never returned to Hawaii, but they were not forgotten, nor was the great discoverer who had proved such an unsatisfactory surrogate for Lono.

It was, of course, possible—probable—that the admirable captain was not the original European discoverer, any more than Columbus was the discoverer of America. Undoubtedly the Islands were sighted from Spanish galleons two centuries before the British raised them; in all likelihood a trickle of Spanish blood flowed in the veins of a few Hawaiians; conceivably there was truth in the legends of shipwrecks that left white Europeans stranded on the Island shores, truth in the story of a marooned padre who established a mission at Kohala, a shade of truth in the folk tale about a band of marauding white men that once had a hideout on the heights of Mauna Kea. But they failed to make a very lasting impression on the outside world and only an apocryphal impression on the Islanders.

After the survivors of the 1779 clash at Kealakekua Bay sailed north, six years elapsed before the arrival of any further white intruders. The display of Hawaiian belligerence had little to do with the delay. In popular conception the Sandwich Islands were "at the ends of the earth," with the continental mass of North and South America blocking the way. Few merchants or mariners were much interested in such remote ocean specks. They were a curiosity perhaps, but no more of a curiosity than scores of other Pacific islands inhabited by blood-thirsty savages.

If Captain Clerke had found a short cut between the Pacific and the Atlantic, the story would have been entirely different, but he did not find it, and geographers were beginning to suspect that no such throughway existed. Moreover, England, France, and a presumptuous little nation known as the United States were too involved in the American Revolution to sponsor Pacific cruises.

It was not for a full year after the end of the Revolution that the official report of Cook's last expedition was even published. Then the one item in it that seemed to interest merchant adventurers was the prospect of lucrative trade in furs between the Northwest and China. Lieutenant James King, who took over as scribe for the expedition after Cook's death, and wrote the last chapters of the report, made it excitingly clear that an enterprising trader with agencies on the west coast of North America could do a fabulous business in Hong Kong. And, incidentally, the Sandwich Islands would provide a convenient way station.

The British Admiralty, too, may have had a hand in the delay. It was in no rush to pass out hard-won intelligence to competing nations and guarded zealously such knowledge as had been acquired on the expedition. In accordance with standing Admiralty instructions, long before the *Discovery* and *Resolution* reached England, the command-ing officer had assembled the entire ships' company and ordered all "to deliver up their journals, and every writing, remark or memorandum that any of them had made . . . on pain of the severest punishment in case of concealment." Every item of information was to be filed, sorted, and sealed for delivery to the Lords of the Admiralty.

But at least one member of the company did hold out, Lieutenant John Rickman of the *Discovery,*—and there were those who suspected the upstart Connecticut Yankee, John Ledyard, of not turning in his fat diary either. Rickman's *Journal of Captain Cook's Last Voyage,* published in London in 1781, anonymously, of course, scooped the official account by three years, and Ledyard's, published in Hartford,

Connecticut, by one year. Although Ledyard freely borrowed from Rickman, he had by far the roughest ordeal in getting his manuscript to the printers. The Revolution was still on. He was obliged to cross the Atlantic with British expeditionary forces, posing as a redcoat, and then desert with all his gear and precious notes.

Once his book was off the press, Ledyard became the self-appointed American propagandist for development of a Pacific fur trade between the Northwest and the Orient—via the Sandwich Islands. With boundless enthusiasm he traipsed from New London to New York, to Boston, to Philadelphia trying to sell merchants on his plan for establishing a post in the Northwest, and he came within a final argument of persuading a Philadelphia syndicate to underwrite a trading company that would have altered the next century of history for the Northwest and Hawaii.

He failed, and the first trading ship to put in at the Islands was a British brig, in the autumn of 1785, loaded with a prize cargo of sea-otter pelts from the very region Ledyard had wanted to exploit. Europeans, not Americans, took the first step in depriving the Hawaiians of their isolation.

Six months later a pair of English fur traders, the *King George* and the *Queen Charlotte*, en route to Nootka Sound, stopped for three weeks, and the commanding officers were so favorably impressed with the climate and the hospitality that they later returned for the winter. The same year brought the celebrated French Captain Jean François de Galaup, comte de la Pérouse, fresh from honors won in his attacks on British forts in Hudson's Bay and now on another search for the Northwest Passage or any other discoveries he could make on the periphery of the Pacific. He gave his name to a bay where he anchored off Maui and then sailed south to mysterious disaster.

In 1787 another fur trader, *Imperial Eagle*, flying the flag of the Austrian East India Company, stopped long enough to drop off an Irish physician, John Mackay, who had spent a rough year doctoring the Nootka Indians in the Canadian fur country and was now ready to try his hand at doctoring the Hawaiians. Skipper Barclay liked the Islands so well that he extended his stay, and his wife improved her

time by persuading a sparkling young girl—*wahine*—to join the cruise
to the Orient as her abigail.

For lack of a more pronounceable name, *wahine* was contracted
into "Winee." She was the first native to be lured away from the
Islands, and under Mrs. Barclay's tutelage developed into a charmer.
Not to be outdone by the *wahines,* when the *Nootka,* bound for China
with a load of furs, dropped anchor off Kauai later in the year, a
handsome chief, Kaiana, begged Captain John Meares to take him on.
Kaiana so readily proved his worth as sailor on long voyages to China,
Alaska, the Northwest, and back to the Islands that Hawaiians were
soon in demand as crew members for every shorthanded ship.

A total of six traders visited Hawaiian waters in 1787, and after
that they kept coming—mostly British—until Robert Gray, a Rhode
Islander, dropped anchor off Waikiki in 1789, displaying the stars and
stripes on the *Columbia Rediviva,* her holds crammed with a cargo
of sea otter pelts. At last John Ledyard's propaganda was paying off,
but the *Columbia* came from Boston, rather than Philadelphia, and
Ledyard did not have a hand in the enterprise. Long since, his patience with the Americans had given out, and he had taken his ideas to
France where he was no more successful; in utter frustration he had
set out on a four-thousand-mile tramp across Siberia—a different
route to the Northwest.

Robert Gray had been sent out by a group of Boston merchants,
headed by no less a celebrity than the New England architect Charles
Bulfinch. After Gray's call at Maui, he went on to Canton and around
the world, the first American navigator to circumnavigate the globe. It
was he, too, who discovered the Columbia River, magnanimously naming it for his ship, rather than himself.

Already the Sandwich Islanders had a grandstand seat for the
march of Pacific history, but they failed to detect any notable difference between the exploits of explorers and the transactions of traders.
Frequently little distinction existed between the two. The explorers
dabbled in commerce, and the traders kept on the watch for new
landfalls. Cook and Clerke found it rewarding to mix barter with the
business of exploring. Even the great George Vancouver combined the

two. He promoted trade in the Northwest, gave his name to the largest island off the west coast of North America, and brought cattle and oranges and assorted plants to Hawaii in the interest of future traffic. The Islanders saw him repeatedly at the height of his career. And they saw Portlock and Dixon, Broughton and Ingraham, Lisiansky, Kotzebue, and a dozen others, all of whom helped to create a sea lane to Hawaii.

Most of the visiting captains succeeded in inducing a few Hawaiians to join their crews—as human souvenirs to be displayed in the homeland. And the carelessness with which masters discharged these seamen and sea women in foreign ports, leaving them to fend for themselves and find passage back as best they could, became notorious.

They were sometimes treated with honor and respect in faraway lands; more often they were little more than exhibits for country carnivals; they succumbed to common Mainland diseases; they became public charges and wasted away from homesickness. So many stranded Hawaiians were found in New England a few years later that they were the mainstay of a mission school started at Cornwall, Connecticut.

Mrs. Barclay's "Winee," "a girl who possessed virtues that are seldom to be found in the class of her countrywomen, and a portion of understanding that was not expected in a rude and uncultivated mind," was left to her own devices in Canton, and would probably have perished there, had she not been chivalrously rescued by Chief Kaiana, who wangled a roundabout passage for her back to the Islands. But the poor girl had suffered so much misery in China, was so wasted away from homesickness, seasickness, and other ills that she died at sea before reaching the one land she loved—an end tragically prophetic of the fate to be met by countless others.

To the first commercial invaders, the inhabitants were pagan savages who had not yet earned a place in civilized society. And the invaders were equally cavalier and unconcerned about regional politics in the Islands. They were not interested in the social makeup, as long as the pork, vegetables, firewood, and water were delivered without a fuss. Whether they knew it or not, their dealings were with kings and chiefs who ruled the different islands or sections of them. Some were cordial and accommodating; others were sly and acrimonious.

One native with whom the traders all liked to do business was Kamehameha, the young ruler of the northern end of Hawaii, the "Big Island"; Kamehameha maintained a residence at Kailua on the Kona coast, benevolently reigning over a kingdom of more than two thousand square miles. Foreigners took to him naturally; they liked his looks, his straightforward manner, and his humor.

"His carriage was majestic," George Vancouver wrote enthusiastically, "and every action told of a mind which under any circumstances would have distinguished its possessor. His eyes were dark and piercing; he seemed capable of penetrating the designs and reading the thoughts of those about him; before his glance the most courageous quailed. His general deportment was frank, cheerful and generous. In form and stature a Herculean savage; in abilities and character a man that any country might have been proud to acknowledge as her son."

Kamehameha thought no less of Vancouver. The two struck up such amiable rapport that the Hawaiian wanted to cede his kingdom to Vancouver's king as a protectorate; he confided to the Britisher his ambition to create an empire that would unite all the Islands, and Vancouver did his best to serve as arbitrator in the threatening inter-island clashes.

Between 1792 and 1794 the English explorer paid three visits to Kamehameha, consulting, admonishing, consoling, counseling him; then he went his way, and the ambitious king continued with his battles for Island unity. Goddess Pele had acknowledged her loyalty to Kamehameha by annihilating a small force of the enemy in a rare explosive eruption of Kilauea in 1790, preliminary to the conquest of the rest of the Big Island; he won a major naval victory in the spring of 1791 using European cannon; in the bloody battle of Iao Stream above Wailuku, he added Maui to the kingdom; he conquered Molokai and Lanai; he landed at Waikiki and drove the defenders of Oahu up Nuuanu Valley and over the Pali.

By 1795, he had almost achieved his ambition. Except for Kauai,

Hawaii was one kingdom. An invasion of that island in 1796 was thwarted by a storm, and Kauai was not added to the realm until Kamehameha resorted to trickery almost a decade and a half later and kidnapped the king. But Kauai, off by itself to the northwest, offered no serious threat to the conqueror's sovereignty during the interim; the unification of the southern islands in the group was what mattered, and under that unification trade prospered as it never could have under assorted rulerships. Kamehameha was already a converted internationalist, eager to maintain orderly and equitable relations with foreign shippers and to advance the welfare of himself and his kingdom through commerce.

The opening of the Columbia River Basin presaged a boom trading era for Yankee fleets in the Pacific—ships like the *Lady Washington,* the brig *Hancock,* the brigantines *Hope* and *Iphigenia,* and the sloop *North West America.* Companies in Boston, New Haven, Mystic, New London, New York, and Nantucket backed expeditions to the Northwest and Hawaii, but for a long time trade was by no means a Yankee monopoly. Merchants in most of the major shipping centers of the world became vitally interested in this new commercial frontier.

Patrons in remote ports like Bengal dispatched vessels. The governments of England, France, Spain, and Russia joined the race, sometimes in apparent competition with private concerns of their own nationals, like the East India Company, the Hudson's Bay Company, the South Sea Company, and the Russian American Company.

Regardless of the country from which the traders came, the idea was to make a double killing. Loaded with cheap trinkets, beads, brass buttons, earrings, calicoes, tin mirrors, flashy blankets, hunting knives, copper kettles, chisels, liquor, snuff, and tobacco, a ship made its way to the fur outposts. There the chattels were swapped with the American coast Indians for hides and furs; the next leg was across the Pacific to Oriental ports where the cargo was exchanged at enormous profit for tea, silks, and assorted eastern luxuries; then the trader would head for home at the end of two or three years of voyaging to collect another fortune.

Going or coming, sometimes both, a stop was made at the Sand-

wich Islands for supplies and crew refreshment. Scurvy was the
bugaboo in all this traffic, and Island produce its readiest cure or
preventative. But from the point of view of the crews, and officers too,
the refreshment program was as important as the antiscurvy measures.

That program was principally a long bawdy bender at the expense
of the easy virtue of native girls. "The head chief came down," reported the supercargo of a typical trader, landing at a typical Hawaiian village, "and taking me by the hand, walked me from the shore . . .
into a circle of about sixty girls, who partially rested themselves with
their elbows on their knees, and by their expressive signs told me if I
had come for a wife, I could take who I pleased."

Cook's men had demonstrated the elemental appetites of foreign
visitors, and the chiefs learned quickly what to provide. The sunshine,
the surfing, the wrestling matches with the natives, and the change in
diet added to the refreshment, too, and the pork and yams loaded
aboard during the letdown furnished variety to the menu on the voyage ahead. The break in the Islands was all that saved many an
expedition from disaster.

Proceeds from the Pacific commerce were astonishing even to
penurious merchants back home. The *Neptune,* sailing out of New
Haven, sold a cargo of eighty thousand seal skins in Canton for $280,-
000 and made almost as much again on the tea, silks, nankins, and
chinaware brought back to Long Island Sound. By comparison, the
total cost of the voyage was incidental, and the most significant expenditures en route were the kegs of nails, scrap iron, some spare
canvas, a barrel of pitch, and a second-hand kettle exchanged in the
Islands for food—not counting the abundance of ribbons, earrings, tin
looking glasses, and bright beads bestowed upon the *wahines* for favors rendered.

All that traffic and trade, however, were not carried on without
frequent flareups. Some captains deliberately incited natives, and some
natives were very inconsiderate of their customers. Private misunderstandings, most of them the result of petty larceny, tended to develop
into free-for-alls. Encouraged by chiefs, the commoners were developing a latent sense of acquisition and were becoming avid souvenir

collectors. The temptation to secure foreign curios was more than they could resist. Stealing had never been recognized as a Hawaiian sin; an unguarded object was common property, and that included the belongings of foreigners.

In all likelihood the curiosities or useful devices lifted from a ship by commoners, who were still under the thumb of the chiefs, promptly went to superiors for a nominal reward. So, given the opportunity, natives would walk off with anything in sight. "On no account suffer more than one or two on your decks at a time," advised an experienced trader. "Keep people constantly in your tops, with arms ready, your guns loaded, and never permit the natives to swim about the ship; or most assuredly you will have your cables cut." They wanted the iron.

The worst quarrels invariably were stirred up by tough old salts who had no intention of making more than one visit to the Sandwich Islands and therefore had nothing to lose by being roughshod; they took every advantage of the no-account savages and showed their superiority by repaying minor offenses with major recrimination. Such a veteran was Captain Simon Metcalfe, a fur trader wintering at Maui during the early months of 1790. Under his command were the *Elinora*, a sturdy, square-rigged snow, and a small schooner, *Fair American*, skippered by the captain's son, and normally serving as the *Elinora*'s tender but temporarily separated from the mother ship.

Anchored alone off the west coast of Maui one night, the *Elinora* lost a dinghy, along with the guard sleeping in it. Rumor quickly reached Metcalfe that the boat had been stolen by natives from the village of Olowalu, broken up for its nails, and the guard killed. The captain immediately shifted anchorage to Olowalu, where he circulated a counter rumor that the thieves would be handsomely rewarded for the return of the seaman's remains and any remnants of the dinghy.

The bones and a few fragments of the boat were promptly delivered; and to witness the presentation ceremony, as well as to participate in friendly trading, Mauians by the hundreds gathered in canoes off the starboard side of the *Elinora*. As if he wished to address them in a body, Metcalfe insisted that the craft close in, gunwale to gun-wale, bow to stern, until they formed a solid mass.

The savages wanted iron, so he gave it to them. The ports to starboard were suddenly hauled up, the battery run out, charged with musket balls, nails, scrap iron, and rusty chain. "Fire," he ordered and then stood by to grin with satisfaction as the point-blank barrage burst over his target and volleys of musketry added to the slaughter. Only then was he convinced that his account with Olowalu was settled.

"It is painful to record the depravity of untutored heathen," lectured the early historian James Jackson Jarves; "how much more the vile passions of a civilized being whose outward form masks him for a man, while his actions prove him a devil. In the annals of Hawaii, the foul deed of Metcalfe stands alone."

But the captain had his deserts coming. Since he was *persona non grata* on Maui after the "foul deed," he retreated to Kealakekua Bay on Hawaii, where his indispensable boatswain, patient, humane John Young, deserted him—or was "detained" by Kamehameha. And when the tender *Fair American* inopportunely arrived at Kawaihae in search of the mother ship, it was unceremoniously impounded as an addition to the king's navy, and its skipper and crew thrown to the sharks, all except the wary mate, Isaac Davis, who succeeded in escaping and joining his friend John Young. The *Elinora* was obliged to leave Kealakekua before her captain could learn of the loss of his son, crew, and tender.

In a less civilized land, the two captains, Young and Davis, would have been regarded as particularly fitting specimens for sacrifice on the altars of the gods, but Kamehameha was too canny to indulge in expensive spite. He needed capable foreigners with the white man's learning and, instead of torturing them, welcomed them as men of mark, befriended them, adopted them, eventually promoted them to the status of chiefs with broad authority, elite wives, and vast estates, and made them important cogs in the kingdom. Davis became the power behind the throne on Oahu, while Young was accorded similar authority on Hawaii.

Kawaihae, on the lee side of the northwest coast, was the exboatswain's bailiwick. There, on a small bay that offered some slight protection from the fierce trade winds sweeping down from the mountains, the king located his navy yard; there, under enormous thatch canopies, were built his largest canoes and his ships; there he erected his warehouses, centralized his salt production, set up his smithies, make-shift forge, and carpenters' shops. As long as the king was in residence on the Kona coast, Kawaihae was a major center of commerce. John Young was in charge.

Gradually traders coming from any quarter of the globe evolved a routine itinerary for Island calls. They put in first at Kawaihae for hogs, salt, and garden produce brought down from the Waimea plateau; went on to Maui and Oahu for water and supplementary supplies; and finally to Kauai and Niihau for yams, more pork, fruit, and vegetables.

The British navigator John Meares, who made the circuit twice, pictured the typical Kawaihae trading scene, canoes plying between beach and ship loaded with live fowls, squealing pigs, heaps of taro root, bunches of bananas, and bundles of sugar cane. "Before night, upwards of 400 hogs were purchased," he calculated. "The decks were loaded and the boats filled with them and the vegetables. Indeed, such was the profusion of these articles that many of the canoes returned without being able to dispose of their cargoes. By sunset we had purchased a sufficiency of fresh provisions to last us to China; and we therefore prepared to make sail for Kauai and Niihau . . . The Islanders appeared to have no other pleasure but what arose from showing kindnesses and exercising hospitality to us. They received us with joy and saw us depart with tears."

Frequently the Islanders were not all left behind. Their supreme pleasure was cadging free passage on a white man's ship from one island to the next, and some incautious skippers returned hospitality for hospitality by letting the best traders stay on board. The trouble, however, was that if two were taken on, they soon had a dozen friends who could not be left behind, and the dozen were sure to round up fifty neighbors, relatives, wives, and children to accompany them.

A little British bark made the mistake of accepting a few barterers as passengers for a run from Honolulu to Hawaii, and before the vessel left port, there were no less than four hundred uninvited excursionists and no way of dislodging them without incurring collective resentment. "There was scarcely room to move on the decks or in the cabin," vouched an officer. "Even the chains, tops and bowsprit were crowded with them. In crossing the channel we were near upsetting the vessel, being top heavy from the number on deck and about the rigging."

As time passed, the value of iron for exchange rapidly depreciated. It took a very large nail to purchase a very small pig, and the owner of the pig usually required that the nail be shaped into a dagger or hook before it would be recognized as currency. Hawaiians were discovering the uses of all kinds of tools, gear, and gadgets, and wanted to barter for saws, chisels, cutlery of any kind, utensils of any kind, blocks and tackle, chains, broadcloth, canvas, axes, guns and ammunition, liquor —and more liquor. A couple of quarts of cheap rum could purchase a plump hog in any port.

Natives were learning the tricks of bartering, too. They were born imitators and found the Yankees good teachers. With time on their hands, they would gamely dicker by the hour. They also learned from the Yankees the art of disguising flaws and misrepresenting goods. When a bundle of tapa was unfolded, it all too frequently was found to be stained, torn, or incomplete on the inside.

Even Kamehameha developed haggling as a hobby. He carefully watched a supercargo from Connecticut measure out the twenty quarts of rum he had ordered; then, Yankee fashion, he maintained there were only nineteen; when the tapster volunteered to measure it over again, the royal barterer cheerfully agreed to accept the purchase a quart short for the price agreed upon. "Do not consider this dishonesty or meanness in him," defended the Yankee, "for he is free from either. It was rather a piece of wit he wanted to exercise."

But traders were no longer obliged to deal exclusively with the witty natives. Before the turn of the century a few *haoles*—white foreigners—had taken up residence in many of the villages frequented by visiting ships. They included a handful of decent souls who had fallen in love with the climate or the scenery and, of course, there were the king's counselors, Davis and Young, but for the most part they were a sorry lot, deserters, mutineers, fugitives, escaped convicts, derelicts, all living in sin with local daughters.

Most of them gravitated to Kawaihae or Honolulu. They preferred not to answer questions about their past. Ebenezer Townsend encountered half a dozen of them at Kawaihae in 1798: a fellow named Shacklesby, who was making himself handy on the waterfront, assisting Young in the construction of a brig for the king; a disreputable Irishman named Martin; a Jew whom Kamehameha had enticed from some ship to serve as a cook; Homes, an "illiterate but honest" Yankee from Plymouth, Massachusetts, who had been in the Islands long enough to acquire a native wife and two children; a nameless Italian; a Britisher, answering to the name of Steward, Captain Steward, who had something to hide and was in no haste to leave.

A few years later, the talented, crippled British gadabout, Archibald Campbell, counted over fifty white people on Oahu alone, about a third of them American and the rest English. "But the number was constantly varying," he hedged. His roster was no less heterogeneous than Townsend's, including John Hairbottle, harbor pilot for Honolulu; a William Moxeley from Norfolk, Virginia, acting as the king's interpreter; a clever shipbuilder named Boyd; James Beattie, the king's blockmaker, who at one time had been on the London stage and occasionally put on performances in Honolulu; William Stevenson, an escaped convict from New South Wales, who had turned into an industrious farmer and liquor distiller near Pearl Harbor and "conducted himself in general with great propriety."

Particularly around Honolulu there were a few bona fide ex-captains and relatively solid characters who saw a future in setting up businesses for themselves. They opened shops and traded with the traders, dealing in any kind of merchandise that came into port and selling fancy foreign finery to chiefs, with rum as the principal lubricant for their transactions.

From the Hawaiian point of view, the great handicap in commerce was lack of substantial export resources. Pigs and yams were not enough. Kamehameha had wasted no time in catching on to the alien conception of trade; he wanted to break in on it and share some of the profits. He wanted ships; he wanted a market. But he had nothing to sell.

In 1791 came a false alarm. Two merchant venturers thought they had discovered sandalwood on Maui and Niihau. They knew the value of it in China, where every orthodox temple reeked with its essence, and they knew it was in short supply. All the sandalwood the Islands might produce would sell in Canton at prices comparable to those paid for furs. The news was received with exultation. Cords of it were lugged from the hills and shipped to China, where it proved to be worth so much common kindling. It was not real sandalwood at all.

But the sandalwood idea died hard. Ten years later the genuine article was identified, and some five tons of it were shipped out. This time the Chinese raised no questions. They wanted more. Kamehameha turned industrialist. Like all produce of the Islands, the sandalwood belonged to him. Orders went out to the chiefs and from the chiefs to the commoners for quotas of sandalwood. Regardless of the season or the preoccupation of the people, they were commanded to quit what they were doing and search for the precious wood.

Cut in short lengths and bundled, it was all toted on the backs of the woodsmen on treks of ten, twenty, thirty miles. It sold by the Chinese picul, 133 pounds, and was worth about ten dollars a picul. But not a farthing of the proceeds went to the men who cut and carried it. The king claimed two-thirds and the greedy chiefs the rest.

For once, the commoners found no joy in a community occupation. Collecting sandalwood was sheer back-breaking drudgery, in which they could take no pride and for which they could see no remotely visible rewards. They hated everything connected with the trade; they hated the very smell of sandalwood and were accused of destroying it deliberately, pulling up the young trees, so that their children would never have to endure the misery they were suffering. The king retaliated by tabooing all sandalwood and proclaiming that whoever should "break down the small shoots of sandalwood in the mountain shall be fined one hundred rafters each five yards long." The ancient serf system was coming to a head-on collision with imported capitalism.

While the forests were being slashed, the taro patches went untended, grass huts in need of new thatch rotted away, fishing canoes were beached, gods were neglected, the festivities of *Makahiki* were abandoned. Sandalwood searchers had to tramp higher and higher into the mountains, often camping there for weeks, exposed to chilling winds and cold rains.

Without proper clothing, food, or shelter, they contracted strange fevers, digestive ailments, and lung diseases. Hundreds died during a period when there was already a dire shortage of manpower resulting from a scourge of plague or cholera that wiped out over a third of the population in 1804 and 1805. Whole villages faced famine, impoverishment, and obliteration. Kamehameha was a man of wisdom, occasionally a humane despot, but he was also a victim of avarice, with a passion for foreign refinements, which only wealth would bring.

The heyday of the sandalwood trade did not come until the second decade of the century. In one peak year nineteen thousand piculs were shipped to Canton alone, and foreign vessels looking for extra cargoes of the wood arrived in the Islands at the average rate of one a week. For one shipload, Kamehameha enriched his storehouses with such luxuries and useless imports as 50 silk hats, 1 iron hearth, 135 pounds of large glass beads, 1,000 large beads, 2 dozen cotton stockings, 2 crystal lamps, 12 Chinese chairs, 10 boxes of silk handkerchiefs, 12 black straw hats, 50 Chinese cutlasses, 3 pieces flowered flannel, 3 boxes of sweets, 1 large coat.

When delivery of the bundles of wood from the mountains was slow, the king cheerfully signed IOU's, in sandalwood, for tons of such goods, and even for ships in which he hoped to develop a commerce of his own. He seemed to assume that the supply of sandalwood was inexhaustible and would last forever.

At the height of the boom, another customer moved enigmatically onto the scene, looking for a share of the wood to supplement a thriving fur trade—Russia. The Tsars had been tardy in sponsoring

Pacific exploration, despite the fact that the Russian shore line extended all the way from the Sea of Okhotsk to the Gulf of Alaska. But their periodic probings were at last under way, and the Russian American Company had established a fur center on Sitka Sound, only five hundred miles north of Vancouver.

The yield in furs there was fantastic, but it took over a year to pack the catch across Siberia and longer to get return supplies. At times the colony was on the verge of starvation. A source of food and dry goods nearer to Sitka had to be found, and California or Hawaii were the logical choices.

Kamehameha was inclined to greet all comers exuberantly, and so he greeted the Russians in their first overtures, pledging complete cooperation as well as commercial preference. Not until representatives of the Russian American Company had erected a solid fort on Kauai and were brazenly starting to construct another in Honolulu did the king conclude that his neighbors to the north were looking for more than commerce.

They were summarily expelled and Russian-Hawaiian relations for a time were clouded. Finally the distinguished explorer, Otto von Kotzebue, was dispatched to the Islands to offer an apology. All the fort building, he explained, was a mistake, a preposterous scheme hatched by the fur-company people without the knowledge of their government and entirely contrary to the Tsar's wishes; the Russian authorities had no desire to establish settlements in the Islands.

Kamehameha graciously accepted the apology, and for years Russian ships moved peacefully in and out of Honolulu, hoping to pick up cargoes of sandalwood to add to the fur freightage. But the calls no longer paid off. Nor did the calls of ships from America or Europe. The mountains had been stripped of the prize wood; little but scrub growth remained. In a desperate effort to locate more sandalwood, searchers adopted the practice of setting fire to impenetrable jungle and sniffing downwind to catch a familiar odor that might lead to a new find. Thousands of acres were recklessly burned, adding to the wanton forest destruction that had already occurred, for by merely opening trails into the woodlands the devastation of timbered areas and watershed had started.

Slowly the trade petered out, and the energies of a people petered out with it. Sandalwood had purchased wonderful new luxuries, such as brilliant textiles of silk and cotton; ingenious inventions like paper and glass; superb tools, furniture, and utensils; showy mirrors, wall paintings, rugs; commonplaces like soap, pins, and scissors. But with the bargains came the white man's diseases, his aggressive drive, his sins and morals, his superiority complex, his firearms, his liquor and tobacco, his passion for getting rather than giving.

The Hawaiians lacked the social experience to cope with the sudden influx of ideas and things. They were receptive to all innovations, good and bad. The concept of profit making alone was enough to destroy what they had always lived by. They were overwhelmed by it all, bewildered, demoralized.

Contact with foreigners was destroying their confidence in the gods and the *kahunas*, confidence in the taboo system, and confidence in themselves. They could not miss observing how traders ignored or defied Hawaiian gods and not only survived but prospered, how they scoffed at taboos and went unpunished. Brothers had sailed away to other countries and returned with reports of a deity less demanding and less punitive than their galaxy of gods. Indeed, they brought the rumor that in the ancestral land of Tahiti, their own gods had been overthrown. And individual Hawaiians could check their consciences and recall that no punishment had followed secret violations of taboos like eating forbidden fruit, trespassing a chief's property, sharing food with a woman.

Kamehameha was aware of the loss of faith among his subjects, but even his unwavering faith and example were not enough to restore it to his people. "Be loyal to the gods and all will be well with you," he pleaded to the last, as though he were defending a cause already lost.

The great monarch who had succeeded in uniting the Hawaiians, only to witness the beginning of their disintegration, died in 1819, and the ensuing orgy of self-flagellation, wailing, and public prostitution gave every indication that the old customs were inviolably fixed. But appearances were deceptive; the ancient order was irreparably broken.

Kamehameha's successor quickly recognized the futility of attempting to retain the taboo system in the face of encroaching civilization, and, coaxed into action by the queen mother and other women of the court, in one simple, dramatic gesture, he dared express his conviction merely by seating himself among the women at a public feast and sampling their food. Such deliberate sacrilege had never before been committed. The royal edict was unmistakable, but the new king let the guests at the great state occasion proclaim it in an astonished, jubilant chorus: "The taboo is broken! The taboo is broken!" That meant all taboos, all restrictions. And without the taboos, the gods, too, were dispensable.

Orders were issued to demolish the *heiaus* and destroy the idols. The sacred relics of ages went up in flames, and a people, already confused and perplexed, were left without a faith, a frame of statutes, or a code of values. All that remained to give continuity and stability in the kingdom were the remnants of the traditional feudal system.

Yet even this revolution could not alter the fundamental Hawaiian character. The lightheartedness, the sense of humor and love of play were indestructible. "They are happy as children, and one soon becomes like them when living amongst them," declared a German artist accompanying von Kotzebue's Russian expedition. "As happy as any people on earth" and "certainly the most cheerful," Ebenezer Townsend added. But the lingering spirit of happiness was something inherent; the invaders from the west had contributed little to it.

III
Hopes for Eternity

To a God-fearing New Englander, anyone anywhere not living in the Puritan image was a little wicked. The Pacific islanders, who had never heard of the Puritans, were, therefore, very wicked indeed. But the gap in the enlightenment of these infidels was about to be closed. The Connecticut missionaries were coming.

Not quite all the evangelists who saved Hawaii were from Connecticut, but a majority was, and the rest might as well have been, for the Hartford and New Haven code was pretty standard religious fare in New England and upstate New York. Except for a sprinkling of Presbyterians, who did not stray far from the code, they were undeviating adherents of Connecticut Congregationalism, the "established" religion of that state for over two centuries; they were under the influence of Connecticut's Yale—or the colleges and seminaries fostered by sons of Eli; under the spell of Connecticut Calvinism, of Connecticut's Jonathan Edwards and his Great Awakening.

The Awakening had established the principle that salvation was the only thing in life worth striving for, that the humble man must accept absolute dependence upon God and divine Grace for redemption, and that only the souls of the elect, through regeneration, stood a chance of being saved. The doctrine permeated every aspect of life from the bedroom to the legislative chamber, and had once inspired the citizens of Milford to vote unanimously in a regularly constituted town meeting "that the earth is the Lord's and the fullness thereof; that the earth is given to the Saints; that we are the Saints."

At town meetings was transacted all official business of the church. No fine line was drawn between civil and ecclesiastical affairs. Until 1818, when "established" religion was demoted and at least legally balloted out of existence, the state was merely the secular arm of the Congregational Church. But alteration of the law did not materially alter realities.

Ministers of the gospel continued to be among the recognized leaders of the state, and, for the most part, they deserved that recognition. They were great men, well-informed, vigorous, outspoken, men of intellect, men of action. In the most honorable sense, they were expected to be practicing politicians and political spokesmen. They preached and prayed politics. For generations their election to pastorates had taken place in town meetings. They were part of the government.

This was the religion, with its political accent, that was to be transplanted to Hawaii. It was a seven-day-a-week faith, with emphasis on the Sabbath. On all calendars were six profane days in which worldly affairs could be carried on with impunity, as long as morning, evening, and mealtime interludes for prayer and Bible reading were observed, but the seventh day was the Lord's. All work ceased, all socializing, all temporal transactions, all travel, except necessary transit to church. This had long been the law.

The missionaries had been brought up, schooled, and edified in this kind of society. The thou-shalt-not attitude extended far beyond the Ten Commandments; it was antitheatre, antidance, antisex, anti-card-playing, antiextravagance, anti-indulgence of any kind; it was so anti-Romanist that as late as 1835 there were only a few hundred Catholics in Connecticut and only two wooden Catholic churches.

Religion had become involved with agriculture, too. Farming was the employment of the majority, and what was necessary for crop and cattle raising was likely to be beneficial to religious life. "My father was Gaylord Coan of Killingworth, Connecticut," proudly boasted the Reverend Titus Coan, one of the most energetic of the Hawaiian evangelists. "He was a thoughtful, quiet and modest farmer, industrious, frugal and temperate, attending to his own business, living in peace with his neighbors, eschewing evil, honest in dealing, avoiding debts, abhorring extravagance and profligacy, refusing proffered offices, strictly observing the Sabbath, a regular attendant on the services of the sanctuary, a constant reader of the Bible, and always offering morning and evening prayers with the family."

Among the seven-score gospel messengers who brought the Word to Hawaii were few who could not offer similar testimony regarding their parentage. They had profited from proper family upbringing, established rapport with the Almighty and with their community pastors, and gone on to a college like Yale or Bowdoin or Williams or Amherst or Middlebury or Union, where they usually received the "call." They were thoroughly familiar with the church-state conception of society, and were ready to pass on their built-in didactics to any in need of an Awakening. They had to do it Connecticut style.

Lock, stock, and barrel this Connecticut way of life was transported to Hawaii in 1820 and imposed upon a people whose previous introduction to the Son of God had been principally in the profane outpourings of *haole* drifters and deckhands.

The transposal was not an isolated event. In the early decades of the 1800's missionary work was being elevated into a kind of fad among high-minded teenagers and collegians. Inspired by recurrent religious revivals, students went off on emotional jags that led to tours on the paths of righteousness and pledges to devote their lives to conveying the Christian message to places difficult to find even in the geography books. Nor were the decisions ephemeral. Often they stuck;

the converts went on to Andover Theological Seminary and from there to the outposts of civilization.

A collective enthusiasm of this sort among undergraduates at Williams College brought about the organization of a needed clearing house for the pool of Protestant missionaries ready to volunteer for service anywhere on the globe—the American Board of Commissioners for Foreign Missions. Yale formed the "Washington Band" for converting the Indians of the Northwest. Middlebury for a time concentrated on "darkest Egypt" and the Near East and then graduated a go-getter named Hiram Bingham who had an obsession to do something for the Sandwich Islands.

The focus on Hawaii came as a natural result of the arrival of scores of foot-loose *kanakas,* dropped off at the eastern ports by Pacific traders. Hawaiians had proved to be such excellent sailors that practically every skipper calling at the Islands tried to recruit a few. One took on a total of sixty. They were considered expendable, and frequently disappeared at ports of call along the way, but many stayed with the ship all the way back to New England or New York waterfronts, where, not uncommonly losing contact with their captains, they turned into vagrants and public charges or occasionally accepted the charity of some philanthropic patron or society.

Tales of benighted souls in the Pacific islands were being circulated by loquacious sea captains and crew members; the stories were getting into print, reviewed in pulpits, editorialized in missionary magazines, and discussed on college campuses. Stray Hawaiians, meanwhile, were put to work on farms, were sent to district schools, taken to church, displayed as heathen curiosities, and even used as exhibits by ministerial fund raisers canvassing for foreign missions on door-to-door drives. There were enough of them, scattered particularly through Connecticut and Massachusetts, to make a considerable impression.

Finally a few homesick Hawaiian lads were rounded up and sent off to chilly Cornwall, Connecticut, to attend a new "Foreign Mission School for the Sons of Unevangelized Barbarians." In this bucolic environment they were introduced to cravats, tea cups, and church

manners, to studies in English grammar, mechanics, natural philosophy, and Biblical chronology, and, for them, to such wholly extrane-
ous old stand-bys as Latin, Greek, Hebrew, and quadratic equations.

Head and shoulders above any other student at Cornwall was a
young native from the Big Island, Opukahaia, a name more or less
Anglicized into "Obookiah," to which "Henry" was prefixed for civ-
ilizing effect. Henry Obookiah had lived an eventful past. As a child,
he had witnessed the brutal slaying of the rest of his family in a feudal
skirmish with ironhanded chiefs, had been rescued from slaughter,
himself by a relative and sent to a *heiau* for training as a priest, had
escaped from that confinement and attached himself to an American
trader. In 1810 he sailed off to America and a few months later, like
scores of his contemporaries, found himself stranded in alien New
England. A group of Yale students discovered him in New Haven and
began putting him through tutorials. They were astonished at the way
he caught on.

When academic life paled, he was farmed out for several years
successively to wholesome Yankee rustics, to parish pastors, school
preceptors, and church deacons. Gradually he acquired a fair command of English, a respectable Christian education, and a fixed ambition to return to the Islands to convert his heathen brethren.

If he had returned, Henry would have given a providential lift to
the missionary cause, but at Cornwall he caught typhoid fever and
teetered between life and death for weeks. Finally on February 19,
1818, passing the torch to classmates circling his bed, he urged them
to love God and take the gospel back to the Pacific and died, reportedly, with an *Aloha oe* on his lips.

The death of Henry Obookiah made news in New England. Immediately, an enterprising mission board published a tract giving all
the harrowing details of his life and death. It was the sectarian best
seller of the year and went into edition after edition. Hundreds of
thousands read it. Henry became a martyr to the cause of Christianizing the Islands. The publication of that booklet, guaranteed to bring
not only tears but sobs from the most callous reader, was Hawaii's

first big advertisement. The Islanders had to be saved. The response from the salvation set was electric.

As one of the set later explained, "Hasten, *hasten* was the watchword that went from church to church. Six marriages were solemnized; two missionaries were ordained; a band was gathered from a dozen different churches to go forth as messengers of the churches to the far distant land of Obookiah. . . . Obookiah from on high saw that day. He saw the darkness fleeing away from Hawaii, and that a mission family, so hastily fitted out, was going forth to carry the Bible to a nation without a God."

One reason for the hasty marriages was that the American Board did not care to take the risk of turning unattached divinity students loose among the Hawaiian maidens they had heard about. The first company consisted of two ordained ministers, two teachers, a physician, a farmer, a printer—most with young brides—and four of the late Obookiah's Cornwall classmates.

The sacrifice that the volunteers were making could not stand belittlement. Not one of them ever expected to see his homeland again. Their farewells were final. They were literally giving their lives, and most of them assumed that survival would be short once their doctrine came in conflict with the doctrine of infidel priests.

Nor did the missionaries intend to make any life-saving concessions to idolatry. In fact, there were to be no concessions at all. New England culture and all its trimmings went with the religion—from long, wordy sermons to long woolen underwear, from the cast-iron constitution to the cast-iron kitchen stove. The Yankee accouterments were part and parcel of Congregationalism.

The first wave of this army of the Lord descended upon Hawaii on March 30, 1820, a little the worse for wear. The eighteen-thousand-mile journey around the Horn, aboard the trader *Thaddeus,* had taken five months—157 days. And, as if the agony of the permanent good-bys in Boston and the memories of that agony were not enough, they had been put through a nightmare of tribulations on the way, wretched quarters, wretched food, squabbles among themselves, ridicule from the crew, condescension from Captain Blanchard, violent seasickness, the gnawing terror of what lay ahead, and, perhaps worst of all, the painful adjustments of all the newlyweds to their partners, who in several cases had met only a few days before sailing. It was no honeymoon.

Kohala, on the northern tip of Hawaii, was their landfall, and the natives swarmed out to meet the ship, as they did any trader, quite unaware of the special nature of this voyage or of the fastidiousness of the mixed company on deck. "The appearance of destitution," moaned Hiram Bingham, who had already assumed leadership of the company, "the appearance of degradation and barbarism among the chattering, almost naked savages was appalling. Some of our number with gushing tears turned away from the spectacle. Others with firmer nerve continued their gaze, but were ready to exclaim, 'Can these be human beings! How dark and comfortless their state of mind and heart! How imminent the danger of the immortal soul! Can these beings be civilized? Can they be Christianized? Can we throw ourselves upon these rude shores, and take up our abode for life among such people for the purpose of training them for heaven?' "

Though Bingham had refrained from discussing it with others, all along he had been considering Kamchatka, of all places, as an alternative destination for the mission, if they were not permitted to land in Hawaii. Kamchatka seemed very inviting to him as he looked upon the natives and the rugged shores of Kohala. But, as the *Thaddeus* sailed around the tip of the island to Kawaihae, to dispel his own doubts as well as those of his squeamish associates, he answered his rhetorical questions with a resounding "Yes." There would be no turning back, no wavering.

And it was at Kawaihae, still virtually the port of entry for the Islands, that Bingham and his cohorts first learned that half the battle they expected to fight was already won for them—the taboos had been broken and the idols destroyed. King and chiefs held sway as of old, but at least there was no recognized religion to suppress. Instead of the boiling caldron readying for a cannibal feast, instead of the shower of arrows and spears with which some of the missionaries had expected to be received, they were greeted with cheers and boatloads of gratuities.

From a safe perch in a cabin window, Lucy Thurston, twenty-four-year-old wife of the senior minister, took the liberty of waving to a canoe of natives in "revoltingly scanty" attire, and was soon courageously exchanging sea biscuit for bananas. Delighted with her first social conquest, she called out the one word of Hawaiian that she could remember in all the excitement, *"Wahine!"*

The response was startling. A dozen canoes gathered under her window and Lucy soon had more bananas than she knew what to do with. *"Wahine maikai! Wahine maikai!"* (Good girl! Good girl!) her suitors acclaimed. "That interview through the cabin window," she acknowledged triumphantly, "gave me the strengthening touch in crossing the threshold of the nation."

One of the Hawaiian boys from Cornwall hurried ashore to circulate the novel proposal that, out of deference to the ladies, natives coming aboard might care to wear something more than loin straps and wrap-arounds. Chiefs, wives, royal associates, and several of Kamehameha's surviving wives who happened to be at Kawaihae, quickly donned their finery and made for the ship, chiefs sweating in sack coats, chiefesses masquerading in faded formals, all looking out of character and uncomfortable.

For the *alii* this was an unprecedented event. The wife of a captain had occasionally been seen on the deck of a trader but never before a coterie of white *wahines*. The wealth of aloha that the Hawaiians brought aboard was as overwhelming as it was unexpected—beaming smiles, sympathy, merriment, warm hand clasps, open arms, and smothering embraces.

Even the haughty Bingham was touched and astounded at the extraordinary reception, but not for long. Once the royal welcomers had paid their respects and found the missionaries more informal than formidable, piece by piece the party attire was unceremoniously doffed, and the royalty were savages again. "Trammeled with clothes and seated on chairs, the queens were out of their element," suggested one of the Yankee wives. Not only did the women strip themselves, but they proceeded to stretch their three hundred voluptuous pounds on deck, as though the ritual of greeting had exhausted them. The men were herded into the cabin. Then and there Lucy Thurston made up her mind that the first necessary step in Christianizing the ladies was getting garments on the backs—and fronts.

Anxious to discharge his passengers as soon as possible, so that he could get on about his business, Captain Blanchard joined Bingham in trying to signify that the white ladies and gentlemen wished to go ashore, that they planned to remain in the Islands, that they brought a new religion with them, and, to teach it, that they wanted to establish missions. All was beyond the comprehension of the chiefs.

Cordial and disarming as the native spokesmen attempted to be, the New Englanders were informed that only King Liholiho could grant them what they wished and that he was in residence some forty miles down the coast at Kailua. He would have to be consulted. Graciously the chiefs and their wives, two dowager queens of Kamehameha I, their guests, and retinue offered to go along for the ride to Kailua, and Captain Blanchard grumpily agreed to let them remain on board.

But just as he was preparing to haul anchor, the vanity of one of the undressed queens brought everything to a halt. She had taken a fancy to the chaste, straight-lined dresses worn by the missionary women and insisted that she would have to be dressed in the same style for an appearance before the king. She could not allow the visiting ladies to outshine her. Had they an extra dress, or could they fashion one for her?

Sensing that this was a God-sent opportunity to satisfy her resolve to get the ample flesh of the queen under cover and realizing that nothing in the missionary wardrobes could possibly encompass her, Lucy enthusiastically agreed to make a dress if the queen could supply the material. The captain paced the deck while a messenger was dispatched ashore for a bolt of cambric.

The fabric was delivered; the *Thaddeus* set sail; and on the open deck the ladies formed the first Hawaiian sewing circle. Long before the ship reached Kailua, the dress was hemmed—an historic event in the annals of Pacific fashion. The finished product was the original *holoku*—Hawaiian Mother Hubbard. Lucy and the queen had styled a favored Island cut in women's wear for the next 145 years.

Upon arrival of the *Thaddeus* at Kailua, the king expressed his admiration for the queen's new dress, but he was not so sure about the dressmakers and their husbands. A new religion? It could be very upsetting to the kingdom. He took his time about making up his mind. While he consulted his chiefs, his conscience, and John Young, the captain grumbled about having his ship and crew tied up so long, and the missionaries fidgeted over the delay in soul saving. A week passed without a decision, ten days. The captain was losing his patience. Bingham was thinking of Kamchatka again.

At last it was John Young who resolved the dilemma. For years he had been ardently advocating a policy of Hawaii for the Hawaiians. Keep out the *malihinis,* he had advised both Kamehameha and his successor Liholiho; they would only bring *pilikia.* But now he remembered his Christian upbringing, changed his mind, and urged the king to let the missionaries stay. The old religion was dead. Let the visitors bring in a live one. The people and the kingdom would surely benefit.

Liholiho was still reluctant; so he settled upon a compromise. He would give the Americans a trial of one year, one year only. Then they would leave, or there would be a new decision. To Bingham, a foot in the door was as good as being inside. He was jubilant. He was sure, Asa Thurston was sure, and all the others were sure they could show their indispensability in twelve months. They were right.

No military task force with a carefully mapped strategy could have operated more effectively than that little band of missionaries, the first of eleven companies to invade the Islands over a period of twenty-five years. The reasonable way of organizing a campaign of righteousness would have been to set up one exemplary station in a place like Kailua or Honolulu or Lahaina, and let the Word emanate from it. There was more than enough labor to occupy all at such a center; they would have had each other's company; life could have been not too unpleasant and the work not too strenuous.

But Bingham did not reason that way. "If we would see the Gospel take effect on a nation," he decreed, "its light must be diffused over the whole nation. The mass must have opportunity to see it simultaneously. Christianity should be made by precept and example to radiate from many different points so extensively that all the tribes may have the means of judging its merits. To teach a single village or to limit missionary influence to a few, while all the rest are left to darkness would require an age to make any perceptible diminution of the mass of heathenism."

The leader had his way. He set up headquarters in Honolulu, and other couples were paired off and dispatched to stations on the outer islands, accompanied, when possible, by one of the Cornwall alumni to serve as interpreter. Each in his own fumbling way became a gospel bearer, beginning with the ABC's of the Christ story and Connecticut morality, each slowly picking up the rudiments of the Hawaiian language until a simple sermon could be delivered, each modestly and patiently laboring with individuals as well as with congregations of the curious.

If the circumstances had been prepared to order, they could not have been more advantageous. The Hawaiians had just lost their old religion and instinctively craved one to replace it. The emphasis on love, unselfishness, and charity, was not entirely unfamiliar, and little by little they caught onto the value of such fresh ideas as self-restraint, forgiveness, temperance, and pacificism. From the start, the taboos of the Bible seemed to hold an appeal among commoners that the taboos of their priests had never acquired.

Nevertheless, the missionaries were confronted with all manner of unexpected resistance, resistance from traders and ships' masters, who resented interference with their sly bartering practices and their "refreshment" programs; open opposition from merchants, who saw the chiefs accepting counsel from the missionaries rather than themselves; occasional hostility from chiefs, who did not like to have their social order challenged; conflict even with the American Board in Boston, who felt that its emissaries were making converts too readily or too slowly and were spending altogether too much money in the process.

Despite the resistance, each quickly won the love and loyalty of the masses, and the familiar title "Father"—*Makua*. As re-enforcements arrived from New England, they extended the light of salvation to thousands and tens of thousands; turned what had been strictly an oral tongue into a written language; set up printing plants at Honolulu and Lahaina and printed millions of pages, including hymnals, textbooks, periodicals, and the Bible they had translated; built hundreds of churches and schools; trained native teachers and pastors; gave Hawaii a democratic constitution, a system of laws, and a respectable government.

The Connecticut idea of broad church-state responsibility was written into the instructions from the American Board: "Your views are not to be limited to a low narrow scale. You are to open your hearts wide and set your marks high. You are to aim at nothing short of covering these islands with fruitful fields and pleasant dwellings and schools and churches, and of raising up the whole people to an elevated state of Christian civilization; . . . to introduce and get into extended operation and influence among them, the arts and institutions and usages of civilized life and society."

It was a large order, and they filled it. But triumph did not come easily. No group of apostles in the history of Christendom ever worked harder for what they accomplished, and they rarely made the mistake of requiring from their proselytes anything that quite equaled the demands they placed upon themselves.

Personal discomforts had to be taken in stride. New Englanders, who had been brought up in tidy homes with kitchens, parlors, comfortable second-story bed chambers, fireplaces, cellars, and butler's pantries, lived for years in huts little better than those occupied by the natives. A few sensitive wives never did get over the shock of their introduction to the hovels in which they were expected to set up housekeeping, dark, musty, wind-torn, flea-ridden haystacks, with the kitchen range set up in the back yard, where all the cooking, washing, ironing, and other domestic duties had to be carried on under the constant scrutiny of a native audience.

To the audience, meal preparations were the most fascinating novelty. Yankee housewives were not going to stoop to eating the food of savages, and rather than dine on pig and poi, they insisted on baking bread and pie crusts from the worm-infested flour shipped from the East Coast, cooking stale salt beef, johnnycake, and Indian pudding.

Even bananas, which few had seen in their home states, were a barbarous fruit, described by one missionary correspondent as different from anything she had ever seen, a little like a peach, but "some like a pear in taste"; similar in appearance to a milkweed pod, only longer, and containing, after stripping off the "capsule," a substance resembling a muskmelon in color and as "soft as fruit."

Unsophisticated twenty-six-year-old Lucia Holman, wife of the doctor at Kailua, complained that not only the fruits and vegetables but everything produced in the Islands "tasted heathenish"; she was sure that "the sunshine of the gospel" was the only thing that could ever sweeten the produce.

Subjected to unsavory food, living discomforts, and general deprivations, the missionaries often were a little sorry for themselves. "Committing ourselves to the care and protection of our ever-watchful Heavenly Father," Bingham wrote lugubriously, "and putting ourselves in the power of strangers and pagans, untutored and destitute of the feeling of moral responsibility, intemperate, lewd and thievish, as they were, we unhesitatingly entered into this new mode of life, and as missionary pilgrims, cheerfully took up our abode in that dark, ruined land, which we looked upon as the place of our sojourn and toil while on earth, and the resting place of our bones when our brief pilgrimage should end." Almost a decade passed before the fatalistic Bingham moved from thatched hut into the security of a frame house with doors he could bolt.

All the parsonages followed the same pattern, distinguished from the huts of the natives only by the kitchen range in the yard and the long underwear, the petticoats and diapers hanging on the clothesline. But parishioners recognized the difference and soon put the *haole* homes to use as chapels, hospitals, schoolrooms, council chambers, and confession booths.

The natives were there at all hours of the day and night. At daybreak they were waiting outside. Toward midnight the last of the visitors had to be dismissed. They trooped in singly or in delegations, invariably to sit at the feet of the missionary or his wife, where they pleaded for advice. There was no freedom even for meals. Fifty or sixty at a time managed to crowd into the bantam shelters. A day without a few hundred callers was dull.

"Such is the propensity to flock to our house for religious instruction," one of the wives wrote back home, "that we found it necessary to have restrictions. During the forenoon, the house was under a *kapu;* that is, the people were not allowed to visit it. Yet to this general rule the chiefs and principal teachers must be made an exception. In the afternoon our doors are open to any and all, and our house has been thronged. The principal chiefs take chairs, but the common people enter, and as it is their habit, seat themselves at our feet saying: 'We have come to declare to you our thoughts; we are sinners; we are thieves, and liars, and adulterers, and murderers. . . . Teach us.' "

Periodically the wives had to take care of all the callers, while the husbands were making the rounds of the scores of villages that composed a "parish." These tours would take them on hundred-mile circuits and last for two or three weeks, with visits to half a dozen villages a day. At each a sermon was delivered, in addition to the baptismal ceremonies, the weddings, the funerals, the public and private rebukes to backsliders.

Titus Coan, who arrived with one of the later "reinforcements," went at his job in Hilo as though he had to make up for lost time. Within a few years, he built up a congregation totaling more than seven thousand. Outside of Hilo, Father Coan's parish extended along the coast north and south for over a hundred miles and inland for another ten, a field of close to a thousand square miles. His home and church were constantly overwhelmed with the penitent, but more than half his time had to be spent on tours.

For years there were no roads out of the village of Hilo, no bridges over the countless streams that crossed his domain, and no available horses. The trips had to be made on foot, and his visits scheduled well in advance, so that the congregations would be prepared for him. That meant that he had to keep moving, come rain or shine, hell or high water.

The high water was his worst impediment, for the entire coast north of Hilo was broken by a succession of sheer canyons, the watershed of mighty Mauna Kea. To get from one village to the next necessitated ascending and descending the precipitous divides of these canyons and crossing the rivers at their depths. In the dry season there was no problem; Coan waded the streams, vaulted them on a pole, or crossed leaping from rock to rock. But most of the seasons on that line of coast were wet, and a downpour high on the mountain any day of the year could send a six-foot wall of water down a stream bed, converting a lazy brook into a raging river in minutes.

Many a time he raced an approaching avalanche of water across a gully and cleared it by a hairbreadth. If the torrent already filled the bed, he had to resort to other measures. Waiting for the stream to go down could disrupt his meeting schedule for a week. He had to cross. For a narrow flood of a hundred feet or so, natives would sling a rope across and tie it on the banks so that he could pull himself hand over hand through the foaming current. Or if the bed were too wide, they would somehow manage to pass or swim a series of ropes from shore to protruding boulder to well-grounded snag, and on to the far shore before he was permitted to attempt his hand-over-hand crossing.

More frequently he rode the shoulders of a sturdy native, gripping the bushy hair of the porter, who worked his way along the steep, slippery river bottom, leaning upstream against a current strong enough to sweep an unpracticed pathfinder into kingdom come, moving one foot at a time sideways among the slimy boulders and sliding the other cautiously alongside. "Thus feeling his way slowly across," Coan airily commented, "he would land me safe with a shout and a laugh on the opposite bank."

So complete was the pastor's confidence in his Hawaiian porters that he once allowed himself to be inched across a river in full flood at the only point where the water was not over the head of his bearer, just above the brink of a thundering 426-foot waterfall.

When a land route was impossible to follow, he took to the sea in a canoe, and often that proved to be more precarious than the river crossings. On one occasion after a heavy storm, he spent an entire night outside the line of breaking swells, bailing for his life, as waves kept washing over the bow. His crew of paddlers were experts, but they refused to risk the life of Father Coan by attempting to take the canoe through thirty-foot surf into a narrow, rock-bordered inlet, the only possible landing place. Not until daybreak, when members of the congregation he was coming to address, spotted him from a headland and saw his predicament, did there appear to be much hope of survival. They risked their lives by swimming to the rescue, and he was brought ashore through the tricky channel, triumphantly riding the crest of a roller in his canoe at breakneck speed, as if it were great sport.

A friend accompanied him on the longest of his routine tours to the barren, lava-strewn regions of South Point, where fishing and salt making were the only sources of livelihood. There lived the most uncivilized and impoverished groups of all the Islanders, but Titus Coan had already brought Christianity to them. His visits were the great events of their lives.

"The day of his coming was marked by a white stone on their calendar," explained the companion. "He knew them all by name; he examined the progress of the children in their lessons at school; he prescribed medicine for the sick, even going so far as to enter the realm of minor surgery with his jackknife. He visited the widows and orphans, counseling them with regard to their welfare in this life as well as the next. He made it a point to see and exchange a few cheerful words with everyone in the throng. . . .

"The periodical review being thus complete, the faithful were called together by the sound of the conch-shell trumpet, for the crowning mystery of the day—the celebration of Holy Communion. The believers sat in rows upon the matted floor, reverently bowing their heads in prayer, as the rites of baptism and of admission to the church were performed.

"Then the dusky deacons carried around to each one a morsel of wheaten bread—emblem truly sacred, for never elsewhere did they taste such provision—and a cup that contained molasses and water, representing the wine of the Holy Feast. . . . Having thus assailed his parish, Father Coan took up his staff and we traveled over the black lava toward the next station, a distance of eight or nine miles from the seacoast."

From South Point on Hawaii to the villages on the northern shore of Kauai, the missionary visitations were much the same. No community was too remote to escape the evangelical ministrations. Inhabitants of settlements where there was no regular Sunday service tramped en masse ten, twenty, thirty miles, to centers where there was one. In the autumn of 1826, a congregation "estimated at no less than 10,000" gathered at the little port of Kawaihae, "probably the largest assembly for that purpose ever convened in the Islands," claimed the secretary of the American Board.

That service had to be held in the open, but ordinarily there was an enclosed sanctuary of sorts. Every sizable village had one, always crowded—and structurally a bitter disappointment to the missionary builders. They had hoped to construct white-steepled churches like those left behind in New England, but without sawmills and adequate lumber, it was out of the question in the early years.

The only solution was to accept the heathen way of building, put up bigger and bigger grass shacks, and enlist the natives to do it. The enlistment came easily; Hawaiians were used to tackling that kind of community project, took pride in their workmanship, and were eager to participate in any endeavor sponsored by their beloved cleric. But the engineering was not so easy.

The basic rule of thumb in grass-house construction was to keep the building small and, if more enclosed space was needed, to build more small shacks. The weight of rain-soaked thatch, the force of gusty winds, and Kona gales made it necessary. Yet a church had to be big, had to be large enough to hold a congregation, and that meant that it must be supported, beamed, and buttressed with tall timber instead of bean poles.

Plan after plan was drawn up by Yankee divines at different stations, and enormous structures built from the plans. Wise old chiefs said they would not stand; that they were top-heavy; that if high winds did not bring them down, the rains would; that they would collapse under the weight of water absorbed in the thatch. But stubborn New Englanders were not deterred.

Disciples were sent back into the same mountains where they had once cut sandalwood for the China trade and giant *koa* for war canoes, this time in search of straight, solid virgin *ohia*. Steel axes were still rare, and whipsaws rarer. In a congregation of a thousand there might not be more than three or four axes, and nothing but lava on which to sharpen them; yet with these three or four, volunteers would fell and trim trees harder than oak and four feet thick at the butt, shape them into timbers a foot and a half square by fifty feet long, and then snake them out of the woods by hand.

"When the timbers are cut," reported Elias Bond of Kohala, who knew something about lumbering from his Maine upbringing, "from eighty to one hundred and fifty persons of both sexes lay hold of a long rope made fast to one end of the timber, and after a day of work dragging the heavy load up and down the precipitous banks of our frequent ravines, through woods and brush, they deposit a single stick of timber on the ground for building. Oxen could do nothing if we had them, because of the thousands of ravines at all depths from thirty feet to twelve hundred, which continually intersect one another. . . . One stick of fifty or more feet in length and fifteen or sixteen inches square occupied four days of the severest labor in drawing."

At Hilo it was the same. "Such labor was considered no hardship," vouched Dr. Henry M. Lyman, famed scientist and traveler, who witnessed the scene in his youth. "The natives had always been accustomed to this mode of transportation for their canoes and other weighty objects. A day in the woods after a big log was regarded as a picnic rather than a laborious task. Many a time in the gloaming did we hear the cheerful songs of parties thus returning home with the trunk of a mighty tree gliding like a monstrous serpent in the grass behind them."

Missionaries themselves were not averse to joining these expeditions, wielding a dull ax, and heaving on the homemade *hau* bark rope. "On such occasions," testified a typical parson, "we usually, on our arrival at the timber, unite in prayer, and then, fastening to the stick, proceed to the work. I have often gone with them to the forest, laid hold of a rope and dragged timber with them from morning to night."

"No conversation is allowed," he added, "except by the marshall, who seems to feel it is his privilege to make noise enough for all. About once in half a mile all stop to rest, and then proceed again. The marshall has a thousand smart things to say to arouse their zeal and provoke their muscular energies—'Bow the head! Blister the hands! Sweat!' All is done in good nature."

And after the timbers were assembled, in the same good nature the loggers helped carpenters raise uprights and tie beams and rafters, assisted in gathering and lashing in place thousands of cross poles, aided the grass gatherers and the thatchers, until at last the women were ready to unroll the great carpets of woven *lau hala,* layer after layer, to serve triple duty as floor, pews, and cushions.

It was all labor for the Lord, the builders were assured. But worldly *haoles* offered their contrary contention; they continually fumed that the missionaries were working the congregations to death. And they had a point. The huge brown haystacks proved to be highly destructible, just as the chiefs had predicted. In dry weather fierce winds tore off the roofs; in wet weather rafters and ridgepoles sagged under the weight of soaked thatch; stray cows munched on the side walls until they were bald; the structures were so inflammable that a few went up in spectacular conflagrations; church after church collapsed.

The life of a straw sanctuary was seldom more than three or four years. But such was the devotion of a congregation and its pastor, that, without too much disconsolation, they would salvage what could be salvaged and start in all over again. Not until 1832, when the mission at Lahaina completed the first stone church in the Islands, was there a meeting house that faintly resembled the Connecticut pattern. Five years later the massive lava stone edifice at Kailua was erected, and in 1842 the coral-block Kawaiahao Church in Honolulu.

But these stone buildings were all too elegant for the tastes of commoners. They liked the gospel as it was served up under a roof of thatch. The worship there could be more informal, and their pet pigs and dogs could be smuggled in more easily. Before the shift from thatch to stone, a *haole* worshiper confessed that he had been persuaded most unwillingly to attend "the great Hawaiian church in Honolulu, the Royal Chapel, where Father Bingham held forth in the presence of the king and his chiefs and a vast concourse of the common people." He was impressed with the immensity of the grass structure, nearly two hundred feet long and over sixty wide, but he was not impressed with the proceedings. "The congregation, some 3,000 in number, squatted native fashion on the floor. Dogs swarmed everywhere, in spite of the strenuous efforts on the part of numerous doorkeepers to keep them out of the sanctuary. Father Bingham was gifted in prayer, having on one occasion publicly addressed the throne of grace for an hour and a half without intermission. This time he prayed only forty minutes. How long he preached, I know not, for my sleep was profound and refreshing."

In New England the prolix prayers were salted with "eye openers," shocking revelations of local conduct announced factually for the edification of the Lord and the public, with petitions for appropriate censure or forgiveness. Eye openers in profusion were incorporated in the Hawaiian prayers, for this means of exposing sin and shortcoming was regarded as nonlibelous, irrefutable, and instructive, and helped to keep the audience alert and attentive.

But prayers, at their shortest, were the most unpopular part of the service, because Hawaiians associated them with the ancient and hated practice of "praying people to death," supplications so effective psychologically that the subject against whom a priest prayed commonly did succumb. So superstitious members of the congregation were always a little uneasy during prayers and frequently took advantage of the minister's closed eyes to make surreptitious departures.

On the other hand, everybody enjoyed the hymn singing—*himeni.* Without the *himeni,* Christianity would have found hard sledding in the Sandwich Islands. The catchy gospel tunes were what made Congregationalism immediately palatable; Hawaiians, who had never known real melody, loved them, and the missionaries made the most of it by translating hundreds of old favorites.

The stanzas, taught line by line in the New England fashion of "lining," soon replaced many of the native *meles* and hulas, were just as popular for weekday as for Sunday rendition, and in time were freely aped in composing impious new popular songs. But until the choristers learned to adjust their four-note scale to an octave, the musical effect was often punishingly discordant. Instead of singing higher or lower, congregations merely shrieked louder. Even contrite missionary children occasionally contracted uncontrollable cases of the giggles during the song service.

Added to the dissonance in *himeni*, the cautious withdrawals during prayers, and the general commotion of dogs, adults, and restless children was the informality of costume. Pulpit exhortation about appearing before the Maker in decent apparel slowly took root, but not as was intended. Women more frequently came to church with covered bosoms and covered heads, rotund bodies enveloped in *holokus* or shapeless *muumuus* and heads shrouded under outlandish representations of sun bonnets and palm-leaf hoods.

The Reverend Charles S. Stewart of Lahaina averred that he had seen a high-ranking, "monstrously large" chiefess on her way to church dressed in a flimsy white muslin slip, heavy woodsmen's boots on stockingless feet, carrying a distinguished silver-headed cane, all topped with an immense and fashionable French chapeau.

All these passed inspection. The men, however, were inclined to be content with any symbol or tag end of western attire. For one, a pair of elephantine trousers held up by gaudy galluses took the place of a *malo*; his brother proudly wore a *malo* and the jacket that belonged to the trousers; another member of the family appeared in *malo* and crimson vest. Even an open umbrella was considered an adequate substitute for shirt and pants, or a pair of shoes, which would squeak down the aisle and then be passed through a break in the thatch to a friend waiting outside for his entrance, the same pair serving half a dozen churchgoers.

Yet when one overlooked the vestments, turned a deaf ear to the tortured hymns, and forgot the other distractions, a church service could be a very impressive ceremony. From offshore, an officer, serving as chaplain on a warship, once watched the long lines of natives streaming into Hilo on a Sunday morning, hordes of people, hundreds, thousands. The paths were outlined with them far back into the hills, and the ocean was dotted with canoes. It was so incredible that he decided to join the procession.

He went out of curiosity, expecting perhaps to be diverted. He was stunned. "I can scarcely describe the emotions experienced in glancing an eye over the immense number," he exclaimed. "They were seated so thickly on the matted floor as to seem literally one mass of heads covering an area of more than 9,000 square feet . . . a demonstration of the power of the Word of God on untutored men, which is without a parallel in existing events, if not in the records of history.

"The depth of the impression rose from the irresistible conviction that the Spirit of God was there: it could have been nothing else. The breathless silence, the eager attention, the half-suppressed sigh, the tear, the various feelings, sad, peaceful, joyous, discoverable in the faces of the many, all spoke the presence of an invisible but omnipotent power. It was, in a word, a heathen congregation fully sensible of the darkness and despair of their original state. The simple appearance of that obscure congregation . . . did more to rivet the conviction of the Divine origin of the Bible and of the holy influences by which it is accompanied to the hearts of men, than all the arguments, apologies and defences of Christianity I ever read."

The naval officer was witnessing Father Coan in action. The Great Awakening had at last come to the Islands, and the Hilo evangelist had brought it. For a few years in the middle thirties the early enthusiasm for churchgoing and the gospel had seemed to wear off because of a slacking of royal interest and the criticism of foreign skeptics. But Coan turned the tide. The revival he started swept over the Islands like contagion itself. During that revival, which lasted for three or four years, twenty thousand were taken into the church. Eventually even the king, his cohorts, and a few foreign dissidents joined up. Yankee Congregationalism became a Hawaiian fixture.

Although a muster of over 150 clergymen, dedicated wives, teachers, medical missionaries, agricultural missionaries, typographical missionaries, helpers, and assistants had a hand in the big venture, seldom were there more than fifty on the job at any one time. The less hardy played out. They died of overwork and mysterious diseases. They could not endure the isolation and the strain, and made no bones about admitting it. They begged for furloughs, got them, and found excuses for not returning. The fifty who bore the burden did the work of five hundred—on salaries ranging from $140 to $600 a year, half of which might go into the church collection plate.

They could not have carried on without handouts of food from the natives, their own attempts at gardening, furniture making, house building, and side enterprises—and the "boxes" from home. Those boxes, arriving once or twice a year from charity societies in the States, filled with castoffs and hand me-downs, made all the difference between existing and living and frequently were what kept the missionaries and their numerous offspring clothed in threadbare decency. They were the real morale builders that could advance Christmas from December to August or April. They were presumptuously prayed for by elders and children alike and, when they came, were recognized as answers to prayer.

Anything could be expected in the boxes from shoes, saucers, and squash seeds to a wheelbarrow or even a knocked-down farm wagon. The favorite benevolence of the home missionary society was a patchwork quilt, preferably an "album quilt" with the signatures of the seamstresses stitched into the squares. The names constituted a kind of endorsement, and though nothing was much more useless in Hawaii than down-stuffed bed coverings, they were prized possessions.

Stockings, books, bonnets, aprons, a scarred fiddle, unwanted woolen coats, hollyhock seeds gathered from a familiar back yard, blue denim, caddies of tea, gingham dresses, water pitchers, all might be found in the same surprise package, and out of the chinks and pockets rattled such delicacies as dried apples, chestnuts, kernels of corn for popping or parching, not to mention the fragments of broken tumblers and tea cups.

But display of the contents of these boxes brought rancorous criticism from white settlers who did not own such refinements. Anyone who possessed tailored clothes—however unfashionable—anyone who could serve tea in rosebud chinaware, afford a fiddle for the boy, and make generous donations to the church had to be pretty well off. Missionary work must pay handsomely, whispered the foreigners—or are the preachers robbing the natives? White critics never seemed to realize that the missionary families lived on charity and often gave to the church, not a tithe, but every penny in their pockets.

To supplement the meager salaries and secure enough income to support families of half a dozen children, all of them had to develop sidelines. They tried raising sugar cane, took up surveying, tried growing coffee, made cigars—though their doctrine banned smoking—experimented with silk worms, raised cattle, attempted innumerable farm ventures.

Many of the experiments were actually parish projects. If a church were going to be self-supporting, reasoned the missionaries, the community had to be self-supporting first. They promoted little plantations and then bigger ones. Father Bond, determined to make his church self-sustaining and independent of the American Board, set an example at Kohala. He started a sugar plantation, and for years it was a losing proposition. He went deeply into debt before it began to pay off. But it did pay off; not only was a dying community revived, but the Kohala church was the first to declare its independence of the American Board. Others saw the merit in his achievement and followed his example.

Conscientious apostles took very literally their original charge about "covering these islands with fruitful fields" and introducing the people to "the institutions and usages of civilized society." They quit their evangelical assignments to serve in such worldly capacities as royal councilors and government plenipotentiaries, secular teachers and commercial agents.

But political or financial attainment was hard on the reputation of an ex-missionary. Father Bond, who contributed to the American Board and other charities many times what he ever received in salary, was dubbed "King of Kohala"; Father Bingham became "King Bingham"; medical missionary Dr. Gerrit Judd, who gave up doctoring to reorganize the Hawaiian government, was "King Judd," the "White King."

Those most devoted to Island causes gave up all thought of returning to New England and adopted Hawaii as their permanent home, and for some it was a mistake. They were hopelessly behind times, expounding outmoded ideas, still living in the 1820's, unbudging in their intolerance, oblivious of all the changes that had taken place in the United States since they had left there.

Missionaries of other faiths felt it their duty to establish stations in the Islands, too, and the Congregationalists fought them off. Repeatedly they used their influence with royalty to expel French padres, and they were equally inhospitable to the Mormons and the Anglicans. They wanted for Hawaii an "established religion" like the one that Connecticut once sheltered—and had long since abandoned. Eventually other churches did form permanent missions—the Catholics in 1839, the Latter Day Saints in 1850, the Episcopalians in 1862, but each such intrusion was regarded by the Congregationalists as a failure on their part.

The world heaped more criticism than credit upon them, and the British were perhaps the most cutting. Declared England's Consul-General in Honolulu: "They have been wrong in their hot-house plan of forcing Christianity on an unprepared people, endeavoring to make them run before they could walk or even stand alone. . . . They have been wrong in using their great influence with the native government in urging a hard repressive system of legislation. They have been wrong—at least they have been unfortunate—in the personal qualifications of many of their teachers for their task, when so much of a missionary's success depends upon appearance, manner and knowledge."

Yet a Frenchman, a member of the Chamber of Deputies, a citizen of the Catholic nation which had been insolently repulsed by the missionaries, Count Agenor de Gasparin, had the last word. "Where," he asked, "can we find in the annals of Government a social transformation which can compare with that which sixty poor American missionaries have affected upon 130,000 savages?"

The missionaries went to Hawaii to transplant a Connecticut

Calvinist society, and they succeeded. If the world took exception to what was accomplished or the way it was accomplished. Calvinism and Yankeedom had to share the stigma. New Englanders, who by the tens of thousands, had contributed pennies or dollars, held a stake in the enterprise, and fund raisers for the American Board never let them forget it.

Over and over again the story was told of the Massachusetts wheelwright who reluctantly gave a dollar in 1820, feeling that he might as well throw it away. Yet within thirty years that wheelwright received from Hawaii orders for twenty pairs of cartwheels and bodies at $90 a pair. "If men wish to invest money where it will yield a dividend of 1800 per cent," exhorted the missionary stewards, "they had better put it in the treasury of missions." Altogether, Yankeedom drew an even better rate of interest than the wheelwright.

After spending approximately a million dollars on the Hawaiian experiment, the American Board virtually withdrew support in 1863, thereby acknowledging that the Islands had been effectively Christianized. By then there was plenty of both material and devotional evidence that the transplant had taken hold.

The last missionary families had crawled out of their grass shacks and were living in neat New England frame houses with all the fixings, and natives were learning to build with two-by-fours, too. The haystack sanctuaries had long since blown down or rotted away and been replaced with stone edifices or white-steepled chapels that would not have been out of place on any eastern village green.

Honolulu merchants grumbled indignantly that the Blue Laws of Connecticut had become the laws of Hawaii. They resented the obligatory closing of shops on Sunday and the complete absence of traffic, except the sanctimonious movement of Hawaiians on their way to church. One was infuriated when he sent a valise to the wharf on the Sabbath, only to have it seized and confiscated, just as it would have been a few years earlier in New Haven or New London.

Traveler-journalist Charles Nordhoff was awed and rather dumfounded at finding in the mid-Pacific islands white frame houses with green blinds, whitewashed picket fences, stone walls, barns, scanty pastures, frame churches, and schoolhouses. "All are New England," he drawled, "New England genuine and unadulterated . . . brought over to these milder suns by the incorrigible Puritans who founded this bit of civilization. . . . No doubt they sought from the beginning to make New England men and women of these Hawaiians; and what is wonderful about it is that to a large extent they have succeeded."

The Hawaiians were not unappreciative. Speaking for them, Timotea, a church deacon at Waimea, sedately addressed the secretary of the American Board: "During the forty-three years the missionaries have resided on the Islands, much seed has been sown, much labor performed, and wonderful have been the results. We were once all dark, buried in darkness, sunk to the lowest depths of ignorance; roaming about the fields and woods like wild beasts; without clothing; our naked bodies most shamefully exposed and blackened by the sun; without books, without Bibles, without Christianity; plunging into the darkness of hell. Now we are clothed like civilized beings; we are Christianized; we are gathered into churches; we are intelligent; we are supplied with books, Bibles and hymn-books; and are living for God and for heaven. All this through the labors of the missionaries you have sent us."

IV

Halcyon Days of Whaling

By tradition, whaling ships had the most roisterous and iniquitous crews that ever sailed the deep; cruising from the Christian Atlantic to the pagan Pacific, they allegedly hung their consciences on the Horn and neglected to retrieve them on the way back; they raised hell in every port they touched and brought trouble, torment, and frustration to well-meaning souls like gospel ministers and missionaries.

But Pacific whalers and Hawaiian missionaries had more in common than either wanted to admit. Both commonly were New Englanders, both a little homesick, both sufficiently cloyed with the tedium of their respective occupations and the sameness of their respective associates to appreciate a contrast in company. In jest whalers could agree carelessly among themselves that "a missionary island was a howling wilderness"; yet in a serious moment half of them could be shown up as hidebound Puritans, unable to shake off their heritage. The average Yankee, after five or six months on the high seas, was mighty glad to set foot on one of the Sandwich Islands where there was some token of home, though it was only a white steeple or a picket-fenced parsonage.

Particular as the director of Hawaiian missions felt he had to be about the society he kept, Hiram Bingham made a point of cultivating whaler captains. They were among his best friends. He could rattle off by the dozen names of key men in the industry, celebrities in North American and British ports—Gardner, Allen, Weeks, Arthur, Bunker, Swain, Coffin, Stetson, Brayton, Turner, Starbuck, Best, Green, Morgan.

"We looked upon them as neighbors, whom we were glad to meet in their long and toilsome voyages," he acknowledged in his inescapably pious diction. "From such men we received repeated tokens of kindness, which alleviated the trials of our earthly exile, while we were able to promote their security among the people who furnished them supplies, and to call their attention to the pearl of great price, by which we were seeking to enrich the sons and daughters of long-neglected idolaters."

Though havoc was wrought at gospel stations by riotous whalers, among them also were some of the most sympathetic backers and benefactors of the mission cause. They were the good Samaritans who delivered the mail from home, passed on personal greetings from Connecticut and Massachusetts neighbors, brought those wonderful boxes of castoffs and hand-me-downs from stateside missionary societies, and occasionally passed the hat around deck for a family in need. Many were induced to attend church services; they sat up front, joined lustily in the *himeni*, and paid handsomely for their sins when the collection plate was passed.

As a type, they were stoutly defended by the youthful apostle, Charles S. Stewart, who en route to his station at Lahaina, delivered a sermon aboard the *Winslow* of New Bedford. "The crews of American whale ships," he declared, "are generally composed of respectable young men, of a class altogether superior to ordinary seamen. Intelligent, active and enterprising, they cannot be regarded with indifference."

Sailing west with light cargoes or in ballast, skippers willingly shipped out quantities of supplies for the missions, freight-free—bulk lumber, books, type, tons of paper, furniture, flour, farm tools, and, on one occasion, the prefabricated frame and furnishings for an entire church. They provided cut-rate passenger service for wives, sons, and daughters returning to New England on furlough or on their way to school and college, and whalers like the *Averick* and the *Thames* of New Haven transported whole companies of re-enforcements to the Islands.

Captains, officers, and crews inconvenienced themselves no end by taking on a mixed troupe of genteel passengers. With all-seeing, all-hearing parsons and wives on deck, crews were obliged to watch their language, avoid stark-naked appearances, and restrict their gambling, drinking, and story-telling sessions to quarters. Officers had to give up their rooms and mess and move in with the crew. Captain and mate doubled up and took turns using the same bunk. It was no small generosity for a trip of five months.

This did not mean, however, that missionaries received first-class accommodations. They got whatever space could be made by re-shuffling ship's company, freight, whaling gear, and hogsheads. On the *Averick* four newly wed couples drew the "bridal suite," a cramped little cabin already stowed to overflowing with trunks and boxes destined for the Islands. Against the bulkheads, wooden bunks thirty inches wide, with two feet of head clearance, were specially constructed, and each couple was assigned one. All the privacy the ship afforded, for themselves and their personal belongings, was that thirty-inch bunk.

"Within this small space," one of the bridegrooms cheerfully recorded in his journal, "we sleep, have shelves for our books, a writing desk, nails for our brushes, looking glass, etc. At the foot stands a large trunk that answers for our sofa. Our trunk containing clothes for the voyage is my footstool, there being no other place in the whole habitable part of the ship. As we sit on this trunk, over our heads and behind us are cloaks, towels and other things for daily use. A curtain drawn before the berth forms the only place for retirement. . . . Dear wife, may the Lord give her strength to endure the hard time she is having."

Dining space and equipment were still more restricted. Someone had forgotten to requisition extra chinaware and silver, and they were so short that even with two sittings, each couple was obliged to eat from the same plate and take turns with the same knife and fork. Yet the captain was so solicitous of the comfort of his passengers that upon observing how cramped they were and how sportingly they accepted the dining facilities, he immediately set the carpenter to work improvising a better arrangement and then deserted his own mess to sit at the head of their table. The passengers won him over completely; in a few days he had scheduled not only regular Sunday worship but morning and evening devotional services as well, and was urging the crew to attend.

But before the *Averick* crossed the equator, the missionaries became fully aware of the fact that transporting passengers was definitely a secondary pursuit of the ship. Its real objective was driven home one afternoon with a yell from aloft, as one of the less nautical of the company claimed he heard it: "A whale! A whale! There! See her blow!"

"Down with the boats! Heave to the ship! and away went four of our boats with their implements of war," continued the theology student. "Soon we saw the hostile parties approaching and a terrible battle followed. As the ocean grew red with blood, it seemed as if all the monsters of the deep were moved with wrath; for rapidly onward, and marshalled in dread array, they hurried toward the contest a mile ahead. . . . The whole spectacle was too horrible. Of a school of forty whales, three fell before their weapons. One they lost; and two were towed to the ship, monsters indeed, . . . the mouth of one large enough to swallow not merely Jonah, but any giant of fabled history.

"Soon upon the deck were fragments of blubber, found on the outside of the whale, not more than a foot in thickness and containing pure oil. . . . Early next morning I went to the caboose, an establishment for making oil, consisting of three exceedingly large pots placed over brick furnaces. Into these the blubber, thinly sliced, is thrown. As it dries, it is dipped into a larger vessel, thence through a strainer into a pot, and finally, a hogshead. . . . Each whale will furnish between 30 and 40 barrels of oil."

By the time most missionaries reached Honolulu, they were pretty well indoctrinated in the trade of whaling, and the acquaintance served them well, for they had to live with it. Besides all the other close alliances between harpooning and soul saving, the first representatives of both callings arrived in Hawaii within a few months of each other; by historical accident their heydays of activity closely coincided, and both shared the same period of gradual decline.

Over a course of two centuries, whaling voyages had been steadily increasing in distance and duration for both European and American venturers as old haunts were exhausted and new ones discovered farther afield. The American Indians and the early colonists went after the monsters from shore, particularly off Long Island, Cape Cod, and the Maine coast. As demand for whale oil increased, voyages of six weeks or two months became common. But by the 1800's the trips had lengthened to two years or more. Ships were going halfway around the world to satisfy the demand for oil—oil for lamps, for leather tanning, for preparation of woolen textiles, for soap, paints, varnishes, and lubrication, and whalebone for hoops, corset stays, and ornaments.

Earlier expeditions were primarily in quest of the ordinary "right" whale that haunted the temperate waters of the world and roamed into the Arctic. Discovery of the sperm whale, rarely found outside tropical or subtropical seas, altered the whole industry. Its oil was of far superior quality, and in the "case" of the massive upper part of the head was a reservoir of twenty or thirty barrels of pure liquid spermaceti that had only to be bailed out and barreled.

The whaling fleets headed for southern seas and the sperm. In 1791 the first American vessels rounded the Horn in the great search. Schools of sperm whales were found along the coast of Chile and a few years later in the "Offshore Grounds," some fourteen hundred miles west of Peru. It took only a few years to thin these schools, and whalers began going still further afield. In 1820 the Nantucket wonder, Captain Joseph Allen, ventured far into the north Pacific in his *Maro,* and in the Sea of Japan eyed the greatest conflux of sperm whales that had ever been seen, open waters boiling with the monsters as far as his glass could scan.

With every last barrel on the *Maro* filled to the brim, he jubilantly started on the long voyage home, put in at Honolulu for refreshment, and confided his story to fellow New Englander Hiram Bingham, who had arrived on the scene only a few weeks before. Allen was Hiram's first conquest of the whaling world. They talked together, and they prayed together. While the *Maro's* men were making conquests of a different sort in town, the missionary outlined his plan for the conversion of the Islanders. In Allen he found not only an openminded listener, but a very openhanded one. Considering the wealth of his cargo, the captain could well afford to be generous.

They parted fast friends, though certainly with widely differing points of view. Allen foresaw Honolulu emerging as a rip-snorting good rest stop en route to the Sea of Japan; the Islands were squarely in the middle of the expanding Pacific industry; they could not have been better located. As for Bingham, he foresaw, with alarm, that the intrusion of a whaling fleet could be very damaging to missionary endeavors.

The foresight of both was valid. If anything, they underestimated the probabilities. By 1830 as many as 150 whalers were using the Islands as winter headquarters. In the forties and fifties, any season with fewer than 400 visiting whale ships was lean. The one year 1846 saw a total of 596 vessels, and some 20,000 hell-bent, slaphappy, philandering seamen taking their fling in the ports.

True, these invaders from New Bedford, Nantucket, Edgartown, Sag Harbor, and New London did bring tidings and gratuities from the home folks. Many did attend church services and make unexpected donations to the cause of righteousness. But they seemed to possess two characters—one that made itself apparent in the company of respectable church people and the other in the company of shipmates and loose women. And, of course, there was the minority of profligates who avoided any attempt at shrouding their character.

"You seemed to behold busy devils scouting about one of the breathing holes of hell and chuckling with Satanic glee over the human victims they were making ten-fold more the children of hell than themselves," ranted a traveling clergyman and writer, Henry T. Cheever, in describing a typical Island whaling port.

"Liquor and lust have done their best to inflame many of them, and your ears would be shocked by ribald oaths, and the language of lewdness, caught up and repeated by native boys; and you would see some reeling to and fro at their wits end, and hustled along by some less drunken comrade; and others without shame, caressed and hung upon my native girls, who flock here in the ship season from other parts to get the ready wages of sin. The populace of both sexes were out to get what was a-going, and to catch the contagion and cant of vice. It was a scene of vileness, disgust and abomination which no virtuous man, if possible, would see but once . . . a sight to make a missionary weep and any foreigner, in whom virtue and shame have not become extinct, to blush."

Yet Francis Olmsted, a brilliant, discerning, and devout young adventurer, who had left Yale and joined a whaling crew to find out for himself what the life was like, saw the other side of his shipmates' character, and he knew it well. To him they were understanding, alert, circumspect young men "with whom the stirring scenes and dangers of the whaling business have a romantic charm, which comports well with their adventurous spirits. . . . Coolness and intrepidity in danger, those indispensable qualifications in the character of a seaman, are taught by exposure to every variety of peril."

"It is true," Olmsted conceded, "that many masters of vessels with their crews have conducted most shamefully in their intercourse with the natives, and have placed every obstacle in their power in the way of the missionaries; yet there are many instances of these devoted men having received great assistance and encouragement in their labors, seconded by the good wishes and efforts of pious masters of whaleships."

There, presented by two equally competent witnesses, were the two clashing aspects of character, which neither the missionaries nor anyone else could ever quite reconcile. The Yankees usually listened to reason, for American skippers at least made a pretense of remaining on the side of righteousness and Father Bingham. But the British showed no such inclination. The whaling season, accordingly, was a nightmare for the missionaries. Lahaina furnished a realistic example.

The town, lamented a responsible resident there, was "a sink of iniquity," where prostitution, debauchery, and the sale of ardent spirits were the most profitable businesses, where choruses of naked trollops performed obscene dances for the entertainment of whalers, where men, without compunction, hired out their own daughters and wives; while the whalers were in port, there were "upwards of four hundred instances of intercourse with sailors daily."

Naturally, it was the duty of the Reverend William Richards, who had been in charge of the Lahaina mission since 1823, to do something about it, and he did. A product of Williams College and Massachusetts farmlands, wiry, dogmatic, impetuous, Father Richards was not one to yield on any point of principle. In effect, without first weighing the consequences, he persuaded the chiefs to put a complete taboo on all association of local young ladies with whaling crews.

In the fall of 1825 the first whale ships of the season came streaming into Lahaina Roads, every man on board looking forward to the two-month orgy of fun and frolic with the girls. But as they dropped anchor and furled sail close inshore, there was none of the customary splashing of the aloha damsels between anchorage and beach. The sailors were dumfounded. Not a single water nymph appeared; none was in sight on the shore.

It did not take long for the eager males to learn that a new order was in effect, that the gloriously bawdy days and nights of the past were ended, that there would be no girls at all this season, and that preacher Richards was responsible. The Yankees accepted the edict without too much defiance and talked of moving on to Honolulu. But that fall there happened to be more British ships in the Roads than usual, and the limeys were not for a moment going to have a meddling Yankee tamper with their prerogatives.

The crew of the *Daniel* took things into their own hands, with the blessings of their captain, William Buckle. He was in no position to interfere, for he still had in his cabin one of the Reverend Richards' former star pupils, the charming Leoiki, whom he had picked up for $160 on the spring call at Lahaina. A delegation from the crew was sent ashore to present to Richards their ultimatum, an immediate repeal of the taboo.

The representatives thundered on the missionary's door, and once inside they thundered on his table. They demanded girls. They demanded that he inform them where they were. They threatened the pastor's life and left no doubt of their intention to carry out the threat, if he did not cooperate. They might as well have threatened a stone monument. Richards was conceding nothing, telling nothing.

The delegation reported back to the *Daniel* and Captain Buckle was persuaded to intercede for them. He went ashore and tried the light approach on the stubborn missionary. "Let the girls come off," he laughed, "and all will be peace and quiet." Richards was not interested in that kind of peace or quiet and put the captain on the defensive by making impertinent inquiries on the whereabouts of Leoiki. Buckle dropped his front of conciliation and left in raging anger.

The stage was set for a riot, and it came late in the afternoon when the whole crew of the *Daniel* stormed ashore, armed with knives, and advanced upon Richards' house, demanding *wahines* or his life. Arm in arm, the missionary and his wife stood before their door. The reverend squared his shoulders and proclaimed resolutely, "Our lives you may take, but the girls you shall not have."

From behind trees, rocks, and grass houses suddenly appeared most of his Lahaina congregation. Slowly they circled the crew and closed in. A Britisher made a pass at a chief, who pushed forward to shield the missionaries. "The play is over," the chief quietly challenged. "Go after them." Out came the clubs and stones that the Hawaiians were hiding. In seconds the Englishmen were dispersed and hightailing it for the beach. Next morning the *Daniel* sailed for Honolulu, and the girls were summoned back from their refuge in the hills.

Richards was so elated by his victory that he impetuously penned a full account of the escapade, naming names, citing sordid details, making accusations, not disguising his own heroism in the fray, and sent it off to the American Board in Boston. Recognizing the story as a real scoop in the war against sin, the Board promptly released it to the press. Overnight Lahaina, Captain Buckle, and the Reverend Richards became famous on the Mainland.

Buckle did not learn of the free publicity until he returned to the Islands a year later. He set course for Lahaina, with lynching in mind. As soon as the *Daniel* appeared offshore, the *wahines* again trooped off to the mountains, and the congregation gathered protectively around the parsonage.

The crew blustered menacingly about Lahaina for days, but this time neither the girls nor Richards were to be found. Not until the whalers left for the Sea of Japan were the girls allowed in town and the missionary recalled from the Big Island where he had been "vacationing," working on a Hawaiian translation of the Gospel of Matthew.

But Richards was not yet in the clear. Two years after the first outrage, the British were still on his trail. Affairs came to a head late in October of 1827, this time with His Majesty's whaler the *John Palmer.* In the intervening months a few of the *wahines* had lost sympathy with the aims of their protectors, and, in defiance of the taboo, a handful of them had slipped out to the ship, and were held there captive.

Such a serious crisis was stirred up as a result that Maui's Governor Hoapili intervened to demand the release of his subjects. Three times he issued the order to Captain Clark, and three times he was rebuffed. The governor himself quoted the captain's stern words of refusal: "Your efforts are vain. It is not right; it is not thus in Great Britain; it is not right for you to withhold women from Englishmen. Do not keep back the women . . . otherwise a man-of-war will come and destroy you all."

Upon the first appearance of Captain Clark on shore, the governor had his dinghy confiscated and the adversary taken into custody as hostage. Observing the turn of events from deck, the mate ordered every gun on the *John Palmer* primed and pointed at the heart of Lahaina. That did not cow the governor. "If you do not give me back the women, you and I shall remain here on shore and you shall never return to your vessel," Hoapili warned, holding his hostage in direct line of fire.

Clark replied with the threat to bring a fleet of vessels to Lahaina, blow the town to shreds, and burn every hut in it. And as if to demonstrate that there was nothing idle about the threat, at that moment a broadside boomed from the *John Palmer* and six cannon balls crashed around Richards' home, barely missing the roof.

It was the darkest hour in Lahaina's history. The port was threatened with extinction. In that exigency, the man who had started all the fuss in the first place was called into consultation. But where Richards had previously stood forth as bold as a David before Goliath, his bluff was now gone. Facing a real showdown, he quailed and advised the the captain be released. Hoapili silently accepted the ignominy.

The captain returned to his ship and set sail the following morning for Honolulu, with the captive girls still aboard. Richards backed down again a few days later by sending a letter of apology to Captain Buckle of the *Daniel,* which was once more back in Hawaiian waters, reportedly organizing an expedition against Lahaina to accomplish what Clark had failed to do. The apology kept the *Daniel* in Honolulu, but the missionaries had already lost the first battle of Lahaina.

Fully as aggravating to the gospel warriors as these out-and-out antagonists were the whaler captains who professed sympathy for the missions but admitted helplessly that they could do little to restrain the crews. Their problems were multiple, too; they were always in a tight spot, perennially harassed with threats of shortage in ships' complement. By the time a vessel put in at Honolulu or Lahaina, crew morale was often at the breaking point, with plenty of loose talk about desertion. To hold the men, a master had to give them shore leave, no strings attached. He could advise the Hawaiian authorities to handle the ruffians with severity, but he was in no position to rein them himself.

There was a subtle difference between discipline on a whaler and discipline on a merchant vessel. A captain could not exercise quite the tyranny over temperamental specialists in whale butchery that he could over boatswains and riggers. Artists of the trade, like harpooners and the daredevils who risked their lives in rough weather spading blubber off heaving carcasses, had to be treated with deference. The relationship hampered the management of men on shore leave.

Then, too, there were some pretty solid hypocrites on the roster of whaling captains, gentlemen who reverently bowed their heads during grace at a pastor's table, who dutifully attended church services in port and made handsome gifts for carrying on the work of the Lord, while behind scenes a well-greased chief was recruiting an attractive lass for him as "compagne de voyage."

His example was enough to discourage the crew from practicing much self-restraint. In an attempt to reduce the free dissipation, a catalogue of penalties was posted around the Honolulu docks in 1844, a vivid digest of the more common offenses anticipated by the authorities:

$10.00 for coming ashore with a knife, sword-cane or any other dangerous weapon.

$2.00 for every seaman seized ashore after 9:30 P.M. at firing of second gun from Fort.

$1.00 to $5.00 for hallooing or making a noise in the streets at night.

$6.00 for striking another in a quarrel.

$5.00 for racing or swift riding in the streets or frequented roads.

$6.00 for desecrating the Sabbath for the first time; $12.00 for second time; fine doubled for every repetition.

$6.00 for catching deserter near harbor; $12.00 if 10 miles off.

$6.00 for drunkenness.

$10.00 for lewd, seductive and lascivious conduct.

$5.00 for fornication.

$30.00 for adultery.

$50.00 for rape.

$60.00 fine for any captain who leaves on shore any man without written leave from the government.

Hanging as a murderer for knowingly and maliciously violating those laws whereby a contagious disease is communicated on shore.

Despite the high cost of high living in Honolulu, the price tab did not serve as an effective deterrent. Similar measures were tried in other ports with the same results. "The influence of the seamen is unspeakably pernicious," came the complaint from Hilo. "Men who have families at home and wish to maintain a good character there, do not hesitate while here to wallow in iniquity."

Sometimes it appeared that the sole purpose of calling at the Islands was to turn the crews loose and let them raise hell. But that was a biased view. The main object was replenishment of ship's supplies, reconditioning of hulls, making general repairs, and securing new gear. The supply business alone soon developed into a whopping trade that completely altered the economy of Hawaii, furnished a livelihood to thousands of natives, and for a few decades turned the temperate uplands into vast truck gardens.

The fleet gradually worked out a regular schedule of two Island visits a year, one in March or April en route to the Arctic, the other about October or November en route home or to southern waters. The Hawaiian base, after a time, made it possible for ships to postpone the return to New Bedford or Nantucket for an additional year or two. They could spend the summer months in the Yellow Sea or the Sea of Japan, the winter months off Chile and Peru, return to Honolulu for refreshment, and then repeat the cycle, often transferring cargoes of accumulated oil to a fast clipper bound for New England.

The increased dependence on the Islands for goods and gear of every kind brought in an era of such boom and boon that New England backers began to grumble about Hawaii's bleeding them of their rightful profits. Indeed, all the Islands profited, even Kauai, a hundred miles to the north, regarded sometimes as a political and commercial stepchild. Forty, fifty, and sixty ships a season often anchored off the little village of Koloa.

On Kauai they wanted salt and pumpkins, sweet potatoes and pigs, butter, beef, and firewood, quantities of firewood to supplement the blubber scraps used for trying fuel. Such expanses of Kauai's virgin timberland went up in smoke under the trying pots of the whalers that a resident claimed "the forests gradually receded from the plains and foothills."

The cleared land was laboriously converted into crop land, again for the benefit of the whalers. Plantation after plantation was hacked out of the rough terrain and seeded with vegetables. A single provision corporation at Koolau, Standefer and Deeren, the first of its kind in the Islands, developed a six-hundred-acre farm and concentrated on raising corn, beans, and sweet potatoes.

Kawaihae on Hawaii had lost its importance as a first port of call, but it regained some of its former popularity as a shipping point for Kohala's fruit, vegetables, and sugar, and for Waimea's beef—beef freshly slaughtered, corned beef, or beef on the hoof. Many a whaler left Kawaihae with so many cattle corralled on deck that it looked like a stockpen.

The appetites of Yankee crews could never be quite satisfied with tropical substitutes for spuds, like sweet potatoes, taro, yams, or breadfruit. Nothing could take the place of a good mealy baked Irish potato. Whaler captains handed out a few bushels of the shriveled tubers that had survived the trip from New England and told the native traders to take them back into the hills, cut them up, and put them n the ground. The strange vegetables were lugged to Kula on Maui where they sprouted and produced prodigiously in the rich light soil.

The Irish potato experiment turned into an industry, next to beef the most profitable venture in the Islands. Within a few years Kula, on the slope of Haleakala, was one vast potato patch, some ten miles long and more than a mile wide. A vessel had only to sail into Maalaea Bay off Kihei and raise a white flag, the potato signal for the Kula growers up on the heights of the mountain. As soon as the barrels could be headed, a straggling human pack train started down the trail, and along with the potatoes came hens, turkeys, hogs, squashes, and melons.

The hillsides and valleys above Lahaina, Hilo, and Honolulu yielded more produce, everything from onions to bananas, pumpkins to pineapples, oranges to arrowroot, cabbages to coffee. At an advanced native school above Lahaina, where agriculture was part of the educational program, the whaling trade threatened to break up school keeping when students began to realize how much money there was in it. Surplus vegetables in the academic fields brought in three hundred dollars over a six-week period. The boys lengthened their rows and could soon make sales of two or three hundred dollars from any ship—during a period when several hundred anchored offshore in a season.

Honolulu drew its share of the take from fruit and vegetables, but the merchants went all out for bigger game there. New Bedford claimed the distinction of being the whaling capital of the world, but the little village on Oahu was a close runner-up. As the Pacific field base, 90 per cent of the fleet seasonally operated out of Honolulu.

The financial dealings there grew larger and larger. It developed into a kind of shipper's bourse. Whalemen had to be paid off in Honolulu, and before that could be done, the seasonal price for oil and bone had to be fixed. In the absence of any other impartial referee, the responsibility for price control fell to the United States Consul, and a touchy responsibility it was; owners lobbied for a low figure in order to minimize the share that would have to be divided among the crew, and the crew, who were payed by the "lay," or fractional part of the net proceeds, naturally enough argued for a high figure.

Once the fixed value and the "take" of a vessel were determined, the men lined up for their cash stake, and wealth began to flow into Honolulu. "Sailors, receiving so much money in a lump, had to be shown how to spend it in the short time at their disposal," a factor's clerk facetiously explained. "The crimps get hold of poor Jack and give him cash in advance at frightful premiums, and minister to his wants and fancies. Then the harpies pounce on him and poor Jack is held in bondage of sin for six weeks and finds his 'lay' has been spent, and he has got to get a heavy advance against next season."

No less gullible prey for the hawkers and harpies were the masters. "What a carnival those months brought!" ruminated the clerk savorously. "The breathless anxiety with which the list of vessels and their reports of catches were received, for that was the basis of everything. Then the rush of pilots to see who could earn the most and fastest. Next appeared the 'agents' to embrace the masters as they landed, one hand locked in the dear skipper's right, and the other thrown lovingly around his shoulder, whilst they walked to the office. How are you, Tom? How are you, Dick? How are you, Harry? Oh, so inseparable! So fond!

"Meanwhile we folks ashore live merrily on the proceeds. We do not touch the dirty man's wages, but we provide for the wants of those who do. Have we not been laying up stores of flashy prints and costly silks and satins and hats and perfumes and fine English ales and the best, at least the strongest, of brandies to meet the demand of the glorious carnival?

"The charm shops and dance houses are open every night, and the lights and sounds of revelry are incessant. Troops of Hawaiian maidens come from country homes to Honolulu for the carnival, and few of them ever return. . . . The agents take in boarders and many a good ten dollars a week is charged in the accounts when the season is over. There was no hotel and no bank. . . . There was no way of providing beforehand for the money required to pay off the crews. Money was therefore in great demand, and exchange on New Bedford sold at ten, fifteen and twenty percent discount. . . . Those were the halcyon days, I promise you, when money was plentiful and everybody wanted a share in a whaler."

The supremacy of Honolulu as the principal whaling base of the Pacific was never actually challenged. It had the most protected harbor in the Islands and offered facilities for repairing, stocking, and refitting that could not be duplicated anywhere in the Pacific, but high pilotage charges and higher anchorage fees were so spitefully resented by frugal captains that they shifted to other ports whenever the special services were not required.

Lahaina was second in popularity, and occasionally more ships anchored in the Roads than in Honolulu. Hilo and Koloa both claimed third place, and temporary anchorages were made off many other villages, depending on weather, trading produce, and the supply of women. At all the landings there were perennial scuffles, and Honolulu was no exception.

Any day of the spring or fall seasons two or three thousand

swarmed through the streets of that port looking for trouble and creating plenty of it. Bingham's life and household were threatened no less dramatically than Richards' had been at Lahaina, and in one glorious riot the whalers burned down the Honolulu jail and held the town virtually captive for two days.

To supplement the seasonal demonstrations on Oahu was the year-round disruption caused by deserters and by malcontents who had managed to get their discharge from whale ships. During poor years when the "lay" was immoderately small and life at sea an interminable bore, they jumped ship by the hundred. At Honolulu they went native, turned into tramps and beachcombers, shacked up with local women, and defied all authority. The constabulary took into custody the more offensive customers; the tractable ones came under the jurisdiction of the United States consuls, who were obligated by law to provide them with at least survival dole until they could be shipped home.

So many destitute and indisposed Americans were on the dole that the annual cost to the federal government rose from $5,690 in 1840 to $44,212 in 1864. For compensation of $10 per man, masters were legally required to transport derelicts and invalids to eastern ports, on demand of the consul, but the rate was so niggardly that after a time homeward-bound ships skirted Honolulu whenever possible.

They also skirted Hilo, where the aggregation of prospective deportees periodically ran the town. Their official residence was the jail. This, however, was nothing but an outsized grass shack; so the impoundment was only nominal. "Our jolly jack-tars accepted the hospitality of the jailor at mealtime, or when it rained," jeered a resident, "but the balance of their time was joyously occupied with the society of their numerous friends. They sometimes, as a concession to uncharitable public opinion, allowed a native policeman to guide them in their walks abroad; but if not sufficiently complaisant, he was soon clubbed into submission."

A gang of some forty of these prisoners once had the audacity to raise a piratical skull and crossbones and, armed with bludgeons, marched around the town, roaring ribald songs, shouting defiance, and proclaiming their conquest of Hilo. While civil efforts were being made to get word of the town's plight to Honolulu, they held control for three months and were not subdued until a warship came to the rescue.

To replace the crew casualties of the whale ships, there seemed to be an endless reserve of Hawaiians who preferred the rough adventure of the sea to pounding poi. They happily went off in teams of ten, twenty, fifty, were superb whalemen, fearless, tireless, and reckless, but, as in the merchant marine, thoroughly incapable of adapting themselves to cold-weather employment and prone to inflate the commonest Yankee ailments into mortal afflictions.

The mortality rate was high, but enterprising masters learned to make allowances for the expected loss and double the number of recruits. As the whaling era progressed, New England towns were industrializing, and whalemen found more rewarding jobs in the factories; so owners deliberately sent out shorthanded ships to the Pacific, with orders to supplement the crew in the Islands. At the peak of the trade, as many as two thousand Hawaiians a year were on the high seas. Less than half of them ever found their way back.

Fortunes were being made in whale oil and bone. But it was a speculative business; one trip might gross a quarter of a million dollars, the next only a few thousand, depending on weather, whale migrations, and luck. Hawaiians were good gamblers, too, and could not resist entering the business. Chiefs made investments in whaling cruises of their own, and Honolulu firms horned in on the trade.

In 1831 a sharp Oahu wholesaler Henry A. Peirce purchased the British ship *Denmark Hill* and organized an expedition commanded by an old-timer, Captain G. W. Cole. The *Denmark Hill* came back with a thousand barrels of sperm, when oil was selling for about a dollar a gallon. Others were confident they could match the bonanza. The brig *Waverly* was hastily outfitted and went forth with just as high expectations from her owners. It was a total loss. On her first voyage she met disaster in the Caroline Islands, where the ship was set afire by the natives and all hands murdered. Despite such setbacks, other ships were converted to whaling, and by 1858 nineteen were displaying the Hawaiian flag in various parts of the Pacific.

Hawaiian survivors of whaling expeditions came home with new *haole* ideas, *haole* dress, *haole* manners, and prestige. Their experiences in foreign ports had given them orientation; they were sobered by the discovery of the vastness and complexity of the world beyond Island horizons and ready to challenge old traditions. Even the missionaries granted that natives of character who had withstood the ordeals of long whaling voyages became better Christians and stronger citizens.

Sandalwood traders had made the Islanders conscious of the refinements of civilization and brought these symbols within reach of the *alii*; the whalers made them accessible to commoners. Only a few years before, a native with a few precious nails tucked into his *malo* considered himself wealthy; now he had a white man's pockets and wanted to fill them with coins. Most of all, the whalers brought a touch of worldly sophistication; they brought disease, death, and disruption, but they also brought a social awakening that the missionaries never could have provided.

On the side, they imported unwelcome contributions like fleas and flies, roaches and rats. In the spring of 1827 the American whaler *Wellington* arrived at Lahaina after an unsuccessful circuit of southern waters, so unsuccessful that half the oil casks still held the water which had originally been poured into them to prevent the heads and staves from shrinking. To change the foul water for fresh, they were emptied into a stream at Lahaina, rinsed, refilled, and bunged.

It was only a few days later that natives in the area began to be plagued by a small insect that sang in their ears, lit on their skins, and raised welts that itched unbearably. Until then the Hawaiians had never heard of a mosquito. The wrigglers had arrived in those barrels, and they were such a vigorous stock that they bred prodigiously, laid seige to the whole of Maui, and soon spread to all the other islands.

They took to the wet regions as if the Islands were their natural habitat, creating such a revolution that missionary son Henry Lyman defensively maintained that neither his missionary parents nor any of the other missionaries were responsible for clothing the natives. The "suppression of the nudities," said he, could be attributed entirely to *Wellington* mosquitoes.

Through a shocking example of disrespect for law, order, and common decency, the whalers even inspired groups of Hawaiians to respect law, order—and sobriety. At least a few of the Christianized natives had too much pride to lower themselves to the depths they saw in the men of New Bedford, Nantucket, and New London. In considerable numbers they turned into teetotalers after witnessing the conduct of foreign tipplers, and when conscientious captains began to realize the disastrous impression their crews were making on the Islanders, they took the side of the natives and climbed on the wagon.

The missionaries received the credit for establishing the first prohibition laws, and they certainly had a hand in it, but Liholiho's brother, Kamehameha III, would make no such concession. "Should it be said that the American missionaries are the authors of one law of the kingdom, the law respecting the sale of rum," he bristled, " . . . I would say a number of captains of whaleships commenced that thing and thousands of my people supported them." Of all unlikely places, Lahaina gave birth to Hawaii's first Total Abstinence Society in 1834, and the charter members, indeed, were sixteen repentant captains and their officers.

The boom era of Hawaiian whaling came between 1843 and 1860, but the peak year was 1846, and a slow decline set in after that. The number of ships remained high, but the take steadily decreased. The California gold rush was the first notable distraction. White whalemen and *kanakas* alike were more interested in the prospect of getting rich fast in the Sierra than taking chances on getting rich in Arctic seas. Honolulu, as a source of supplies for the gold fields, was much nearer to San Francisco than New York or Boston, and for a few years the bulk of the Kula potatoes and Oahu merchandise was diverted from the Okhotsk and Bering Seas to the West Coast.

Then in rapid succession came a long series of events, all of which contributed to the decline of the golden age of whaling. The sperm fisheries off Japan became exhausted, and the right whale grounds began to play out too. In the early fifties Japanese ports, weeks nearer to the center of operations, were opened to whalers, and the Islands lost out commensurately.

In 1859 Edwin L. Drake struck a well of oil at 69 feet outside Titusville, Pennsylvania, and the best spermaceti could not match the product of that well. The Civil War brought disaster to the industry, particularly from the devastating raids of Confederate cruisers *Alabama* and *Shenandoah*. They took a toll of fifty Yankee ships. Forty more were purchased by the Union government and sunk in Charleston Harbor to help blockade the port. Half the whaling fleet had been wiped out by the end of the war.

The increase in the cost of outfitting whalers, the whole uncertainty of the business, and the rapidly rising demand for factory workers in New Bedford and adjacent cities all had their effect. The gold rush turned San Francisco from a village into a port city with facilities that Honolulu could not equal, and the completion of the first continental railroad made it a terminal with which Honolulu could never hope to compete.

But to the last the whalers preferred Island anchorages to San Francisco Bay for recruitment and refreshment. Mark Twain supplied the most obvious reasons: "A whaleman don't amount to much in San Francisco, but here he is the biggest frog in the pond. Up there the agent lets him dance attendance until more important business is attended to, and then goes out with him and assists him in just such of his concerns as absolutely require assistance, and then leaves him to paddle his own canoe with the remainder; but here the agent welcomes the old salt like a long lost brother and makes him feel that he is a man of consequence—and so he is . . . and the agent attends closely to all the whaler's shore business of every kind whatever, and thus the captain's stay in port is a complete vacation."

In 1871 the whaling fleet tempted fate by remaining in the Arctic too late in the season, and 33 ships were abandoned in the ice floes. It was a crushing blow to Honolulu and the subject of endless contention, for if the crews had remained with their ships another two weeks, instead of attempting a hazardous escape in small boats through a narrow channel of open water, most of the fleet could have been saved.

On October 29th of that year, as the last of the survivors of the catastrophe were arriving in the Islands, the Reverend Samuel C. Damon conducted in the Seaman's Chapel an extraordinary service to memorialize the lost fleet and eulogize the refugees. His text was the passage from Psalm 107 that even those whalemen who conscientiously avoided churchgoing knew by heart: "They that go down to the sea in ships, that do business in great waters . . ."

"Methinks I see that long fleet of boats, loaded with provisions and manned by these hardy crews, commencing their long journey along the narrow passage barely wide enough for a single boat," he orated grandly for the benefit of survivors in the audience who had been through the harrowing experience. "Onward moves the procession of more than a hundred boats, retiring—aye, fleeing from the relentless grasp of that icy enemy. . . . Inch by inch they contended, but silently and surely the icy barrier pressed down upon the fleet. There was no alternative but to retire, and that with all possible haste."

That sermon was almost the funeral oration of Hawaii's whaling era. People read symbolism into the words about retiring "with all possible haste."

For years afterward there were seasonal visits of ships going down to the seas for big game, but never in any great number. One by one the weather-beaten hulks were ingloriously retired to the back bays and inlets of the Massachusetts, Connecticut, and Maine coasts, with seldom a hint of homage for their part in creating a port called Honolulu on the other side of the globe.

V

Triumph of Man over Nature

Until the planters began blanketing Hawaii with cane and pineapple fields in the late 1800's, the Islands had a naked look from the sea. Mountain slopes were defaced with countless solidified cascades of lava; broad lowland stretches were barren, arid, treeless, often clouded with windswept sand. Except on the windward side of the Islands, in valley recesses and on mountain heights, vegetation was sparse everywhere.

It was as though the Creator, after raising the Islands from ocean depths, had stopped short of garnishing the creation. With all their transplantings from the South Seas, the Polynesians had made a good start at augmenting the work of nature, but the bald contours were still in need of a vast amount of embellishment. Once explorers started spreading word of the dearth of vegetation, Hawaii never again lacked volunteer landscapists. They came with the same fervor that possessed the missionaries, as intent on converting the land to productivity as the gospel bearers were intent on converting the people to Christianity, an invasion of benefactor-naturalists, Johnny Appleseeds and John Bartrams, planters and breeders, amateur and professional.

Included in the gear of well-equipped explorers was a kit of seeds from the home country to try out on newly discovered lands or to plant for survival if marooned. When shipping space permitted, live-stock was carried for the same purposes. Hawaii benefited richly from the handouts of the early voyagers. On his first visit Captain Cook left melon, pumpkin, and onion seeds, along with a few goats and pigs—which did not survive. British Captain Charles Barkley delivered sample turkeys and more seeds in 1787. Six years later George Van-couver brought grapevines, orange and almond saplings, sheep, and cattle.

From other donors came guava, coffee, mango, plum, shower trees, cactus, ironwood, eucalyptus, evergreens, quantities of flowering shrubs like poinsettia, bougainvillaea, and plumiera, new varieties of palm, and algarroba, the *kiawe* that was to line the shores and create impenetrable thickets where nothing else would grow. The mission-aries, whalers, and traders added to the offerings. Within a generation after the discovery of the Islands, Hawaii was growing plants from the temperate and tropical regions of six continents. Still they made rela-tively little impression.

Topping the list of contributors to the Island nursery during the early years was a green-thumbed little Spaniard, Don Francisco de Paula Marin, called by friends and foes alike "Manini," the stingy one. Don Marin, who arrived in Honolulu from one of the Alta California missions in the early 1790's, shortly after John Young and Isaac Davis, was a man of more talents than he or any one else could count—linguist, agriculturist, navigator, medico, mason, merchant, philosopher, carpenter, blacksmith, trader, tailor.

While serving an apprenticeship as shipbuilder and stonemason, he mastered Kamehameha's language with such facility that the king shortly conscripted him as official interpreter for the kingdom. He represented the crown on a succession of trading expeditions, served as economic adviser, doctored the king's ailments, cut and stitched three pairs of royal trousers, and then at last was released to work at the one employment that really fascinated him—gardening.

In gratitude for services rendered, the king gave him a choice tract of land on the north side of Nuuanu Stream in Honolulu, and there Don Marin set out acre after acre of grapes. Honolulu's Vineyard Street still bisects the former bounds of that vineyard. Near the bank of the stream, Manini erected an adobe house, fenced in a few acres of yard, and started the first agricultural experimental station in Hawaii. Behind the fence the ingenious gardner learned to his satisfaction what would or would not grow in the Islands.

Both Kamehameha and Liholiho heaped honors upon him in the form of royal-blooded wives and additional acreage. He was granted a second estate at Kaneohe, on the windward side of Oahu, given a still larger plantation on the Hamakua coast of the Big Island, and ceded all of Ford Island in Pearl Harbor, where he raised rabbits and goats.

Never satisfied with his crops or his experiments, he kept up a flow of correspondence with the rancher-padres on the California coast and maintained a steady exchange of plants and animals with them. Every sea captain that came into Honolulu was befriended and buttonholed; on their return trips they brought rare cuttings and pottings from Bangkok or Boston, Lima or Lisbon.

Self-reliance was his motto. He supplied his populous family with bread from home-grown wheat, molasses from his own cane, honey from imported bees, small beer from his hops and barley, coffee and wine from the Nuuanu plantation, cigars from his tobacco field, magnificent roses from the front yard, and peaches, figs, plums, mangoes, luscious melons, lemons, oranges, tomatoes, and turnips from the back yard. Cucumbers and peppers were pickled in brine seasoned with homegrown spices. His sun-dried raisins were the supreme delicacy of Oahu.

But even with an occasional gift bouquet of roses for the missionaries or a bucket of fruit for officers of a visiting ship, Don Marin could not overcome his reputation for miserliness. He burned his prunings rather than give them away. He was not generous in distributing seeds. His exotic fruit and vegetables had cost him a great deal of labor and money; he would sell them at his price but let them rot on the ground rather than pass them out freely. Moreover, his enterprises had brought him great wealth, and he made no attempt to purchase a better reputation through contributing to local causes. He was Manini, the stingy, to the day of his death in 1837.

As years passed after his demise, however, the fences around his estates were breached or felled. Poachers took advantage of the family decline, until there were few front yards or back yards on Oahu that did not possess some souvenir of greenery originally propagated by the spirited Spaniard. More than a decade elapsed before his benefaction was fully appreciated, and then belatedly the Hawaiian Minister of Foreign Affairs paid him the tribute he had earned.

"Most of the present wealth óf these Islands," he asserted at a public meeting, "is owing to the seeds, roots and plants introduced by this one man. In my opinion, it may be fairly questioned if there ever existed in these Islands or exists at the present time, any man to whom the Hawaiian people are so generally indebted."

Yet, with all of Don Marin's legacy, the dooryards, the public grounds, and the broad stretches of dusty plain had hardly acquired a verdant look. Even thirty years later the Island scenery failed to excite the polished English journalist, C. F. Gordon Cumming, who had been everywhere and seen everything from Paris and the Pyramids to the Taj Mahal and Tahiti.

At first glance, she was rather scornful of Hawaii. The dismal black mountains of the Big Island reminded her of nothing more attractive than three gross stranded whales; the "howlishly dreary" shores of Maui were the most distressingly ugly coast she had ever seen; Oahu was "a pile of hot, uninviting, red and yellow volcanic hills without any apparent herbage;" and Honolulu "a somewhat pale edition" of what she had seen in Fiji and Samoa. "All that makes this place delightful," she concluded, "is artificial, . . . idealized by imported vegetation." To her the borrowed Hawaiian greenery hinted a plagiarism of nature.

Later Miss Cumming prettied her appraisal, conceded that the "imported vegetation" was "a marvelous triumph of man over na-ture," and wrote two flowery volumes about the Islands, but she never retracted her allegation that there was a degree of plagiarism in the scenery. She was one who had traveled far and wide enough to detect the fact that practically everything that flourished in both the vegetable and animal kingdoms in Hawaii had come from somewhere else.

If the introduction of all the assorted vegetation was a long slow process, the introduction of barnyard animals was even more tedious, and the end result hardly a triumph. Nevertheless, the visionary pa-trons who were intent on converting the Hawaiians into herdsmen, shepherds, and stable keepers unquestionably were prompted by the highest motives. Where they failed in quality of stock introduced, they more than made up in quantity.

Captain George Vancouver was the first visionary. On a goodwill mission, with only the faintest political overtones, he picked up a shipload of sheep and longhorn cattle at the Monterey Mission in Alta California early in 1793 and altruistically set out for Hawaii with the hope of "establishing a breed of these valuable animals in the Sandwich Islands." Most of the cattle died on the long passage, and when he dropped anchor at Kawaihae in the middle of February, the only chance of life for the few sickly survivors was getting them ashore and into pasturage immediately.

But as luck would have it, he ran smack into the middle of one of the king's general taboos; no boats were stirring from shore, no light-ers were permitted to land, and, worse, a fierce Kona storm blew in. To save his ship he was obliged to put to sea again, and for three days, while the precious cattle showed fewer and fewer signs of life, his *Discovery* was buffeted by tempestuous seas and hurricane winds. In the darkness brought on by cloudbursts and violent thunderstorms, the ship was barely saved from wreckage on the jagged lava shores of Hawaii.

Providentially the morning of February 19th dawned fair, and the seas subsided. He returned to Kawaihae and once more risked arous-ing the wrath of the chiefs by going ashore to explain the purpose of his call and the plight of the cattle. Toward noon the taboo was temporarily lifted and a flotilla of double canoes put out from the beach.

One look at the savage black brutes with their evil horns was enough to convince the native boatmen that they were not interested in cattle. They refused to ferry them ashore. The captain tried to convey some hint of their value; he pleaded with a chief "to lend assistance in securing for himself and countrymen so important a benefit." It was fruitless. Vancouver himself was so exasperated that he was beginning to lose interest in cattle and philanthropy.

Then, by chance, he held up a worthless trading bauble that caught the fancy of the Islander. His eyes glowed. *"Auwe!"* For that, he would indeed endanger his life to please the white captain.

"Instantly," the captain recalled, "he waived all his former objections. The bull and the cow were soon comfortably placed in his canoe, in which there were some vegetables that the bull ate, seemingly with much appetite. This gave me great pleasure, as I was now in hopes that he would soon recover by the help of properly nourishing food which the shore abundantly supplied."

The day was saved. The pair lived and flourished as cattle never flourished on Mexican pasturage. A few days later the other surviving remnants of Vancouver's herd were put ashore at Kealakekua, and with more specimens delivered on subsequent calls, Hawaii was off to an early start in ranching—decades before American cowboys had discovered the Wild West.

On Vancouver's advice, a strict ten-year taboo was placed on the longhorns. They were driven back into the Kohala hills, given the run of the uplands, and treated like the sacred cows of Hindustan. They multiplied prodigiously. Within five years small ravenous herds were counted in dozens; within ten years they had migrated to the slopes of Mauna Kea, where they ran in herds of hundreds and the natives ran in terror before them. All of Waimea became an open cattle range.

Calves were caught and shipped to Oahu, Kauai, and Maui to be bred with more of their kind periodically brought in by other philanthropic explorers and traders. In Mexico, in Upper California and generally in the Southwest, these ugly black creatures with a three-foot spread of horns were well-known for their viciousness and fighting fury, and they became equally well-known in the Islands. At the Spanish missions they were corralled and more or less domesticated, but in Hawaii they went completely wild. Under the taboo they had prior rights to the land, including the private taro patches, yam, cane, and banana plantings. What they did not eat they trampled.

Commoners started building higher walls around their huts and cultivated plots. The cattle climbed over them. Whole villages were enclosed in six-foot walls, and still the fierce longhorns got in. They terrorized the natives, destroyed gardens, browsed off the house thatch. When the ban on killing the intruders was finally lifted, there were thousands in the Waimea region, and villages were being evacuated.

The white men had brought in the cattle, and now they were asked for advice on how to get rid of them. "Shoot them," proposed councilors Issac Davis and John Young. For the next twenty years the cattle were slaughtered in droves, shot in self-protection, shot for hides, shot for tallow, and occasionally for the tough, stringy beef. But they reproduced faster than they were killed.

In 1823 missionary Joseph Goodrich of Kailua reported that he was obliged, in making an ascent of Mauna Kea, to skirt herd after herd, "so wild and ferocious that the natives are afraid to go near them." Foreigners did most of the shooting for sport or pay and employed Hawaiians for a pittance to transport salt and kegs into the mountains, dress the carcasses, pack the meat in brine, and carry the heavy kegs of pickled beef on their shoulders to Kawaihae for shipment. Hides were lugged to market in the same fashion.

Almost a decade later, Lorenzo Lyons, who had taken over the mission at Waimea, deplored the slavish labor, charged that the whole district was "a cattle pen," grumbled that the inroads made by the beasts on every growing thing were "the greatest evil from which we are now suffering." A hundred acres of the choicest tillage land had been given up, he claimed, and people were no longer planting anything. To escape the cattle, his converts were moving farther and farther back into the wilderness.

The king and chiefs were well aware of the destruction, not only to crops but to the woodlands and valleys. Acre upon acre of once luxuriant ti plants on all the islands had been grazed clean; forests had been invaded and irreparably damaged; gullies and swamplands were drying up, as a result of stripped watershed.

To contend with the menace, one foreigner after another, posing as an authority on American cattle, was commissioned by the king to help with the eradication. Trader William French held a commission for a time, and he hired an Irishman named Harry (Jack) Purdy and a Yankee from Newton, Massachusetts, John Palmer Parker, as his chief cattlemen.

Both Purdy and Parker were ex-seamen who had taken a liking to the Island climate. Jack was a born frontiersman, content only in open spaces, accompanied by four or five dogs, a gun, a knife, a hatchet— and a bottle. John was another jack-of-all-trades, who had left Boston in 1809 to make his fortune in Northwest furs, but had been sidetracked into China sandalwood shipping, and had finally taken up residence in Honolulu as Kamehameha's supervisor of fishponds.

From Honolulu he gravitated to the Big Island, took a job as blacksmith, carpenter, and cowpoke with William French, and then persuaded his former employer, King Kamehameha, to give him a try at domesticating some of the wild Waimea cattle. At that point the king was ready for any kind of experiment that might reduce the deluge of complaints that were pouring in. Parker was given the go-ahead.

He established himself at Puuloa, one of the upper Waimea villages, started building paddocks and enticing wild stock into them. He tamed the calves, tamed heifers and steers, segregated wild bulls, built up a dairy, and fattened steers for beef. The whalers soon learned that Parker's less gristly meats were for sale at Kawaihae, and he was in business. He was granted permission to take as bride an eligible young chiefess Keliikipikaneokaolohaka, and the gentleman from Newton was ready to change his address to Waimea for life.

But neither puritanical Parker, nor impious Purdy, nor William French's gang, nor any of the king's private appointees was really licking the wild-cattle problem. The prolific longhorns were spreading like a tide over the northern and western reaches of Hawaii. Waimea, formerly one of the most thickly populated areas on the island, was getting a deserted look; coastal villages were thinning. To forestall a similar evacuation of Kailua, the chiefs set their subjects to work building a formidable stone wall eight miles long to circumscribe the village and hold back the invading herds.

Kamehameha I failed to solve the dilemma, and Liholiho did little better, but in 1832 Kamehameha III tried a new tack. Three celebrated Mexican cowboys, Kussuth, Luzada, and Ramon, were induced to come to the Islands and contend with the problem professionally.

These three "Espagnols," along with other Mexican friends, relatives, and full-blooded southwestern Indians, who soon joined them, changed the character of the cattle capital and halted the migration. The Hawaiian boys idolized them. The colorful costume and gear of the newcomers caught the imagination of the natives, the elaborately adorned saddles, the broad-winged stirrups, the hair rope in alternate strands of black and white, the red bandannas, the broad-rimmed flapping hat turned up in front, the gay serapes, crimson sashes, and studded leggings, the braided lariat.

Paniolos they were called, since "Espagnol" couldn't be pronounced in Hawaiian; and Juan became "Huana," José, "Hoke," Joaquin, "Hoakina." Locally the language was spiced with Spanish, and after a few years a considerable number of the younger generation in Waimea took on a Spanish cast as well as costume. The *malo* was given up for the split-legged Spanish riding breeches; the *kihei* for the serape; the fringed red Spanish sash became the Hawaiian sash, as standard a part of an Island performer's getup as his lei.

Even the Big Island missionaries came under the spell of Mexican costumery. On receiving a heavy woolen shawl in the barrel of hand-me-downs from a New England missionary society, Father Lyons wrote appreciatively to his benefactors that he had converted it into a poncho by cutting a hole in the center. "I wear it instead of a cloak. This is the fashion on these islands."

The Mexicans brought with them their own mounts, and it was not long before everyone in Waimea wanted to ride that descendant of the old Moorish horse, the bronco. A model of the Mexican cart was imported, and local wainwrights began producing clumsy rigs with solid wooden wheels cut from cross sections of *koa* trees, and yokes of oxen were soon drawing over the hills reasonable facsimiles of the vehicles known at the California missions for over a century.

New home industries sprang up, and Mexican saddles, bridles and bits, pack saddles, and spurs began coming from the shops in Waimea. The tan pit, the smithy and, in a land where old and young had previously gone barefoot, the cobbler flourished. To the long repertory of Hawaiian games were added roping and lasso whirling. The one ambition of any energetic Hawaiian youngster was to join the roundup—*hoohuli pipi.*

Followed by a train of willing apprentices, the Mexicans went after the wild cattle with a vengeance. If killing them off was all that was wanted, they were just the men to do it, though they thought it an awful waste of beef and bullets. To both the *paniolos* and the newly indoctrinated Hawaiian huntsmen, it was magnificent sport. Waimeans forgot their terror and took to the chase as naturally as the marauding kine had taken to their taro patches. The slaughter was vengeful, ruthless; the flanks of Mauna Kea fairly flowed with blood.

"Not tens, but hundreds of thousand of skeletons bestrewed the sides of that old mountain," claimed one of Father Lyons' honest sons. In fact the conquest for a time appeared to be too final. Beef shipments at Kawaihae all but ceased. Natives and foreigners alike complained that a quarter of beef was hard to come by. In 1840, eight years after the first Mexicans had arrived, observers maintained the havoc had been so great that there was scarcely a bullock left on the side of Mauna Kea facing Waimea, except on private lands. So once more a royal taboo was proclaimed. The Mexicans were out of business, and the economy of the Big Island sagged.

But this time the taboo was not accepted quite as literally as it had been in the days of Kamehameha the Great. There were still ample wild cattle back in the high fern and *lehua* country, and they came out of hiding as soon as their professional enemies were off the mountain. That gave the rustlers a chance.

And there were plenty of rustlers scattered over the broad mountain saddle between Kawaihae and the Hamakua coast in the 1840's. The area was a refuge for scores of the most-wanted men of the South Pacific, a recognized refuge for Island outlaws and for sailors absent without leave, a superb hideout for crooks and criminals from the West Coast, the adopted home of a shipload of British convicts who had escaped from the infamous Botany Bay penal colony at Sydney, Australia, shanghaied a ship, sailed to Hawaii, and scattered in the hills after scuttling their vessel.

These were the men who helped set the character of Waimea almost as much as the Mexicans. They lived off the land and off the natives, moved in with Hawaiian girls, shot wild cattle freely, trapped them in camouflaged pits, and brought endless *pilikia* to the missionaries. Father Lyons, who felt the brunt of their evil influence and was often threatened by them, repeatedly confided his distress to superiors in Honolulu and Boston over "certain foreigners who are wicked and abandoned, and live not far away."

"In my field are sixty or seventy of them, from seven or eight different nations," he wrote. "They are beef catchers, sugar manufacturers, shoe makers, merchants, tanners, sawyers, carpenters, blacksmiths, comb-makers, masons, doctors, farmers and what not. They have intermarried with the natives and have families growing up. . . . Many are bitter enemies. . . . They are like mad men."

These "mad men" did most of the cattle killing between 1840 and 1844, occasionally slipping to Father Lyons a cut of contraband beef as peace offering. The taboo lasted only five years. By 1844 it was obvious that the animals, far from extinct, were coming back stronger than ever. However, a great change was taking place. Private ranches were starting up all around the circumference of Mauna Kea and Mauna Loa, stocked with tamed longhorns, here and there crossed with better breeds.

At Pookanaka, five miles east of Waimea village, Jack Purdy, to supplement his income from indiscriminate hunting, was developing a dairy. He owned a huge herd and specialized in making butter for trade at Kawaihae. John Parker, one step ahead of his competitor, picked a magnificent site for himself and Keliikipikaneokaoeohaka high on the slope of Mauna Kea, seven miles from Waimea. There he built his ranch house, walled in a home lot, and, duplicating everything he had at Puuloa, started constructing corrals and paddlocks for his cattle herds.

Presumptuously he gave a name to the place, Manaaiole, and, after living there as squatter for two or three years, he confidently petitioned the king for a royal patent. The old superintendent of fishponds had not been forgotten. For a consideration of exactly ten dollars, the "faithful and loyally disposed subject" won the property in fee simple forever.

The deed was a significant document. That ten-dollar purchase was the start of the vast estate that was eventually to become the largest private ranch in the world. With a headquarters definitely in his name, Parker began purchasing adjacent acres; then he bought detached plots at distant points and gradually acquired title to the land in between. "It was a pleasure to all, especially to him," commented a contemporary, "to see the cattle and calves, thousands of them, grazing on the plains between Mana and Waimea."

From these herds went forth quantities of corned beef and live stock to feed the whalers; more was shipped to California during the hungry gold-rush days, and to Tahiti and other Pacific islands. Mauna Kea steers furnished hides for Mainland shoes and tons of tallow for cheap candles and soap.

Big ranching, however, was not limited to the island of Hawaii. On Oahu, Maui, and Kauai, herds were not quite as large, but the longhorns were ever present, and beef and beef products were among the major exports. During the late 1830's Honolulu was shipping out some five thousand hides a year, along with thousands of barrels of corned beef. Cattle grazed freely on the slopes and plain in back of town and made almost daily invasions down residential streets to browse on roof thatch and home gardens.

They were such a menace in 1831 that all the natives were conscripted to turn Honolulu into a walled town. A mightly barricade of stone, six feet high and six feet thick, was constructed around the main commercial area. It was like the old days of *heiau* building. Every chief was responsible for the erection of one fathom of wall. Two thousand people were employed at one period, and their encampment around the town looked like that of a beseiging army, while merchants complained that trade was at a standstill. Yet even this barrier was not entirely effective. Somehow the strays managed to get over or around it.

Too much beef was the problem on Kauai, too, though the wild herds there preferred the seclusion of the mountains and did not conflict too seriously with the domesticated cattle in the lowlands. Two cents a pound for fresh sirloin was the going price, but there were so few takers that half a carcass often went to waste. As long as whaling lasted, two or three thousand barrels of corned beef were shipped out annually. However, the steadiest market with whalers on Kauai was cattle on the hoof. They were penned on deck and not slaughtered until a ship was far north, where the meat could be hung in the rigging to freeze. All this made little impression on the supply, and for years most of the Kauai cattle went into soap, candles, and lubricants. "It seemed a sad waste," moaned Charles Nordhoff on a visit to the island, "to see a hundred head of fat steers driven into a corral and one after the other knocked on the head, slaughtered, skinned, cut up and put into the boilers to be turned into tallow. But it is the only use to make of the beasts."

The whaling crews that purchased their beef alive taught the *paniolos* the trick of swimming the stock to the ship, a practice quickly adopted as standard at all ranch moorings. Cattle were herded into corrals or holding pens on the beaches, and from there one steer at a time was hauled by a mounted cowboy through the surf to the side of a whaleboat, where the head was lashed to the gunwale, well out of the water. Five more were brought out in the same manner, and then, with a trio of fighting-mad animals adrift on each side, the whaleboat was towed to the ship. On belly slings they were hoisted by the davits one at a time over the rail and onto the deck. The resulting aquatic pageantry was the most colorful show of the ranching business, and has not yet been entirely abandoned.

As the sugar plantations expanded during the fifties and sixties, longhorn steers were tamed and trained as oxen, and Hawaiian *paniolos* turned out to be the most expert ox trainers and drivers west of Vermont. The missionaries taught them. Natives had all the time and patience the job called for, and nothing delighted them more than to exercise command over these plodders that could haul such enormous loads.

Starting with a few yoke, plantation managers increased their stock until herds of several hundred were an indispensable feature of every up-and-coming sugar operation. On muddy roads it was a common sight to see a single cane cart drawn by six or eight yoke. Until mules and portable railroads took their place, the whole sugar industry was dependent upon ox power.

But Yankees and Britishers, who were used to gentler bovines in their barnyards and pastures, never quite forgave Vancouver for not donating to Kamehameha a pair of English Shorthorns, Scotch Galloways, Dutch Holsteins, or French Jerseys, rather than those ill-tempered Mexican longhorns. It was quite a gamble to transport domesticated cows and their mates from the Atlantic coast all the way around the Horn to Hawaii; so for decades, even the most serious husbandmen in the Islands tried to be satisfied with what they had.

In fact, there was almost too much satisfaction. "I doubt if the graziers in any other part of the world have been more successful than in these islands," declared Honolulu judge and amateur Island economist William L. Lee in 1850. "With no winters to contend against, the labors are comparatively light, the increase in their flocks certain and rapid, and the owner of a small herd is sure, with a reasonable degree of care and attention, to become wealthy in a few years. Beyond question, the raising of cattle has thus far been the most successful pursuit connected with the soil yet undertaken in the islands."

George Vancouver would have appreciated those words, but at

best those lean Mexican imports made poor steer beef and very poor dairy cows. Good cattlemen knew it and already were beginning to substitute quality stock from the Mainland for the degenerate long-horns. The effort was frustrating, however, for with so many dominant descendants of the longhorns on the loose, it was next to impossible to keep a pure-bred herd uncontaminated.

Some of the most dedicated pioneers in the new endeavor were not cattlemen at all. They went into stock raising by accident or happen-stance, men like Britisher Henry H. Greenwell, graduate of the elite Royal Military College at Sandhurst, who sold his commission and sailed to Australia to raise sheep, to California to dig gold, and to Hawaii to sell merchandise and grow oranges before finding his real métier in raising fine cattle and starting the Greenwell ranching dy-nasty on the Big Island; or Captain James Makee, who miraculously survived an attempted hatchet murder on his whaleship *Maine* to be-come Honolulu's wealthiest ship chandler, exporter, importer, sugar planter, entertainer of royalty, and founder of Maui's million-dollar Rose Ranch, renamed Ulupalakua, still one of the largest and most profitable ranches in the Islands.

By insisting on nothing but quality stock, Greenwell, Makee and a few of their contemporaries helped rid Hawaii of the unworthy legacy from Mexico. John Parker, who had originally set the pace for ranch-ers, never did succeed in purging his herds of the longhorns. He died in 1867, and his heirs did not inherit the paternal aptitude for ranching. Not until Manaaiole was placed under professional management at the end of the century did the modern Parker Ranch begin to take shape. Belatedly the scrawny Mexican cattle were killed off and replaced with shiploads of registered Herefords, Holsteins, and Durhams; and so much acreage was added that at one time the ranch possessed approx-imately a fifth of the four thousand square miles that make up the island of Hawaii, an area considerably larger than all of Oahu, an empire almost the size of Rhode Island, extending from the snow-crested heights of Mauna Kea to the palm-fringed beaches on the coast.

Hundreds of smaller ranches were cut out of adjacent lands and many more incorporated on the other islands. Cattle raising continued as a major industry, but it was not for long entitled to the expansive praise Judge Lee had accorded in 1850; it was not Hawaii's most successful agricultural pursuit.

Even in 1850 a few were already totting up the cost of the cattle invasion in terms of ruined woodlands, dry stream beds, eroded pasture, and displaced villagers. The evidence was everywhere, even on Oahu, where the herds were never as large as on the outer islands. Tramping from Honolulu to Waialua in 1853, an elderly missionary bemoaned the fact that the forests of ti plants which once covered the central hills of Oahu were gone. He pointed out that cattle had utterly denuded the uplands above Pearl Harbor and, with nothing to hold the soil, so much had been washed down in heavy storms that the harbor was becoming a shoal and the pearl oysters that gave the inlet its name were drowned in mud.

At best Vancouver's gift was a mixed blessing. Quite aside from the loss of thousands of acres of lush upland and the conversion of vast expanses into seasonal desert, the principal beneficiaries of the gift in the end were foreigners, not Hawaiians for whom it was intended.

The effect of another benefaction, the horse, was even more disruptive. Until 1803 the only natives who had ever seen the animal were those who had gone off on expeditions with traders and explorers. It was as foreign to the Islands as the polar bear.

Pacific adventurer Richard Cleveland, captain of the *Lelia Byrd*, was the first to conceive the idea that horses could be a salvation to overworked and underprivileged Hawaiians. He took his appeal to the padres of St. Joseph's Mission in California. *"Imposible!"* exclaimed the friars. The Hawaiians know not the horse, a beast older than civilization? They would be delighted to supply a few specimens for the enlightenment of such backward people.

Certain that he had a bequest no less magnanimous than Vancouver's, Cleveland swam a mare and her foal ashore at Kawaihae on June 24, 1803, to the terror and delight of the fishermen, shipbuilders, and salt makers at that little port, and then sailed over to Maui to present a mare and stallion personally to Kamehameha, who happened to be in residence at Lahaina.

The king was disappointingly unimpressed. He boarded the *Lelia Byrd,* eyed the animals perfunctorily, and left without a word of appreciation. Even after the horses had been landed and a sailor had demonstrated their usefulness by galloping down the beach on the back of the stallion amid shouts of admiration from hundreds of spectators, Kamehameha remarked with an air of indifference and sarcasm that "he could not perceive that the ability to transport a person from one place to another in less time that he could run, would be adequate compensation for the food he would consume and the care he would require."

"Our present was not very highly appreciated," the captain glumly concluded. But Cleveland's gift was only a starter. After that, visiting ships frequently brought presents of horses; traders and merchants imported others, ostentatiously demonstrating their usefulness. Kamehameha's prejudice wore off, and soon the king, queens, princes, and high chiefs all coveted fine stallions. Foreigners insisted that they could not carry on their businesses without them. By the twenties, the demand was so great that when the French three-master *Héros* arrived in Honolulu with an entire shipload of horses from San Diego, they were all sold at high prices within hours.

The first imports, like Vancouver's cattle, were merely turned loose to breed in the wild. On the Big Island they were joined by work horses that had been let to pasture and defied recapture. These crossbred with the wild horses, and within a few years hundreds were seen on the slopes of Mauna Kea and Mauna Loa. Occasionally groups of them were driven into paddocks by the cattlemen to be broken and stabled; more were shot and slaughtered by Hawaiians who developed an appetite for horse meat, claiming it was better than beef.

Yet, for almost half a century after Cleveland's visit, horses were largely a curiosity among commoners, an emblem of status for the *alii* and rich *haoles.* In 1840, claimed missionary son Sereno Bishop, who knew Honolulu intimately, "there were no saddle horses, or practically none," and the only wheeled vehicles to be seen in the city were handcarts, oxcarts, the equipage of the king, and carriages of a few merchants. A few years later he observed that saddle horses were still uncommon and very expensive, costing from $75 to $150.

But an astonishing change was on its way, and it came with a rush. "You never saw such a company of equestrians in all your life," exclaimed Laura Fish Judd, wife of the medical missionary, in describing the parade for an exciting holiday celebration in Honolulu just before midcentury. "Men were stationed at different places to count them as they passed. There were nearly four thousand."

By 1860 horses were everywhere, and a fair mustang could be purchased for ten or fifteen dollars. A whole pedestrian population that had long been distinguished for its unwearying trampers, its stalwart runners, its carriers and haulers of great weights over great distances was taking to the saddle. Of all the revolutionary material changes imposed upon Hawaiians by foreigners, this was one of the most sweeping and the most devitalizing.

The triumph of the horse was best exemplified in Honolulu on a Saturday afternoon after the markets closed at four o'clock—any Saturday afternoon between the late 1850's and the 1880's. The city became a carnival, a population on parade. The squares were filled. The streets were crowded. The open plains stretching east of the city toward Waikiki were thronged. Everyone was on the move, going nowhere in particular, but going—on a horse. If a Hawaiian didn't have a trotter of his own, he climbed on someone's else; two or three would be astride the back of a single broken-down mare, sometimes the whole family.

Altogether, the animals were sorry samples of horseflesh, scarcely a mount that would not have disgraced a third-class livery stable. There were nags on their last legs, roans that looked as though they had never seen a nose bag, young colts with the spirit already whipped out of them, ancient plugs all legs and bones, droop-headed broomtails that should have been turned loose to their final pasture long since, yet were being ridden by rotund three-hundred-pound matrons as though the mounts were Arabian chargers.

The looks and spirit of a horse didn't matter. The riders made up in gaiety and energy for the deficiencies of the steeds. They rode as if walking had become a vice. "The broad road was so thronged with brilliant equestrians that I thought we should be ridden over by the reckless, laughing rout," chronicled a sightseer of the day. "There were hundreds. . . . The women seemed perfectly at home in their gay, brass-bossed, high-peaked saddles, flying along astride, barefooted, with their orange and scarlet riding dresses streaming on each side beyond the horses' tails, a bright kaleidoscopic flash of bright eyes, white teeth, shining hair, garlands of flowers and many-colored dresses, while the men were hardly less gay, with fresh flowers round their jaunty hats, and the vermillion-colored blossoms of the ohia round their brown throats.

"Sometimes a troop of twenty of these free-and-easy female riders went by at a time, a graceful and exciting spectacle, with a running accompaniment of vociferation and laughter. . . . In the shady, tortuous streets we met hundreds more native riders, dashing at full gallop without fear of police."

Honolulu had blossomed into the horsiest city in the civilized world. The fact became more evident whenever a ship stood in toward the pier. There was an ocean of hacks, warehouse vans, and omnibuses with their teams waiting on the wharves, but in the background were saddle horses by the hundred tied to rails, coconut palms, and lamp posts. As far as one could see from the deck of the ship was a scattered cavalcade advancing from the direction of Waikiki, from Ewa, and from the mountains.

The splashy, contented, singing throngs that came to see a ship dock never failed to stun a newcomer, but the brigade of horses was even more impressive. That unexpected and incongruous sight made the most sophisticated globe-trotter wonder if the paradisiacal isles had not jolly well gone wild west. They were more colorful than California and, with all the riding accouterments of the Southwest, as Mexican as Mexico.

Nor was the passion for riding limited to Honolulu. It was the same everywhere in the Islands. A fad had become a craze. In fact, the farther one ventured from a town, the greater the number of horses. Rural villages boasted more horses than people. A family of grass-shack dwellers owned a dozen. And they were as cheap as they were multiple. A ridable beast could be purchased for three or four dollars; old nags sold at auction for twenty-five cents. Even the children had their own. "You can buy a horse for a song," chuckled Mark Twain, "and a week's hay for another song, or you can turn your animal loose among the luxuriant grass of your neighbor's front yard without a song at all."

"One miserable jade of a beast was all the town of Hilo possessed in the way of horseflesh," claimed Mrs. Judd in 1837 when she wanted to make a trip to Kilauea. Yet at the height of the horse craze, when famed horsewoman Isabella L. Bird arrived in Hilo, she found for a modest local celebration "fully a thousand horses tethered on the grass by the sea."

"Every man and woman, almost every child has a horse," she added. "The beach and pleasant lawn above it are always covered with men and women riding at a gallop, with bare feet and stirrups tucked between the toes. To walk even two-hundred yards seems considered a degradation."

But the Hilo breed was no better than that found in Honolulu or in any other town, except in the stables of the affluent. The horses pur-chased by the natives for two or three dollars were the castoffs of the elite, the inbred stock from the mountains, the foals of tired, uncared-for mares.

These were the animals that the Horse Committee of the Royal Hawaiian Agricultural Society complained about so vehemently, de-ploring "the lamentable increase in the miserable creatures, . . . a curse and nuisance to the country," while a less official critic referred to them as "a perfect plague of badly bred, badly developed, seedy looking animals, . . . sorry, lean, undersized beasts, looking in general as if the emergencies of life left them little time for eating and sleeping . . . heavy-headed and heavy-hearted, with flabby ears and pendulous lower lips, limp and raw-boned."

The Society for Prevention of Cruelty to Animals had existed in

England since 1824, but its tenets had not yet reached Hawaii. No descendants of Eohippus were ever treated with less consideration. The horses went unwatered, unfed, unshod, were spurred mercilessly, ridden with open sores under their saddles and deep cuts under the rough girths. Though they were regarded as more essential than anywhere else in the world, they were neglected and inhumanely maltreated.

Only a generation or two removed from an existence in which no allowance was made for physical agonies in another human or animal, the Hawaiians were not yet prepared to comprehend the sensitive nature of a horse. In shifting from barefoot gait to stirrups, they appeared to be incapable of exercising fellow-creature sympathy.

To them the horse was a nerveless automaton, expected to go anywhere its rider formerly walked, up the steepest rock-strewn *palis* and down them at a castastrophic pace, over treacherous lava beds, where a native could make his way only with painful difficulty, along stream beds of canyons, dry or flooded, across island deserts where the nearest supply of brackish water was twenty miles away.

Newspaper editors, with more sympathy for horses than for the irresponsible riders, furthered the complaints of the Royal Agricultural Society by charging that horses were the main cause of the habits of laziness and vagrancy among the natives, especially among the lower classes, who considered themselves rich—*waiwai*—as soon as they became horse owners, refusing to labor for themselves or anyone else and depending on the work of their horses for support. "Except for short shopping distances in Honolulu," observed one censor, "I have never seen a native man or woman walking."

The editors were on the right track. Horses were a last straw in the breakdown of native physique. The Islanders not only gave up walking and much of their working, they also abandoned their surfboards and canoes for saddles. Instead of indulging in their challenging old sports, they wasted their time in aimless riding from place to place. To them riding was more an amusement than a sport.

In their obsession for horses, a standard of living, already low, sank lower. By nature they were subject to distraction, gregarious, relaxed, easygoing, unworried. Discovery of a less exertive way of getting about enabled them to revert to their natural leanings, to let well-enough alone, to put off until tomorrow what they were not obliged to complete today.

They never again caught up with the morrow. It was forever lost. Cleveland's benefaction, like Vancouver's, did not work out as intended. It seemed that most of the presents brought to Hawaii by altruistic patrons to help along the triumph of man over nature were destined to benefit someone else more than the Hawaiians.

TAHAINALUNA

VI
Send Us Teachers!
Send Us Books!

On January 7, 1822, a year and nine months after the pioneer delegation of missionaries arrived in the Islands, the first printed pages in the
Hawaiian language came off the little mission press in Honolulu, not
the Ten Commandments, the Lord's Prayer, or the Beatitudes, as
might be expected, but a simple, practical, mundane primer, a four-
page Hawaiian hornbook.

Every chief in town was summoned to witness the event, and one
of them was given the honor of swinging the lever on the old Ramage
press to make the first impression. The witnesses had seen the writ of
the English and the French; yet they were still skeptical about the
ability of any magician to convert fleeting Hawaiian speech into letters. Not until printer Elisha Loomis peeled the proof from the type

and deciphered the characters were they convinced that they had a writ of their own.

That ceremony marked one of the great moments in Hawaiian history. The chiefs were so intrigued by the printed word and so fascinated by the marvelous machine which could fix speech on paper that from that day on Loomis had more volunteer printer's devils than he could use. He needed mass support, for before he was through with the hornbook, its reprints, supplements, and new editions, over one hundred thousand copies had been printed.

All the spare-time scholarship that a half-dozen overworked parsons and wives could muster over a period of twenty-one months went into those four unpretentious pages. Before a sentence could be composed, the words of countless speech variations had to be sorted and distinguished; before the words could be set down as a vocabulary, a spelling system had to be devised; before spelling was possible, an alphabet had to be invented.

They identified ninety-five different sounds in the language and were tempted to create an alphabet of that many characters, but if they did, they knew very well they would never induce a totally illiterate people to master it. In the end they cut the alphabet to the bone. They concluded, for example, that the symbol *P* could take care of the *B* sounds, too; *T* and *C* could be eliminated and shifted to *K*; the *R* sounds could be lumped with *L*; *D* was a problem because in different localities its sound was hard to distinguish from those of *K, L, N* or *T*, so *D* was scrapped, as also were *J, Q, X, Y*, and *Z*.

The missionary linguists took a great many liberties with the language, but they wound up with just five vowels and seven consonants, an alphabet of twelve heavily burdened letters. Of course, it would be a desecration to distort Bible names too freely; so nine additional consonants were held in reserve as "third-class letters" to be taught as needed in Sunday School.

The phonetic decisions were final. By explorers and traders Honolulu had commonly been spelled *Hanaroorah*, *Kamehameha* as *Temaahaah*, *Hawaii* as *Owhyhee*, with a great many variations, and there were hundreds of similar inconsistencies. In one bold stroke the confusion was eliminated and the linguistic laws declared unimpeachable. Even the king was defied. When he informed the missionaries that his name was Rihoriho, he was imperiously overruled and told that henceforth it would be Liholiho.

"It would hardly be possible to write any language in the world with a more simple and limited alphabet," gloated Hiram Bingham, who had slaved over the sifting of the letters and the compilation of the hornbook. "To make the spelling and reading of the language easy . . . was a matter of great importance, almost indispensable to our success in raising the nation."

Bingham did not overestimate either the problem or the achievement. With the alphabet settled, other difficulties of formulating a written language were easily resolved; and with a simple hornbook to use for instruction, the missionaries were ready to lead a quick-step march into literacy. That march proved to be one of the most sensational campaigns in education ever conducted.

In January 1822 not a Hawaiian in the kingdom could read or write, except the handful of boys who had been to Cornwall, Connecticut. Within a decade there were almost a thousand schools and some fifty thousand pupils were attending them; a third of the Island population was more or less literate. By mid-century practically everyone had taken to learning and religion—*palapala* and *pule*—leading the English Consul-General Manley Hopkins, who never credited the Americans with anything not self-evident, to concede that education in the Sandwich islands "embraced a larger proportion of the population than it has ever done in Great Britain, in Prussia or New England," and prompting Mark Twain with his usual jocularity to declare the Islanders "the most universally educated people outside of China." The twelve-letter alphabet and the simple primer were responsible for the transformation.

But the natural curiosity and the native intelligence of the Hawaiians could not be overlooked. Within days after their arrival, every mission family took in a handful of promising young men and women, assigned them household chores, fed them, clothed them, and indoctrinated them. The response was astonishing. They were ready in a few months to go forth as knowledgeable exponents of Yankee ways and as initiated Christians. Then there were small select classes of students being trained as interpreters, emissaries, and instructors, and the trickle of Cornwall alumni, who were the best educators of all.

From these three sources, a corps of native trainees was picked to serve as the first teachers as soon as the four-page speller was off the press. All of them unwittingly had lent a hand in composing it, for the missionaries had learned from their pupils almost as much as the pupils had learned from them. At sea-front villages, in remote valleys, in rugged mountain back country, in the most unlikely places, schools immediately began to spring up, as though it were all part of a calculated plan of infiltration.

Fortunately it was not necessary to wait for the American Board to appropriate funds for school construction or to supply teaching equipment. Except for the hornbook, there was no equipment, and the pupils themselves built the schools, simple grass umbrellas that could be completed in a day or two. They could get down to their lessons at once.

News of the wonderful trick of putting speech on paper spread over the Islands like wildfire. To fun-minded Islanders it *was* a trick, a sport, an exciting new game. Everybody wanted to play. It was more fun than gambling, than rolling *maika* stones, than *noa* and *puhene-hene*. And sessions were brief enough not to tax the span of interest, lasting only for a couple of hours in late afternoon once or twice a week.

At the sound of the teacher's conch, students swarmed to school, as they had once swarmed to the beach for surfing when the sea was high. Adults came, not children. There was no room for the young ones yet. Chiefs claimed priority; elders of status were next in line, and then the commoners. The old gaming haunts were all but abandoned in favor of schoolrooms.

Father Bingham and his linguists had made a hit with their twelve-letter alphabet far beyond their most extravagant hopes. It was so simple that the dullest oldster could master it in a few days. Chiefs and gray-haired commoners alike showed an unabashed love for school and schooling. Once they had memorized the alphabet and learned to read a few words and sentences, they wanted to copy them, to write their speech.

As abecedarians turned into scholars, educational materials became a necessity. From the far corners of the Islands frantic calls came in to mission headquarters for paper, slates, ink, pencils, books and more books, anything. Of course, no one was prepared for the demand. There were no such quantities of supplies. Poor Elisha Loomis was having a hard time finding paper enough even for reprints of his hornbook.

By slow boat to Boston the frantic appeals were relayed to the American Board: Send us books! Send us teachers! Send us paper! Hang the cost! "The necessary expense ought not to be thought of for a moment," ran an urgent petition. "You need have no fear about pecuniary means to meet the expense. . . . Let not this consideration delay you a moment. The Lord and his people will provide the necessary pecuniary means."

At best it would take a year and a half to get a response from any appeal, and too often the Board merely returned a complaint that the missionaries were spending too lavishly, expecting too much. They begged for paper from every ship that called at Honolulu, and even then Loomis frequently could not keep stations supplied with the speller. Chiefs inconsiderately demanded them by the score, and a school in the hinterland would have to get along with a single copy for a class of fifty.

"It is astonishing how so many have learned to read with so few books," speculated a *haole* mentor. "They teach each other, making use of banana leaves, smooth stones and wet sand on the beach. Some read equally well with the book upside down or sidewise, as four or five learn from the same book with one teacher, crowding around him as closely as possible."

And they were not content merely with learning to read. As pupils made the discovery that there was such a thing as arithmetic, they wanted to be taught figuring. Gradually, as native teachers got the hang of it themselves, the third R was added to the curriculum. Heavy doses of Scripture memorizing and moralizing had to be included, and it was not long before geography, Bible history, and singing could be put on the agenda.

As fast as good students could be tested in their progress, they were "graduated" and sent on to set up new schools of their own. Compensation was not the incentive either. No one among the hundreds of teachers received a penny in pay. They taught for the love of it, but mostly for the prestige. Their status was recognized by chiefs who saw to it that they lived tax free and were suitably housed and fed by their pupils. Indeed, the prestige of a schoolhouse keeper was almost as elevated as that of a gaming house keeper. Never could he have hoped to attain such respect in any other employment.

But the gloss of learning not infrequently went to the teacher's head; he took advantage of his learning, basked in his newly acquired status, and let the pedagogy suffer. Foreigners who looked in at some of the schools complained that there were no seats, no tables, no school apparatus; the scholars were in wild disorder, talking, laughing, quarreling, and the teacher ineffectively fretting and storming after them with a heavy rod. Missionaries were accused of squandering the time of the pupils, encouraging desultory habits, leading them to starvation through neglect of gainful occupation.

The same foreigners would criticize any missionary accomplishment, and Hiram Bingham well knew that the love of *palapala* was too strong to permit many such scenes. "It is not very difficult," he hit back, "for good men to sneer at the shabby appearance of the Hawaiian schools, the incompetency of the native teachers, and the magisterial patronage they enjoy . . . but it is a consolation in the toil of bringing a nation to an acquaintance with letters, morals and true religion to find at length that a large portion of the people of all ages can be induced to collect in schools." And, as though riddance of native diversions were the prime purpose of the schooling, he could always rejoice that "the heathen sports of the nation have nearly disappeared."

As more paper was shipped out from Boston, the real test of the effectiveness of missionary education was seen in the demand for books and more books. Between editions of the speller, the mission printers worked day and night grinding out tracts, texts, and teacher's manuals, Bible verses to memorize, hymnals and hygiene treatises, catechisms and compendiums of history, arithmetic books, geography books, grammars—a wide and wild miscellany including such items as *The History of Beasts, Sixteen Sermons, Attributes of God, Tract on Popery, Tract on Lying, Tract on Marriage, Tract on the Sabbath, Tract on Intemperance.* They were read until there was nothing left of the pages but indecipherable dog-ears.

Pastors in the various parishes all doubled as school superintendents and examiners. They went the rounds several times a year with a satchel of new books, with questions, encouragement, and chastisement, and they took upon themselves the responsibility for personally examining every student before he could be declared a reader or writer. But the sheer size of the student bodies made the examinations little more than a perfunctory frisking for information.

With twenty or thirty different schools scattered through a parish, the examination process became an ordeal that went on day after day for weeks, · requiring the cleric to race daily from one village to the next. Six thousand pupils were checked off by a single examiner in 1832 in the course of three weeks, and though he never revealed his secret for differentiating between the learned and unlearned, he declared at the end of the period that two thousand "ranked as readers."

When making the rounds for purposes of ranking became a physical impossibility, the students from all the schools of a region were assembled at a central point for the ceremony, and it was turned into a public exhibition, with a mass parade, a mammoth luau, and an academic procession, for which the Hawaiians borrowed ideas from the pomp and ceremony of royal cavalcades and the missionaries threw in their recollections of commencement and class-day extravaganzas.

Everybody came, parents and grandparents, brothers, sisters, relatives from far and near, foreigners, if they would deign to accept an invitation, and chiefs by the score to add dignity and prestige. Proudly describing a typical spectacle at Waimea, Father Lyons recounted almost breathlessly, "Great and enthusiastic preparation had been made—bowers erected, meeting houses adorned with evergreens. At last the march commenced . . . men in front, children next, women bringing up the rear, each division with some flag, children with *kahilis.* For want of a more skillful person, I was obliged to act as captain. . . .

"*Kahilis* were waving, banners flying. People were decently, some richly, dressed. Men wore shirts and pantaloons, many teachers white frock coats. Women appeared in white and calico dresses, with shawls and handkerchiefs tied very tastefully about the head for bonnets. Ladies made quite a display of bonnets, veils and even shoes and stockings."

After marching up and down the center of the village, with frequent pauses for concerted recitals of psalms, song, and catechism, the whole throng, thousands strong, "repaired to a bower" for the luau— and Lyons scurried off to the next engagement in Waipio Valley, where three thousand residents and the students of four valley schools pooled their efforts in an even more elaborate performance. "The people appeared perfectly astonished at the display of civilization which they found themselves capable of making," Lyons exulted. "New life flowed in every vein; joy sparkled on every countenance."

Competition in colorful costume was the fad one year when Honolulu saw thousands traipsing into town from both windward and leeward sides of Oahu for the final examinations, men in tapa *kiheis,* women in wrap-around *paus,* pupils from each district wearing a distinctive color, crimson, brilliant yellow, spotless white, stunning black, and brown. Even foreign dissidents had to admit it was stirring to witness a block of five hundred, all arrayed in one color, recite in perfect unison the Sermon on the Mount or the fifteenth chapter of John.

But Kailua on Hawaii had to be credited with the most remarkable and suspensive performance of all time. For that occasion the schools from the entire Kona district were invited to the old capital for their examination fiesta; but they did not appear as scheduled. Their audience waited until after sunset, and not a student had yet turned up.

Just as darkness settled down, and odd glow flushed the slopes of

Hualalai, the mountain with the majestic upward sweep from Kailua Bay. The chiefs gathered around in chilled astonishment. Was it an eruption? As they watched, here, there, and everywhere against the blackness of the vast slope appeared flowing avenues of light. It was not lava. The illumination was coming from long torchlight processions, dozens of them, scattered over the face of the mountain. They wound back and forth until the heights were alive with streams of moving light.

Gradually the lines merged to form one immense fiery column moving toward Kailua, and, as a climax to the show, thousands of conchs in a thousand pitches blasted forth "with as much spirit as if they expected the fortification of darkness were about to fall before them."

To Hiram Bingham, who was present for the great occasion, the display was "a sort of celebration of the arrival of the light and the deliverance from idols, and was to the poor people something like the fireworks of Boston Common . . . and the sober examination of those numerous schools the next day proved the existence of many little torch lights-kindled along the dark shores."

Those torchlights were all held by adults. For almost a decade the missionaries shied away from attempting much kindling of learning among the younger generation. There simply were not enough teachers or texts or schools for the children. Moreover, as a missionary wife put it, "The children are not yet tamed. . . . They are considered bright, but too wild to be brought into the schools."

But by 1830 they had benefited sufficiently from the example set by their elders to be given a try, and it was quickly decided that the taming problem had been overemphasized. In the hands of a pedagogue who did not spare the rod, the young hellions lapped up spelling lists and called for slates, learned to multiply and asked for long division, gulped down the Scripture excerpts in their copies of *Daily Food* and begged for Bibles. They took to learning as omnivorously as had their fathers, and the school sessions met daily instead of once or twice a week.

Commuting distances of eight or ten miles meant nothing to them.

They walked to school in drenching downpours and blistering sun; they came on surfboards and in canoes. In lush, remote Waimanu Valley on Hawaii, bottomland long since deserted by man and reclaimed by nature, they swam to school naked, merrily making their way up and down the river holding bundles of clothing out of the water with one hand.

The home office in Boston was beginning to appreciate what was happening educationally in the Sandwich Islands and supplied the children with instructional aids that their parents had never seen, such refinements as wall maps, real blackboards, pencils, and foolscap. Makeshift desks were fashioned from mud bricks and discarded surfboards or hewn by hand from green timber.

Literacy was no longer a novelty. It had to be shared by all. Within a few weeks after the arrival of medical missionary Dr. Gerrit Judd and his wife in 1828, Mrs. Judd, with the assistance of Mrs. Bingham, had started a school for queens, dowagers, princesses, chiefesses, and their retinue of ladies in waiting and boasted of having as pupils the most distinguished blood in the realm.

Such dignitaries could not be summoned to school by a conch, like the common herd, and since Honolulu had neither clocks nor bells, the preceptresses settled on the simple expedient of raising a flag when classes were due to start. The fact that the emblem had the word "Superb" across its folds was accidental; it had been salvaged from the little freighter *Superb* that foundered off the island. The banner with the bold letters was accepted as both school motto and rallying signal.

The ladies of the court showed themselves worthy of it in their mastery of sentence structure and sewing. In the absence of Liholiho, one of them, Kaahumanu, widow of Kamehameha I, had already taken the liberty of issuing a decree that everyone in the kingdom would be obliged to learn reading and writing; she then aptly demonstrated that she could comply with her own orders.

The law was now on the side of the missionaries, and they made the most of it. Not content with the widespread system of public education, they began to promote a rash of specialized institutions—

trade schools, female seminaries, teacher's institutes, boarding schools for boys and boarding schools for girls, schools for sons and daughters of chiefs, for particularly gifted youngsters, for foreign children, for part-whites—the *hapahaoles*—a theological seminary for training future Hawaiian preachers, even a college preparatory academy.

The seminary at Lahaina—Lahainaluna—was the first experiment in "higher education," and 1831 the year. The most urgent need, postulated the missionaries, was a place where teachers and religious leaders could be properly imbued and disciplined, a school for exemplary male adults who had already been tamed.

All that was needed for such an institution, according to the Island educators, was a roster of eager students and an eager disciplinarian. Missionaries at different stations would furnish the students; the Reverend Lorrin Andrews, another Connecticut migrant who had found his way to Hawaii via Ohio and Kentucky, would furnish the discipline. The fact that he had no buildings in which to conduct the school and virtually no books or equipment was not considered an overwhelming obstacle.

Carefully selected students began arriving at Lahaina early in September, with their wives and children, and none seemed the least perturbed at finding no living quarters or classrooms ready for them. They at once started to attend classes in the open, high on the barren hillside above Lahaina where there was not even a shade tree; between lectures they proceeded to build their own huts and lay mud-brick walls for a recitation hall.

Once the walls were up, lumber for rafters had to be secured; so Andrews packed his Bible and lecture notes into a calabash and led the student body off to the mountains to cut timber. They were gone five weeks, and returned to find that the rains had dissolved the mud walls and all would have to be rebuilt with stone.

For most of a year the principal extracurricular activity was carrying boulders by hand over the uphill miles between shore and campus. The construction was never allowed to interfere with classes. Andrews continued to lecture in the open, sometimes dripping perspiration, sometimes dripping rain, while students held slates over their heads to shade their eyes or to keep their notes from being washed away.

These preliminary inconveniences merely seemed to whet appetites for learning; so attractive was the curriculum that while the recitation hall was going up, school enrollment jumped from twenty-five to sixty-seven. With a roof finally over their heads, the students thrived on a diet of such delicacies as Greek, Hebrew, geometry, trigonometry, sacred geography, interpretation of Scripture, archaeology, and elocution.

There was little else to thrive on the first year or two, for the student body was also held responsible for raising its own food, and crops were slow to start on the dry hillside. At length, one of the undergraduates promoted the idea of appropriating a stream in the nearest valley and channeling water to Lahainaluna. Once that irrigation system was in operation, every student spent an hour or two in the fields before breakfast, and the student menus markedly improved.

By the opening of the second year, most of the students had desks, which they hewed out of timber themselves, and work was starting on another class building. The school kept growing despite Andrews' rigorous academic regimen. Lest his pupils be left with spare minutes, vocational training was added to the curriculum, carpentry, masonry, wood turning, cabinet making, printing, binding, engraving, cartography, calligraphy, instrumental and vocal music.

Into the sophomore program went algebra, navigation, surveying, world history, and ancient languages. Juniors and seniors took advanced mathematics, natural and moral philosophy, church history, astronomy, chemistry, and sacred theology. Altogether the course of study was not far short of what was being crammed into four years at a New England college.

Perhaps a college was what Lorrin Andrews had in mind for Lahainaluna, and it was a magnificent location for one, backed by the Gothic lines of the West Maui Mountains and, commanding a stupendous view of seemingly uptilted ocean, the bold bulk of Lanai, Molokai, and, in fair weather, the mountains of Oahu on the far horizon. But Andrews ran into campus moral problems less theoretical than those on which he lectured in his philosophy courses. While the boys were busy at the books, wives of the married students were cutting up. It was a dull existence for the girls, and they improved their time by shopping around among their husband's classmates for more exciting companionship. It was the undoing of Andrews' early plans for the school.

Six years after the propitious start, Lahainaluna had to be abandoned as a training ground for wedded adults, a grave educational casualty, for the school had established an enviable reputation and made so much progress in practical arts like typography, engraving, and map making that its productions were going to be collectors' items for the next century and a quarter. Nowhere west of the Rockies was there a school which could match the erudition offered at Lahaina.

But the institution did not close its doors, far from it. Lahainaluna was merely remodeled to take in boys from eight to twenty in a combined grammar school, high school, and seminary, presumably for males of premarital age, with a graduate school in theology. Dormitories were substituted for the cozy family huts, and in a few years enrollment was well over the hundred mark.

To compensate for the local loss of feminine companionship, Andrews warmly endorsed the creation of a seminary for females, as a high-class matrimonial bureau and training ground for prospective wives of Lahainaluna alumni. But it was located at Wailuku, a safe distance from Lahaina, with the all-but-unscalable mass of the West Maui Mountains between the two.

The seminary curriculum was designed to complement that of the brother institution, so that lucky lady graduates, through courses in subjects like Christian religion, moral philosophy, and natural theology, would have at least a conversational knowledge of their husbands' enlightenment and at the same time gain a familiarity with such branches of the liberal and household arts as reading, writing, drawing, geography, arithmetic, composition, spinning, weaving, and sewing.

Founder of the female seminary was Jonathan Green, one of the few apostles with a prevailing sense of humor and a little latitude in his convictions. But the formidable matrons he drew for teaching and chaperoning were endowed with neither humor nor latitude; the girls were sequestered like so many nuns, routed out of their dormitory at daybreak to hoe in the school gardens under close supervision, herded to prayers at six thirty and breakfast at seven, put to work at general housekeeping until nine, and subjected to supervised study and recitations most of the day; at four, they were marched back to the fields with their hoes, for, like the boys at Lahaina, they had to grow their own food.

But there was variety in the program. Afternoon classes were devoted entirely to household arts, among which spinning and weaving took precedence. Cotton was being produced on Maui in considerable quantity at the time, and Father Green had ideas of developing a profitable industry by teaching the girls how to process it. A staid spinster, Lydia Brown, was imported all the way from New Hampshire to carry out the project, and in one period of five months some ninety yards of cloth were produced, but it was discovered later that Lydia had done most of the weaving. The girls never proved very adept at the craft.

Under strict chaperonage they were occasionally paraded for the benefit of the Lahainaluna males, and enough of them evaded their guardians to help fulfill the conjugal objectives of the two schools. "Love to thee . . . thou must precious of the daughters of the earth," ran one of the intercepted billets-doux from a Lahaina suitor. "Thou beauty of the clear nights of Lehua. . . . Love to thee, O Pomare, thou royal woman of the Pacific. . . . Where art thou, my beloved, who art anointed with the fragrance of glory. Much love to thee. . . . O, thou art joined to my affection, who art knit to me in the hot days of Lahainaluna. . . . I was overwhelmed with love like one drowning. When I lay down to sleep, I could not sleep; my mind floated after thee. Like the strong wind of Lahaina, such is the strength of my love to thee. . . . At the time the bell rings for meeting on Wednesday, great was my love to you. . . . Forsake not thou this our love. Keep it quietly, as I do keep it quietly here."

The Wailuku female seminary may have had academic and administrative shortcomings, but its matrimonial services were a rousing success.

Back in Honolulu, meanwhile, the ever squabbling merchants and missionaries had at last found a common cause. Both agreed it was high time some sort of English school was devised for educating the throng of *hapahaoles,* mostly illegitimates fathered by transient seamen and beachcombers, the by-product of ships' refreshment programs.

Actually such a school had been started by the missionaries in 1820, shortly after their arrival, but it was quickly dropped when they were reminded by the mentors in Boston that these children of sin hardly came within their field of responsibility. With the passing of a dozen years, however, they were ready to reconsider the question and furnish a teacher, provided the foreigners would supply the physical necessities.

The hat was passed. It may have been conscience money; it may have been openhanded liberality; but the funds rolled in, hundreds of dollars, a novel experience for mission folk who were generally unable to wheedle even token gifts from the merchants. Collectors, fortified with sentimental tales about the woes of Honolulu's fatherless brats, went the rounds of vessels in the harbor, and doubled the take in conscience money.

Before the campaign was over, the hat-passers had enough cash for a splendid coral building and funds left over for dormitories and a teacher's residence. The Oahu Charity School was going strong by 1833, with close to a hundred students, and it had one New England accessory that impressed the natives more than the fancy desks, blackboards, and other apparatus—a belfry and bell, which clanged the call to classes every morning at eight.

Then as a deterrent to further increase in the *hapahaole* enrollment at the school, there arrived from New London, Connecticut, as a gift from whaling magnate Thomas W. Williams, the makings of a spacious new Honolulu church, a seamen's chapel. The Bethel, as it was known, was also an educational institution, with a library and classroom, as well as a sanctuary and a full-time chaplain-pedagogue in charge. Without doubt it contributed to the short life of the Oahu Charity School, for in a few years the school ran out of *hapahaole* waifs to educate and had to be given up.

But for every school that outwore its usefulness, at least two were opening elsewhere. Regardless of his location, every missionary of vigor and imagination seemed to have a compulsion to found an old-fashioned grammar school on the order of the one he had attended in New England. He felt it his duty to pass on that educational legacy and to provide a discipline that the native teachers in their schools naturally could not give.

At Hilo, in Titus Coan's territory, it was a self-supporting boarding school. Titus was too busy with his evangelistic services to undertake the supervision; so he turned it over to David Lyman and his wife. They evolved something better than a grammar school. Long before vocational courses had come into vogue in the States, the Lymans established a model trade school that incorporated most of the classical program, too. The courses ranged from farming and woodworking to tailoring and dairying, from the three R's to the three A's, astronomy, anatomy, and the Apostles. The Lymans worked hard at it from four in the morning until nine at night, classes interspersed with prayers, planting, weeding, and harvesting, and overtime drill on manners and music.

Manners and music were a Hilo specialty. At mealtime the Lymans went all out to remove the last vestige of the barbarian; they insisted that the students sit on benches around wooden tables instead of on the floor and knocked knuckles when pupils reached for food with fingers rather than with a civilized fork or spoon. Many a clumsy boy who could not manage a fork went hungry until he could.

But music was the cultural triumph of Hilo. Mrs. Lyman was a talented soprano and versatile instrumentalist, who did not hesitate to attempt instruction in strings, woodwinds, or brasses which she had never played herself, fretting out the lessons as she went along. A ship captain, who took a shine to her accomplishments, presented her with a flute; in no time she mastered it and so did several of her pupils.

They began making flutes and fifes out of bamboo, and she had a woodwind orchestra.

Other visiting captains dug up an accordion, a cello, and assorted brasses. A band concert given by a naval vessel put the students into a frenzy of excitement. They wanted a band, too, and soon organized it, complete even to homemade trombones. Moreover, on Sundays Father Coan could boast of a choir accompanied by flute and viol.

The fervor for *haole* music, so utterly different from the scant melody in old Hawaiian chants and hulas, spread up and down the coast and back into the hills of Waimea, where Father Lorenzo Lyons, more famed for the Hawaiian hymns he composed than the sermons he expounded, was trying to encourage an interest in sacred song. The two influences met and fairly exploded into harmony. Choral clubs were the rage from Puako to Waipio. In his field, which stretched in a broad band from the east to the west coast of Hawaii, Lyons spent as much time organizing singing classes and training voice teachers as his colleagues spent on their boarding schools.

"Great enthusiasm continues in singing schools," triumphed the maestro, ordinarily given more to restraint than exaggeration. "They have spread like wildfire. Multitudes interested, young, middle-aged and gray-haired. A few Catholics join with the Calvinists in singing. Some individuals, wild and strangers to any sort of meeting house, when they come within the sound of the singing, are so enchanted that like Saul of old, they are afterward found, if not among the prophets, yet among the singers. . . . Heretofore I myself was the chorister and perhaps the only singer in the house. True, others would strike up their notes, but they were anything but musical notes. Now the native choristers set the tune and perform the music. . . . What a change I have witnessed!"

Education, in one form or another, was changing everything. Even the young sons and daughters of the chiefs were attending a plush school of their own in Honolulu under missionary guidance. Bingham had had a hard time justifying this sort of segregation. But these children were too arrogant or indolent to attend other schools, and unless special classes were provided them, the future rulers of the kingdom would be growing up with less education than their subjects. The Chiefs' Children's School was bilingual, English and Hawaiian, and the Reverend Amos Cooke and his wife Juliette were the instructors. Amos was another of the Connecticut Congregational clan, a martinet who firmly believed that the quickest way to spoil a child was to spare the rod. The chiefs' children, however, were already badly spoiled; not one of them had ever been disciplined. Each was trailed by a string of attendants—*kahus*—ready to carry out every bidding of the young upstarts, and anticipate the bidding if possible.

Their futures were secure; all were in line for the throne, or at least a governorship. Neither Amos nor Juliette were unaware of the weight of their responsibilities; errors in handling the youngsters could bring upon the entire mission immediate parental antagonism, while misguided pedagogy could affect the kingdom for years to come, when the pupils themselves were rulers. In the face of these inevitabilities, it took a heap of courage not to stoop to indulgence.

The army of *kahus* was dismissed on the first day of school. At the parting they cried, and the children yowled. Never before had the royal sons and daughters been left for a moment without their beloved protectors. Some of them bawled all night. Amos and Juliette let them bawl. That was the beginning of their discipline.

The long-pampered pupils soon learned that all coddling had ended; they had new "*kahus*" who issued demands rather than fulfilled childish whims. And once they discovered that there was no disputing the authority of their teachers, they took to the books and studied ravenously, English, mathematics, history, and theology, just like the students at Lahainaluna or Hilo. They were superb scholars.

The Cookes applied common sense in not trying to divorce them entirely from their past life and provided all kinds of supervised fun that was not on the educational calendar for commoners—riding, sailing, surfing, hiking. They played ball, flew kites, rolled hoops, celebrated the Fourth of July with genuine firecrackers, formed an accordion quartet. The school was such a success for several years that even a few missionary children were allowed to attend as day students.

But as the royal heirs matured, the errant ways of parents seemed to reappear in the teenagers. To the horror of Amos, one of the boys turned up late at night thoroughly intoxicated. He had escaped through a window. In fact, the truth was soon revealed that two or three of them had been slipping out at night, time and again, for bibulous entertainment; they had been dancing, and only the good Lord knew what else they had been up to.

The coeducational plan of the school was not working out quite as the Cookes had intended either. On a hunch, Amos burst into the girls' room one noon hour. His suspicion was well-founded. There in broad daylight were two of the boys bundling two of the girls—in bed.

Amos had a frank little talk with the boys, and Juliette took on the girls. Their expression of shame and contrition appeared to be genuine, and for a while educational affairs went along more smoothly. Then everything went wrong at once and built up to a climax.

The old *kahus* were back on the job surreptitiously supplying intoxicating beverages to the boys, who were drinking continuously. A series of letters, accidentally found, revealed that two of the young royalty were plotting an escape, making arrangements for a long sea voyage that would take them far beyond the reach of their disciplinarians.

One of the girls blithely admitted that she was with child by a royal classmate. An extramural husband had to be found for her. And, alas, an incorrigible culprit had to be expelled because of a liaison with none other than the queen. One might expect it of a queen, but certainly any student of the Cookes should know better. Fortunately most of the group had finished the planned course of study about that time; so the school was closed with little sorrow on the part of anyone.

Out in the rural areas the schools for commoners were doing much better. At Waialua on the other side of Oahu, a "manual labor boarding school" for boys flourished; at Waioli on Kauai an all-purpose "select school," partly vocational, partly teacher training, partly preparatory for admission to Lahainaluna, enrolled some seventy-five boys. David Lyman's boarding school for boys had set such a fine example at Hilo that Father Coan's wife Fidelia opened a similar one for girls—on a budget of four hundred dollars a year for twenty students.

At every station was at least one select school run by the missionaries themselves for a group of twenty or thirty especially promising students. The Bonds in isolated Kohala supervised three in their spare time, a boarding school for boys, a seminary for girls, and, after 1842, a normal school, the first one in the Islands. Father Bond thought his one-day-a-week teacher's college held a more important precedent than that; never having heard of Samuel Read Hall's Columbian School in Vermont or of the State Normal School in Massachusetts, he was convinced that he had invented a new branch of professional education. He had; but during his long absence from cultural centers, someone else had done the same.

In all the preoccupation with lighting so many lamps of learning among the heathen, the most neglected youngsters were the missionaries' own children, and by the 1840's they were a considerable body, well over two hundred. From the very first shocking recognition of Hawaiian moral standards, the parents had agreed upon a complete segregation policy for their offspring. They would have absolutely no association with the natives, and to preclude the possibility of their overhearing any oddments of evil, they were forbidden to learn the Hawaiian language.

Missionary mothers gave most of the elementary instruction around the living-room table; fathers did the tutoring in advanced subjects like algebra and Latin, and as soon as arrangements could be made with friends, relatives, or charitable societies on the Mainland, the sons and daughters were shipped off to New England, where there would be no further danger of pagan contamination.

The pathetic partings of parents and young fry were the sorest affliction the families ever suffered, and a few, like the Thurstons at Kailua, took a firm stand and resolutely refused to subject themselves and their children to the agony. What the mission most needed was a segregated school for American boys and girls—in the Islands. For years the subject had been tossed around at meetings of the brotherhood and sisterhood. They had sent repeated appeals for funds to

Boston, but neither discussions nor appeals seemed to produce any-thing tangible.

In 1842 Lorrin Andrews brought things to a head in a way no one had thought possible. He quit as head of Lahainaluna over a disagree-ment among the brethren on the right to acquire personal property and real estate. Most of his colleagues insisted that all such acquisitions should be turned over to the mission organization. Andrews, who had put a lot of energy into establishing a Lahaina farm that he considered his own, dissented. He severed all connections with the Honolulu and Boston mission and, to support himself and family, opened a seamen's chapel at Lahaina, continued the farming, printing, and engraving started at Lahainaluna, and then, to add fuel to the burning contro-versy, announced the opening of an English school of his own for white children.

The last thrust was all the incentive needed to get a program under way in Honolulu, without aid from Boston. Out of their meager re-sources, each of the local missionary families subscribed fifty dollars. A brand new building was hastily erected at Punahou, two miles from downtown Honolulu, on land that the governor of Oahu had once given to Hiram Bingham. The Reverend Daniel Dole and his wife Emily, who had arrived from Maine the year before, took over as authoritarians and teachers, and before the end of the calendar year could count fifteen boarders and nineteen day students.

The original building was nothing but "a low whitewashed adobe structure thatched with grass." Punahou School and Oahu College grew from that modest beginning. It thrived on Greek, Latin, Euclid, and prebreakfast hoeing, steadily expanded, drew students from Cali-fornia during the opening of the West, and in the half-century after its founding developed into the greatest preparatory academy west of the Rocky Mountains.

In one way or another all of the missionary schools contributed toward Hawaii's nineteenth-century reputation as the most school-minded nation in the world. Punahou contributed in a very special way; its educational facilities were a tempting invitation to the sons and daughters of the missionaries to remain in the Islands after graduation. Scores of them did remain, and those Punahou alumni, inheritors of "the moral backbone of New England," were the men and women who fixed the future tone and character of Island society.

Just as the mission organizations gave the churches their independence as soon as they could support themselves, so the native schools were released one by one to government control. By the 1850's most of them were under the supervision of a minister of public instruction, an ex-missionary, of course. All of those hundreds of native schools, started on a shoestring, were merely the forerunners of a modern system of primary, secondary, and higher education that could compare more than favorably with that of any part of the United States mainland.

The Yankee missionaries wrought an educational miracle in Hawaii the like of which could be found in no other country, and for years serious educators attributed the miracle solely to the Puritan pedagogy and the Congregational conservatism that modeled it, assuming that there would have been no miracle under different guidance and extending little of the plaudit to the receptive, adroit students themselves.

Not until other church organizations, like the Roman Catholic, the Episcopalians, and the Mormons, had been given a chance to put into practice utterly different philosophies of education and had achieved equally remarkable results, was there any objective reappraisal of the Congregational accomplishment.

Late in the century, Sisters Mary Clara and Phoebe, representing an order of the Church of England, established a school for girls at Lahaina. The curriculum was quite similar to what the Americans presented, but the school atmosphere had a difference.

"I never saw such a mirthful-looking set of girls," asserted a discerning critic in 1875 after visiting the school. "Whenever they spoke to the Sisters, they clung about them as if they were their mothers. . . . To say that they were free and easy would be wrong; it was rather the manner of very frolicsome daughters to very indulgent mothers or aunts. It was a family manner, rather than a school manner. The Sisters are very wise in adapting their discipline to the native character and circumstance. Strict obedience is, of course, required, but the rules are few and lenient. Hawaiians are a dancing people and will dance, or else indulge in less innocent pastimes. . . . I have been told by many who on most points are quite out of sympathy with the Sisters, not only that their work is recognized as a most valuable agency, but that their influence has come to be regarded as among the chiefest of the blessings of Lahaina."

The Yankees were not the only schoolmasters capable of bringing redeeming education to the Hawaiians.

VII

Converted to Commerce

Despite its squalor, its drab disorder, and sheer ugliness, Honolulu had won its status as the undisputed commercial capital of the Hawaiian kingdom before 1850—"one of the least inviting spots on the face of the earth," as a missionary son brought up there remembered it in his worldly-wise adulthood. The town was still a sea of grass shacks, but it was incongruously accented here, there, and yonder with importations of foreign architecture. Except for the haystack houses, every structure, like the vegetation, seemed to have been borrowed from some other land.

The conglomeration of sheds and warehouses at the landings duplicated the waterfront scene at San Francisco or San Diego; the massive walls of the fort that occupied half the harbor shore and served as a perch for useless rusted cannon reminded incoming sea captains of fortified ports in Brittany; the church steeples, Charity School belfry, and mission community were strictly New England; the new multi-verandaed royal palace was a naïve adaptation of British Victorian;

Nantucket widow's-walks topped the domiciles of retired whaler captains; high-pillared Charleston porches fronted the stately retreats of two or three successful merchants; and the dominant architectural accent in the business district was straight out of Mexican California, a western frontier setting of adobe shops, false-front stores, and groggeries complete with narrow stoops and hitching posts; the loungers, the horses, the saddles, the signs, and even the wares in the windows had the western cast.

But the harbor front offered the most striking evidence that an invasion of commerce and commercial men was slowly transforming Honolulu from an unattractive native village into a less attractive Pacific market place. That whole section of town was an unsightly hodgepodge of shaky wharves, blacksmith shops, slaughterhouses, and fish sheds projecting over the filthy waters; ramshackle warehouses smelling of oakum, dried fish, and spilled liquor; cattle pens and temporary pigsties; towers of barrels and trading goods awaiting transportation in or out.

In an effort to give dignity to the area, a pretentious government building, housing a post office, customs, and treasury department, had been erected in the middle of the chaos. But it failed in its purpose. The structure merely looked as though it should have been somewhere else, particularly the monumental arched gateway with a glittering replica of the royal crown overhead.

Nor did the crumbling fort belong where it stood. Started by the Russians and completed by Hawaiians, no one had ever thought of a good use for it, except to enclose the governor's house, the jail, and barracks. Certainly the defunct cannon and ancient brass pieces, which had once cost a dozen times their weight in sandalwood, were no match for the guns of a modern warship that might choose to let loose a broadside. The rampart was now an anachronism obviously cluttering the path of commercial progress.

Directly across the street from the upper wall of the fort, as if hugging it for protection, was a huge, low-slung adobe structure that looked more formidable and impregnable than the fort itself. What few windows it had were closely barred. The great doors were swung open only while a ship was in the harbor and were promptly closed and bolted as soon as a vanload of supplies eased in or out. There was an air of mystery and secrecy about the building.

Those who had managed to get a glance into the dark, cavernous interior saw that it was stowed to the rafters with a rich miscellany of barrels, boxes, and bales. It was the warehouse of the Hudson's Bay Company, and most of the goods inside were destined for trade with Indians on the northwest coast of America, though the company never shrugged off any business it could grab from the whalers or interisland dealers.

New England whalers had put Honolulu on the map, and the Hudson's Bay Company apparently had every intention of reaping the major benefits thereof. Hudson's Bay—the "Great Company"—was a name to be reckoned with anywhere in the North Atlantic and North Pacific. Wherever it moved, its governor, Sir George Simpson, aimed at nothing short of monopoly, and monopoly was what Sir George had in mind for Hawaiian commerce.

But he was encountering too much competition for his comfort. New England salesmen were not to be bluffed out of business by any British giant. The Yankee peddlers, who for over a century had been dispensing tin pans and buckets, hats and shoes, lanterns and cure-alls, teapots and wooden nutmegs, had outworn their welcome in the United States, moved on to more lucrative levels of commerce and industry, and a few of the more enterprising hucksters had given up their carts for ships to exploit a new clientele in the Pacific, anywhere from Chile to China.

In the deep South they had been regarded as a pestilence "on the list of plagues next to yellow fever, and before locusts, taxation and a wet spring." In the Islands they were greeted as a boon. The poorest native could somehow earn enough pennies to purchase a tin thimble, a handful of brass buttons, or a licorice stick. A wonderful new world of trinkets was opened to Hawaiians by the peddlers.

It was equally wonderful for the salesman. In the Sandwich Islands he did not have to hawk his wares from door to door and spiel his way into a five-cent sale; the customers came to him. On Market

Street or Beretania he quickly graduated from peddler to merchant and became a man of standing in the community.

Many were worthy of the promotion, for it took a wealth of enterprise as well as a substantial reserve of capital to freight a shipload of merchandise from an East Coast port to Honolulu, and only the most resourceful ever made a success of it, usually in a complicated deal with a ship's master or trader who knew his way around the Pacific and knew how to contend with the almighty Hudson's Bay people.

British Consul Robert C. Wyllie declared in 1844 that the prosperity of the Sandwich Islands was entirely dependent on the whalers. "Were the whale fishery to fall off," he conjectured, "the Islands would lapse into primitive insignificance." The Yankees proved him wrong. In lean whaling seasons, it was their vision and their undertakings that kept both Hawaiians and foreigners from going hungry, and when the oil business finally did fall off, they were the ones who kept the Islands from lapsing into "primitive insignificance."

The peddler-merchants were the real economic stabilizers of the kingdom, the possessors of the kind of ingenuity it took to tide over from one business pursuit to another. They were pioneers in diversifying Island industry and in the long run contributed far more to the future of Hawaii than the hordes of harpooners. They even gave the missionaries spirited competition in molding the character of the populace.

Although several American salesmen preceded him, the first to do much real molding of Island character and destiny was the irrepressible Vermonter William French, of the same ilk as that other William French of Brattleboro, Vermont, who a full month before the battle of Lexington shed the first blood of the American Revolution. French, a jack-of-all-trades with a partiality for salesmanship, got his introductory view of Hawaii in 1819, a few weeks before the arrival of the missionary ship *Thaddeus*.

He was en route to Canton at the time but was so favorably impressed with the possibilities of shopkeeping in Honolulu that he was soon back in the harbor aboard the brig *Nile* with a cargo of general merchandise. His empire rapidly expanded from the proceeds of that shipload, retailed at a generous markup in Kawaihae and Honolulu.

He settled in the Islands, and, almost annually thereafter, one cargo followed another to his wharves—pots and pans, cotton prints and sea biscuit, clocks and playing cards. In New England it had been demonstrated beyond any doubt that the only salesman more glib, more audacious, more persistent than a Connecticut peddler was a peddler from the Green Mountains of Vermont. French proved it again in Hawaii.

From general merchandise he drifted into general management. As fast as he could find reliable clerks and assistants, he branched out into ventures that paid bigger dividends. He dipped his dexterous fingers into more Pacific pies than his contemporaries could count. After a time, he owned not only the ships that brought his supplies to the Islands but the wharves where they docked. He possessed stores and warehouses, a blacksmith shop, a slaughterhouse, a Honolulu hotel—modestly referred to as "tenements"—a cooper's establishment, and a tinsmith's shop.

He operated an enormous cattle ranch at Waimea, Hawaii, and an experimental sugar mill at Waimea, Kauai, from which he shipped out what was probably the first exported sugar, eight thousand pounds, along with some eight thousand gallons of molasses.

When his schooners, the *Victoria* and the *Unity*, could not handle all the trade he generated, larger vessels were chartered. He dealt in hides and beef, livestock, hardware, whale oil, cotton goods, cane products, horses, and liquors. From his base in Honolulu he dispatched cargoes to the Russian colonies in Alaska and to the Mexican ports of Monterey and San Francisco. His routes of commerce extended across the Pacific from Siberia and the Sea of Okhotsk to the Gulf of California. On Oahu his industrial speculations ranged from a rum factory in Honolulu to a sheep ranch and cotton plantation at Ewa.

In some of his trial ventures he suffered damaging losses. The Kauai sugar mill failed to pan out after two years and set him back three thousand dollars. He could not get a satisfactory land lease for the Ewa cotton plantation and had to give that up. He accused Hiram Bingham of responsibility for a loss of seven thousand dollars when the missionaries prevailed upon the chiefs to outlaw his rum distillery. But the small fortunes he accumulated in fur barter with the Russians, in horse trading with the Mexicans, and in dealings with the New England whalers, the Chinese, the Australians, and the American Indians more than made up for any deficits.

Like other farsighted Honolulu merchants, it was inevitable that he would have to lock horns sooner or later with the Hudson's Bay Company. The conflict came in 1835, when intelligence reached London that he was encroaching upon Northwest territory that the Great Company considered its special province.

"It appears that Mr. French, an American at the Sandwich Islands," read the dispatch to the Hawaiian office, "carries on an intercourse with the Russian Company, and has a contract with them for the supply of certain articles, and that he combines with this a fur trade along the coast on the return of the ship to the Sandwich Islands. It would be of importance, if it can be accomplished without loss, to interrupt this intercourse by offering to supply the Russians on better terms."

The Russians received better terms from Hudson's Bay agents, and the Sandwich Islander was squeezed out. Then in 1840 French made a large mistake. Intent on extending his empire, he formed a partnership with an English merchant, Francis John Greenway. Though previous partners had watched over his affairs in China and Australia, French was by nature a lone operator, not a corporation man. In less than two years the finances of French and Company were in such a tangle that an international scandal was in the making.

Greenway went into bankruptcy. The partnership was dissolved and ex-partner Greenway shortly adjudged insane by a duly constituted jury. It took years and the creation of a Hawaiian court of chancery to untangle the strands. English residents were embattled against the Americans and both against the Hawaiian government over issues involved. And the irony in the complication did not come to light until the attorneys and accountants had sorted out all the figures to discover that the firm was not bankrupt after all, only "temporarily embarrassed."

French died a few years later, a sadder, wiser, and poorer man for his indiscreet choice of a last partner, but still fairly well off. Despite the embarrassment, the Vermonter had established a pattern for big Island business, a pattern large enough to outdo Hudson's Bay, a pattern soon to be copied by other wheeler-dealers, the great Hawaiian companies known as "factors." Moreover, he had passed on the secrets of his success to a few of his more imaginative employees like rancher John Parker and Captain Charles Brewer.

Don't put all your eggs in one basket, he chided in describing his formula for commercial prosperity. Cater to the captains of industry who in twenty minutes run up accounts of four hundred dollars for marine supplies, but be just as polite to the native who spends twenty minutes picking out a ten-cent jackknife. Purchase a plantation or two on the side; lease the land if it is not for sale; contract to operate it, and handle all the business, if it is not for lease. Don't let a dollar lie idle when it can be making money in another enterprise. Instead of worrying about setbacks, plunge into another venture. Take chances, but be sure first that the prospects lean a little toward your side.

Those were the lessons drilled into Stephen Reynolds, another Honolulu merchant who served an apprenticeship as one of French's clerks. Reynolds was a fellow Yankee and a sharp one, who had been peddling goods off and on in the islands for a decade before he settled there permanently in 1823. He was a short, self-important little man, sunburned to a crisp, quick on repartee, and a devastating critic of those who crossed him.

Typical of the small shopkeepers who helped give the market district such a shabby appearance, he was never fired with quite the ambition of a William French. He was content to close up shop and serve as harbor pilot on the side and pose as legal authority in a town that had no professional lawyer. He hated formalities of any kind, particularly of dress, and, whatever the occupation, his standard uniform of the day was a sloppy, broad-brimmed Panama hat, white cotton shirt in need of laundering, and a pair of yellow Chinese trousers sagging on his hips for lack of suspenders.

His emporium, at the corner of what would eventually be Nuuanu Avenue and Market Street, was the customary country store for general merchandise where everything from liquor to pitchforks and the latest gossip was dispensed. The building itself would have fitted into a western mining town without an alteration, even in the sag of the false front. From morning to night a string of tousled horses stood at the hitching rail, and a parallel line of tousled town characters squatted on the rickety porch, Reynolds usually among them officiating as raconteur.

In this gathering were hatched most of the diatribes against the missionaries. For years Reynolds was a thorny irritant to Hiram Bingham—whom the storekeeper regarded as "an impudent puppy" —and to the apostles in general, all of whom were dismissed as "blood-sucking, cash-sucking, lazy, lying wretches." They never forgave him for teaming up with French to start the Honolulu rum distillery or for his slurs in the galling little *Island Gazette,* of which Reynolds was part owner for a time.

Moreover, he set an invidious example by carrying on with assorted damsels of indifferent reputation and producing a brood of little ill-mannered *hapahaoles.* Worst of all, he opened in the center of town that anathema of all Connecticut Congregationalists, a dancing school, and night after night the streets in the area echoed to the scrape of his fiddle and the chortle of his pupils.

Reynolds did, however, take occasional interest in constructive community projects. He worked tirelessly and idealistically for the Oahu Charity School, so that his *hapahaole* offspring might benefit from an education, and he was probably more responsible for its success than anyone else.

Reynolds' general store never made its owner wealthy. On one occasion he noted in his diary that he had grossed only $8.37½ in a week and wondered how he could continue to feed his dusky brood on that kind of income. He complained too about the competition from the Hudson's Bay Company, which he declared was undercutting the

Yankees until they would be driven from the Islands and out of the Pacific.

Long after his insufferable enemy Bingham was gone, he felt compelled to accept the fact that he could not lick the missionaries, so he joined them in the formation of a stock company to provide capital for raising tropical crops suitable for export; but that venture did not pay off.

The diversification doctrine of William French failed to take effect with him until late in life, when he secured a half-interest in the Haliimaile Plantation on Maui and through a lucky foreclosure won title to the rest of it. Into the plantation went just about all the capital he had managed to set aside while merchandising. But country life was too much of a strain on him; he missed the company of the loiterers and scandalmongers of his Market Street store. In 1855, like poor Francis Greenway, he surrendered to dementia, disappeared from the scene, and the Reynolds plantation became the Brewer plantation.

But there were plenty of merchants and shopkeepers to absorb Reynolds' trade in Honolulu, some thirty or forty of them, like E. & H. Grimes; Paty and Company; C. L. Richards and Company, Ship Chandlers; Makee, Anthon and Company; E. O. Hall & Sons, a mission printing family that had switched to hardware; a German corporation, W. H. Hackfeld and Company; and a respected British firm, Henry Skinner and Company, not to mention the would-be monopolists, Hudson's Bay.

Nothing, however, was sacred about the retention of business labels in Hawaii. They changed faster than people could forget the old ones. Progressive companies were in a constant state of flux, with mergers, new partnerships, reorganization, and realignment of stockholders regularly and pridefully being advertised. A shopper might purchase a set of fine chinaware on partial credit at the sign of J. Hunnewell and be obliged to settle the account a few months later at the same store, relabeled Peirce and Brewer.

Financial embarrassment and bankruptcy were responsible for some of the metamorphoses. For half a decade the dissolution of the great Ladd and Company was the talk of the town. Its demise came late in 1844, and the locked doors and boarded windows were mute testimony to the termination of its affairs, but the fading sign "Ladd, Brinsmade and Hooper" continued to memorialize the expired partnership.

Theirs was a weird and pathetic story. In the early thirties, the report of what the missionaries were accomplishing in Hawaii caught the imagination of the high-minded New Englanders, William Ladd and Peter Brinsmade. Since they were not equipped with theological training, they decided to take a fling at exposing the heathen to the one thing they did know, Christian commerce.

Like the missionaries, they sought out two openhearted girls who could share their principles, married them, talked a friend, William Hooper, known for his talents as a practical manager, into joining them, arranged for a shipment of general merchandise, and set sail for the Islands. Arriving in 1833, they put out their shingle, and since Ladd was the originator of the scheme, they were incorporated as Ladd and Company, even though Brinsmade was the senior partner and, as it developed, their real spokesman.

It was rumored in the Islands that Ladd and Company shared not only the blessings and prayers of the Boston Missionary Board, but liberal "pecuniary assistance" as well. In any case, the partners were given a warm reception by the Honolulu gospel set, and both they and their wives sipped many a cup of weak tea at the homes of the missionaries. Though they were reasonably successful as merchants, their emphasis on "mercantile morality" did not seem to net any more substance than did the principles of less moral merchants.

Brinsmade quickly emerged as the leader of the trio, and he was described by a not entirely sympathetic British acquaintance as "one of those rapid, intelligent, all-sided men which the social hot-bed of the United States produces so quickly and in such numbers—a man, who, if his practice as a surgeon fell off, would turn merchant; if he failed at that, would become an editor; or meeting with disappointment in the last vocation, would without hesitation climb the steps of the rostrum as a preacher; and even at a pinch would offer himself as a candidate for the Presidentship."

Under such gifted guidance, the company was soon scanning broader horizons. Possibly their Christian principles entitled them to privileges and exemptions not available to more worldly tradesmen. They were granted Honolulu wharfage rights and warehouse sites which a dozen merchants coveted and could not acquire; and when they decided to branch out as planters in the William French manner, for an incidental fee of three hundred dollars a year they managed to acquire a fifty-year lease of a thousand choice acres at Koloa, Kauai, which others had been unable to lease at any price—and the Maulili waterfall was thrown in as a mill site without additional charge. Even the Kauai chiefs balked at the deal.

Despite almost insurmountable difficulties, a plantation and sugar mill were in operation by 1836, and the quiet, practical partner, William Hooper, was left to manage things. In essence his instructions were to keep the natives gainfully employed so that they would stay out of mischief and support the church and themselves. Ladd and Brinsmade returned to Honolulu to mind the store, dictate plantation policy in absentia, and think up more grandiose schemes.

They quickly came up with a dazzler, still based on those "purely Christian principles." If the chiefs would back them they would be glad to put *all* unemployed Islanders to work and make everyone self-supporting and church-supporting simply by extending the Koloa Plantation idea over the whole archipelago, with Ladd and Company as factors.

It was a chimerical proposition that only a slightly mad utopian would have dared dream up, much less present in all seriousness to a monarch. The House of Ladd wanted King Kamehameha III to cede them "the full right and privilege of occupying, for the purpose of manufacturing agricultural productions, any now unoccupied and unimproved localities on the several islands of the Sandwich Islands, suitable for the manufacture of sugar, indigo, flour, raw silk, *kukui* oil, or any other production of the country, by water power, steam power, or animal power . . . and all the natural advantages of water, building materials and all other conveniences thereunto pertaining."

Much of the readily tillable land was already taken, but "unoccupied localities" were increasing with the same rapidity as the native population was decreasing, and there were, besides, vast acreages that could still be reclaimed by clearing and irrigating. Possession of such a carte blanche would give Ladd and Company a principality of hundreds of thousands of acres; it would be a commercial coup that would put all competitors forever in their places.

Incredibly, the king endorsed the plan and agreed to a contract.

In return for the cession, Ladd and Company magnanimously agreed "to stimulate and encourage habits of industry" among native landholders, "to manufacture or purchase on fair and equal terms the produce that may be developed by their industry, and to use their conscientious and steady endeavors to render the Sandwich Islanders an industrious, intelligent, civilized and independent nation." Kingpin Brinsmade was committing himself to industrializing the Islands and selflessly reaping what profits might accrue.

France, England, and the United States were all demonstrating an overweening interest in Hawaii at the time, giving the king constant concern for his political security. As a rider to the agreement, therefore, he stipulated that the proposition would not be effective until the independence of his kingdom was acknowledged by the three powers. The contract was signed November 24, 1841.

A gargantuan development deal of that nature called for a comparable investment ante. Realizing that the capital was not available in the Islands, Brinsmade took off at once for the United States on a stockraising campaign. In Washington Daniel Webster listened to him politely, but without commitment. His reception in Boston and New York was equally cool. American capitalists seemed to view with a degree of skepticism this unprecedented get-rich-quick scheme in the South Seas.

Brinsmade sniffed at Wall Street and sailed for Europe, where he was certain that financiers would be more appreciative of the opportunity he was offering. But, to his astonishment, the British gave him a cold shoulder, and the French showed little more warmth. Parisians brushed him off with the recommendation that he try Belgium.

By the middle of May 1843, Brinsmade felt he was getting somewhere. In Brussels he found men of real vision, and after interminable parleys, he agreed to transfer all the Hawaiian rights and properties of Ladd and Company to the Belgium Company of Colonization, and the Belgium group in turn agreed to organize a subsidiary called the "Royal Community of the Sandwich Islands," with starting capital stock of four thousand shares, each at a par value of one thousand francs, the whole transaction involving well over half a million dollars.

Then Brinsmade's balloon began to deflate. The stock simply was not snatched up, as he was sure it would be. Moreover, the great powers were slow to recognize the independence of the islands on which the original contract was conditioned. No one in Belgium or anywhere else appeared vitally interested in either the Royal Community or Brinsmade. After waiting around for two full years, he gave up and returned to the United States and then to the Islands in March 1846, destitute and disillusioned.

While in Europe he had heard rumors that the affairs of Ladd and Company were getting shaky at home. To his utter consternation he had to face the fact that the store had gone to pot in his absence; the Kauai plantation had failed; the wharves and warehouses were in other hands; he had lost everything. Ladd and Company was no more. And still another bitter pill had to be swallowed; the United States medical consul, Dr. Robert Wood, who had been lending the company large sums to keep the Koloa Plantation running, had foreclosed, taken possession of the property, and was making an exemplary success of it.

By profiting from the trials, errors, and occasional triumphs of these early merchants with an urge to operate plantations, more competent corporations gradually evolved. Borrowing the common British term for big colonial trading syndicates and agents, they were called "factors"; actually they were general merchants, wholesale and retail, and would sell anything on their shelves to anybody, but they served primarily as contract managers, suppliers, and shipping agents for back-country plantation superintendents who did not have the time to go shopping every day nor the time and talents to negotiate all the details of importing and exporting.

The factors stocked, or purchased to order, the tools, equipment and groceries needed on the plantation. Frequently they set up subsidiary stores on the property of their clients. They handled much of the bookkeeping and did the banking, floated loans, and made investments. A good factor in the Islands had to maintain contacts with dozens of shippers and dealers. Orders might be filled directly from the East Coast or be transshipped from ports in Chile, China, the Philippines, or California. To obtain the best rates, it was necessary to keep track of the immense amount of commerce pouring into the Pacific from America and Europe.

Captain Henry Hackfeld, a German—not the expected Yankee or Britisher—was the first model factor in the Islands, and he it was who set up the company that was eventually to become a giant among the "Big Five," American Factors, Limited.

Hackfeld had made a name for himself as a trader on the China coast long before he eyed Honolulu as a center for his operations. He knew the Pacific and made a shrewd guess that of all the island dots, Hawaii had the most attractive future. With a cargo of some eight thousand dollars worth of goods he set up shop in Honolulu late in 1849, sharing quarters with a merchant who had already established himself, C. S. Barstow.

The Hackfeld-Barstow partnership lasted just six weeks. Swan, Clifford and Hackfeld took its place, and that did not last much longer. The German preferred to go it alone as H. Hackfeld, vendor of "woolen stockings, finger bowls, shawls, matting, nanking, handkerchiefs, pongee, backgammon boards, china plates, china couches, cigar boxes, tea caddies, writing desks, camphor trunks, axes, black tea, toweling, . . . parasols, silk waistcoats, bird cages, dinner sets, iron bedsteads, window glass . . ."

Business was so satisfactory that in 1853 he was ready to take on his 19-year-old German clerk, Charles Pflueger, as partner and advertised his concern as "H. Hackfeld and Company, General Commission Agents and Ship Chandlers." The man with the heavy Prussian accent was suddenly recognized as a real mercantile comer in Honolulu, and to him Dr. Wood, new owner of the Koloa Plantation, went that same year with the proposition that he serve as his agent and shipper.

Hackfeld signed the contract and a few months later signed another contract for handling the business of the huge East Maui Plantation, in which Wood had also acquired an interest. Though he modestly refrained from adopting the popular tag for his occupation, he was already a factor.

From that start Hackfeld and Company advanced at a headlong pace until its founder was managing scattered plantations in all parts of the Islands, running a line of packets between Bremen and Honolulu, running an international employment agency, running Honolulu retail stores, promoting vast irrigation networks, serving as agent for innumerable shipping lines, and in spare time making sure that the wives and daughters of plantation managers were supplied with the latest fashions.

Captain Hackfeld retired in 1886, but the corporation he fathered continued to expand under a new generation of German managers. Practically all freight from the Orient passed through the Hackfeld warehouses. The company went into coffee and pineapples, organized a subsidiary fertilizer concern, helped build a giant refinery in Crockett, California, was involved in insurance, technological research, and big-time industrial relations.

It was an all-German company, incompatible with the interests of the United States when World War I came along. The Alien Property Custodian seized it in 1918, and patriotic American management was substituted for German. But the company hardly broke step during the transfer, and as "American Factors" it kept on the march.

However, the Germans by no means had the run of Island trade and plantation management all those years. One by one the other four members of the exclusive Big Five—C. Brewer, Theo. H. Davies, Castle and Cooke, Alexander and Baldwin—entered the commercial race, frequently paced neck and neck. Each of the entrants liked to boast a little about its blue-blooded lineage.

C. Brewer and Company traced its ancestry back to the Pacific trader and pioneer Honolulu shopkeeper, James Hunnewell, who set up a country store in 1826 with three thousand dollars worth of Yankee notions on his shelves. J. Hunnewell, General Merchandise, became Hunnewell and Peirce; Hunnewell stepped out to make it Peirce and Hinckley; Thomas Hinckley could not stand the strain, died on his retreat to New England, and for a few years the sign over the door of the establishment publicized a lonely "Henry Peirce, Merchant." Peirce, meanwhile, had bid Captain Charles Brewer away from William French and sent him voyaging to China, Kamchatka, and the Northwest on his behalf, and the expeditions paid off so well that he talked the captain into a partnership, Peirce and Brewer; and in 1843, when Peirce retired, the firm at last adopted the more adhesive title, C. Brewer and Company.

Charles Brewer personally never did any shop tending or factoring; he merely gave the company his name, prestige, and direction and went back to Boston to let his partners, son, and successors distend the firm into a world-wide complex. "The purchasing and selling of vessels," ran an advertisement delineating the Brewer services in 1859, "procuring and collecting freights and charters; obtaining ships stores and making repairs, and all other business appertaining to shipping; and also the sales of merchandise generally. . . ." And that was scarcely a beginning, for eventually the corporation operated or owned plantations, ranches, and businesses reaching to all the Islands and far beyond.

Theo. H. Davies and Company, Limited, the only British member of the "Five," traced its beginnings back to September 1845, when an English brig docked at Honolulu with a cargo worth eighty thousand dollars consigned to Starkey, Janion and Company. Another alumnus of the school of William French, Londoner R. C. Janion had been around the Islands for years, a peripheral merchant concentrating on beef exports. He had learned the cattle business in Waimea, Hawaii, as chief cowpuncher for French before developing herds of his own and in 1845 was back in Honolulu with his fellow countryman Starkey, ready to replace the defunct Ladd and Company.

Starkey, Janion and Company moved into the vacated Ladd store and gradually built up a business worthy of the attention of financer Theophilus Harris Davies, who insisted that his given name be elided to "Theo." He took over during the fifties, cleverly counting on a wide assortment of flashy yard goods to lure patrons into his emporium. "We had two and sometimes three cargoes in the year," he boasted, "and when the patterns of prints, especially pinks and yellows, arrived, we kept the office doors closed until the advertised times, and there was then a rush of Chinese and other buyers to see who could get the first pick."

But Theo's primary interest was sugar, and he soon entered competition with factors Hackfeld and Brewer in the marathon for the big accounts. His prosperity was accepted with a touch of resentment among foreigners, for many had the erroneous impression that he was somehow associated, like the Ladd company trio, with Congregational missions, and it was indecent for anyone connected with Sabbath preaching to acquire weekday wealth. It was a sensitive issue with Honolulu merchants.

Even before the American Board began to withdraw financial support and the old Bingham organization started disbanding, the fiction was spreading that missionaries were masquerading as merchants, skimming the cream off native trade, selling goods on the side, going into business that gospel ministers had no business going into. Time and again these alleged mercenary interests were used by merchants as an excuse for not supporting the missions.

In part, the popular impression arose from the fact that the Honolulu mission actually did maintain a sort of mercantile establishment, a combined commissary and supply depot called the "Depository." During the early years it was essential to the survival of the scattered mission units. The brothers and sisters depended on it for everything from starch to stovepipe.

But the Depository also stocked a limited supply of cheerless cotton goods and tailoring supplies which could be requisitioned for resale to natives at bargain prices, in order to keep native bodies covered with Christian garments. Though this service never cut appreciably into the sales of merchants, its existence perennially stirred up acrimony among foreigners looking for something to censure.

Finally in 1851, when the decision was reached that the Depository should be discontinued, something had to be done with the considerable quantity of goods still in stock. Samuel N. Castle and Amos S. Cooke, who had general oversight of secular affairs at the time, saw that they were soon going to be out of a job and volunteered to take over the surplus at cost and go into storekeeping, with the understanding that future sales would carry a 5 per cent markup.

Castle and Cooke were anything but optimistic about breaking even on the transaction but soon discovered to their surprise that they were making money. At the end of the first year their accounts showed that they had sold seven thousand dollars worth of goods to nonmissionaries and had cleared over eighteen hundred dollars. Compared to their salaries as mission business agents, this was a lavish income. Samuel went off on a quick trip to New England to arrange with stateside wholesalers for further shipments of supplies.

But success did not go to their heads. They were still partial to the brethren in the gospel, and for them special discounts were always available. For an ordinary wheat-consuming foreigner, flour cost twenty-four dollars a barrel, but missionaries got it under the counter for ten. Amos proudly announced that he would be satisfied to make one thousand dollars where competitors were making ten, and as the fortunes of the partners mounted, he demonstrated that he meant what he said by charging only 10 per cent a year on loans that would have cost 1 per cent a month at other houses; 5 per cent was the usual markup on sales of most merchants, so Castle and Cooke cut theirs to 3 per cent. It was Golden Rule business such as Ladd and Company had only talked about.

Castle and Cooke were quick to learn that the most substantial profits came from ministering to the plantations, and they were soon as involved in factoring as companies with a long head start. In fact, they were so involved before the end of the century that they gave up their wholesale and retail departments entirely and specialized as factors. Despite the contrary canard, the kindly, considerate, charitable Samuel Castle and Amos Cooke were the only two missionaries who ever made a place for themselves among the Big Five.

In Alexander and Baldwin, however, two honorable missionary names were honorably perpetuated, thanks largely to the generosity of

Castle and Cooke. Samuel Alexander had spent most of his youth at Lahainaluna, where his father succeeded Lorrin Andrews as head of the school, and Henry P. Baldwin had spent his down the hill at Lahaina proper, where his father doubled as parish doctor and preacher.

Though seven years apart in age, as they reached their teens they developed a common interest in growing things. Samuel enthusiastically accepted a job as manager of the Waihee Sugar Plantation on the windward side of the West Maui Mountains and shortly found a place for his chum as head overseer in the same company.

They made an energetic team and in 1870 branched out on their own and began buying plantation land on the slopes of Haleakala. Substantial loans from Castle and Cooke, on minimum collateral, made possible the addition of huge slices of adjacent plantations. For the next thirty years the financial affairs of Alexander and Baldwin were so closely linked to Castle and Cooke that the young company looked almost like a subsidiary. With the encouragement of their creditors, Alexander and Baldwin kept expanding, acquiring more land, building irrigation systems, developing transportation, and making improvements on mills.

The bond between Sam and Henry was based entirely on mutual faith, good friendship, and family intermarriage. Not until 1895 did they have even a formal partnership agreement, and they waited five more years to form a corporation. Alexander, meantime, had established a management office in San Francisco, while his associate took charge on Maui. Alexander and Baldwin, Limited—"A and B" to all Islanders—actually did not come into being until July 1, 1900, but they already had an enormous organization in operation, ready to manage their own affairs and to serve as factors for plantations and ranches anywhere in the Islands.

In one significant respect, "A and B" was different from the other four members of the exclusive quintet. While the earlier companies had all grafted functions as agents onto mercantile establishments, the junior member started with agriculture and could proudly boast that its entire organization was build up in devotion to that original interest.

Confronted with the allegation that they were Islands monopolists, the Big Five were destined to take a lot of invective from both amateur critics and professional economists, and no one doubted that there was an uncommon spread of self-protective interests among them and more than a hint of interlinkage and policy concordance. Yet without their constraining influence and their long-range projection, Hawaii could have turned into a Coney Island carnival of commerce. The course originally set by William French was more farsighted than he realized.

Scattered through the Islands during the period that Honolulu was coming of mercantile age were countless little country stores, patterned after those on Oahu, but their life span was short and the goods shoddy. They catered mostly to Islanders who were not too fussy about either quality or fashion. Rarely did Hawaiians themselves go into business. They made poor shopkeepers and were content to let foreigners take the commercial risks.

The only place of trade that native hucksters seemed to regard as their private province was their own helter-skelter outdoor Saturday markets, where fruit and fish, mats and vegetables, leis and hats were displayed in unsanitary confusion. Whether or not the clientele had any intention of making purchases, all thronged to it, as to a fair, decked out in their brightest finery, draped in *leis* and exploding with laughter and noisy chatter. "Really you couldn't see the place for the people," summarized a *haole* sightseer.

In the larger towns they opened restaurants, too, as the old forms of family hospitality slowly died. The idea of a public eating place, where one paid for a meal, was, of course, borrowed from the foreigners, but the restaurateurs got along without any of the civilized appurtenances. A stuffy grass shack was the setting; there were no tables, no knives or forks, no waiters.

Everything was served family style on a greasy floor mat, with a roasted hog and gigantic calabashes of poi in the center. Diners squatted in a circle, each supplied with a gourd plate of raw fish and salt water. On signal from the proprietor, the guests tore into the hog with their bare hands, alternately seizing morsels of pork and dipping fore and middle fingers into the common tub of poi, occasionally varying the course with a glob of raw fish sopped in salt water.

"They feed thus until satisfied, for which they pay six and a quarter cents," observed Dr. W. S. W. Ruschenberger, Philadelphia surgeon, traveler, and author, after watching "the revolting feast" from the door. "This charge includes the feeding of the children and dogs of the guests, which must be a considerable drawback to the profits, if we may judge from the number of children and lank curs among the groups."

Haoles in general never considered what few native establishments there were worthy of their patronage, and aside from putting Hawaiians to work at arduous field, forest, or deck labor, the mercantile class did little to encourage industry of any kind among the Islanders. From the earliest days, traders had balked at revealing techniques or trade secrets that might give Hawaiians a commercial advantage. "An illiberal notion is held by many of the white people," complained humanitarian Archibald Campbell in 1809, "that the natives should be taught nothing that would render them independent of strangers."

He wanted to teach a prominent chief to read English, but the king's counselor, Isaac Davis, slyly cautioned against it: "They will soon know more than ourselves." In England Campbell had mastered the trade of weaving and volunteered to teach Hawaiians how to make canvas sails. He attempted to fashion a crude loom, but white associates did everything in their power to sabotage the effort, maintaining that if the natives ever learned the secret of weaving cloth, a lucrative trade would be ruined.

Few merchants ever altered their "illiberal notion," and missionaries only incurred the collective wrath of professional traffickers by defiantly teaching the crafts they knew. In 1836 Kamehameha III and fourteen chiefs took the initiative and dispatched a plaintive appeal to the American Board in Boston. "Love to you, our obliging friends in America," they wrote. "This is our sentiment as to promoting the order and prosperity of the Hawaiian Islands. Give us additional teachers, like the teachers who dwell in your own country. These are the teachers whom we would specify: a carpenter, a tailor, mason, shoemaker, wheelwright, paper maker, typefounder, agriculturists skilled in raising sugar-cane, cotton and silk and in making sugar; cloth manufacturers, and makers of machinery, to work on a large scale; and a teacher of the chiefs in what pertains to the land according to the practice of enlightened countries; and if there be other teachers, who would be serviceable in these matters, send such teachers also."

Bingham and the brethren submitted a similar appeal, adding only that the teachers be pious men, but nothing ever came of the petitions. Such an educational project would be "too secular" in nature, the Board maintained; they might well have indicated also that New England industrialists would have objected as strenuously as the Honolulu merchants.

In the end, Hawaiians were the victims of commerce, rather than participants and profiteers. Without raising a voice in self-defense, they stepped aside to let foreigners take advantage of their dearth of business talent and squandered their scant earnings to support the intruders by purchasing quantities of gaudy goods, products of Connecticut and Massachusetts factories, trash and trinkets, cheap liquor, cheap tobacco.

Except where missionary influences prevailed, they widely adopted the vulgarities of the peddlers and habits that the produce engendered, swaggered about in incongruous symbols and remnants of foreign attire, became alcoholics, and perhaps the most confirmed tobacco addicts in the world. Men, women, children, even two-year-old babies took to the imported weed. They swallowed the smoke from their short homemade pipes, freely circulated the common family pipe, and even roused themselves occasionally during the night for a few puffs.

Year after year the government remained in debt to the tradesmen who had sold kings and chiefs refinements they could not afford, such as elaborate uniforms and wardrobes, yachts, mahogany suites, regal couches, bolts of silks and satins, fine horses and equipage. And as commoners gradually became independent of chiefs, they, too, adopted the same reckless spirit of spending.

The craving for foreign possessions, for a standard of living which they were not yet socially prepared to adopt, for profits they did not have the knowledge and aptitude to accrue led to excruciating frustration. It added up to individual debasement and national decadence. For the Hawaiians that was the principal legacy of the invading Yankee peddlers and foreign merchants.

THE DOCTOR

VIII
Death and Doctors

The doctors didn't come in time.

Chiefs were dying; commoners were dying; the kingdom was losing its bloom. It was a sorry paradox. The Islands that Captain Cook discovered were one of the most healthful places on earth. Isolation had kept them virtually antiseptic. None of the bacterial disease producers common to the continents was there. Hawaii was a rare asylum where the worst human ailment was a stomach ache or old-age infirmity, where wounds had a chance to heal without infection, where a *kahuna lapaau*—curing expert—could readily relieve ordinary complaints and injuries with simple poultices or cathartics.

The discoverers found an energetic, hardy, prolific population; yet fifty years later the people were being described as sickly, indolent, unproductive, a disappearing race. Cook's lieutenants guessed that the total number of inhabitants might be 400,000 or half a million, but in 1823, when the missionaries took a census, they could account for only 142,050, and by the early 1850's that total was cut in half.

To nineteenth-century sociologists it was axiomatic that aborigines perished before the march of civilization, but not at that rate, not in a climate as ideal as that of the Sandwich Islands, not a people relatively well-nourished and at peace with those bringing the civilization.

Cook and his men were undoubtedly overenthusiastic in their calculations, failing to take into consideration that the same mob of greeters might have appeared twice in different places. In any case, later accountants took the liberty of auditing his figures and suggesting that the count should have been nearer three hundred thousand. Still the cut was not made without protests. "Subsequent voyagers confirmed the correctness of the estimate," argued scholarly Artimas Bishop in 1838. "The accounts of older and more intelligent natives, as well as indications of a country once extensively cultivated, corroborate the probability of its truth, and prove the fact that there was once a teeming population flourishing throughout the whole cluster of islands."

And David Malo, the most literate native educated by the early missionaries, saw nothing inconsistent in the statistics of Cook's aides. "The kingdom is sick," he cried in 1839. "It is reduced to a skeleton, and is near to death; yea, the whole nation is near to a close."

Along with the Bible, the alphabet, and clever gadgets, foreigners also imported all the diseases and disorders their ancestors had been hatching for thousands of years, as well as enough bacteria and insect life to keep the Islanders everlastingly supplied with afflictions.

Yet Hawaiians were perishing en masse before the march of civilization. Actually they had been indulging in an orgy of self-destruction long before the influx of disease-carrying foreigners, so great an orgy that only a phenomenal birth rate could account for anything like a "teeming population." For them life was cheap, and death held no fears. They could afford to live recklessly and kill recklessly. The carnage of their pitched battles taxed credulity; the scale of their wars was Homeric.

Nearly a century after the coming of the white men, acres of battlefields, like Diamond Head Crater on Oahu and Keei on Hawaii, still glistened with bleached skeletons of slain warriors. And these bones represented only a fraction of the total casualties. Victorious armies relentlessly sought out the families and supporters of the vanquished enemy to prolong the slaughter over periods of weeks and months. "When discovered, they are cruelly massacred on the spot," lamented William Ellis, "or brought down to the king and chiefs . . . to die perhaps, to live perhaps." John Young testified in his old age that he had seen thousands massacred in the wars of extermination.

The mortality from interisland and intertribal clashes alone would have prostrated a less resilient and less prolific people. And between wars the demand of priests for human sacrifices and the enforcement of capital punishment for violation of taboos constituted a steady drain on the population. Temple *kahunas* possessed a powerful incentive for the enforcement of taboos, for violators all made acceptable candidates for sacrifice on the altars of the gods.

"The restrictions of the chiefs and priests were like the poisoned tooth of a reptile," observed the dispassionate young adventurer Francis Olmsted. "If the shadow of a common man fell upon a chief, it was death; if he put on a mantle or *malo* of a chief, it was death; if he went upon the house of a chief, it was death. If a man was found standing on those occasions when he should prostrate himself, viz., when the King's bathing water or his tapa or his *malo*, were carried along, it was death. So, too, if he continued standing at the mention of the king's name in song, it was death. . . . If he was irreligious, he suffered death; if he indulged in connubial pleasure on a taboo day, he paid the same penalty; if he made a noise while prayers were saying, he met a like fate. If a woman ate pork, cocoanuts, bananas, a certain kind of fish, or lobster, it was death. So, too, was it death to be found in a canoe on a taboo day." Added to these were a great many other causes of premature death, like participation in too dangerous and chancy sports, settlement of private feuds, addiction to *awa* drinking, accidents at sea and in the high mountains, not to mention the occasional depopulation of whole villages by tidal waves and lava flows. Flirting with death was a favorite Hawaiian occupation.

Yet, despite this rampant slaughter, in the years before the intrusion of foreigners, the throngs of growing youth always seemed to keep pace with the death toll. Women started childbearing in their early teens. Families of twenty children and more were commonplace.

And this propagation was heartily encouraged by chiefs, since the importance of their domains was measured in part by the number of subjects they could claim.

To be sure, little sentiment was expended by parents on their young offspring, and many of them never survived. Family ties were loose, principally because few mothers could ever be quite sure who had fathered a child. "For husbands to interchange wives and for wives to interchange husbands," explained historian Sheldon Dibble, "was a common act of friendship, and persons who would not do this were not considered on good terms of sociability. . . . When a solicitation is made, they seem to imagine . . . that to comply is generous, liberal and social, and to refuse is reproachful and niggardly. From this confused state of things . . . it will be understood at once that there could be little or no attachment in the various domestic relations."

Children came easily and regularly, and there were so many of them that they were seldom kept together as brothers and sisters. They were freely exchanged or given away like other possessions, so that many children never knew who their real parents were, and the parents themselves lost track. Deformed, sluggish, or ill-tempered babies were unceremoniously put out of the way; others were neglected; sickly ones were placed out of sight and sound where their cries would not be disturbing, and allowed to languish and waste away.

In an amoral society, there was no one to condemn either abortion or infanticide. Both were accepted without qualms of conscience. Still the survival rate of the young at least balanced the death rate of adults.

All this had been going on for untold generations. And then in 1778 Cook's men left at Niihau a killer with which the natives were totally unfamiliar, a slayer to supersede all others, the scourge of venereal disease. In civilized lands where exposure to communicable maladies over the centuries had built up a margin of resistance, syphilis and gonorrhea were grim enough, but in a land virgin to such infection, it was devastating.

Unsuspecting natives, never given to constraint in relations with the opposite sex, spread it as freely as the trade winds carried the scent of the sea. By the time the captain returned for his second visit, syphilis had swept over all the Islands. It maimed and mutilated by the thousands and tens of thousands, and every vessel that followed the wake of the *Resolution* and *Discovery* added to the curse.

Twenty-five years later a swifter and more virulent exterminator came in on a foreign ship, a disease for the moment more ghastly than slow-maturing syphilis. Strong men were healthy one day and dying in agony and horror the next. The pestilence reached its climax in 1805. Hawaiians called it *mai ahulau* (sick people heaped up). It was one of the great local epidemics of modern history, and may have wiped out as many as half the inhabitants of the islands.

Old survivors in the missionary period claimed it took the "majority," a disaster of such appalling proportions that few Hawaiians seemed capable of describing it coherently. To this day, its nature remains a mystery, but it was probably either cholera or bubonic plague, the Black Death that had wiped out half of Europe almost five hundred years earlier.

The pestilence ran its course, leaving regions of the Islands desolated, but the other killer, syphilis, strode on unchecked. In the 1830's even the *American Journal of Medical Science,* which normally concerned itself with diseases nearer home, felt obliged to report that "words would fail to express the wretchedness and woe" in the Sandwich Islands. "Foul ulcers . . . everywhere abound and visages horribly deformed—eyes rendered blind—noses entirely destroyed—mouths monstrously drawn aside from their natural position, ulcerating palates, and almost useless arms and legs, mark most clearly the state and progress of the disease among that injured and helpless people." Nor did the *Journal* see any prospect of eradicating the effects, gloomily predicting that "the prevailing and inveterate habits of promiscuous sexual intercourse will serve still to perpetuate and extend the disease."

With the cooperation of natives, seamen on the sandalwood, fur-trade, and whaling ships saw to it that the prophesy was fulfilled. The chief reason for the popularity of Hawaii among sailors was the revelry provided by the women. Entertainment was cheap, plentiful, and erotic. While vessels were anchored off Honolulu, Lahaina, Hilo, or a dozen lesser villages, the libertine carnival went on day after day, night in, night out. Declared Dibble with Old Testament indignation: "Many ships . . . are no better than floating exhibitions of Sodom and Gomorrah."

For the natives it was a lucrative trade. When girls at the ports had lost their attractiveness, their sisters from country towns flocked in by hundreds. If daughters did not go voluntarily, procurers rounded them up or parents delivered them, often selling them outright for a few dollars or a little finery, for $60, $150, depending on youth, health, and the length of services required. Not infrequently they were taken off on long voyages. Seldom did they return to their homes and, almost invariably, sooner or later, they were deserted, diseased and destitute.

"Foreigners have lent their whole influence to make the Hawaiian islands one great brothel," accused disillusioned David Malo, and he was scarcely exaggerating reality. Long after the missionaries had prevailed upon royalty to outlaw prostitution, the situation was not greatly changed. Unregenerate women still found their way to the ships.

American and English sailors were wise to the diversions Honolulu afforded; the French, who put in less frequently, were slow to be initiated, and when Frenchman Edmond Le Netral arrived on the *Héros* with a cargo of horses in 1828, he was astonished at the "entirely new and unexpected performance," some sixty or eighty "quite pretty and especially very beautifully formed" damsels climbing naked over the side to satisfy a crew of thirty-two.

"These beauties," he explained naïvely, "usually swim out and come on board without being seen—a custom adopted by the islanders and by almost all the vessels which anchor in the port of Honolulu." In fact, he added, "there were more women than the crew wanted."

The natives invited their own disaster. Except in the back country, where proud villagers refused to have anything to do with the white scavengers, whole districts of the kingdom appeared to be stricken with Gallic disease. The word "common" was not strong enough to describe the contamination; it was "prevalent." Children as well as adults were afflicted. "All the people of the Islands are miserably diseased," claimed Malo.

Under influence of the killer, what little family adhesiveness once existed deteriorated further. The incentive for bringing up large families was lost. Raising children was not worth the struggle. They were expensive in labor and taxes, an extravagance, a burden, an encumbrance. Infants became the unwanted. The rate of conception was unchanged, but the number of surviving children was shockingly reduced. Where there had once been families of twenty sons and daughters, two were more than enough.

Puzzled by the small size of family groups, William Ellis pried into the reasons for it on his extensive tour of Hawaii. "We have long known that the Sandwich Islanders practised infanticide," he concluded, "but had no idea of its extent until we made various inquiries. It prevails throughout all the islands, and, with the exception of the higher class of chiefs, is, as far as we could learn, practised by all ranks of people. However numerous the children among the lower orders, parents seldom rear more than two or three, and many spare only one; all the others are destroyed sometimes shortly after birth, generally during the first year of their age. . . . It is painful to think of the numbers thus murdered."

Missionaries commonly agreed that at least two-thirds of the children had perished at the hands of parents. Fathers and mothers unconcernedly admitted their complicity, giving as reasons the trouble of bringing them up, the handicap of roving about with young ones in tow, the annoyance of their crying, the bother of feeding them, deformities and trying illnesses of one sort or another. In fits of jealousy mothers killed the favorite child of their husbands, and in retributive fits husbands killed the wife's favorite. They suffocated them, strangled them, beat them to death, dashed them on stones, but most frequently buried them alive.

"As you are passing the outskirts of some city or village," dramatized historian Dibble, "you behold a wretched woman carrying something to a secluded spot. You observe her as she stops, lays down her burden and digs a pit in the earth. Ah! What is that she is about to bury? Her own smiling infant. The child perhaps is sick and troubles her. . . . She stifles its cries for a moment with her hand, thrusts it into the grave prepared, covers it with a little earth and tramples it down while struggling yet in the agonies of death.

"But wait and look around a little," he continued, "and you will find that this is not the first grave she has dug. Perhaps this may be the fifth or the seventh child she has disposed of in the same way, and for many of them perhaps for no better motives than to rid herself of trouble or to leave herself more free for sensual pleasure and vicious indulgence."

A missionary wife accidentally discovered that her own serving girl, Pali, and the young brother who always accompanied her were the sole survivors of a family of ten children. The other eight had all been buried alive, and the brother lived only because Pali had followed her mother to the burial place and promptly disinterred him.

David Malo, who loved and defended his fellow Hawaiians passionately, nevertheless maintained that "few women had any desire for children;" that mothers, fearing premature old age, "pierced their unborn children" or "drank such medicines as would prevent conception."

For a hundred years every thoughtful visitor to the Islands expressed astonishment at the evidence of population decline, particularly among the younger generation, and expounded his own theories of the fundamental cause. To Hiram Bingham, who spent twenty one years there during some of the heaviest decimation, it was the work of the Almighty.

In the language of a Jeremiah he declaimed in 1836: "The angel of the Lord had kindled a fire upon the nation, which will burn to its entire destruction unless it is speedily extinguished. . . . According to the present ratio of decrease, it will be but a few years before the pall of death will be spread over the whole land, and these valleys once full of people will be solitary. These shores once teeming with myriads will either become silent as the house of death or be peopled with a new race of men. . . . We greatly need help to apply at once, and in every part of the islands."

Help came. But it was always too little and too late. What Hawaii needed was an invasion of medical men like the invasion of merchants, preachers, and sea captains, but doctors never came in companies. The American Board sent out one medico at a time, when twenty would have been too few, and the single emissary seldom stayed for long.

On the roster of 175 Protestant missionaries, wives, teachers, assistants, and repatriated Hawaiians dispatched from Boston between 1819 and 1854 only ten had professional medical training. Four of the ten chose to remain in the islands the rest of their lives; for the other six the average tenure was less than five years.

Government vessels calling at Hawaiian ports usually carried a surgeon, and many of them performed heroic services in emergencies. Half a dozen nonmilitary and nonmissionary doctors put out shingles in Honolulu during that same period. But with all the comings and goings, there rarely were more than two or three physicians to serve the whole archipelago, frequently but one, and none at all for periods of many months.

Attacking the real problem, the survival of a kingdom, was utterly impossible. As one missionary doctor explained, his first duties were confined to the mission families; his second to the natives, which meant primarily the royal family and chiefs; his third to foreigners. Day-to-day crises and the hours or week it took to race from one medical crisis to the next occupied all his time.

His office might be in Honolulu, but he was obliged to answer calls to Kahuku or Kaneohe on the opposite sides of Oahu and from there respond to the summons to attend the imminent birth of a missionary babe in far-off Kauai or Maui or Kailua, Hawaii. He was gone from his home base for months at a time. More than half his days were spent on the road or the high seas.

However, the major problem anticipated by all doctors going to Hawaii, the resistance of superstitious natives to any treatment by a foreigner, was pretty well resolved by the very first resident physician, Thomas Holman, fresh from medical school, and a member of the original missionary company of 1820.

From visiting ships, from advisers like Don Marin and John Young, the Kamehamehas had developed a profound respect for foreign medicine, and King Liholiho was so intrigued by the prospect of having a white doctor at his disposal that he virtually commandeered young Holman as soon as he landed at Kailua and even assigned John Young's son to him as a personal interpreter.

John, Jr. was no fool. He frankly advised the doctor that he was assuming a post of perilous import; the jealousy of the native *kahunas* was so keen that the loss of one distinguished patient could cost him his job and probably his life. Holman accepted the challenge. Before there was a chance to unpack his 93 pounds of medicines, he had more referrals than he could take care of, including a popular queen and several royal attendants. Luckily, the disorders were uncomplicated. Within a day the patients were on their feet, and the fame of the miracle worker had spread abroad.

But a more severe test came almost immediately when Liholiho personally summoned the doctor to attend his closest friend, captain of the royal guard. Holman hurried to the patient, diagnosed his ailment as "bilious colic" and saw that he was close to death. Under the circumstances, the doctor elected not to accept the guard as a patient, frankly informing Liholiho that he could do nothing for the spent captain and would only be blamed for his death. Perhaps it would be better to call in the *kahunas*.

Here, alas, was the showdown between the magic of the native doctors and the magic of a medical missionary. The king had to choose between the two; he chose Holman, assuring him that he would in no way be censured for failure to save the chief. In effect, that decision constituted a repudiation of the old healers and charlatans.

Dr. Holman went to work and lost his patient within a few hours, as predicted. Liholiho, rather than reproaching him, promptly made good on his promise by presenting the doctor with a taboo wand and instructing him to carry it henceforth as a protective symbol of royal recognition. The incident was more than an expression of confidence in Holman; it was an endorsement of missionary materia medica for the entire kingdom. Never after that did any foreign doctor need to be unduly concerned about the consequences of unsuccessful ministration to Hawaiians high or low.

Holman's real failure came in a personality clash with his fellow missionaries, rather than in an inability to establish rapport with the natives. He could not endure the holier-than-thou airs of the Binghams and Thurstons, and after being confronted by Bingham with a docket of unmissionarylike malefactions—insubordination, misappropriation of common property, holding hands with his wife in public, neglect of duty, and finally desertion—he was ignominiously excommunicated at the end of eighteen months, though his log of cases showed scant cause for such treatment. His doctoring had included all manner of exemplary and successful practice, from curing a shipload of sailors desperately stricken with dysentery to bringing the first missionary babies into the world. Among the hundreds of patients he attended, only four were lost, including the captain of the king's guard.

On the surface it looked as though the Holmans had signed up with the American Board for a world cruise—around the Horn to Hawaii, a few months on the Kona coast, three weeks at Lahaina, a brief stay in Honolulu, several months on Kauai, back to Oahu to catch a ship to the Orient, then around Asia and Africa to the Atlantic and home. He was probably the first American doctor to circumnavigate the globe and his wife the first American woman to do the same.

He was anything but a quitter. As a pioneer practitioner on pagan Hawaiian soil, he opened the way for the doctors who followed, set the patterns that they adopted, and created the picture of the country doctor hurrying from patient to patient under sail rather than under horsepower. The medical work he performed during his year and a half of duty would have been enough to establish the reputation of a young surgeon in any land untenanted by a Hiram Bingham. The trouble was, he stole the show, and that did not set at all well with his less popular colleagues.

To Bingham, even a doctor had to be more concerned with saving souls than bodies, and the missionary colony was obliged to get along without a successor for more than a year and a half, while the Boston

Board was deluged with reports of all the apostolic ailments and with hysterical appeals for an enlightened doctor constitutionally and educationally equipped to preach as well as practice.

The replacement, Dr. Abraham Blatchely, finally came late in the spring of 1823, but to the chagrin of Bingham he was not primarily a saver of souls either. At first the missionaries were sure he would be an improvement over Holman, but they were disappointed. He could not be everywhere at once any more readily than his predecessor. Moreover, he failed to rally his first distinguished patient, queen mother Keopuolani. It was, however, a great comfort to have him on hand for the arrival of missionary babies, who were spaced about as regularly as Hawaiian babies.

For three years he was kept constantly on the go, Honolulu to Lahaina, to Hilo, to Koloa, to Kailua, mostly at the beck and call of indisposed Yankees, and never on schedule. Notifying Bingham that he might be away for as long as ten or twelve weeks, he went off to the Kona coast and found so much employment there that he was gone for ten months.

He treated members of the missionary circuit for everything from dyspepsia to dropsy and fought his way through an epidemic of influenza. But the one epidemic he feared most was smallpox. It was killing off American Indians by tens of thousands, and he was so sure of its hitting the Islands sooner or later that he sent all the way to London for vaccine. A year and a half later a large supply of it arrived, completely useless from mishandling in transit.

By 1826 he was worn out, suffering constantly from "low fever," sure that his death was imminent. Fearing also for the health of his wife, he submitted his resignation. The mission refused to accept it, in view of the hopelessly long list of invalids and expectant mothers he would be deserting. So he left anyway, returned to Connecticut, and then moved out to Ohio—where he lived to the ripe age of 73.

Again Hawaii was without medical counsel for a year and a half, and the casualties of that period, including the death of a missionary wife and an important chief, pointed up more sharply than ever the necessity for a dependable and devoted physician. Dr. Gerrit P. Judd arrived on March 30, 1828, and was recognized at once by both *haoles* and Hawaiians as the man they needed.

He was a whirlwind of energy. Four days after disembarking, he was making professional calls naturally and confidently, as though he had always lived in Honolulu. He and his wife made such a hit with the queen regent Kaahumanu that they admitted they were treated like "pet children." And he was equally popular with commoners.

Unlike Holman and Blatchely, Judd did appear capable of being everywhere at once. He looked over the pallid missionaries, immediately decreed that they had to have a sanitorium, and soon set one up on the mountain heights of Waimea, Hawaii. He summoned the courage to operate on the revered chiefess Kapiolani for cancer of the breast and, in an excruciating ordeal for the patient, removed the breast without benefit of an anesthetic.

He made a hurried trip to Wailuku, Maui, to investigate the cause of a "new disease" running rampant at the female seminary. After taking a cursory look at the students and putting a few questions to them, he dismissed the girls and called the preceptress to task. In an effort to civilize her pupils, she was trying to feed them on a Yankee diet and starving them in the process. He prescribed fish and poi, as much as they wanted, and all symptoms of the "new disease," malnutrition, quickly vanished.

He was the first doctor to be seriously disturbed about the rapidly declining Hawaiian population and in spare time made a general analysis of Island diseases. There was nothing wrong with the climate, he concluded, either for natives or foreigners. He attributed the high mortality rate to "unfavorable circumstances among the natives themselves," to improper care, food, and medication by native *kahunas*. Later when he saw more of the ravages of imported epidemics, he unhesitatingly placed the blame where it belonged.

With the hope that students at Lahainaluna might go into medicine themselves, he wrote the first medical treatise in Hawaiian, a sixty-page, illustrated *Anatomia*. Judd was just beginning to hit his stride as a medical savior of Hawaii when, perhaps impetuously, he resigned from the mission to devote all his time and energy to Island political affairs, which, he maintained, were in as dire need of cures as the sick population. Though he continued to take emergency calls, his principal work for over a decade was government service. He did not resume his medical practice until 1853, and then it was as private physician rather than missionary.

Dr. Judd had an advantage over his pioneering predecessors; he was not obliged for long to tend all the patients in the 16,000 square miles of the Sandwich Islands. In 1830 an English doctor, Thomas C. B. Rooke, who had been binding up the wounds of seamen on a whaleship, decided he had seen enough of the deep and opened a private office on Honolulu's Fort Street. To the delight of royalty and commoners, he married one of John Young's eligible *hapahaole* daughters, at once became a part of the community, and eventually Court physician, chamberlain, member of the Privy Council, and cofounder of Queen's Hospital.

And there were more missionary doctors, too. At last in 1831 Hiram Bingham's prayers and pleadings for a man trained in theology and medicine were answered with the arrival of Dwight Baldwin. Unfortunately his sponsors in Boston had assured him that medicine would be a secondary occupation; so he came prepared to spend more time in the pulpit than at the bedside.

It did not take him long to discover that he was required to frequent both places with inordinate regularity. After brief assignments in Honolulu and at the new health station at Waimea, where the mountain winds and rains to him were more baneful than bracing, he settled at Lahaina as a life-termer to become one of the pillars of Hawaii, a provocative preacher, genial physician, and imaginative agriculturalist.

The roster of residential doctors jumped to a total of four in 1832 when Alonzo Chapin unexpectedly turned up in the fifth company of missionaries—without a degree in theology—and from the way he was put to work it appeared that Bingham had concluded three medical men were enough. As a spare, he assisted Judd in Honolulu, was temporarily assigned to Kauai, shifted to Lahaina, sent on to Waimea, recalled to Honolulu, and again assigned to Lahaina, where he was induced to give up medicine for a while to engrave maps and teach mechanical drawing at Lahainaluna. Someone, after a time, remembered that Hawaiians were still dying at a fearful rate, and once more he was ordered into medical service at Hilo, then back to Lahaina, and again to Hawaii.

Chapin was the most versatile professional man in the missionary family, pinch-hitting here, there, and everywhere for preachers and teachers, treating diseased and damaged whalers in season, bringing into the world most of the missionary babies at outlying stations, and in-between extracting teeth, amputating arms, serving as consultant, and nursing a perennially ailing wife, performing any kind of chore that called for talents no one else possessed. Bewildered by it all, he quit at the end of three years to take his sick wife back to Massachusetts, where he continued to mix medicine with postmastering, authorship, and politics.

By the middle thirties, doctors, either missionary or nonmissionary, were no longer a rarity in the Islands. One was not always available on the right island at the right time, but if an invalid could suffer along for a few days, a spry messenger would sooner or later show up with a medic, the medicine, or a gospel minister.

Ministers who had not known the difference between a purgative and a palliative before they left New England learned fast on the job in Hawaii. Along with the Bible and the sacred elements, they always carried a bundle of ointments and pills on their field trips, and the home reception room often became half dispensary and half confessional.

At outposts never visited by doctors, they performed minor surgery, sat at sick beds, doled out colored pills, used leeches freely. For most of the ten years that the Reverend Artemas Bishop was stationed on the Kona coast he also doubled as doctor, and a young son, who was occasionally called in to assist in an operation, remembered far more vividly the pharmaceutical display than any display of Biblical works, "shelves full of medicine bottles, also a chest of drugs, which, when opened, dispensed a sickening odor of aloes."

"A prominent drug," recalled son Sereno, "was red precipitate of mercury, which he used to dust upon the fearful syphilitic ulcers which disfigured so many of the people's limbs and faces. Salts, bluepill and calomel were leading drugs which I heard much of. Blood-letting was a constant remedy. . . . Binding the arm, he would prick the lancet into the swollen vein, and the dark blood would spurt three feet into the basin held to receive it."

The professionals did not always approve of the amateur efforts, and as more trained physicians arrived, the unprofessional ministrations were less necessary. Dr. Robert W. Wood came in 1839 to supervise a Hospital for American Seamen in Honolulu and stayed on to open the first drug store in town, to enter general practice, and to become one of the first successful sugar plantation owners. Later he shared the Honolulu field with half a dozen other private practitioners, including the French doctor George Trousseau and the German Edward Hoffman.

Medical missionaries also continued to trickle in—Thomas Lafon, another physician preacher, but an outspoken abolitionist, who soon broke with the Board because he refused employment by an organization that would deign to accept donations from southern slave owners; Seth Andrews, for nearly a decade the sole physician on Hawaii, where he claimed a clientele of sixty thousand and medical responsibility for seven mission stations; James Smith and L. H. Wetmore, both of whom cast their lot with the future of Hawaii and remained for the rest of their lives; and Luther Gulick, who spent six years in Honolulu but scarcely counted as a mission doctor, for most of his time was occupied as secretary of the Hawaiian Mission.

There was no question about the devotion even of part-time doctors to their calling, but they were not doing much to counter the invasion of death among Hawaiians. Despite their labors, the population continued to decrease at an appalling rate. Epidemic followed epidemic.

The year 1848 brought four of them—diarrhea, measles, whooping cough, and influenza—one after another in such rapid succession that patients rallying from one siege fell victim to another. Nearly every child born in the kingdom that year died.

Between October and December Honolulu was all but paralyzed.

Whole families were wiped out. "I remember one day walking through the deserted streets of the town when not a person was in sight," attested Henry Lyman, "but from every house could be heard the sound of coughing and the moaning of distress." The sick buried the dead, only to follow their kin to the same burial sites a day or two later. So great were the fatalities that Hawaiians were obliged to give up their customary ceremonies for the deceased.

In one day alone three hundred victims of measles were carried out from Waikiki for disposal at sea. Measles itself was not the most frequent cause of death, for eruptions were not unusually severe, but ignorant patients, tormented by fever and irritation, would rush to the nearest beach or river to "cool off"—and contract pneumonia or dysentery.

At Waimea, a typical village of the outer islands, the mortality was less severe, but still grim. There was no doctor. Father Lyons took over and, as he could spare the time from doling out medicine, comforting the dying, and officiating at funerals, jotted in his diary the course of the affliction from day to day: "A thin meeting. Many sick with the measles. . . . Only five at Sunday School. Thirty or forty at church. All sick with the measles. . . . Yesterday and today spent visiting and waiting on the sick. Our natives nearly all sick. . . . Little children are dying as well as old people. Diarrhea and dysentery are carrying off the people. . . . The whooping cough is on the islands and perhaps here. . . . Multitudes sick with coughs. . . . Attended four funerals. . . . Twenty-six deaths in Waimea. . . . Attended two funerals. . . . Visited sick and dying. . . . In some cases hardly anyone to perform burial. . . . Attended two funerals. At one not a solitary mourner. The grave dug by strangers . . ."

When the epidemic was over, a new census taken in Father Lyons' "field" showed a population of 4,067—" probably somewhat too small," he commented hopefully. Fifteen years earlier the count had been 15,000.

The last victims of that quadruple pestilence had been in their graves less than four years when the disease the doctors had feared most for years struck Honolulu, smallpox. Allegedly it came "in some

trunks of old clothes sold at auction and scattered among the natives."
The first two cases were light and diagnosed so tardily that a whole
neighborhood was infected before any attempt to confine it was made.
Those who had been exposed were terrified to learn of its seriousness
and took to their heels, spreading the disease along their escape
routes.

Dr. Judd abandoned other government emergencies to struggle
with this one. In an effort to augment the supply of vaccine, he tied a
cow to a tree in his back yard and inoculated it with fresh human
virus. The cow failed to cooperate. Queues a half mile long lined up
for vaccination, but measures to check the spread were futile. No
hospital facilities existed and no nurses. During July and August
smallpox raced over Oahu like flame in a forest. Cases mounted into
the thousands, mostly among Hawaiians and practically all fatal.

Amateur surgeon Artemas Bishop had been shifted to Ewa, west
of Pearl Harbor. While he was frantically inoculating the entire populace of his parish and attempting to keep his people segregated, a
young *wahine* gaily slipped through the guards and went gallivanting
off to Honolulu. She quickly contracted the disease and in terror hurried home, where she summoned all her friends and relatives to bid
her farewell. One by one they kissed her, then returned to their own
huts and died. The *wahine* recovered. Bishop saved hundreds through
his precautionary measures; yet he sorrowfully reported that half of
Ewa died.

Upon hearing of an outbreak on Hawaii, Dr. Wetmore, stationed
at Hilo, called a public meeting at which he explained that all were to
be vaccinated and that he had to have a hospital. The doctor went to
work on the vaccination and the men on a hospital. The builders won
the race; in exactly three days they constructed a stout, thatched long
house, fifty-eight by fifteen feet, just in time to receive the first patients. Wetmore decreed a policy of strict isolation and in the end took
pride in reporting only 75 deaths in his district.

On Maui Dr. Baldwin went into action before there was an outbreak. He rushed from village to village by horse and canoe demanding that no one be permitted to land, urging villagers to drive off

visitors from other islands with clubs, if necessary. But Maui had too much shore line and too many beaches to police. Smallpox was distributed all around the island before the doctor or anyone else realized it. He established a quarantine camp near Lahaina, ordered that all cases be brought there, and, thanks to the respect he commanded, kept the death count down to 250.

On Kauai Dr. Smith was more successful. Boats were not allowed to land, and the few cases that did develop were isolated so quickly and efficiently that there was no epidemic. Landings on Molokai were guarded with arms, and not a single native was stricken.

Back in Honolulu merchants were more worried over the disaster a smallpox scare would bring to the whaling trade than over the disaster in Hawaiian lives. Moreover, they were furious with Dr. Judd at the time for his diatribes against commercial prostitution, which, if curtailed, would also cut into local trade. While he was working day and night to combat the disease, he was charged at a public meeting with having deliberately started the smallpox epidemic; angry antagonists petitioned the king for his expulsion from office, hinting that there would be riot, revolution, and a downfall of the kingdom if the doctor were not ousted. Judd resigned.

The epidemic gradually diminished during the late summer and fall. No one could ever make an accurate count of the dead. Around ten thousand was a good guess, and that checked reasonably well with the tally of an 1854 census, which showed that the population had declined eleven thousand in three years. And this was only the first smallpox epidemic, for three more were to come in 1861, 1873, and 1882.

Native preachers likened their tribulations to those of the Children of Israel, and, as if the Children of Hawaii were not receiving adequate punishment for their backsliding, in the very same year of the great smallpox scourge, Honolulu's German doctor, William Hillebrand, announced that he had identified a case of leprosy in a coast village of Oahu.

Missionaries, thoroughly familiar with all the gruesome diseases of the Bible, were horrified, and they in turn horrified their congregations. But no one in the 1850's knew what to do about leprosy; so the doctors and the government temporized. They temporized for a dozen years. By 1865 cases of the disease "much like leprosy mentioned in the Scriptures" were being spotted on all the islands. It was evident that drastic action had to be taken.

On recommendation of the Board of Health, a law was passed requiring that all lepers be isolated in a temporary hospital at Kalihi on the outskirts of Honolulu. Victims pleaded not to be sent to this house of inevitable death. They went into hiding. Parents, relatives, and friends concealed distorted caricatures of human beings under matting in corners of grass shacks, in lava tubes, in the deep bush, while sheriffs went the rounds. Months were lost in uncovering the hideaways. And as the "hideous deformities" and "breathing corpses" were rounded up, there proved to be far more than had been supposed. The Kalihi hospital was neither large enough nor isolated enough.

On the north side of Molokai the ideally segregated spot was found, a peninsula of several thousand acres bound on three sides by open ocean and on the other by an almost perpendicular precipice rising to the height of almost half a mile.

In 1866 the first shipload of 140 lepers embarked for Molokai. None of them ever returned. After that, the *Kilauea* or other inter-island ferries offered regular one-way passage to the settlement. Many lepers went under duress, fighting to the last for their freedom; some went peacefully, too ill to care; some gave themselves up voluntarily before anyone but themselves knew that they had the symptoms.

Bill Ragsdale went like that, Bill, the popular Hilo pettifogger and interpreter to the legislature, known everywhere in the islands for his wit, ready eloquence, and shady morality. He merely wrote a letter to the sheriff, giving himself up, offering to be expatriated at once, but begging the sheriff not to come for him and requesting that he be allowed to go aboard the steamer alone and unguarded.

No one had suspected Bill's condition, and when the news leaked out on the day of his departure, he was the hero of the hour, rather than a condemned exile. "He was riding about all morning," pictured a witness to his departure, "taking leave of the people and of the pleasant Hilo lanes which he will never see again, and just as the steamer was weighing anchor, he walked down to the shore as carefully dressed as usual, decorated with leis of ohia and gardenia, and escorted by nearly the whole native population.

"Tears and sobs accompanied him, and his countrymen and women clung to him, kissing him to the last moment, whilst all the foreigners shook hands as they offered him their good wishes. He made a short speech in native, urging quiet submission to the stringent measures which the government was taking to stamp out leprosy. . . . His last words as he stepped into the boat were to all: 'Aloha, may God bless you, my brothers,' and then the whale boat took him the first stage towards his living grave."

Eleven hundred and fifty-four had already preceded Bill Ragsdale to Molokai's Kalaupapa and Kalawao settlements, described in 1872 as among "the most horrible spots on all the earth; a home of hideous disease and slow-coming death, with which science in despair has ceased to grapple; a community of doomed beings, socially dead, whose only business is to perish; wifeless husbands, husbandless wives, children without parents, and parents without children; men and women condemned to watch the repulsive steps by which each of their doomed fellows passes down to a loathsome death, knowing that by the same they too must pass."

At Kalaupapa Bill Ragsdale became "Governor Ragsdale." As volunteer superintendent, he devoted the rest of his short life to bringing what order, comfort, and humor he could to the stricken community. The Belgian priest, Father Damien, whom the world would soon acclaim as one of the most selfless Good Samaritans of all time, was already there, and Brother Dutton was coming.

Because of the widespread horror of leprosy in nineteenth-century Europe and America, it was dramatized as a major killer in the Islands, but the lives it took were few compared to casualties from repeated epidemics of smallpox, measles, and influenza and subsequent epidemics of scarlet fever, whooping cough, mumps, diphtheria, consumption, Asiatic cholera, and bubonic plague. In overlarge measure Hawaii was obliged to make up for the long immunity it had held.

"A large business in one of the back streets of Honolulu is the manufacture of plain coffins," declared journalist William Root Bliss gloomily in 1873. "Marriages between the natives are not prolific, even when the married are in comfortable circumstances and of industrious habits. Offspring are regarded as a calamity. Settlements are vanishing; cottages are vacated and destroyed; and we ride for miles in parts of the country, which were once populous, without seeing a new hut or hearing the voices of children, or meeting a human being. . . . Decreasing population, diminishing production, lack of enterprise . . . foretell a dismal future. . . . Those who have studied the subject most believe that the native race is destined to disappear soon."

Directly or indirectly foreign doctors were responsible for all the measures to counter disease—laws on quarantine, sanitation, compulsory vaccination, birth registration, prostitution; the creation of a Board of Health; the drilling of artesian wells for safe drinking water; the building of one temporary hospital after another, culminating in the construction of Queen's Hospital in 1860.

But none of these measures saved the Hawaiians. By 1900 their total population, exclusive of *hapahaoles,* was down to less than thirty thousand, one-tenth of what it had been before foreigners inflicted upon the Islanders their diseases, their western worries, their monetary values, their horses and cattle, their standards of civilized living.

There had to be a popular scapegoat to carry the blame for such decimation, and the handiest one was the body of missionaries, non-medical and medical. By insisting on dressing the natives in *holokus* and cotton pants, by helping to destroy their dance and sports, by discouraging bathing in the nude, by tampering with the superior diet of fish and poi, by introducing them to culture and letters that completely changed their manner of living, the missionaries undoubtedly contributed to the physical decline of the natives. But if the merchants and traders had been given a free hand, without missionary intervention, the Hawaiians most certainly would have been virtually annihilated. The few that remained in 1900 owed their lives to pompous Hiram Bingham and his colleagues.

Late in the century clusters of journalists without too many chips on their shoulders, men like Richard Henry Dana and Mark Twain, weighed the arguments and went on record unequivocally in favor of the missionaries. But no affirmation counted for more than that of worldly John Young, who knew the kingdom intimately both before and after the arrival of the New England apostles. "Whereas it has been represented by many persons that the labors of the missionaries in these Islands are attended with evil and disadvantages to the people," he solemnly avowed, "I hereby most cheerfully give my testimony to the contrary. . . . I am persuaded that nothing but Christianity could preserve the people from total extinction."

ROYAL COUNCIL IN SESSION

IX
Government by Snip, Snub, and Snarl

By all the laws of political chance, the Sandwich Islands should have been a British colony. A Britisher discovered them. Through Vancouver, Kamehameha I made at least a feint of ceding them to England. Other kings pleaded to have them tucked under the protective wing of Great Britain. And for a few months in 1843 the Union Jack did fly tentatively over the royal palace in Honolulu. Great Britain lost Hawaii through default.

To a mid-nineteenth-century analyst, the islands were "a kind of little plum pudding," into which too many nations were poking their fingers without much appetite for the stuffing. None of the great powers wanted the bloomin' dots, except possibly Russia and France, and they were not sure.

Charles Nordhoff voiced the sentiment of both England and the United States when he acknowledged that "to annex the Islands would be to burden ourselves with an outlying territory too distant to be cheaply defended; and containing a population which will never be homogeneous with our own; a country which would neither attract nor reward our industrious farmers and mechanics; which offers not the slightest temptation to emigration. . . . We should not encumber ourselves with territory which by reason of unchangeable natural causes . . . will not become in time Americanized."

Tactful agents from national capitals avoided reciting any such generalizations, but on one point there was no equivocation: each wanted to make dead certain that no other nation worked itself into a position of favoritism with kings and chiefs so that Hawaii could be grabbed without a deserved holler from the rest of the world.

Nevertheless, England could have won the Islands without priming a cannon or flexing a diplomatic muscle, if she had had in residence at Honolulu between 1824 and 1846 a more gracious and perceptive consular representative than Richard Charlton. London did not need to put into words its contempt for a fourth-class dominion; sending a fourth-class agent expressed it more subtly.

Charlton's sole qualification for the consulship was his previous experience as a Pacific trader. In his case it was not a redeeming qualification, for he had not been a very successful trader; he owed enormous debts in Valparaiso and other ports and needed a refuge on a remote beach where he could keep out of touch with his creditors. He was a rude, corpulent, beefy-faced opportunist, constantly making trouble for himself and the missionaries. He hated missionaries.

Through Boki, the governor of Oahu, who shared the consul's disaffection for New England preachers, Charlton acquired ambiguous title to considerable property, built himself a respectable consulate, established a side business of cattle ranching and merchandising, and also on the side acquired a native mistress or two, in addition to a bona fide British wife. Charlton recognized no system of law, order, or rectitude but his own.

"Whatever good points he may have possessed," summed up a

biased English observer, who normally went out of his way to be more than generous in evaluating his fellow countrymen, "the English consul was unfit for his position; he was hasty in temper, uncouth in his communications . . . a careless, free-living man . . . not disliked by the native population, but deficient in diplomatic knowledge"—all polite understatement.

The little rapport he had with the natives abruptly ended one day when he looped a rope around the neck of one of them, hitched the other end to his saddle, and galloped through Honolulu, dragging the *kanaka* in the dirt behind him—Charlton's conception of appropriate punishment for the rascal who dared take a pot shot at one of his stray cows. Those cattle, for which the consul seemed to expect an extension of his diplomatic immunity, were the trial of the town, forever browsing on gardens and roof thatch. Though their owner had been admonished for it time and again, the marauders kept coming, and desperate natives kept chasing them off with sticks and stones, until Charlton finally caught the culprit who dared use a shotgun and who had accidentally killed a longhorn.

Not satisfied with having crippled the good marksman in towing him through town, the representative of the British crown next demanded that laws be enacted immediately for the protection of foreigners and their property; he wrote home about the cow, insisted on redress, tried to blow up the slaying into an international incident, and was not silenced until an aggressive Yankee captain hove into port and told him off.

When the Reverend Richards complained about the treatment of Lahaina lasses by British seamen, Charlton threatened to seize the pastor and destroy his mission. On one occasion he menaced Brother Bingham with a horsewhip and swore that he would have him shipped off the island. On another, he actually attacked editor James Jarves of the *Polynesian* with the same horsewhip and howled louder than Jarves when he was assessed a fine of six dollars for assault and battery. Kamehameha III even sent a personal letter to William IV of England suggesting a replacement of the consul. But Charlton remained in office; England lost face and, eventually, another colony.

Without the missionaries to compensate for diplomatic deficiencies, the Americans, too, might have lost a potential territory and state, for the caliber of the first United States representative was little higher than that of the British. John C. Jones put in an appearance as American Consul—or Commercial Agent, as he was called—only three months after the arrival of the missionaries. At the mission he was at once accepted as an agreeable addition to the community, but the harmony was of short duration.

He became almost as avid a missionary hater as Charlton, maintaining that the preachers were ruining millions of dollars worth of trade by shedding "enlightenment" upon the natives and ruining them in the process, cramming religion down their throats, degrading them, trampling on their rights under the pretense of saving souls, and leading them to famine and destruction.

To Jones the Hawaiians were "children of nature" who ought to be accepted as such and not confronted with the problem of eternal damnation for neglecting to live, act, and dress like civilized people. He joined the "children," bid adieu to the mission, borrowed Hannah Holmes, one of Bingham's most likely female candidates for salvation, and set up housekeeping without benefit of clergy.

Later he took a shine to Lahilahi, a captivating young daughter of Don Marin, invited her in, too, and the three lived together in bigamous bliss, with a miscellany of children, to the utter mortification of the missionaries. And still later, on a business trip to California, he picked up a lovely señorita, brought her back to the Islands, and abandoned the other consorts. All this seemed deliberately calculated to embarrass the missionaries, who naturally felt that the Americans should be setting a marital example.

Charlton was regarded as leader of the antimissionary clique and Jones as his deputy. The two saw eye to eye on all matters relating to the immoral welfare of the Islanders, and when the British consul went off on one of his temper tantrums, Jones was close behind to keep the rancor warm.

The commercial agent actually did a great deal to promote American trade; he drafted Hawaii's first "Treaty of Commerce and Friendship," sent home hundreds of stranded whalers and ship deserters, found jobs for others, and though he made no effort to live as an exemplary citizen of the nation he represented, he upheld the rights of the Yankee peddlers. It was Jones who contributed the bell for the cupola of the Charity School for *hapahaole* children, and long after his sins had caught up with him and he was recalled by President Van Buren, the bell continued to ring out loud and clear as his memorial.

French representation was no better than British and American. For years France had two obsessions in its commercial and political relations with the Islands, the importation of low-duty spirits and the importation of high-spirited Catholic clerics. Hawaii had no right, insisted the French, to harbor a grudge against Burgundies and cognac and less right to begrudge the priesthood any favors extended to Yankee Puritans. Consular agents spent most of their energy wrangling over these two issues, though they did manage to find almost as much time for *le sport* as Charlton and Jones.

In the idyllic little village of Honokahua, a dozen miles by trail north of Lahaina, Professor Chester Lyman of Yale once stumbled onto the French consular staff off duty. They had come out to shoot ducks, explained the vice-consul with a guilty look, before the professor had a chance to inquire what brought them to such a remote spot. Lyman accepted the statement at face value, though he saw neither shotguns nor ducks, and passed on to the next valley, where he found more unarmed agents, also on a "hunting trip."

"The truth is," Lyman learned from his guide, "these men are in the habit of coming out each week to this retired nook for the purpose of hunting—but more especially for the purpose of dissipation and licentiousness. They spend the night here and ride back to town on Saturday afternoon. Of course, among Hawaiian females . . . they find little difficulty in obtaining objects of their lust."

The quality of foreign diplomacy in the Sandwich Islands during most of the nineteenth century was as low-grade politically as it was morally. In any of the capitals of Europe or America, Hawaii was considered a puny little kingdom that merited no top-hat envoys. It was the ideal outpost for the banishment of untalented government functionaries. Seldom was any government encumbered with a more singular lot of amateur diplomats, bumbling, bickering, backbiting, and so arrogant that when it came to a showdown they attempted to dictate policy and procedure.

The basic trouble, of course, was that the Hawaiian government itself was strictly amateur, with an unseemly amount of internal bumbling, bickering, and backbiting. The end of the reign of Kamehameha I marked the end of an epoch. With uncanny insight, he understood his childlike subjects and knew what was good for them in the face of encroaching civilization. He, too, was an amateur among rulers of sophisticated states, but he had a gift for brushing off political intruders who might be damaging to his conception of Island welfare. His successors lacked that gift.

In the three-quarters of a century after his death, a procession of six kings occupied the throne, Kamehameha II through V, followed by Lunalilo and Kalakaua, and finally Queen Liliuokalani. None of them could match the shrewdness and dynamic energy of the founder of the Kamehameha dynasty. Two or three were playboy kings given to drunkenness and debauchery, distinguished primarily for the brevity of their reign, and all six seemed to lack resolution in a moment of crisis. Yet despite their weaknesses, they were virtually worshiped by their subjects and given credit for achievements made by advisers, fellow chiefs, island governors, regents, premiers, and diplomats.

Under Liholiho—Kamehameha II—1819 to 1824, the taboo system was broken; the missionaries were allowed to introduce Christian enlightenment and a written language; the first systematic commerce with other nations was established. But Liholiho was restless and unstable, incapable of restraining his wanderlust and willing to let his more gifted and aggressive premier or *kuhina nui*, Dowager Queen Kaahumanu do most of the ruling.

He abandoned the ancestral royal residence at Kailua and moved to Honolulu; yet he had no fixed capital. He roamed from island to island as whim and mood directed and in 1823 left for England, with his favorite queen and a retinue of chiefs, to survey the realm from which his father had once sought protection. Both he and the queen died there the following spring—of the measles.

Lahaina Whaling Spree, Maui

Hamakua Coast, Hawaii

Menehune Fishpond

Spouting
Horn

Hanalei Valley,
Kauai

Hanauma Bay, Oahu

Waimea Pastoral, Hawaii

Diamond Head, Oahu

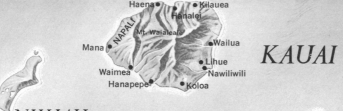

Haena • • Kilauea
Hanalei
NAPALI
Mt. Waialeale
Mana • • Wailua

KAUAI

Waimea • Lihue
Hanapepe • Nawiliwili
• Koloa

NIIHAU

Waimea • • Kahuku
• Laie
Waialua
Bay
Kaena Pt. • Haleiwa • Punaluu
Makua • Wahiawa
KOOLAU RANGE
WAIANAE MTS.
Schofield
OAHU Makaha • Barracks • • Kaneohe
Lualualei • • Kailua
Pearl • Waimanalo
Harbor
Ewa • • Makapuu
Barbers Pt. • Honolulu • Point
Waikiki Diamond Koko
Head Head

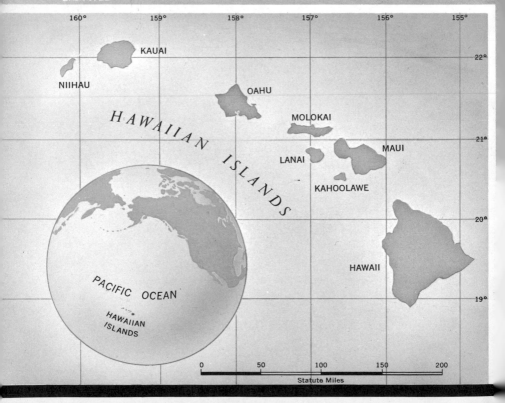

MOLOKAI

Ilio Point
Kalaupapa
Hoolehua
Kaunakakai

MAUI

Honokahua
Kahakuloa
Kaanapali
WEST MAUI MTS.
Waihee
Spreckelsville
Lanai City
Lahaina
Kahului
Keanae
Iao Valley
Wailuku
Makewao
Olowalu
Kihei
Kula
Hana
Maalaea Bay
Haleakala Crater
Makena
Ulupalakua
Kaupo
La Perouse Bay

LANAI

KAHOOLAWE

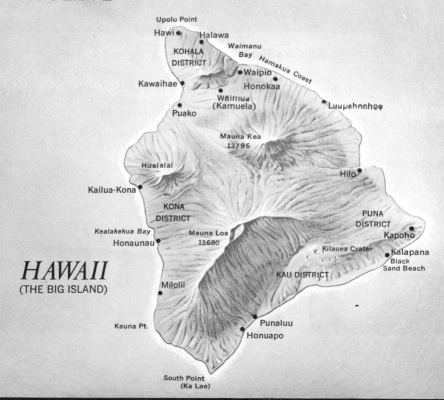

Upolu Point
Hawi
Halawa
KOHALA DISTRICT
Waimanu Bay
Hamakua Coast
Waipio
Kawaihae
Honokaa
Waimea (Kamuela)
Luupahoehoe
Puako
Mauna Kea 13796
Hualalai
Hilo
Kailua-Kona
KONA DISTRICT
PUNA DISTRICT
Kapoho
Kealakekua Bay
Mauna Loa 13680
Honaunau
Kilauea Crater
Kalapana
Black Sand Beach

HAWAII
(THE BIG ISLAND)

Milolii
KAU DISTRICT
Kauna Pt.
Punaluu
Honuapo
South Point (Ka Lae)

Kilauea's Mammoth Crater, Halemaumau, Hawaii

(*Left*) Kilauea Forest Devastated by Cinder Eruption, Hawaii
(*Center*) Kilauea Iki, Hawaii
(*Right*) Haleakala's Latest Lava Flow, c. 1750, Maui

Cane, Maui

Honolulu Harbor, Arrival of the *Lurline*, Oahu

The Pali, Oahu

Remnants of Ancient Hawaii

Mooring *pukas* chiseled
in lava, South Point

Sections of the
King's Highway at Puna
and Kailua-Kona, Hawaii

Heiau at Kawaihae

Taro Patches and Lush Tropical Jungle of Keanae Area, East Maui

Cattle Roundup, Hawaii

Puako Petroglyphs. Samples of the thousands of Kilroy-Was-Here doodles carved in lava by roving Hawaiians, Hawaii

Moonlit Reefs, Maalaea Bay, Kihei, Maui

Waipio Valley, Hawaii

Examples of the Missionary Legacy   (*Left*) Village churches at Keanae, Maui
(*Center*) Kailua-Kona, Hawaii (*Right*) Waimea, Kauai

Hanalei Mission Church, Kauai

Seining, Kalama Park, Maui

Pineapple Hill, Honokawai, Maui

Waikiki Skyline, Oahu

Waimea Canyon, Kauai

Haleakala Crater (Mauna Loa and Mauna Kea across channel), Maui

(Center) Crater Plunge, Hawaii
(Left) Hapuna Beach, Hawaii   (Right) Lahaina Harbor, Maui

Mount Waialeale, Wettest Spot on Earth, Kauai

Black Sands Beach, Hawaii

To forestall the calamity resulting from just such an exigency, before leaving Hawaii Liholiho had designated his nine-year-old brother, Kauikeaouli, as his successor, and temporarily relinquished all royal authority to Queen Kaahumanu; so the kingdom was in good hands. Kauikeaouli deferred claiming his crown until he was almost twelve. His favored stepmother reigned during the interim and continued as regent after his enthronement. Thanks to his youthful start, Kamehameha III had the longest reign in Hawaiian history, 1825 to 1854. That was the period during which the kingdom came of age. Accepting the counsel of a succession of foreign officials in his government, he approved the first written constitution in 1840, established a limited monarchy, with a legislative and judiciary system; he came to grips with the growing strife between Protestant and Catholic missions and granted religious freedom to all his subjects; he extended to commoners the privilege of owning real estate and brought about a division of the ancestral lands—the "Great *Mahele,*" and in one way or another he staved off defiant moves of both the French and English to absorb the kingdom. At the time of his death in 1854, he was ready to sign a treaty of annexation with the United States.

In fact, historian Henry Cheever in 1851 was so confident of statehood for the Islands that he pictured Hawaiian senators and representatives seated in Washington "with members from Minnesota, Utah, Deseret, New Mexico and Santa Fe." "The Star of Hawaii," he envisioned, "may yet blaze in the flag of the American Union; and the sons of her past missionaries, together with native-born *Kanaka Maoli* from the Island Heart of the Pacific, may yet mingle in debate on the floor of the American Congress, and the voice of Senatorial eloquence from the luxurious tropics may yet awaken echoes from the hardy North. May propitious Heaven speed the augury!"

The augury, however, was not to be sped, due, incongruously enough, to the intervention of a Jim-Crow-baiting transportation official, some eight thousand miles away in Philadelphia, Pennsylvania.

Alexander Liholiho—Kamehameha IV—was the aristocrat of the line. He had the benefit of a good education at the Chiefs' Children's School, had toured Europe and America, and married a distinguished Islander of culture and refinement, the granddaughter of John Young.

But Alexander had no love for the United States and warmly rejected the attitude of his predecessor regarding American annexation. If the decision had been left to him, he would have made sure that the Islands never came under Yankee jurisdiction.

The prejudice went back to the incident in Philadelphia during a tour of the States with his two brothers. Everywhere they had traveled, in England, France, Canada, and New England, they were honored as princes, but not in the City of Brotherly Love, where a conductor mistook them for Negroes and ordered them off the train. "Confounded fool!" fumed the prince. "I was treated like a dog, to go and come at an American's bidding. . . . They have no manners, no politeness, not even common civility to a stranger."

The Philadelphia conductor came close to altering the course of events in Hawaii, but Alexander spent most of his brief reign, from 1855 to 1863, trying to check the steady decline in native population rather than in molding international relations. "Our first and greatest duty is that of self-preservation," he proclaimed. "Our acts are all in vain unless we can stay the wasting hand that is destroying our people." Alexander himself fell victim to "the wasting hand" when he was still in his twenties. But before his death, he and Queen Emma had personally raised funds for construction of a Honolulu hospital for his afflicted people. Queen's Hospital stood as a major memorial of his short regime.

Alexander's brother Lot—Kamehameha V—was of an entirely different cut, determined to restore some of the character of his grandfather's dictatorship. First and last he wanted to make Hawaii and the world aware that he was a chief of the old order, the authoritarian order. He shared Alexander's prejudice against the United States, and was convinced that Americans were deliberately attempting to convert the kingdom into a republic, with the prospect of annexing it as soon as it became one; encouraging universal suffrage was the American way of destroying a monarchy.

Highhandedly he abrogated the former constitution and in a welter of dissension imposed a new one which made the king unquestionably supreme. His was a dictatorship that dictated. With all its defects,

Lot's system of law remained in force for nearly a quarter of a century, which was longer than any other constitution of the kingdom.

But the gusto of the chieftains seemed to pass into limbo with the death of Lot in 1872. Lot's successor, Prince Lunalilo stooped to the march of democracy, despite the constitution, modestly submitted his name as a candidate for election by the people, and was voted into power by an overwhelming majority. He was the generous humanitarian, in contrast to his predecessor, but died at the end of his first year in office.

With the new and booming sugar industry stabilizing the economy, Kalakaua, who followed in February 1874, brought the greatest period of prosperity the Islands had ever known. He was scholarly and literate, the internationalist and the pro-American, who traveled across the United States to be received in an impressive ceremony by President Grant and to win the Reciprocity Treaty of 1876 that introduced free trade between the two nations.

The dissentient idea of a republic was in the balmy air of Hawaii when Liliuokalani succeeded her brother in 1891. She was a gracious and brilliant sovereign, but no match for the revolutionary forces working against her. *Pilikia* over sugar production was her real woe. In 1890 the American Congress reneged on the sugar deal, substituted the McKinley Tariff Bill for the fourteen-year-old reciprocity treaty, removed the tariff on all foreign sugar imports to the United States, and gave a bounty of two cents a pound to production within the country.

The effect on what had become Hawaii's chief industry was disastrous. Sugar interests now saw that the only way out of the dilemma was to make Hawaiian sugar American sugar through annexation. Liliuokalani was not yet ready to surrender her kingdom to the barons. Instead of accepting what American advisers considered inevitable, she chose to buck the plantation owners and strengthen the monarchy by attempting to proclaim still another constitution that would reassert sovereign authority.

Her cabinet refused to endorse the move. The crisis erupted into riot, political turmoil, and threat of violence. Citizens took matters into their own hands and appointed a "Committee of Safety" to form a provisional government. Disbanded volunteer military companies were reorganized. At a mass meeting on January 16, 1893, the committee's proposals for a new democratic republic were ratified, and the U.S.S. *Boston* promptly landed a force to protect American interests. The "revolution" was over.

Next day, under vehement protest, Queen Liliuokalani abdicated, to be replaced by a provisional government under Sanford Dole, son of the old Punahou teacher. The dynasties were broken; Hawaii became a republic, then a Territory of the United States, with a succession of *haole* governors leading the way to statehood. As if bidding farewell to the ancient regime and offering an unresentful welcome to the new, it was Liliuokalani, the last of the Hawaiian sovereigns, who penned the plaintive and imperishable refrain "Aloha Oe."

But no brief summary of the roles played by the kings could more than hint at all the promptings from behind scenes during the turbulent century. The kings and queens were billed as the principals; they held the spotlight. Yet seldom did they carry the action, and all too frequently they muffed their lines at the dramatic moment, turned exposition into burlesque, tragedy into melodrama, comedy into farce. It was an extravaganza that starred the bit players, the prompters, and the amateur directors—seen most advantageously in their bizarre trappings and makeup on the opening day of parliament.

Journalist William Root Bliss witnessed that performance in 1872, with its pageantry of silk stovepipes, *kahilis,* and feathered cloaks. He noted that the first man on the rostrum was the chancellor, "a New England born gentleman"; then the king, followed at a respectful distance by his ministers and staff officers, all *haoles* "caparisoned with barbaric glory."

"There was the American-born banker," he detailed, "a scarlet ribbon around his neck, from which hangs the sparkling insignia of Hawaiian knighthood. There is the little minister of finance, an excellent American-born dentist. There is the tall, scheming minister of foreign affairs, also minister of the navy, that is yet to be, and of war, not yet declared, once an American lawyer. There is the dignified minister of the interior, general manager and police supervisor of the kingdom, once a crusty Scotch physician. There is the attorney-general of the crown, who recently went to New England and married a wife. All these men in cocked hats and blue broadcloth, brilliant with gilt bands, laces and decorations; the rapiers buckled at their sides, and they themselves appearing to be very uncomfortable."

Mark Twain saw them in forensic action. He boasted of having attended enough legislative sessions in other parts of the world to be a competent judge of parliamentary order and flatteringly ranked the mental caliber of Hawaii's assembly on a par with that of the most advanced nation, adding that the observation was not intended as a compliment, for "a comfortable majority" in any senate or parliament "knew just enough to come in when it rained, and that was all."

"This Legislature is like all other Legislatures," he concluded. "A wooden-head gets up and proposes an utterly absurd something or other, and he and half a dozen other wooden-heads discuss it with windy vehemence for an hour . . . and then a sensible man—a man of weight—a big gun—gets up and shows the foolishness of the matter in five sentences; a vote is taken, and the thing is tabled."

Through the stream of complaints from antimissionary business and consular agents, the world had been given the impression that legislators were all missionaries, their sons, or cousins, which was far from the truth. Gospel ministers and their relatives did get into the legislative show, along with foreign merchants, doctors, second-class lawyers, and first-class hecklers, but missionaries were the minority, although the seniority. They had been the first educated outsiders to become deeply involved in affairs of government, and took leading parts not because they wished it or had the slightest political ambition. Circumstances demanded their involvement.

Soon after his arrival, Hiram Bingham became a power behind the throne by invitation. Among a pagan people being exposed to the first indoctrination of civilization, no line could be drawn between Christian worship and Christian everyday life. The new religion reached out inevitably into matters of personal conduct, into community conduct, into means of regulating that conduct, into set prohibitions, and therefore into legislation, governmental administration, and measurement of justice. Bingham avoided accepting any title that might officially link him with such secular activity, but he could not shield himself from the political conquests he won or the errors he made. And he was unfortunately reluctant to admit that he was an amateur at politics.

In 1838 Kamehameha III begged William Richards, the Maui reverend who had made himself so unpopular with the whalers and their girl friends at Lahaina, to accept a government post as royal confidential adviser. After long and prayerful consideration, Richards decided it was his duty to accept and accordingly resigned from the mission.

He had translated seventeen books of the Bible and was an able scholar in the Hawaiian language, a good orator, and a wise counselor, but a rank amateur in politics. By kingly edict he became overnight the recognized statesman of the realm, started studying books on government, translating them, and lecturing to the king, the chiefs, and Lahainaluna students on political economy. Unquestionably he was the most influential foreigner in the Islands. His word was law.

Malcontents who had been searching for someone at whom they could direct their choler immediately aimed at Richards. Skippers and shopkeepers were brutal. Even the missionaries, who looked askance at anyone who would give up the gospel for government, eyed him with jaundice. The bilious British were hardest of all.

"A man originally distinguished for his insignificance," was the label scornfully fastened on him by Consul Manley Hopkins, one of Charlton's successors. "A well-meaning, pious, industrious person without any great intellectual power . . . a sort of conscience to the king . . . his interpreter, or rather his spokesman. He put off his definite character of a minister of religion to assume the task of making laws and governing a people. Alas! ambition sometimes dwells beneath unstarched white cravats and suits of black alpaca." Nevertheless, Richards was a tower of strength. He had to be. A lesser man would have buckled under the weight of derision heaped upon him.

Lawmaker Richards could not handle the situation alone. He was credited with conscripting another amateur statesman, Dr. Gerrit

Judd, who became a still more conspicuous power behind the throne. Judd was the best surgeon in the Islands, an excellent pharmacologist, and he had a winning bedside manner, particularly with chiefesses and princesses. He was a man of many talents, but he knew no more about political science than Richards. He learned as he went along.

His first exposure to native politics came quite naturally in bedside counseling, while diagnosing royal ailments, prescribing pills, or cupping blood. The Dowager Queen Kaahumanu was one of his steadiest patients. Among the *alii*, clinical consultation was soon subordinated to gubernatorial consultation. When a princess had a political problem, the doctor was summoned.

It was not entirely in the capacity of medical adviser that he accompanied the king's retinue on interisland expeditions. He was good company, quick-witted, and a sharp observer. Years before the public was aware that he had any connection with the government, he was superintending in spare time the affairs of the premier's office, which included such matters as maintenance of tax records, registry of vessels, correspondence with consuls and commanders of ships, and supervision of the treasury.

His official career in government began in 1842, when Richards was sent off to Europe as treaty maker and the doctor was invited to take over during his absence. Since the kingdom had somehow managed to get along up to that time with little semblance of either treasurer or treasury, and was obviously in need of both, Judd counterproposed that he start organizing state finances and omit some of the busy-work in which Richards had been engaged.

The conditions were accepted and Judd took the post, at $750 a year. For appearance's sake, he soon resigned as mission doctor, even renounced American citizenship and swore allegiance to the king. The following year he was elevated to the position of Secretary of State for Foreign Affairs and in succession later held such titles as Minister of the Interior and Minister of Finance. But the title mattered little; Judd ran the government. Unofficially he was prime minister; and his more contemptuous critics also conferred upon him the rank of "King."

Around him he rallied the best staff of *haoles* he could find. He needed a lawyer desperately. In fact, every businessman in Honolulu was also screaming for a lawyer, notably those who objected to the way the government was being run. The first one to step ashore, was an energetic young pettifogger named John Ricord and, in 1844, before the opposition had a chance to hire him, Judd had created the post of Attorney General and sworn him in.

Then too late, he began inquiring into the lawyer's background, and uncovered a cloud of rumors, a Mainland client allegedly fleeced of thirteen thousand dollars, an accusation of insolence that had caused his ignominious dismissal from a Michigan court, a jail break while waiting trial on a charge of grand larceny for pocket-picking in Buffalo, and no telling what sort of reputation in Louisiana, Texas, Florida, and Oregon, where he had lived and practiced law.

In Honolulu a lawyer was a lawyer, regardless of his reputation. Ricord watched his step, signed a temperance pledge to please the ex-missionary, went to work on a complete revision of Hawaiian laws, developed into a fiery prosecutor and, to all appearances, an honest attorney general.

A few months later a frail, soft-spoken Scottish doctor, Robert C. Wyllie, disembarked at Honolulu, thoroughly indifferent to the destinies of the Island kingdom. He was a bachelor who had made a lot of money in South America and Mexico, and was taking one last fling before returning home to the clan, indulging in a round-the-world trip by way of China. He visited Honolulu only because the ship happened to call there.

Judd by chance met the fellow professional on the pier, liked his looks, ordered his luggage brought ashore, and in no time had him signed up as Minister of Foreign Affairs, an office Judd himself relinquished to become Minister of the Interior. The Scot pleaded ignorance of protocol and the operation of either foreign or domestic affairs, but that did not matter. Judd liked amateurs. The new minister never did get back to Scotland; he died in office twenty years later after establishing a record more distinguished, if anything, than that of the man who hired him.

In similar fashion, Judd snatched another New York lawyer, William L. Lee, off a ship bound for Oregon and quickly had him appointed as judge, though his experience had all been below the bench. He was a superb addition to the cabinet Judd was building. When William Richards returned from his European mission, he joined the group, though demoted to the Ministry of Public Instruction. Then to give the cabinet the right cast, he had *hapahaole* John Young, Jr., installed as titular premier, though John well understood who the real premier was.

Actually Dr. Judd was not trying to usurp the throne. He was stalling for time until native sons, graduates of Lahainaluna and some of the select schools, were qualified to assume cabinet posts. "Do you think that I can do the work of a white minister?" asked Young who considered himself more Hawaiian than *haole* and therefore able to take the side of his people in justifying the strong foreign representation in the government. "No. The chiefs will, we hope, be qualified, but now we must have these white men."

By 1851 there was a grand total of forty-eight foreigners in the government service of Kamehameha III, all neophytes, all amateurs. They made quite a team, and it was that team which drafted the laws, organized and reorganized the financial structure, settled international problems, argued with local merchants, contrived the Great *Mahele*, held together "the incongruous elements of Government," as Judd phrased it, and did what they could to make their action look as though the king were the inventor, sponsor, and executor.

Harmony was never a conspicuous feature of the teamwork. Meetings occasionally broke up in abusive spats of name calling and fist clenching, and for long periods Judd was kept at wits' end trying to patch up the rifts. Even his placid foreign secretary once angrily accused him to his face of governing on a system of "snip, snub and snarl." The discord sometimes disintegrated into a comedy of errors, and when a real crisis arose, the amateurs could be frightened into paralysis or thrown into hysterical confusion.

Years before Judd had built his cabinet bulwark, William Richards established the pattern for ruffled government reaction. On July 9,

1839, the French frigate *L' Artémise,* commanded by Captain C. P. T. Laplace, blew into Honolulu harbor, bearing a money-or-your-life ultimatum; the king would at once welcome the Catholic religion, designate a free site for the construction of a church, release any and all prisoners of the Catholic faith from custody, and present a tribute of twenty thousand dollars as a guarantee of future amiability toward Catholics in general. Three days of grace were allowed for complying with the terms. The alternative was war, "with all the devastations and all the calamities which would be its unhappy but necessary results." *L' Artémise* carried sixty guns, more than enough to level Honolulu.

There was no possible misinterpretation of the threat. Captain Laplace intended to take the Islands either through surrender or conquest. No one denied that Catholics had been persecuted in the interests of protecting the imposed state religion, Congregationalism, but their maltreatment was now being used as a pretext for subjugation; and the blackmail set high enough so that there would be no possibility of a payoff.

Humanely, he sent word ashore that during the bombardment he would be pleased to provide asylum aboard the frigate for all foreigners except Protestant clergy, "the true authors of the insults given to France." Missionaries, he insited, would have to be lumped with the natives and undergo "the unhappy consequences of war," which they had brought upon themselves.

The king was at Lahaina, and it would take at least three days to fetch him. Richards was in charge, the fate of a kingdom in his hands. He was beside himself. The fastest crew of boatmen he could assemble was dispatched to Maui with orders to hurry Kamehameha III back to Honolulu. Judd, not yet officially in power, but indispensable in an emergency, was off on a tour of inspection at the far end of Oahu. A runner was sent for him. When located thirty miles to windward, the doctor learned, among other extravagant intelligence, that "the French ship carried guns which could fire around mountains and send balls all over the island." Judd mounted his horse and raced for Honolulu, urging along the files of natives that already clogged the trail over the *Pali.*

Ulterior motives for this war of the two religions had been accumulating for years. Following the example set by Spanish padres in other parts of the world, French priests had been planting missions all through Oceania, mellowing aborigines for political absorption and getting military protection from France when it was needed.

The Sandwich Islands had not been overlooked; rather, the Yankee Protestants got there first and established a sort of ecclesiastic right of eminent domain. Nevertheless, the French were inclined to regard them as intruders in their Pacific sphere of influence; even Louis Philippe had been persuaded that "the means of procuring the annexation of the Hawaiian Islands lay in the introduction of the Roman Catholic religion."

The first French priests had arrived at Honolulu in 1827, and were treated just as hospitably as they would have been in most any New England village at the time—invited to leave. Bingham convinced the chiefs that this different variety of Christianity, with emphasis on symbols and statues, would merely confuse the natives, and the chiefs faithfully conveyed the message to the priests.

"We do not want you," Premier Kaahumanu formally confirmed in her most diplomatic diction. "We have put away our idols, and abandoned our old system of religious forms and penances. We have received the Word of God by the hand of teachers whom we love and with whom we are satisfied. Our kingdom is a little one. We do not wish the minds of our subjects distracted by any other sect. Go away and teach destitute countries which have not received the Bible."

The premier undoubtedly drafted the rebuff, but she had not been able to eliminate from it all the Yankee seasoning. Finally the delegation had to heed the edict; the priests were deported. But they kept coming back or sending other members of the fraternity. They stole ashore surreptitiously; they came in disguise; they came openly and defiantly. They managed to erect a chapel or two and made easy converts of natives who had been read out of the Protestant church for various transgressions. Laws were coded against participating in this new form of idol worship, and violators were treated as roughly as they would have been in Connecticut. A few of them were imprisoned, flogged, and tormented. There was no question about it; it was persecution.

Captain Laplace was not the first French representative to reproach the authorities for the harsh treatment of Catholics, but he was the first to issue such an ultimatum. In it he referred to "the enormities of the Hawaiian Government towards French subjects"; "the indulgence and long-suffering of France"; "the cruel persecution while Protestants enjoyed the most extensive privileges." "To tarnish the Roman Catholic religion with the name of idolatry," Laplace summed up, "and to expel it under this absurd pretext, was to offer an insult to France and its sovereign." The captain was not bluffing. He intended to get reparations, twenty thousand dollars worth, or exterminate Honolulu and take over the Islands.

Hundreds of armed natives milled around the city during the three days of grace. Many were organized into units that did not look very military. The rusty guns at the fort were manned. Chiefs, the amateur statesmen, consuls, merchants, and missionaries argued themselves hoarse day after day and into the night. They talked of resistance; they talked of conciliation; but mostly they talked of submission.

When the king failed to show up at the end of the third day, Laplace was persuaded to extend his period of grace another forty-eight hours. The arguers resumed their conferences. On the fifth day they were still arguing, and the king's flotilla was not yet in sight. A decision had to be made without the king. Submission was the only way out. Twenty thousand dollars had to be raised.

Richards, Judd, and worried chiefs abandoned the council chambers and started making the rounds of local merchants. They were astonished at the hidden wealth they turned up. No one had any idea that so much ready cash had been lying around. The tradesmen anted up with generous loans of twenty-five, fifty, a hundred dollars, and more at extortionate interest rates. And the real hero of the hour was Captain Charles Brewer, who happened to be in port and came through with a munificent sum to carry them over the top.

Just before the deadline, to the consternation of Captain Laplace, twenty thousand dollars in cash was delivered to *L' Artémise*. Hawaii was saved from French occupation, saved from the exclusive sway of Calvinism, saved from the barrage of those cannon that could pitch curved balls around mountains. The persecution of Catholic martyrs was at least temporarily halted. Honolulu was rescued from extermination, and its skyline was going to be graced with a spire topped by the cross.

But Laplace was so unhappy at having underestimated the assets of Honolulu that he began making new demands. Only the previous year the king and council had been induced to prohibit the importation of hard liquors and to lay a heavy duty on wines, another insult to the French crown. The captain now insisted that the Hawaiian prejudice against brandy also be discarded along with the prejudice against bishops.

Belatedly the king, who had signed the law, arrived from Maui to find Richards and his lawmakers stewing over the second ultimatum. Either the duty on brandy must be reduced or *L' Artémise* would summon a larger force and make a shambles of the Islands. The king resolutely refused, but when reminded of the alternatives, he hurriedly placed his signature on the rider to the "Laplace Treaty" and the French frigate sailed away. Perhaps it was only by linguistic accident that the Hawaiian world *palani* means both brandy and France as well as a detestable person or something with a foul odor.

Sending for a warship, as the French consul had for *L' Artémise*, was standard procedure for settling international disputes, and, remote as the Sandwich Islands were, an American, French, or British man-of-war never seemed to be very far over the horizon. If a Yankee merchant were having trouble collecting a debt from the government, the appearance of a gunboat usually brought a quick settlement. If the British consul had been crossed by the governor, a salute from one of His Majesty's vessels was effective in producing an apology.

After the signing of the Laplace Treaty, French flagships dropped anchor more frequently to check on importation restrictions on brandy and bishops. Honolulu at last had become the focal point for all the rivalry of great powers seeking status in the Pacific. Sometimes there was considerable congestion in the harbor—and worse congestion in the offices of the amateur statesmen trying to maintain Island peace and independence.

To Richards, to Judd, to any official, native or foreign, willing to face realities, it was clear that some power sooner or later would invent a firm pretext for seizing the Islands and be less clumsy about it than Laplace. The sense of insecurity mounted until Richards was finally bundled off in the spring of 1842 to see what he could do about negotiating a joint agreement with England, France, and the United States that would guarantee Island independence. Hardly had he sailed when it became evident that he had not gone soon enough; troubles began bursting out all over, troubles for Judd to cope with.

Early in August word reached Honolulu that the French had seized the Marquesas Islands, and Judd naturally jumped to the conclusion that Hawaii would be next. Within two weeks the half-expected French corvette anchored off Honolulu, without the customary salute, and Captain Mallet sent ashore a new edition of the old grievances.

As paraphrased by an amused witness of the proceedings, "It complained of insults heaped upon ministers of religion; of quiet congregations menaced by subaltern authorities; of converts driven to hear Protestant sermons and to attend Protestant schools; of churches overthrown and of treaties torn . . . and, as the document would not be complete or consistent without something about wine and spirits, . . . of limitations in the sale of brandy to a certain number of gallons . . . for the purpose of eluding this article of the treaty—not to say violating it."

The ultimatum was stronger than Laplace's and avoided the error of offering a cash settlement. In a tactful reply penned for the king's signature, Judd neatly sidestepped the challenge by explaining that a duly authorized minister had been commissioned to negotiate a new treaty with the king of France. If Judd had replied with a forty-gun barrage, the dodge could not have been more effective. Mallet dared not run the chance of incurring his sovereign's ire by interfering with treaty making. He was so nonplused that he hoisted sail and disappeared.

But Hawaii's acting foreign minister was not given much time to gloat over the triumph. Other annoyances awaited his attention, this time from the British. A few days after Captain Mallet's corvette withdrew, the detested Charlton mysteriously sailed for London. Adding a few facts to rumor, Judd was forced to conclude that the sole purpose of his journey was to scuttle the Richards' mission and persuade Great Britain to annex the Islands.

To fill his large boots during what might be a protracted leave, Charlton appointed a pompous young rogue and busybody named Alexander Simpson, a personal enemy of Judd and a great many others. "Don't recognize him," whispered Judd to the king. The counsel was followed.

Being ignored was the one thing Simpson could not endure; he would teach the uncouth Islanders a lesson. He had seen how effectively warship diplomacy worked for the French; so he concocted a dispatch outlining the insults that he, Charlton, and various British comrades were suffering and sent it off to the commander of the British squadron in the Pacific, Admiral Richard Thomas, urging immediate action.

Simpson had to wait for more than four months for the response, but on February 18, 1843, H.M.S. *Carysfort,* under command of Lord George Paulet, carrying discretionary orders from the squadron commander to check into the complaint, breezed into Honolulu harbor and the consul *pro tem* scrambled aboard to give more details of the agonies Englishmen were enduring under the Hawaiian yoke.

In no time Lord Paulet was madder than Simpson and ready for action. As a starter, he gave the government—Judd—just eight hours in which to ponder the wisdom of recognizing Alexander Simpson, Esquire, as Her Britannic Majesty's representative in the Hawaiian kingdom; if a favorable decision were not reached in that length of time, the *Carysfort* would deliver a broadside that would make Honolulu unrecognizable.

Long before the eight hours were up, Judd and the governor had decided in Simpson's favor. But that concession was only a beginning. The king was summoned from Maui, and a tug of war was on. It continued for days. Original demands of three thousand dollars for "damages" gradually mounted to over one hundred thousand. "Ah, those were dark days!" sighed Laura Judd, who each night listened to her husband's résumé of the day's humiliation. "The intention was sufficiently clear, to rob the treasury by extorting large sums of money, and compel the king to yield his sovereignty, to prevent it (they said among themselves) from falling into the hands of the French."

The king squirmed as no Hawaiian monarch ever had before. "I can bear it no longer," he moaned after listening to the recital of peremptory demands for more than a week. "Let them take what they please. I will give no more. I am a dead man."

"They want your islands," Judd explained privately, "and are determined to have them by cession or by conquest. If they take possession by force, you will have no redress; they will keep your islands forever, but if you cede to Lord George Paulet *for the time being,* and refer to Great Britain as umpire, the justice of your cause can be made so clear that you are sure to receive back your sovereignty in due time."

Against the advice of "all the men of influence and wealth," the king adopted the doctor's counsel. The kingdom was surrendered; the Hawaiian flags came down, and Simpson saw to it that they were burned. By chance, the *Carysfort* had a great many extra Union Jacks on board, and they were distributed freely. Paulet and the rogue Simpson became virtual dictators, with Judd representing the king on a four-man advisory commission. Hawaii was part of the British Empire—"for the time being."

To prevent unnecessary communication with the outside world, the remnant Hawaiian governing body was all but quarantined and the port blockaded. The resistance went underground, quite literally; secret headquarters were set up in the royal tomb, and in that tomb was launched a melodramatic program of intrigue and subterfuge that would have done credit to a chamber of Machiavellians. The situation called for duplicity, and Judd proved an artist at it.

In an open meeting of the commission, he enthusiastically endorsed the idea that Simpson embark at once for Great Britain to present his case to authorities in London; in a closed meeting of the underground, he arranged for a loyal Honolulu merchant, James Marshall, to sail on the same ship and smuggle the true facts of the case to London, where Richards and Charlton presumably were already having a free-for-all.

Both were to sail on the *Albert*, which had previously been chartered by Ladd and Company, and Marshall would merely be representing the merchants. The tangle of intrigue was further obfuscated by the simultaneous European ventures of Peter Brinsmade, who was trying to raise funds for that magnificent scheme of putting unemployed Hawaiians to work on the thousands of unoccupied acres which had been conditionally ceded to Ladd and Company. Marshall needed no other disguise than his association with Ladd.

So Consul Simpson and the most treacherous foe he could have scared up, the Envoy Extraordinary and Minister Plenipotentiary of the Hawaiian kingdom, set out together on March 11, 1843, as sociable shipmates, each hiding from the other his official papers. The contradictory documents eventually landed on the same desk in London.

As soon as his emissary was off, Paulet proceeded to set things to rights in the kingdom, freely expurgating missionary-inspired statutes, tampering with the courts, recruiting native troops, liberalizing liquor laws, and, of course, relaxing regulations on prostitution. "This has been an American government; now it is British," Judd was informed summarily in answer to an impassioned protest. He forthwith resigned from the commission, and the king refused to appoint a successor. For five months affairs went from bad to worse.

Meanwhile, with a confusion of rumors and reports drifting about the Pacific, Paulet's commanding officer, Admiral Thomas, got wind of the seizure, could not square the conflicting details with official orders he had received from the British government not to interfere with internal affairs in Hawaii, and put on sail for Honolulu. He arrived on July 26th and, to the humiliation of Lord George, at once declared the seizure "unauthorized" and reversed everything.

Five days later Hawaii regained her independence and made the

most of the occasion. "Lord George was not present," Laura Judd
cattily noted. "Foreign residents of all classes, missionaries and thousands of natives assembled at an early hour. . . . The splendid Hawaiian standard was unfurled. . . . Guns from the *Carysfort* and the other
English ships each poured forth a salute of twenty-one guns. . . . The
roar and reverberations were loud and long. As the cannons ceased,
thousands of human voices mingled in one patriotic cheer. Men and
boys, black, white and red, shouted themselves hoarse. . . . The king
and chiefs proceeded to the stone church, where, in the midst of the
great congregation, they gave thanks to their God for deliverance
from a foreign yoke." And Admiral Thomas won the satisfaction of
having a central square named for him.

Gerrit Judd would have been the last to deny that he was the
champion in that long bout. He was entitled to a little self-approba-
tion, for without his machinations the kingdom could have fallen apart
during those five months of occupation. If the good admiral had found
affairs in chaos, he would have felt obliged to put and keep them in
order, which undoubtedly would have become a permanent English
enterprise. The Islands came that close to membership in the British
Commonwealth.

The other diplomatic tyros buzzing about European and American
capitals all this time could not quite come up to the standard of parley
Judd set at home. They shed no tears upon learning that Simpson and
Charlton had both been relieved of their posts; they succeeded in
getting from England and France a joint declaration recognizing the
independence of Hawaii, but the United States declined to make it a
tripartite agreement. All they could wangle out of Washington was a
pronouncement from President Tyler conceding that the Islands were
independent and a hint that the Monroe Doctrine was being extended
to mid-Pacific. All other effort to get aid and comfort from Europe
and America was a resounding failure.

To Judd and his successors the Paulet incident was scarcely more
than a lively overture. Six years later France was at it again, still
dissatisfied with the Islanders' indifference to bishops and brandy. This
time the Honolulu fort was demolished, the monarchy once more

threatened, and Judd went off to America and Europe himself, prepared to auction off the sovereignty of Hawaii if he could not get a firmer guarantee of the kingdom's independent status.

He obtained little satisfaction in Europe, but he finally did get a commitment from the Secretary of State in Washington that the United States definitely did not want the pesky Islands, essentially for the same reasons that Charles Nordhoff unofficially outlined. Americans, however, reserved the right to change their minds as often as Englishmen or Frenchmen or Hawaiians. The final political decision was left to expediency—and sugar.

Despite the snipping, snubbing, and snarling, the greenhorn foreign statesmen in Honolulu muddled through and turned in a pretty good account for themselves. Their doings were written indelibly into the history of the Islands. As politicians and diplomats, they proved themselves to be not much more prone to error than the professionals for whom they blazed the way.

X

The Conquest of Cane

The Polynesians did not have granulated sugar in mind when they brought cane cuttings all the way from the South Seas to Hawaii. A snip of sugar cane itself was their confection, their substitute for licorice sticks and lollipops. They liked to chew it raw and had such a yen for it that no domestic establishment was complete without a clump. Standing cane served as a fence hedge and windbreak, cut cane and leaves as hut thatch. At lower altitudes it thrived luxuriantly and was so commonly raised that all the early *malihinis* assumed that cane was indigenous.

The Hawaiians grew five bantam-sized varieties, seldom reaching to a height of more than six or eight feet. All five played a part in the evolution of Hawaii's foremost industry, but cane was not crowned industrial king of the Islands until around 1870 and won the distinction then on sweeter, taller, plump-stalked specimens, far superior to what the natives had been gnawing for centuries. Moreover, cane was not eligible for enthronement until practically every other form of vegetation in the seed catalogue had been eliminated from the contest.

For years cotton and coffee were in on the runoff, competing closely with potatoes, oranges, mulberry trees, tobacco, wheat, and a score of secondary crops like corn, coconuts, grapes, bananas, and sisal. The elimination race was more speculative than methodical, refereed exclusively by *haoles,* rarely taking into consideration native appetites and interests. Since Hawaiians could never whip up much enthusiasm either for eating or cultivating imported grains and vegetables, the real planters, planners, and *lunas* were all foreigners; they had to carry the initiative.

Big ideas for growing something different in Hawaii seemed to come in waves, spreading over the Islands like an epidemic. Each new introduction was heralded as a money-maker's dowry that would yield profits shinier than the lucre from sandalwood. Each was pirated from the innovator to be tried out on a larger scale, on superior soil, with a superior strain, cheaper labor, better management, bigger returns. And while all these trials and errors were being made, conservative planters continued to putter away at the one crop they were sure would triumph in the end, sugar cane.

Farmer Don Marin, of course, had tried just about everything. Planters borrowed freely from his demonstrations, and few succeeded where he had failed. Out of all the fruits, vines, shrubs, grains, and vegetables with which he experimented, coffee was the first to be snatched up and developed into an agricultural craze. John Wilkinson, an English consumptive, sparked the fad.

Wilkinson had heard about the genial Hawaiian climate and decided that Honolulu was the one spot on earth where he might shake his ailment and make a fortune in the process, growing coffee. He arrived with George Anson Byron, Lord Byron, cousin of the poet, who brought the remains of Liholiho and his queen back to Hawaii on the *Blonde* in 1825. The immigrant was no agricultural tyro. He had already served his apprenticeship as planter in the West Indies and been highly successful at it, but the climate there did not agree with him. He was confident that Hawaii's weather would be more beneficial and that Hawaiian coffee would be even more productive than Caribbean.

En route to the Pacific he picked up a quantity of young coffee trees at Rio de Janeiro and upon reaching Honolulu persuaded Boki, the governor of Oahu, to grant him a lease of a hundred acres in Manoa Valley, two miles inland from Waikiki. Don Marin readily abetted the venture in view of his own experiments.

The coffee was planted, but the landlord was just skeptical enough of the outcome to insist that the rows be interspersed with sugar cane. Both did remarkably well, so well that Wilkinson was sold on the cane as much as the coffee and dispatched an order back home for a sugar mill of his own design.

The planter had not misjudged the adaptability of Hawaiian soil, but he had misjudged his own adaptability to the climate. Humid Manoa Valley was the worst kind of haven for a consumptive. The work, the worry, and the rain felled him before his first crop could be harvested. The plantation reverted to Boki, who was not imaginative enough to see much future in the red coffee beans. At any hour he preferred a glass of rum to a cup of black brew, so he dismissed the coffee experiment and resolved to use the cane for producing rum. A little pressure from the missionaries put an end to that venture, and the whole area was plowed up and planted to sweet potatoes.

Wilkinson's endeavor might have been entirely lost, had it not been for the ornery British consul, Richard Charlton, who had more vision than his friend Boki and was always ready to capitalize on someone's else initiative. He caught the coffee bug, salvaged some of Wilkinson's plants, imported more from Manila, and established another plantation in Manoa. The craze was on, and everybody suddenly wanted to grow coffee.

Missionaries in Kona heard of its success and persuaded the local chiefs to put commoners to work setting out plants. The Kona natives were fishermen, not farmers, and they made the mistake of tucking the plants into holes in the lava and brushing a few loose cinders around the roots.

It was the most profitable mistake ever made in Kona. The plants took hold in the rich porous lava, grew, and bore prolific crops of beans. An industry was born. From there it spread to Hanalei on Kauai and to other islands. In less than twenty-five years after Wilkinson had introduced the first large-scale plantings, Islanders were growing all the coffee they could drink, were wholesaling it to whalers and traders, and exporting some thirty tons a year. And that figure steadily rose in the following two decades to over two hundred tons.

Everyone was sure that coffee was going to be the real money-maker for the Islands. The prognosticators proved to be right about the success of the Kona product grown in the rough lava, but they were dead wrong about most other localities. The yield was disappointing; the flavor was disappointing; the demand was disappointing. Then a blight struck some of the best plantations on the northern islands. On Kauai the trees withered, died, and had to be pulled out.

It was a terrible setback to planters who had built up a stubborn faith in Hawaiian soil. "Plant sugar instead. That's the crop that will pay in the end," consoled the conservatives. But they were not very convincing. Bankrupt coffee growers turned instead to potatoes, which in the 1840's were becoming the biggest field crop exported from the Islands.

Barreled Irish potatoes were being lugged out of the hills in lots of a hundred at a time. The west slope of Haleakala was banded with a broad ribbon of potato fields stretching for miles. Whalers dined on mealy Maui spuds all the way to the Sea of Okhotsk and back again, and many an Argonaut digging in the foothills of the Sierra was saved from starvation by the same expensive tubers. Kula and a few other upland areas had a potato rush that was compared to the gold rush of California. Natives and strangers thronged up Haleakala, bought land at the exorbitant price of three dollars an acre, and called it "Nu Kalifornia."

But the rush was of short duration. Altogether too many potatoes were planted toward the last. The whaling trade slackened. Nobody bothered to let the Hawaiian growers know when Californians started cultivating their own gardens or when settlers in the Oregon country began to seed hundreds of acres for the California market. Prices dropped. The market was drugged. Then a disastrous drought struck Kula in 1851. The boom collapsed, and potatoes were left in the ground to rot. Hawaiians never did like the taste of them; so no sentiment was wasted on that calamity.

If an export product had to be raised, reasoned some of the more foresighted growers, perhaps sugar would be better in the long run. But the majority were not yet ready to accept the reasoning. Hardly was the Maui potato boom over when another was in the making, a little lower on Haleakala in the Makawao region. This time it was wheat, and Pastor Jonathan Green the advocate of the new indulgence.

Statesman Gerrit Judd had contrived the Great *Mahele,* the last step in casting out the ancient feudal system. Commoners could now possess their own farm plots, or *kuleanas.* To a people who had no conception of private ownership, it took a lot of explaining. Brother Green, who had really broken away from the brotherhood but still pastored his flock at Makawao, did his best to illustrate how the land division would work to advantage by urging members of his congregation to take small pieces of land and plant them in wheat.

Most of the parish followed his advice, and in a few years Makawao was one vast grain field. The wheat craze spread north and south among the Islands like the coffee craze. Green engineered the construction of a flour mill to grind the harvest; another factory was constructed in Honolulu in anticipation of bumper tonnages year after year. In 1855, 453 barrels of wheat flour were exported. Amateur economists were certain that the wheat boom would more than fill the slack of the expended potato boom.

At a meeting of the Royal Hawaiian Agricultural Society in 1852 the Reverend Green bravely asserted: "I feel that examples of practical agriculture would do more for the future temporal, political and moral state of Hawaii than whole pounds of precept. Of the latter there have been tons bestowed upon the Hawaiian race, to how little purpose the neglected fields around us too plainly tell. . . . As the rage for speculation seems to have spent itself, I may be able by another year to communicate on their behalf something of importance."

Green was trying to appear mysterious, but everyone knew he was talking about his great wheat experiment. It never occurred to him that he, too, was speculating; nor did it occur to the president of the Agricultural Society who later not only endorsed the planting scheme but boasted that Makawao flour had been his staple food for months and he hoped "never to eat another ounce of imported wheat."

The enthusiastic president was obliged to eat his words as well as Mainland wheat. By 1857 flour was selling for eleven and thirteen dollars a barrel in San Francisco; at the mills in Honolulu or Makawao it cost seventeen dollars. The millers had to charge that much to make ends meet. Makawao grain, or any other Island grain, simply could not compete with American grain. The boom Brother Green had tried to create died in infancy. Even the frustrated pastor agreed that sugar might make a better-paying proposition.

Meantime some of the other brethren on Maui were talking up silk culture as a means of keeping their congregations busy—and generous when the collection plate was passed. That brainstorm was plagiarized directly from the Connecticut homeland, where the legislature had once subsidized the industry by parceling out half-ounce packets of mulberry seeds to every parish in the commonwealth with planting instructions and where, as a result, factories produced more native silk yardage than in any other state in the union.

Mulberry groves planted around Wailuku, to feed the worms yet to be imported, did so well that Kauai stole the scheme. Two Yankee industrialists, Sherman Peck and Charles Titcomb, subleased some four hundred acres from Ladd and Company just before that trio failed. At Koloa, they planted thousands of mulberry trees, both native black and American stock. They were cutting out a giant-sized operation for themselves.

Silkworms brought in from China throve. Worms from the United States missed their winter hibernation and were a complete failure. Eggs were bottled and packed to the rainy five-thousand-foot crest of Waialeale Mountain to cool off. But they did not respond to that artificiality. Finally someone tried crossing the American worms with those from China and made a great discovery; the composite generations were the most productive silkworms yet developed.

At the peak of the silk fad there were a hundred thousand mulberry trees on the Peck and Titcomb ranch and half a million worms to feed on them. One hill crowned with the trees was such a magnificent sight that it was renamed "Mauna Kilika" (Silk Mountain). As the missionaries had predicted, Hawaiian women and children took to the new occupation as though it were a pastime. They were adept at handling the cocoons and at reeling and twisting the delicate filaments. Prospects were so hopeful that a competing company moved into Koloa, and Peck and Titcomb expanded to Hanalei.

Then, as if the Almighty disapproved of silk, one disaster after another struck. Unprecedented drought withered the mulberry leaves; aphids appeared from nowhere to cover bark and branches like a gauze and to suck the life out of the trees. Enormous spiders, with bodies the size of chestnuts, followed the aphidian invasion and attached themselves to the branches by the million. Day after day fierce dry trade winds battered the groves, and, as a final gesture, Kona gales swept in to whip off every remaining leaf from the trees. The destruction was complete. Peck and Titcomb turned to sugar.

The Civil War set off a new fling at cotton growing, and for a time it looked as though King Cotton might subdue King Cane. The soil and the climate were perfect; Hawaii had advantages that no section of the South could equal. Cotton could be picked ten months out of the twelve rather than for a few weeks in the fall, and, once started, it kept growing and did not have to be replanted more often than every fifth year. Moreover, it was not entirely a blind gamble. As with coffee, potatoes, and mulberry trees, Don Marin had demonstrated beyond a doubt that it matured rapidly and bore abundantly, and others had been making experimental plantings off and on for fifty years.

In 1812 two New England sea captains had surveyed some of the plantings, and were so impressed that they attempted to obtain a shipping monopoly on all future exports. The spinning and weaving classes at Wailuku Female Seminary had at least served as good object lessons in what could be done with cotton and had encouraged one enthusiast, Charles Smith, to start a plantation on Maui. Then, in 1837, the contagion reached the island of Hawaii, and the governor impetuously ordered the construction of a stone cotton factory at Kailua with two hand-operated looms and twenty spindles.

That venture, however, fell short of sensational success. Native mill hands objected to the confinement, the regular hours, and the long day. The gin was ineffective, and the supervision was ineffective. Kailua ran out of enthusiasm and cotton after two years, and the mill had to shut down. But no one was going to accept that experience as a sample of what would happen elsewhere; in time the minor difficulties of labor and operation could be overcome. They had to be overcome when planters showed that long-staple cotton, Sea Island, grew to a height of twenty feet in the Islands and yielded a much as a thousand pounds to an acre.

With the southern supply cut off from Union states in 1861 and prices at astronomical heights, little plantations began sprouting all over Hawaii, individual efforts for the most part, without benefit of centralized organization and technical guidance. There was no longer any need to operate mills near the source of supply, as New England factories were clamoring for all the raw cotton Hawaii could supply.

Inordinate delight was demonstrated over a token export of six hundred pounds in 1863; growers were more pleased when the figure jumped to 3,122 the following year, and they were sure that the boom was on when 22,289 pounds were shipped out in 1866.

But the Civil War was over then, and planters did not reckon on the recovery of the South. Never again was the 1866 record matched. There was a slump both in price and demand as soon as southern states resumed production, and a comparable slump in enthusiasm for Island cotton. Export poundage steadily declined until it was dropped entirely from the Customs House tables in 1875. The cotton growers were shifting to sugar.

With oranges the story was much the same. The seeds and cions that Vancouver and his contemporaries left were augmented with better grafts from far-off places until citrus trees were common landscaping in any back yard. A few planters set out great acreages. Claimed Mark Twain in 1865 after a trip into the Kona district: "We rode through one orange grove that had ten thousand trees in it! They were all laden with fruit." Making tenfold allowance for typical Twain hyperbole, one could safely guess that he saw at least a thousand trees in that grove. Several were of that size.

For years oranges had to be regarded as a fruit for local consumption, since they would not keep on the long voyage to New England. To supply the Saturday markets, natives trudged to town with bulging sacks of them balanced on the ends of their shoulder poles, and a great many were sold cheaply to whalers and trading vessels.

Not until the gold-rush days was there a market near enough to warrant taking the risk of shipping them in quantity, and then they were counted singly rather than by the dozen. Occasionally when there was an oversupply, oranges were used as ballast by ships headed for San Francisco with a light cargo, and complaints about the high rate of spoilage en route did not have to be exaggerated, for the fruit was literally dumped into a hold on a bed of loose hay, with layers of more hay pitched in for added protection.

Hanalei and the adjacent valleys on Kauai produced them by the shipload, and the Honolulu merchant Henry Peirce had a handsome grove in Lihue. In 1856 the old California river steamer *West Point,* heavily laden with oranges, left her moorings at Koloa to avoid a rising Kona storm. She didn't make it, and was wrecked on the rocks before she could clear the island. "For days," recalled a local resident, "the whole coast was yellow with Kauai oranges."

It took ten years for a seedling to become a bearing tree, too long for a profitable venture in Hawaii. And just as the older trees were beginning to show appreciable returns, a brand new aphid descended upon the groves. Like most of the afflictions affecting agriculture, the assault was called a blight. The result was the same, catastrophic. The foliage curled, wilted, yellowed; trees were left bare, except for scattered mangy fruit. "Oranges suffer from blight, and some of the finest groves have been cut down," understated a British traveler in cataloguing a long list of farming woes in 1873.

More pathetic were the reports of growers themselves. "The orchards are now completely clothed in a green carpet," wrote Henry Greenwell from Hawaii. "A few trees which are tolerably healthy are more thoroughly in bloom than I ever before witnessed. It has been usual for one side only of a tree to be covered with flowers, but this season the blossoms are to be found everywhere, from top to bottom and all around. Should the blight keep away . . . there should be a crop of 200,000 or 300,000; but I have no hope of the blight keeping away. The orange trees in the neighborhood are in the same condition as my own."

Greenwell's premonitions were well founded. The blight did not keep away. His trees, like thousands of others everywhere in the Islands, succumbed to the aphids, and were chopped down or snaked out by the roots to feed enormous bonfires. A few of the orchards were converted into cane fields, as though planting sugar were a last resort.

If the grove land had been boggy or better-watered, all the abandoned acres would have been seeded with rice, for rice was the next agricultural craze. Plantings of oriental varieties in the 1850's were not much more successful than coffee or wheat. Then, during the following decade, seed from South Carolina was brought in, and the grain flourished.

In an abandoned taro patch of less than a quarter of an acre a Honolulu physician, Dr. S. P. Ford, tried an experiment with just four pounds of seed, and from it harvested an astonishing yield of 1163 pounds. At that rate, he figured, an acre should produce close to four tons, an incredible harvest, and he made no secret of it.

The response to this revelation was electric. Immediately there was a run on taro patches, abandoned or not. Luxuriant growths of taro were pulled up and South Carolina rice planted in its place. Within a year there was a taro famine, and, according to one stretch of the truth, poi sold for approximately its weight in silver. That turn of affairs stirred a complete reversal; taro patches came back into their own, and there was a glut of poi.

Stabilizing the rice-taro market took a few uneasy years, and then rice leaped ahead until a million pounds were being exported in 1867 and about as much home-grown grain consumed in the Islands. Chinese immigrants, who had cultivated paddy in the old country, caught the fever and made far better rice growers than the *haoles*. They formed tight little companies—*huis*—of a dozen or more partners, leased all the taro patches in a valley, put native tenants to work on the patches, and cleaned up, even when rice was selling for two cents a pound.

The *huis* borrowed big organization ideas from Honolulu merchants and formed "rice factors." Sing Chong, founded in 1868, had some four thousand acres under cultivation on Oahu and, as a factor for other producers, controlled much of the production, virtually dictating the market price for years. That was the company that helped elevate rice to next-to-top place among Island crops and hold it there for a generation. By 1887, the peak production year, scores of individual farmers, as well as the *huis*, were equaling and sometimes surpassing that fabulous harvest of Dr. Ford.

Paddy did not bow to King Cane for the simple reason that it was grown in swampland, in salt marshes, or on hillside terraces entirely unsuited to sugar. But even with that advantage, cane would have crowded it out, had it not been for the unique combination of oriental planters and oriental consumers.

Periodically there seemed to be almost a touch of desperation among growers in the effort to find a real competitor to cane. They tried cassava and field corn, olives and onions, peanuts and *pulu*—the yellow wool on tree ferns. A banana devotee claimed that the Islands could grow twenty thousand acres of bananas; a cigar zealot wanted to plant thirty thousand to tobacco; sisal enthusiasts thought they could outbid Yucatan for the world market in cord fiber, and as many as three thousand acres of sisal were planted.

Mainland lumbermen thought they saw a great future in quick-growing Hawaiian timber and talked of reforesting the mountains. "One of the most profitable investments in the Islands," exclaimed a wheeler-dealer from the Coast. A German forester actually did make a small start on Kauai, and far-sighted conservationists imported dozens of varieties of trees from Europe, Asia, Australia, North and South

America for experimental plots, with the idea of determining what was most suitable for different altitudes. But tree growers had to look far into the future, and no one seemed ready to advance capital for an enterprise that would only benefit his heirs.

Recurrently, for more than a century, distillers kept bringing up ambitious plans for drowning the bourbon makers of the South in a flow of *okolehao,* the Polynesian intoxicant made from ti roots, which would grow anywhere, in any soil, at any altitude, with a minimum of care. Missionary influence quietly overruled that.

One by one the candidates for the agricultural crown were subordinated to King Cane. The elimination took years, but it was a clear victory in the end. Ironically, the contest might have been decided decades sooner, without all the preliminary parrying, if a single veteran Chinese sugar maker, brought to the Islands by a sandalwood trader in 1802, had been induced to remain.

The trader presumably had regaled the Cantonese expert with tall tales of tall Hawaiian cane, persuaded him to pack up his stone mill with the prospect of becoming a pioneer mid-Pacific industrialist, and taken him aboard. But the trader erroneously unloaded the mill and its operator on Lanai, the island with the least cane. The Chinaman did run a few batches of stalks through his rollers and produced a small quantity of sugar. Lanai, however, failed to match the billing of the trader, and it was a long way from home. The expert decided he had been gudgeoned and took the first available passage back to the orient. The mill went with him, and since the owner neglected to leave his card, Hawaii's first sugar maker remained anonymous.

For two decades after that, experimenters puttered around with mills of their own invention, wasting time on engineering problems that the Chinaman had licked. He had taken all his secrets with him. But the one thing he could not take away was an appetite for the sweet crystals that had been fixed among the upper-class Hawaiians.

Natives were put to work pounding cane stalks on their ancient poi boards and boiling down the juice. By March 5, 1811, someone had invented a contrivance that at least helped keep King Kamehameha's sugar bowl filled, for a tourist on the Yankee trader *New Hazard*

jotted in his diary under that date that he had gone ashore with the
captain and inspected the king's mill and boiler. But he kept all the
details to himself.

Eight years later, in February 1819, Don Marin produced sugar
and molasses in his back yard in Honolulu. The ingenious Spaniard,
however, was too preoccupied with wine making and rabbit breeding
to make a career of sugar manufacture. In 1823 an Italian immigrant
named Lavinia engaged a crew of unemployed Hawaiians and established the most streamlined processing plant to date by using great
numbers of poi boards and pounders. Until the monotony of the job
wore down the interest of his hirelings, Lavinia kept his copper kettles
boiling and a modest poundage of sugar moving to market.

Then the Chinese once more came to the rescue. Another trader, a
dealer in hides, enticed two oriental experts with the euphonic names
of Lau Ki and Ai Ko aboard his ship in Hong Kong and brought them
back to Waimea on Hawaii, where they created the first real cane
plantation and mill. The priority of that establishment, of course, is
disputed warmly by numerous community boosters who enter cate-
gorical claims that their locality was first, but Waimea's claim is as
sound as any.

"The cane was ground with mules," asserted an honest old *kanaka*
W. L. Kapu, who in 1908 still vividly recalled watching the operation
in his boyhood. "There were three short logs of wood that stood
upright; the middle one was the highest and to the top of this was
fastened a long timber, and the mules pulled around on this. The cane
was put in on one side of the middle piece and returned to the other.
The juice ran down into a trough and was carried to a larger pot.
When it was boiled, the sugar was taken and spread outside to dry on
mats. When dry the sugar was put in bags."

And without the least compunction, Kapu confessed to a certain
amount of pilferage at that 1825 mill. "I was only a boy then," he
reflected, "and one childish thing we did was this: when the Chinaman
went into his house, we ran and grabbed some sugar. That stuff was
something new, and it was good."

From Waimea Lau Ki and Ai Ko carried their art to Kohala and

Hilo, where they started similar plantations and mills. But, alas, even these experienced Chinese had to admit eventually that all three establishments were failures, commercially speaking. Too much galling labor went into the process for the small amount of sweetness that came out.

Nor did the Chinese hold a monopoly on failure. The mill that John Wilkinson ordered for his sugar and coffee plantation in Honolulu presumably was destroyed after his death, lest it be used for the manufacture of rum. Early mills at Wailuku and Waikapu on Maui met a similar fate. And longer tales of woe came from Kauai.

After giving proper assurance that he intended to make sugar, not rum, William French in 1835 entered into an odd partnership with the governor of Kauai, in which he would furnish the machinery and the governor would supply the cane and the horsepower for the grinding. French kept his rollers and boilers running for two years and at the end of the second season made history by exporting eight thousand pounds of sugar and about eight thousand gallons of molasses, the first sizable export and the first real hint of success in the business.

But the statistics gave the wrong impression. French was losing money fast. Though he was operating on shares with the governor, French was expected to take the risks, while the governor took the profits. He pulled out as soon as he could dissolve the partnership and shipped his mill to Oahu.

French had other reasons for moving, too; he was running into competition from the favored Ladd and Company. Where he had not been able to lease an acre of plantation land himself, the persuasive Ladd and Company partner, Peter Brinsmade, had succeeded in getting almost a thousand, including a waterfall. But French had the evil satisfaction of seeing his competitors encounter trouble also. Regional chiefs highly resented the expropriation of their land and prohibited natives from working for the company.

Not only that, they tabooed the sale of any provisions to the resident partner William Hooper, tabooed any association with him, and tabooed all wild cane with which Hooper had planned to plant his acres and feed his mill. He made no headway until he began paying tribute to the chiefs and buying off the natives, giving his laborers 12½ cents a day, a fabulous wage for men who had never received any regular compensation in their lives. For approximately a penny an hour, Hooper soon found that he could attract all the help he needed. Lacking draft animals, he hitched forty men to a plow and went to work.

With a mill not much better than Lau Ki's, Hooper made nothing but poor molasses the first year. He erected a better mill and turned out sugar that was still hardly marketable. Finally Ladd and Company went whole hog in 1841 and imported a mill with a pitch-back water-wheel that cost over fifteeen thousand dollars.

It produced excellent sugar that was shipped all the way to Sydney, Australia, to Valparaiso, Chile, and to eastern ports of the United States shipped so far that transportation costs absorbed most of the profits. The handwriting was on the wall. Ladd and Company was over-extended. Though Hooper had earned a place as hero among the sugar pioneers, he could not halt the inevitable.

Four years later the company went into bankruptcy, and the property was sold at sheriff's auction. The first successful sugar plantation was a conspicuous failure—until the new owner, Dr. Robert W. Wood, poured more money into it and turned the tide.

By mid-century more and more planters, divorced from oranges or cotton or wheat, were shifting to sugar despite all the failures. There were companies operating on a shoestring, companies with sound financial backing, Chinamen with not much more than their wits for capital, retired seamen and semirctircd professional men looking for something to do, and, of course, the missionaries. Picturesque little mills, with stone or wooden rollers, run by ox power, mule power, and water power, were springing up around the islands, almost as common as maple-sugar houses or cider mills in New England, and almost as crude.

Typical of the amateur operations was a mill operated at Waioli, Kauai, by missionary William Alexander and his parish as a means of financing church activities. They had planted seven acres of cane, hired the only two white carpenters on the island to knock together a small mill on the Chinese pattern, and haggled with a whaler captain until he was convinced it was his blessed privilege to contribute two second-hand iron try-pots to use as boilers. They were all set when harvest time came round: "Power was furnished by the pastor's horse, and the sugar, after being boiled in the try-pots, was dried in mat bags hung up to dry."

At the other end of the Island chain on the outskirts of Hilo was a representative lay establishment, operated by three Chinese, who had rigged up three vertical rollers and a long beam to turn them, then hitched to the beam a pair of half-tamed oxen that plodded round and round in a circle from dawn to dusk. A young Hawaiian boy squatted in the center of the scene, lazily pulling one stalk at a time from the pile of cane and thrusting an end between the rollers, ducking the beam every time it swung around.

Juice from the squeezed cane trickled into a flimsy wooden trough that extended to an adjacent shed, the boiling house. There three try-pots, like those at Waioli, bubbled and seethed under the watchful eyes of one of the proprietors, who darted about in the clouds of steam, pigtails flying, alternately stoking the fire with dried cane stalks and ladling hot syrup from the kettles into porous Chinese earthenware jars.

These allowed the molasses to drain off and at the same time retained the crystalized sugar. To catch the molasses, the jars were set in rough wooden "canoes," and these canoes impressed a squeamish visitor more than all the other makeshift contrivances together, for on the surface of the molasses, which he anticipated might be served at his own table in a few days, floated "dead flies, cockroaches and adventurous mice without number."

Yet that particular Chinese mill was such a success that when the same visitor returned to the site for another inspection a few months later, lo and behold, "the old bullock-mill had given way to a larger system of horizontal rollers, connected with a fine overshot waterwheel turned by a dashing stream."

The conversion of that Hilo mill was symbolic of the haste with which the whole industry developed as soon as planters and millers got together and resolved to move forward with purpose. The quaintness disappeared. Mechanization and capitalization made all the difference, notably when operations had the backing of big names like James

Makee, Paul Isenberg, James Campbell, Vlademar Knudsen, Samuel T. Alexander, Henry P. Baldwin, and Claus Spreckels. Sugar exports jumped from four tons in 1836 to 150 in 1845, to 722 in 1860, to over 7,000 in 1865, and that did not take into account local consumption or that unsanitary by-product molasses, which increased in volume during the same period from 8,000 to over 10,000 gallons a year.

Marvelous technical improvements came in rapid succession. Taller, sweeter cane, imported from Tahiti but called "Lahaina" because the first cargo of cuttings was discharged there, gradually supplanted the "indigenous" canes. Water power took the place of animal power at the mills, and then water yielded to steam. An ingenious Yankee mechanic, David Weston, invented a centrifugal machine that could separate sugar from molasses in minutes rather than weeks. The vacuum pan replaced the kettles. New methods of clarifying granulating sugar improved the quality of the crystals.

"Sugar is now the great interest in the islands," caroled an excursionist in the middle of the remarkable industrial change. "Christian missions and whaling have had their day, and now people talk sugar. Hawaii thrills to the news of a cent up or a cent down in the American market. All the interests of the kingdom are threatened by this one. . . . Were labor plentiful and the duties removed, fortunes might be made, for the soil yields on the average about three times as much as that of the state of Louisiana."

Church pastors, no longer getting financial support from Boston and struggling with the problem of finding some source of income for their congregations as well as themselves, savored the taste of sugar, too. William Alexander's little seven-acre project at Waioli, Kauai, was all right for defraying church expenses, but needed even more was grand-scale industry to fight off poverty in a whole community.

Father Elias Bond had racked his brain for years to contrive a way of halting the economic decline of the Kohala region on the Big Island. One by one he had tried most of the fruits and vegetables with which other mission stations had experimented, and none of them seemed to give Kohala a real lift.

"Finally," he concluded, "it came to me as clear as sunshine that it must be sugar cane, either grappled with at once or come to by a not tardy indirection. It was cane at once and cane only. My mind had become fixed on a prospective sugar plantation as the only possible way of retaining our people in Kohala *nei.* There was no work in the district by which people could earn a dollar. . . . It was a question of life and death." Through an enormous amount of hard work, unerring faith, and a whopping loan from Castle and Cooke, Father Bond established the great three thousand-acre Kohala Plantation, a model community enterprise that restored life to a region dying in isolation.

The wealthy Honolulu merchant and ex-captain, James Makee, created an entirely different kind of community. In 1855 he had given up merchandising for cattle ranching at Ulupalakua, high on the southwest slope of Maui's Haleakala. Within five years he subordinated cattle raising to cane raising and went all out for sugar, planting a thousand acres of cane and creating a baronial establishment overlooking the expanse, a magnificent mansion, guest houses, a village of outbuildings for Chinese and Hawaiian laborers, sugar mill, engine house, boiling house, a church with altar and organ, storehouses, even a billiard parlor and bowling alley. He named it Rose Ranch, and for a few years Rose was considered the largest and most expensive sugar estate in the Islands. A million dollars were poured into it, and some eight hundred tons of sugar annually came out of it.

Makee was as good a promoter as plantation manager and knew the value of fixing in the public mind some symbols for his super estate. He imported hundreds of peacocks to strut through his yards and fields, surrounded his mansion with a maze of flower gardens, roses, fuchsias, lilies, pansies, violets. "Nameless beauties without number attracted the eye at every turn amidst the labyrinth of walks," exclaimed a guest. He entertained the king there in princely style, escorting the royal party up the mountain from his private landings at Makena between files of eighty torchbearers and honoring them with a sumptuous *luau,* band music, and a grand ball.

But his greatest publicity coup came during the Civil War when he and his cane products gained international fame through the contribution of two hundred barrels of molasses to the United States Sanitary Commission, forerunner of the American Red Cross, headed by the renowned clergyman Dr. Henry W. Bellows. The first shipment of a hundred barrels sold at auction in San Francisco for two thousand four hundred dollars in gold, every dollar of which went toward the care of sick and wounded soldiers.

It was that sale that prompted the San Francisco *Morning Call* to publish the popular ballad "One Hundred Barrels More":

> " 'Tis coming, Father Bellows, one hundred barrels more;
> Molasses or the masses from Kamehameha's store.
>
> .   .   .   .
>
> Send on the sweet instalment of the patriot from afar,
> To where in hospital, or field our wounded heroes are,
> Then take the generous spigot out and let the fluid flow
> And let each lick the 'lasses, then on and lick the foe.
>
> .   .   .   .
>
> And let our blessings backward go to isles beyond the sea
> To crown the good philanthropist, the generous Makee."

The virtues of generous Jim Makee and his molasses were lauded across America. Even the Confederate states heard about him. He became the exemplar of Bellows' Sanitary Commission, as "One Hundred Barrels More" was reprinted from Sacramento to Syracuse.

But blessings at home did not crown the good philanthropist for long. In 1871 a fierce Kona hurricane swept across the mountain to level his cane and some thirty thousand eucalyptus trees he had planted, to destroy the mill, the engine house, the church, the bowling alley, and most of the laborers' cottages, to flood the other buildings and ruin all the refined sugar in storage. "It seemed as though the Furies were let loose," wrote Makee. "The hurricane was so terrific that trees, houses and everything about us was flying before the wind. . . . The air was literally full of branches and barrels and shingles."

It looked like the end of Rose Ranch, but Makee cheerfully vowed to "try again." Five years later he was back on his feet. The years

1876 and 1877 brought bumper crops that more than made up for all the storm losses. He started a second plantation on Kauai in partnership with King Kalakaua, a third at the foot of the West Maui Mountains in Waihee, and vastly extended his acres at Ulupalakua.

Then another catastrophe struck Rose Ranch, searing drought that lasted for eight months, from September 1877 to April 1878. Everything from the rose bushes to the cane dried up and withered. It spelled the downfall of the mountain plantation. A few more crops were harvested, but the cane acreage steadily declined until the last harvest was milled in 1883. Cows were turned into the cane fields, and Rose Sugar Ranch became Ulupalakua Cattle Ranch, under different ownership.

Cane raising was the wrong choice for gentlemen farmers. It was becoming increasingly evident that sugar production had to be a scientific operation and axiomatic that a successful plantation had to be a big plantation. The length and breadth of the fields and the size of the mills expanded. Fertilizers were introduced. A new deep plow turned up rich soil that had never before been disturbed. Heavy field equipment developed for use on the western plains, was adapted for use on Hawaiian fields. Steam power and portable railroads gradually took the place of mule, horse, and ox in the transportation of cane from field to mill. An idea was borrowed from the big lumbering operations of the West, and on hillsides where there was an ample head of water, flumes were constructed to float cane to the mills.

Someone figured out that in growing enough cane to make a five-pound bag of sugar, twenty thousand pounds of water had to be brought to the fields. Normal rains dropped that much on the windward sides of the Islands, while sheltered leeward sides went dry. The ultimate future of the cane industry depended on distribution of water.

The planters well knew that water conservation and irrigation were the salvation of California agriculture, and they had seen the remnants of superb irrigation systems built by former generations of Hawaiians. Tens of thousands of arid Island acres could be turned into fertile cane fields by salvaging water from some of the rampaging streams that ran off into the ocean. So they started building ditches that got longer and longer. They were supplemented by tunnels blasted through the mountains to shorten the course and to catch veins of underground water. Then they started drilling wells to cut into subterranean rivers and reservoirs.

Maui offered a prime example. In 1876 two missionary sons, Samuel Alexander and Henry Baldwin, built the Hamakua Ditch, a seventeen-mile irrigation canal that brought forty million gallons of water a day from the wet windward side of Haleakala to their plantation on the barren Maui isthmus. Claus Spreckels, the wealthy Mainland tycoon and operator of the largest sugar refinery on the Coast, saw what they had done, moved to Maui, conned a Hawaiian princess into selling him twenty-four thousand acres of adjacent desert for the scandalous bargain of ten thousand dollars, and built a thirty-mile ditch that would deliver to his land fifty million gallons a day, almost the amount of water used daily by the city of San Francisco. Then he tapped the West Maui Mountains above Waihee for another ditch.

"Sand, sand, sand!" cried the indefatigable tourist Isabella Bird, after crossing the future site of those Maui plantations in the early seventies. "Sand hills, smooth and red; sand plains, rippled, white and glaring; sand drifts shifting; sand clouds whirling; sand in your eyes, nose and mouth; sand stinging your face like pin points; sand hiding even your horse's ears; sand rippling like waves, hissing like spindrift, malignant, venomous. . . . The track from Wailuku to Haiku is over a Sahara in miniature, a dreary expanse of sand and drifting sand hills, with a rare, dismal growth of thornless thistles and indigo. Tractless, glaring, choking, a guide is absolutely necessary to a stranger, for the footprints or wheel marks of one moment are obliterated the next."

Eventually that whole wind-blown Sahara was converted through irrigation into lush cane fields, and in the middle of them was erected one of the largest sugar plants ever built. Yet even that represented a relatively small part of the total Island industry, destined to spread out over a quarter of a million acres and produce over a million tons of sugar a year.

Those expansive Hawaiian cane fields proved to be more productive than any others in the world. But the soil alone was not responsible. In 1900 there were fifty-six sugar plantations in the Islands. Though the acreage after that steadily increased, the number of plantations decreased until the total was less than half that number. The plantations merged; they competed; they cooperated. Cooperation was the fundamental secret of their success.

Resources were pooled to create the Hawaiian Sugar Planters Association and an Experiment Station. The start came in 1895 with the joint hiring of a chemist to do research on fertilizers, and gradually the scope was broadened to include development of hybrid canes better adapted to local culture, control of common pests and diseases, and assistance in agricultural projects unrelated to sugar.

Ten years after starting the Experiment Station, the planters again combined their resources to form a refining and marketing cooperative, the California and Hawaiian Sugar Refining Corporation. It was the readiness of planters to cooperate as well as compete that established sugar as the foremost Island industry.

But just before the turn of the century, one last challenger threatened to start all over again the contest for agricultural supremacy. This time the rival was in the shape of a South American pineapple, an exotic fruit that Don Marin had toyed with in his Honolulu garden more than eighty years earlier.

Don Marin, however, was not entitled to any acclaim for introducing pineapples. They were growing wild around Kailua, Hawaii, before he arrived in 1791. The Hawaiians called them *hala-kahiki* (foreign screw pine or pandanus) because they resembled the fruit of that tree, and no one ever puzzled out how they reached Kailua, unless they were brought by one of the sixteenth-century mystery ships of the Spanish or by Captain Cook, who was credited with starting pineapples in the Friendly Islands, the Society Group, and at several other South Pacific landfalls.

The Wild Kailua variety was puny, acid, and fibrous, and, though the plant was as hardy as a thistle, the fruit was subject to quick rot after the slightest handling. It was more of a curiosity than a potential trade item, and it retained that status until 1882, when an English sea captain with a flair for horticulture, John Kidwell, retired to Honolulu and started growing imports. In the course of three or four years he brought in some three dozen varieties and, giving each a try, planted acres of them in Manoa Valley on land that was to become the campus of the University of Hawaii.

All the varieties were discarded as inferior except the "Queen" and the "Smooth Cayenne." From those campus plots grew an industry that would eventually cover seventy thousand acres. Kidwell's efforts were assisted by another Britisher, E. W. Jordan, who, in the interests of Hawaiian agriculture, had started a plant- and shrub-importing business at Honolulu and who, after seeing what Kidwell had accomplished, took a big gamble in 1896 and brought in from Queensland, Australia, a million Smooth Cayenne plants.

But Hawaii was not yet in the pineapple business. Locally the new *hala-kahiki* was a luscious fruit, but, when picked green for shipment to the Coast, half the pack rotted en route. Canning was tried, and the result was not only unsatisfactory but unnerving. So many of the cans exploded that the warehouse where they were stored echoed with the ruckus of a Chinese wedding, and anyone entering the storage area ran the risk of getting showered with pineapple shrapnel. The industry did not present a very encouraging picture. In 1899 fewer than eighty acres in the islands were devoted to pineapples, and it looked as though some of them might more profitably be turned to onions or alfalfa.

That was the year that James D. Dole, distant relative of the missionary son Sanford Dole, arrived and changed everything. He optimistically planted, as a starter, sixty acres at Wahiawa above Pearl Harbor, organized the Hawaiian Pineapple Company, delved into the chemistry of canning, and on the northern outskirts of Honolulu built a factory that was to become the world's largest fruit cannery. His first pack in 1903 was 1,893 cases; thirty years later it was 5,000,000.

From the beginning, it was clear to Dole that the Hawaiian Islands could produce a lot more pineapples than grocery stores the world over were ever likely to sell; the real problem with pineapples was developing a consumer's taste for them. In one of the first grand-scale household advertising campaigns, he developed that taste and changed his product from a rare luxury to a fruit staple.

None of the pioneering was easy. Pineapples attracted more pests than all the oranges, mulberry trees, and coffee of previous generations put together, and they too would have been given up if a new arsenal of agricultural weapons, chemicals and insecticides had not been invented in the interim to combat the infestation.

In 1922 the Dole company purchased almost the entire island of Lanai and converted it into the "Isle of Pines." But Dole was not the pineapple dictator for long. Competition soon harried the company like fruit flies. To profit from Dole's whirlwind popularizing campaign, big Mainland canning corporations set up huge subsidiaries in the Islands. The industry kept expanding; it produced more than half the world's supply of pineapple products, easily climbed to second place on Hawaii's production scale, and occasionally rubbed sugar for first place.

Pineapples, however, infringed relatively little on terrain that would profitably produce sugar, for they grew either in dry coastal areas where there was insufficient water at the right time for cane or at elevations above two thousand feet, too high for the big irrigation ditches. So the two industries could always prosper amicably.

But prosperity for any Island crop depended on the man with a hoe, a machete, an insect gun, and a strong back. Ever since the planters first began to face the fact that Hawaiians were dying off and the survivors were not enthusiastic field hands, labor had been their major worry. It continued to be.

XI

Invasion by Invitation

The missionary conception of farming was the Yankee conception; barn and barnyard, chicken coop, family cow, family horse, workshop and woodpile, pigpen, pasture and garden patch—everything needed to make a household self-reliant in a pinch. That was what the New England apostles had in mind for the Sandwich Islanders.

To replace the ancient agricultural system dominated by the chiefs, they envisoned little family-sized farms dotting the landscape everywhere, exactly as they did in rural Connecticut, New Hampshire—or Pennsylvania. It was the sensible, orderly way for any people dependent on the soil to make a living.

In advocating a redistribution of the king's realm into fee-simple plots for all the people during the 1840's, Dr. Judd was trying to realize this dream, and he was persuasively abetted by most of his *haole* cabinet. "Even the poorest of Your Majesty's subjects would stand on a footing of independent right," argued the Scotch Foreign Minister, Robert C. Wyllie, to Kamehameha III. "He would know that the land he cultivated was his own and could not be taken from him; and he would have the powerful self-interest to improve it, and make a good dwelling on it." Wyllie and Judd wanted to see Hawaiian common ownership exchanged for the British-American type of private enterprise.

By a slow wearing away at royal resistance over almost a decade, the dividing of the lands into homesteads, the Great *Mahele,* was finally brought about in 1848. The king retained a vast estate, which he considered appropriate to a monarch; he surrendered a third of the remainder to the "government," a third to the chiefs, and a third to the commoners.

But it did not work out according to the master plan of the missionaries and minister Wyllie. By 1855, when most of the parceling was complete, it still looked as though the masses had the raw end of the deal. Crown lands totaled some 984,000 acres, government lands 1,495,000, chiefs' lands 1,619,000, and the private claims of commoners a mere 28,600. Out of a total population of close to 70,000 natives, only about 11,000 families had acquired any land at all, and the private holdings—*kuleanas*—inconsistently ran anywhere from a few square rods to forty acres, with the average plot less than five acres.

The comparative figures did not tell the whole truth; actually the 28,600 acres in *kuleanas* were tillable and well-watered, representing some of the best agricultural soil in the kingdom, whereas the expanses taken by the chiefs, the government, and the king included desert, lava fields, swamp, and forest, along with blocks of more habitable terrain. But even with large allowances for that, there was little equity for commoners.

In most cases, the sites occupied by commoners at the time of the *mahele* could have become theirs for the asking and the payment of a small fee. They did not even bother to file claims. A people that had always considered land indivisible in the same way as sky and ocean were common endowments simply did not understand the meaning and value of private ownership. They were afraid of incurring the resentment of a chief by attempting to take possession of land he had held; a great many interpreted the individual allotment of property as a ruse, a way of encouraging commoners to improve their lands and build better homes, which would then be appropriated by the chiefs.

They could not comprehend how a fold of paper, the title, could represent property. At mid-century, agricultural land was selling anywhere from 25 cents to $1.50 an acre. Fees for surveying and processing claims were $6 or $12, depending on the size; it did not make sense to pay more for filing a claim than the land was worth.

Moreover, Hawaiians soon discovered that after a survey had been certified, recorded, and paid for, it was still subject to dispute. The bounds were seldom marked, or, if marked, the stakes or stones were innocently removed. *Kuleanas* were in every imaginable size and shape, without reference to butts and bounds of adjacent parcels; they overlapped or left narrow strips of unclaimed land between.

The dividing of the lands was done in such haste and by such ill-equipped surveyors that fantastic errors were made. Chains of different lengths were used, ship's compasses and pocket compasses, with no allowance for local magnetic variations. Waikiki, for example, was surveyed by a dozen amateurs, none of whom knew what the others were up to and none of whom bothered to square their bounds with adjoining bounds. Those slipshod surveys were going to plague realtors as long as the Islands rose above the waters of the Pacific.

The Great *Mahele* was far more important politically than agriculturally. Whether or not the commoners realized it, it was almost the equivalent of an emancipation proclamation; they were at last out of bondage to the chiefs; they had won independence, the right to work for themselves on their own land. Serfdom was exchanged for freedom. Yet hard as the missionaries and assorted government officials had tried to prepare them for the new economic and social status, the majority were unable to grasp the implications and profit from them.

The bright vision of little independent farmsteads dotting the shores and uplands, Yankee style, faded quickly. Here and there owners were persuaded by *haole* altruists to plant their newly acquired acres to something like wheat or cane or cotton or coffee in community industrial projects, but few of the schemes survived for long. Hawaiians seemed incapable of catching on to the western concept of a diversified farm, and in many cases the *kuleanas* were not large enough to sustain a family anyway.

Too often the emancipation of the *Mahele* meant freedom from responsibility. Natives had always been addicted to wanderlust. Once out from under the thumb of a chief and on their own, they felt at liberty to come and go as they chose, to the neglect of their holdings, if they had any. They sought naïvely for new tokens of status in *haole* clothes and *haole* habits. Their exemplars lived in town; so they flocked to Honolulu or Lahaina or Hilo.

Unfortunately the liberation came during the period when ownership of a horse was beginning to be accepted as the most conspicuous symbol of wealth and standing. Scant earnings went toward the acquisition of a horse rather than investment in income-producing farm equipment. One horse was not enough. Hawaiians went horse crazy. Every member of the family had to have an animal for his individual wanderings. Many a *kuleana* became little more than a paddock.

Those who acquired land had no idea of its value. Hundreds of individual holdings were unceremoniously abandoned. More were impetuously sold to white speculators or plantation proprietors for small but dazzling cash. Many were leased to planters for short terms, and once a *kuleana* was incorporated in the middle of a sprawling cane field, the landmarks were lost, the boundaries forgotten, and its recovery not worth all the necessary litigation.

Far from accomplishing what Wyllie, Judd, and the missionaries had visualized, the *Mahele* merely opened the way for supremacy of the giant sugar and pineapple plantations, for the subordination of natives into a new kind of serfdom, and for their displacement as Island inheritors by a motley host of *haoles*, Chinese, Portuguese, Japanese, Puerto Ricans, Koreans, Filipinos, the most sweeping invasion yet, a dispossession almost as complete as that of the North American Indians.

It was the defeat of the missionary effort to spot the Islands with those little independent farms that resulted ultimately in Hawaii's being taken over by plantations and turned into a racial melting pot. The displacement came slowly at first. No one could complain that the Hawaiians were not given a fair tryout as farm laborers. They were the only field hands the early planters had, and patience beyond the call of duty was exercised in attempting to put them to work at cane cultivating.

They would work with energy and spirit—for a few days or hours. Then they would disappear. The simple fact was that natives were wise enough to realize that they could supply their primitive living requirements in much less arduous and far more pleasant endeavor than dragging a plow, hoeing cane, or harvesting it, even when earning an enticing penny or two an hour.

For a short time William Hooper of Ladd and Company, who managed on Kauai the first sizable Island cane plantation, was delighted with his employees. But the delight quickly gave way to exasperation. He served as his own field *luna,* supervising some four hundred men, and tried to set an example by working with them, indulging in the same stoop labor, digging, planting, hauling, cutting, putting in the ten-hour day he expected of the natives.

It was hopeless. In desperation he wrote to his partners at the end of three years that his experiments proved only "the complete worthlessness of Sandwich Islanders as laborers on a farm." His four hundred *kanakas,* he claimed, were doing the work of ten poor white laborers or "2½ smart Yankees."

The same reaction was echoed by cleric-historian G. W. Bates, who, after observing Hawaiians at work, concluded: "No beast of prey watches his victim with a closer scrutiny than the *kanaka* watches his employer. In his presence he makes every effort to appear active and useful; but the minute he disappears, it is a signal for a general cessation of work, and one keeps a 'look-out' while the group indulges in every variety of gossip. On the reappearance of their master, the sentinel gives the alarm, and every man is found to be at work as though he meant never to lay down his tools. The owner may have watched them through a clump of foliage; but they will swear him out of the use of his eyes, and insist on it that he was altogether mistaken."

The Ladd and Company plantation had many other problems, but it failed largely because Hooper could not find satisfactory labor, and most of the other pioneering planters failed for the same reason. The help was unreliable, shiftless, lazy. And the sad thing was that these traits did not characterize Hawaiians until the intrusion of civilization had altered their perspective and destroyed their morale.

For almost two decades the planters made do with native labor. They even prevailed upon the king to legislate against laziness. A royal decree of 1842 penalized chiefs for harboring the "sluggard." "Let him obtain his food by labor," demanded the king. Tenants whose land was found overgrown with weeds were to be dispossessed. Tax officers were ordered to pick up idlers and put them to work for the government. Supplementary legislation of 1846 empowered the Minister of the Interior to seize vagrants and apprentice them for periods up to a full year.

But outlawing lassitude had little effect. Plantation labor did not improve. There was less of it because of the declining population and because of the large number who went off on whaling expeditions or to California as gold diggers after 1848, but actually there was no dearth of physically fit Hawaiian workmen during those years. The problem was qualitative, not quantitative. Foreign Minister Wyllie, who was inclined to be more charitable than commercial men, grumbled that nowhere in the Islands could natives be found regularly or gainfully employed, that their average workday, year in and year out, amounted to less than four hours.

For years traders had been bringing back from Hong Kong or Canton delegations of Chinese to experiment with sugar milling, rice culture, or general merchandising. They had settled on all the larger islands and fitted comfortably into the population. *Haoles* regarded them as industrious, cooperative, and enterprising, and by the late forties all the planters were talking up coolie labor. In fact, one of the principal incentives that stirred the creation of the Royal Hawaiian

Agricultural Society in 1850 was the possibility of its taking collective action for the procurement of oriental workers.

Before the society was a year old, it did act. The *Thetis,* under Captain Cass, was dispatched to Hong Kong for a shipload of recruits. It returned in January 1852 with almost two hundred, and they were followed six months later by another hundred. The invasion was on. They were the first waves of the tens of thousands to come.

There was nothing unusual about the coolie recruitment. It was a common practice that belonged to the era, whether the project were gold mining in Australia, harbor construction in South America, or railroad building in the West. An agent called at a Chinese port, set up headquarters in a public place, and advertised for laborers. From the swarms that applied, the ruggedest were chosen. Each signed a five-year contract, under which the Hawaiian planter agreed to provide free transportation; to feed, clothe, and house the emigrant; to pay him three dollars a month; and to repatriate him at the end of five years, unless he decided to renew his contract or remain in the Islands as a free worker.

It was a good bargain for both planter and recruit. The cost of recruiting and transportation came to about fifty dollars per man and maintenance to around sixty dollars a year, so that the total monthly cost ran to approximately nine dollars. And the coolie himself had reason to be equally satisfied. Nowhere in China was an unskilled laborer likely to earn a comparable wage, with keep, and though the "keep" was on the shoddy side, it was better than anything he could count on in Asia and not inconsistent with maintenance of contract labor anywhere else in the world.

In general, the imported Chinese came up to expectations. They took without complaint such indignities as being ordered to strip and stand for inspection of teeth, body, and build, exactly like a slave in the southlands, and if they did not understand directives delivered in clear English, floggings or fist wielding usually brought quick comprehension. They were docile, and they were cheap. Even with allowance for transportation expenses, planters found that they cost less than native laborers and were far more steady and competent on the job. But there never were enough of them. Only thirteen hundred of these soldiers of the sugar-cane fields saw service during the thirteen years between 1852 and 1865.

The most distressing sequel to the importation of Chinese was that very few of them, after their five-year contract was up, could be persuaded to sign on for a second hitch. Nor were they eager to get back to China. They wanted to remain in the Islands. Like the Hawaiians, they drifted into the towns, but unlike the Hawaiians, they took jobs as mechanics, carpenters, cooks, tailors, peddlers, waiters, artisans, gardeners, and handy men, quickly showing that they were just as skillful in these kinds of employment as white men. Worse still, they opened shops, bakeries, restaurants, laundries, and groceries and went into annoying competition with their hosts.

In town and on the plantations, they ganged up, lived together, stubbornly stood up for what they considered their rights once they were acclimated, and were as successful suitors of *wahines* as Americans and Europeans, with one notable difference in the wooing—they married the girls and made good husbands and fathers.

Plantation managers and government officials were wise enough to foresee that foreigners putting up such a united front would soon bring serious problems of control both to the cane fields and to commerce. A closely knit racial group on the plantations could band together and take a frightening stand on controversial issues like living conditions and wages. Needed was a mixture of races that would be incapable of organizing a social solidarity, crews that could be held in check and played off against each other.

Kamehameha III, who heartily resented seeing his kingdom diluted with an entirely new breed of disputatious aliens, sided with the planters and offered his panacea. He wanted to substitute Polynesians for orientals and evolved a scheme for moving the entire population of Pitcairn Island to Hawaii.

Feelers sent to the sons and daughters of the *Bounty* mutineers found them surprisingly receptive to the idea. They could have undoubtedly been talked into packing up and moving north, but when the British Consul insisted that they come as British subjects and remain as British subjects, the invitation was hastily withdrawn.

In 1855 Kamehameha IV revived the plan but applied it to other

South Sea islands. "It becomes a question of some moment whether
a class of persons more like the Hawaiian race could not be induced to
settle on our shores . . . ," he declaimed. "In a few days they would
speak our language with ease; they would be acclimated almost before
they left the ships that conveyed them hither; and they might bring
their wives. . . . Such immigrants, besides supplying the present demand for labor, would pave the way for a future population of native-
born Hawaiians, between whom and those of aboriginal parents no
distinguishable difference would exist."

It was a capital idea, but it had a flaw. Polynesians in the other
islands were dying off as rapidly as their Hawaiian cousins, and foreign governments holding jurisdiction over the domains heartily op-
posed any further diminishing of the population. A few years later,
despite political objections, a few Micronesians and some two thousand Polynesians, mostly Gilbert islanders, were brought in, and again
the king's judgment was at fault. They proved to be highly unsatisfactory and poorly adapted to plantation employment.

Meanwhile, commissioners were scouring the globe for other substitutes for the Chinese. The nationality did not matter, so long as they
were tractable, energetic men, who would not demand more pay than
the coolies and would assimilate with the Hawaiians. In recognition of
the acute labor shortage, an official Bureau of Immigration was established in 1864 to take over the recruiting responsibilities that the
Agricultural Society had previously assumed.

Pending receipt of reports from other parts of the world, Dr. William Hillebrand, Honolulu's respected, nonmissionary German physician, was hurried off to Asia to round up stopgap labor. He foraged
along the coast of southeast Asia, pried into the Malay Archipelago,
and went on to India, all with discouraging results. Finally the best
deal he could make was still with the Chinese, and he left agents to do
the recruiting. They returned the following year with five hundred
contract coolies, trailed by a scandalous reputation for "blackbirding,"
trickery, and kidnapping. It was an ornery, discontented lot.

With the rise in sugar prices during the Civil War and the conse-
quent expansion in cane acreage, planters were desperate for help.

Commissioners again tried to interest Malays and Hindus, without success. Wages were advanced, the working day temporarily shortened to nine hours, flogging banned, and living conditions on the plantations generally improved. Those measures at least helped to retain what labor there was.

To publicize the golden opportunities in the Islands, the Hawaiian government stationed a consul in Japan, and in 1868 he coaxed a group of 148 Japanese to accept three-year contracts. But they did not endear themselves to plantation managers, could not acclimate themselves to the Island way of living, and constantly grumbled about interpretations of their contracts. Forty of them were shipped back home after complaining too bitterly about their ill-treatment. Yet when the contracts for the remainder expired, only thirteen chose to return to Japan. Altogether they had made such a poor impression that Hawaii saw no more Japanese recruits for almost twenty years.

Then, as if responding to a new order of events, Hawaiians started to show more interest in cane growing and began signing up in greater numbers for one-year contracts. Perhaps they had profited from the example set by the coolies; perhaps it was a rebirth of pride; perhaps it was the inducement of earning as much as thirty, forty, and fifty cents a day; but their attitude had changed. Some of the lassitude and the devil-may-care spirit was disappearing. They wanted to work; they wanted particularly to boss other workers, to become *lunas*.

It was such a remarkable reversal that Charles Nordhoff, after observing the natives at work, felt called upon to congratulate plantation managers on their good fortune in having such capable field hands. The sugar planter, he declared, has "a laboring population perhaps the best, the most easily managed, the kindliest and—so far as habits affect the steadiness and usefulness of the laborer—the least vicious in the world." Nordhoff had compliments for the Chinese, too; but the Hawaiians were his favorites. In accepting contracts as plantation workers, they were unconsciously returning to the old paternalistic serf system they had known under the chiefs.

However, it was late for the rightful job claimants to make amends and volunteer their services, and they were now all too few. While their numbers had been declining pathetically, plantation acres had been increasing phenomenally. Thousands of men were needed to cope with a boom brought on by the passage of the reciprocity treaty with the United States in 1875. And, by an odd accident, substitutes for the unwelcome Chinese were at last located on the other side of the globe, substitutes en masse, in the last place any commissioner would have deliberately investigated, the Madeira Islands off the African coast of Morocco.

Dr. Hillebrand had returned to Europe in 1871. While in the Islands, his hobby had been classifying Hawaiian flora; he took the hobby back to Germany with him and a few years later sailed to Madeira for a continuance of his study of tropical botany. But on arriving at Funchal, he temporarily dropped his botany for sociology.

Madeira was as tragically overpopulated as Hawaii was underpopulated. Here indeed, decided the doctor, were the laborers Hawaii wanted. The two island groups had a similar climate, and both were primarily agricultural; so there would be no problem of adaptation or assimilation. The Madeirians were a hardy south European peasant stock, primarily Portuguese, exactly what Hawaii needed. Before Hillebrand left, he had made travel arrangements for 180.

It was the start of a great migration from eastern Atlantic to mid-Pacific. In the next four decades some twenty thousand men, women, and children of Portuguese extraction, from Madeira, the Azores, and the Iberian Peninsula, were to make that trip halfway around the world. They went as permanent settlers, not short termers, and they took with them their wives and families, their belongings, their ancestral traditions, their embroidery, music, appetites, and sentiment.

They readily accepted residence in plantation hovels, without any hankering to open shops, crowd into the cities, or compete with either the Americans or the Chinese, and for years they were the backbone of labor on many a plantation—until they had put aside enough of their earnings to buy a little farm or a perch on the back slopes of Punchbowl in Honolulu. They were superb workers, but never quite accepted as full-fledged *haoles*.

Still the flow of Portuguese was not enough. Repeated attempts were made to induce other Europeans to settle in the Islands. One of the Big Five, Theo. H. Davies, imported Scotch plowmen, teamsters, and clerks and made it fashionable for plantations to be supervised by frugal, hard-driving Scots. Paul Isenberg, whose family controlled another of the Big Five, H. Hackfeld and Company, brought a considerable number of Germans to Kauai. And Vlademar Knudsen, son of the president of Norway, turned Hawaiian planter, was instrumental in recruiting over six hundred Norwegians.

But the planters soon regretted the choice of Germans and Norwegians. These Europeans complained that they had been duped, that promises made by recruiting agents were ignored; the Germans demanded beer and *bratwurst* at their table; the Norwegians demanded butter and Irish potatoes; both demanded better housing and better pay. Unfortunately they were literate and kept writing letters home and to the newspapers about their hardships, until the San Francisco *Chronicle* was accusing the plantations of harboring "modern slavery" and the European press was picturing Hawaii as another Devil's Island. Literacy and *luna* dictatorship made poor companions.

Again coolies had to be summoned to take the place of the wretched northern Europeans. Between 1875 and 1887, over twenty-five thousand more were imported, against reverberating reminders of the "Yellow Peril" they imposed. Oddly enough, a third of them came not from China, but from the United States. The completion of the Union Pacific, the petering out of the gold fields, and mass emigration from the East had left thousands of Chinese unwanted, unemployed, and tormented on the West Coast. Hawaii was the new land of opportunity for them and at least a little nearer home.

Fears were expressed in the early eighties that the Islands were about to be overwhelmed by the Chinese legions, and legislation was passed to curtail their importation. The laws, however, were freely disregarded. Before the end of the decade, they comprised a fifth of the population, and were ganging up more than ever, asserting their rights in no uncertain terms, becoming contentious, and forever squabbling with the natives, many of whom had risen in rank to *lunas* and were bossing the coolies.

Under such conditions, running a plantation called for the patience of a Job and the diplomacy of a Solomon. "If a single instance of injustice were perpetrated," sympathized Isabella Bird, "the factory might stand still the next year."

The idea of reducing troublesome clannishness by having several races represented on a plantation had not yet proved effective. "Why not give the Japanese another try?" queried the planters. They took the query to King Kalakaua, and on a round-the-world cruise in the early eighties, he took it to Tokyo and did his level best to intercede for the planters. The magnificent reception he was given there played on his vanity, and he was ever after a little partial to the Japanese. His personal overtures were unsuccessful, but as soon as he returned to Honolulu, he dispatched an emissary to amplify the pleas for emigrant labor. That mission, too, was a failure.

Finally nature came to the rescue. Southern Japan was stricken with drought. Farmers in Honshu and Kyushu suffered almost total crop failure for a succession of seasons, and peasants were starving. They had to be given relief in some form; so in 1886 the Emperor at last relented and authorized Hawaiian representatives to draft his subjects for the mutual benefit of both nations.

Recruiting agents rode into villages of southern Honshu, of Kyushu, and Okinawa, spinning fairy tales of glorious Hawaiian scenery, the perpetual summer, and overflowing wealth. Peasants applied in hordes. Two thousand shipped out the first year. The bars were down. Before the great migration ceased two decades later, 180,-000 had disembarked at Honolulu.

They did not represent Japan's most distinguished citizenry. Virtually all were from the plebeian farm class, ranking far below the *samurai*, artisan, and merchant groups. They had lived in abject poverty. Compared to provinces they had known, Hawaii was a land of luxury. The plantation masters knew it and never let them forget it.

Everything that the agents had told them about the Islands was true. The mountains and the sea were beautiful; the climate was pleasant; and they were surrounded with evidence of wealth and abundance such as they had never seen at home. The manager's mansion on the hill overlooking the plantation stood forth in awesome splendor; the homes of the overseers were impressive; the mill was a mechanical wonder.

But a worker quickly learned that none of the luxury was for him. The agents had told the truth, but not the whole truth. They had failed to go into detail on living quarters, the exact nature of the work, the character of the supervision, or the lack of freedom to enjoy their surroundings. The new home was a secluded camp in the middle of a dust-swept cane field, a clutter of shacks and sheds into which the men were herded, a dozen or twenty to a dormitory. The only privacy an individual possessed was that of his canvas bunk or, for a married couple, a single room ten feet square, separated from a line of similar rooms by a head-high partition.

Workers shared common, homemade cooking stoves, common outhouses, a common outside spigot. To the furnished appurtenances, the Japanese soon added little shrines, where homage was paid to deceased parents and ancestors, and crude community baths, where men and women could soak together after a day in the fields.

The demands of the work had been underplayed by the agents, too. Planting, weeding, irrigating, cutting, bundling, and loading were all done by hand. In the early stages of field cultivation, the harrowing and hoeing was invariably in a stifling cloud of dust, and worse still was the later interminable task of stripping leaves from stalks in a jungle of cane where no air stirred and the fine shag of the cane leaves irritated eyes, nose, and skin almost beyond endurance.

The workday ran from dawn to four o'clock, ten hours under the eyes of a mounted *luna*, who was not infrequently armed with a black snake whip and always armed with a savage volley of commands that were never quite intelligible. Monthly pay for the onerous employment amounted to $12.50 for a man, $8 for a woman, but there were mysterious deductions never fully explained.

Though the contract signed by the laborer was clear enough, and forthright, it made no mention of the Masters' and Servants' Act to which he was subject in Hawaii, and it was this act that prescribed the dire penalties of imprisonment, wage forfeiture, and added labor that a manager could inflict for failure to meet required work standards. So binding was the contract and so inexorable the law that the only way out of the agreement was suicide or desertion. The Japanese were less inclined than the Chinese to hang themselves; desertion was preferred until the fugitives discovered that the plantations even maintained armed troopers to round them up. The only safe choice was to follow orders and endure the misery.

Few of the Japanese came to Hawaii with any intention of remaining longer than the specified term of their contracts, and few accordingly brought their wives. They had a fierce devotion to the Emperor, their country, their villages, their families and ancestors, and an unshatterable pride in the homeland. Their one aim was to save their earnings so that they could return to Japan as men of affluence and status. But the get-rich-quick dreams faded fast in Hawaii.

Recruits were depressed by the futility of the labor. There were no rewards for hard, conscientious work. It had no future. They were homesick, despondent, frustrated, pathetically nostalgic for family and friends. Yet they stuck it out, and at the first opportunity headed for home—or town.

The majority went back to Japan upon fulfillment of their contracts, but a great many, embarrassed by the small sums they had been able to accumulate on the plantations, determined to prolong their stay. They took jobs as laborers in other kinds of work and found that they could earn more than in the cane fields and that Hawaii was not inhospitable after all. They hired out as domestic servants, went into chicken raising and market gardening, the kind of farming they had known in Japan.

After a time they sent for their wives, and bachelors sent for "picture brides" faithfully selected by parents. More and more families settled in the Islands, always with the expectation of returning eventually to Japan, but, as the years passed, the date of departure was repeatedly postponed, and the very idea of repatriation became increasingly vague.

Countless tales of unhappy plantation life in Hawaii filtered back to Japan, but they never seemed to thwart the persistent efforts of the Planters' Labor and Supply Company, whose agents continued to roam through the villages of southern Japan, picking up new recruits faster than disgruntled ones were returning. Despite all the discontent, before the end of the century Japanese far outnumbered all other nationalities on the plantations.

In the press and from the rostrum the traffic in contract labor and its effect upon Hawaii were discussed as openly, impersonally, and materialistically as dealings in so many cattle. Even a public official like Henry S. Townsend, Inspector General of Public Schools, brazenly spoke his piece for the benefit of *Forum Magazine* readers in July 1898. He considered the Chinese "an objectionable element," because most of them had left the plantations to run private shops and farms; they were industrious and thrifty, he acknowledged, but "too industrious and too thrifty. . . . It is impossible for Americans to compete with them without working like slaves and living like beggars."

The Japanese were no less objectionable to Townsend, not because they were Japanese, but because "so large a percentage of them is of the lower classes. They are not good representatives of the intelligence and the culture of the Empire of the Rising Sun."

The Madeirans were disappointing, too. "Our Portuguese are not noted for scholarship," he snidely remarked. Although they were "industrious, thrifty and law-abiding," like the Orientals, too many had deserted the plantations. "They are teamsters, mechanics, overseers of labor, merchants and landed proprietors. . . . Many have gone to California and many others have returned to Portugal."

Nothing about the labor picture in Hawaii looked good to Honolulu's distinguished educator. And he was anything but optimistic about the remainder of the population, principally the Americans, British, Germans, and Norwegians, "a little community of some 7,000 men, women and children," only about 5 per cent of the whole. "Our census figures have been taken as indicating that they have become 'Asiaticized,' and they certainly do indicate a serious state of affairs."

The planters were as worried about this "Asiaticization" as any others but more worried about what would happen to the labor supply when the Islands were annexed to the United States and Washington closed the door to Chinese immigration under the oriental exclusion laws. In anticipation of that event, they succeeded in getting a waiver on Hawaii's own exclusion acts and got fifteen thousand more coolies under the wire before it was too late.

At the same time, to betoken their good intentions of combating the rising "Yellow Peril," they brought in from Europe a total of 365 Galicians who were actually Poles from Austria, a few hundred Negroes, and exactly fourteen white farm families from New England. It was the best they could do. And when the Galicians caused more trouble than had the Scandinavians, again the planters were obliged to look to the Orient.

After annexation, Chinese were contraband, and so was contract labor in general. But Koreans and Japanese were not yet on the exclusion list. Between 1903 and 1905 the recruiters concentrated on Korea and induced some five thousand of them to take their turn in the Hawaiian cane fields. Nor was there any letup in the recruiting of Japanese, until a series of diplomatic notes between Theodore Roosevelt and the Japanese Government produced in 1908 the "Gentleman's Agreement" that halted most of the immigration from Japan, except for families, wives, and "picture brides."

Next the planters played their trump. As a result of the Spanish-American War, Filipinos had acquired the status of American nationals. In the Philippine Islands was an untouched reservoir of manpower, and agents there could deal with American rather than foreign officials. An entirely new recruitment approach was adopted. There were to be no pretentious promises, no pressure talk; all employment was to be on a strictly temporary basis.

The Hawaiian Sugar Planters Association took charge. Their representatives opened an office in Manila, honestly advertised the particulars of the employment, and required that every recruit be able to pay his own travel expenses to Hawaii. The contracts were for 720 days of work, to be completed within a three-year period, at the end of which the planters would provide free transportation home.

There was a challenge in such an agreement. The first importation began in 1906, and within four years 2,361 Filipinos were working at least part time on the plantations. The arrangement proved so popular that twenty-five years later the total had jumped to sixty-six thousand and Filipinos had replaced the Japanese as the major labor force in both sugar and pineapple production.

But while the Filipinos were pouring into the Islands, the racial amalgam was further infused with 2,200 Spaniards from the sugar country around Malaga in southern Spain, with almost as many Russians from Manchuria, and more thousands from the cane fields of Puerto Rico. The melting pot was simmering—a composite of citizenry almost as diverse as that which was assembling in the United States during the same period.

True, a dying kingdom needed to be repopulated; true, political wisdom was exercised in mixing races and nationalities. But there was more expediency than wisdom. The ingathering was motivated neither by idealism nor consideration for the future welfare of Hawaii. Production of sugar and more sugar, pineapples and more pineapples, were the guides, regardless of what happened to the chemistry in the melting pot. Only by accident did the mix fuse into an interesting and colorful alloy.

Chinese, South Sea islanders, Portuguese, Japanese, Austrian Poles, Norwegians, Germans, Spaniards, Koreans, Russians, Filipinos, Puerto Ricans, a sprinkling of Britons, Mexicans, Irish, French, Scotch, Italians, Micronesians, Hindus, not to mention the different brands of Americans—Yankees, southerners, Hoosiers, westerners, Negroes, and second-generation European compounds—all these composed the blood of Hawaii in the early 1900's. The whalers, missionaries, and merchants had merely tampered with Island sociology; the planters revolutionized it.

Visitors came in waves to extol the marvelous example of racial integration without detecting a hint of the gnawing discord behind scenes. The whole plantation organization was based on a principle of racial segregation. Each race was made very conscious of its position on the social scale through a corresponding wage scale.

At the top of the ladder were the Americans, English, Scotch, and

Germans. Then in descending order ranged the Hawaiians, Portuguese, Chinese, Japanese, and Filipinos. All were aware of the stratification. Policy was determined by the *haole* elite; the Scotch managed; the Hawaiians and Portuguese bossed; the others did the rough work. And the social system as established on the plantations was accepted as the proper pattern for all other Island associations.

Among the managers, the key word that characterized ideal labor was "docile." Every group had to be kept in its proper relationship, cooperative, subjected, *docile*. And every group in turn, as it became acclimated to plantation environment, grew less docile. The immigrants fulfilled their contracts, then moved on, if not to higher wages and greater opportunity, at least to independence.

Many caused plenty of trouble before making the move. Disputes and dissension were followed by rebellion and strikes. The whole history of Hawaiian plantation labor was punctuated with strikes. In 1900 there were twenty of them, two in 1902, two in 1903, ten in 1904 and 1905. Most of these uprisings were minor, but they paved the way for crippling strikes of 1909, 1920, 1924, and at least one major, costly strike in every succeeding decade.

The plantations from the start were operated on a highly paternalistic system, with free housing, free fuel, free water, free transportation to and from work, free medical care. Considering the isolation from towns and the destitution of workers, it was the only feasible system, but it was not fully appreciated, and never offered enough to satisfy the discontented. Each one of the strikes was brought on by a demand for an extension of the perquisites, for higher pay, shorter hours, better working conditions, or better living conditions, and generally the strikers got at least a part of their demand.

More humanitarian treatment, as well as the work stoppages, were responsible for conspicuous plantation changes after annexation. The management was no less paternalistic, but by the 1920's villages of pleasant little bungalows had replaced the shabby camps. Three-bedroom homes, each complete with kitchen, living room, porch, and private outhouse were the rule; there were shade trees in the yards, and hibiscus, croton, and poinsettia hedges in front. Bachelors could live at the company boarding house or double up with their buddies in a bungalow; they could get their own meals or dine at the plantation restaurant, three solid meals a day, for fifteen dollars a month.

A few more strikes brought household electricity and hospitals, bathrooms and baseball diamonds, and just about all the refinements a man in dungarees could hope to merit in any laboring-class society. The paternalism, the perquisites, and the company camps did not begin to disappear until after World War II, when every last Filipino and Portuguese had a car of his own to transport himself to work from the nearest suburb and the plantation workers were so completely unionized that they were calling the turns in Island economy. Moreover, the financial drain of high wages and fringe benefits had made either sugar or pineapple production a nip-and-tuck proposition, industries that could survive only through increased mechanization and decreased manpower.

Plantation labor, originally imported to sweeten Island economy, meantime was declaring its own destiny, each racial group jockeying for recognition and greater respect, each struggling to attain a higher station on the social and economic scale. It was a continuous tug of war.

Minorities like the Galicians, the Norwegians, the Spaniards, and Russians had long since virtually disappeared. The Germans pulled out during World War I. Except for a little group of Samoans on Oahu, the South Sea islanders had lost their identity, and the Koreans and Puerto Ricans were pretty much absorbed in the general population. That left the Chinese, the Japanese, the Portuguese, and the Filipinos as the principal contenders for status among themselves and the *haoles.*

For the Chinese, the goal through the years was to become business entrepreneurs in the Islands; for the Japanese, to be accepted and respected as Japanese-Americans; for the Portuguese, to be regarded as *haoles;* for the Filipinos, to acquire enough financial reserve so that they could return to the Philippines in style.

All four attained their objectives at least in part. In less than three generations the Chinese had forgotten that they were ever coolies, and a majority were industrial proprietors, large and small, merchants, bankers, college-educated professionals, men and women in clerical and skilled occupations. The Japanese, who dramatically demonstrated during World War II where their loyalties lay, had been welcomed into the conglomerate American brotherhood and were proportionately represented in every vocational calling favored by Caucasians. By thousands, the Portuguese had married out of their nationality, and only die-hard *kamaainas* any longer denied them *haole* standing. The Filipinos, whose one objective prior to 1945 had been to get back to their own islands, were electing to stay after all.

Among all the peoples whom the plantations had lured to Hawaii, the Japanese, Portuguese, and Filipinos were the only ones in any great number still working the cane and pineapple fields. They dressed in dungarees and helmets by day, but out of uniform they were indistinguishable from any other laboring groups. Far removed from the old shantytowns, they lived in the TV-oriented, aloha-shirt refinement of tidy villages or bright new subdivisions and took overweening pride in landscaping a more colorful front yard than their neighbor's.

Residential blocks of ethnic groups still existed, but the bounds had become less sharply defined than they once were. Everywhere an older generation persisted in its attempt to preserve some of the ancestral traditions of the fatherland; yet the attempts were not always successful when imposed upon children and grandchildren. The language schools that flourished before World War II to keep alive foreign tongues and foreign loyalties had lost status, and the few that still existed were purely for cultural enlightenment.

Children of many races growing up together, sharing classrooms, matching accented repartee, lining up in the same football squad, habitually judging each other more on intrinsic character than on color or family creed inevitably fostered an interethnic outlook. Close to a third of Island marriages crossed racial lines. Hawaii became one of the few states where differences of race and national heritage were freely overlooked.

Statistics presented the most impressive evidence of the way the invasion by invitation had worked out. The count of 26,000 Chinese in 1900 had advanced to only 38,000 sixty years later, while in the same period the Japanese had increased from 60,000 to 203,000; the Filipinos, from an inconsequential number to 67,000; Caucasians, including the Portuguese, from 26,000 to 202,000; Hawaiian and part-Hawaiian from 38,000 to nearly double that figure; "others," accounting for random miscegenation as well as minorities, from 26,000 to almost 100,000.

Where social demarcations had once been drawn with disdainful frankness, no one now, regardless of his high birth, registered serious aversion to dwelling on the same street with the Matsumotos, the Medeiroses, the Chongs, Goos, Dois, Garcias, Pachecos, Kapohaki-mohewas, Taniguchis—and Smiths.

KILAUEA CRATER

XII
Pele versus Volcanology

Ominous suspense settled over the southern half of the island of Hawaii during the early months of 1868. Rarely had the two volcanoes, Mauna Loa and Kilauea, been known to kick up in concert, but this season, as if to demonstrate their capriciousness, both were simultaneously coming to life with a terrifying commotion.

Fire fountains were spewing sheets of white-hot lava nearly to the top of Kilauea's great crater, occasionally tossing gigantic boulders over the rim. In its depths a churning lake of molten lava was rapidly rising. No one had climbed to the top of Mauna Loa to see what was happening in its *caldera,* but the glow against the clouds at night reflected all the horrors of hell. Almost invariably a violent eruption somewhere on the lower mountain slopes followed such turbulence in a single crater. Here were two prospective outbursts.

Late in March the first signs of imminent eruption were spotted from Kawaihae, fifty miles away. Towering spirals of smoke billowed

266

up from the summit of Mauna Loa, lighted by magnificent spurts of flame. The outbreak came sooner than was expected. Four separate streams of lava poured down the mountain on the southwest side. Then, after a few hours, the flow mysteriously ceased, and almost simultaneously Kilauea, too, quieted.

To seasoned Islanders, the discontinuance of summit activity merely added to the suspense. From past experience they knew that this was only a lull. The vast pressure of liquid lava had to be relieved somewhere, and the halt in visible fireworks meant that the molten mass was forcing a subterranean channel toward another outlet. Where?

On March 27th slight earth rumblings were noted at Kau on the southern side of the Island, along the Kona coast on the west side, and later at Hilo to the east. Gradually the rumblings were amplified into shudderings and foreboding jolts. During the next five days over two thousand earthquakes were counted, coming at an average interval of every five minutes, steadily increasing in intensity and frequency.

They were most severe to the south of Mauna Loa, in the Kau district, where three distinct kinds of motion were felt, undulating waves; sudden, sharp jerks; and a thumping "like a cannon ball striking the floor beneath you and rolling away." And accompanying all three were strange "rattling noises."

At last appeared the first evidence of where the real eruption might take place. In the open ranch country of West Kau, some twenty-five miles from the summit of Mauna Loa, telltale fractures began to show on the ground surface, cracks that sent forth little jets of steam or spurts of lava, cracks and ever-widening cracks on a rough line stretching for miles, as the ground yielded to an irrepressible internal force. By the first of April the shocks, which seemed to synchronize with the creation of the fissures, were continuous.

Then at 3:40 in the afternoon of April 2nd came a culminating quake, the like of which no living man on Hawaii had ever experienced. It was felt along the entire Island chain, including Kauai, three hundred miles to the north. At Waimea, near the northern end of Hawaii, it was like the blast of doom. Father Lyons tried to comfort his terrified flock, who normally thought nothing of earthquakes; later he paced off fathom after fathom of strewn rocks that had been stone walls.

At Hilo, Father Coan, who had adopted volcanic observation as his hobby and pursued eruptions with the fervor of a fire chaser, claimed that the earth was literally convulsed: "First it swayed to and fro, north and south—then east and west—then round and round, up and down in every imaginable direction for several minutes, everything crashing about us, the trees thrashing as if torn by a mighty rushing wind. It was impossible to stand—we had to sit on the ground, bracing with hands and feet to keep from rolling over. The ground itself rose and sank like waves. Horses and men were thrown to the ground—houses destroyed."

The destruction at Hilo was formidable, but the center of the earthquake was in the Kau district, sixty miles to the southwest. In places there, the terrain was so disrupted that it was turned into a network of rifts, smoking with sulphur fumes. Chasms ten and twelve feet wide were rent in the earth. Few structures were left on their foundations. Forests were leveled. Not a stone wall was left standing anywhere. Gigantic boulders barreled down mountain slopes. Cattle and horses stampeded.

Along a fault line near Waiohinu, a lateral shift of eighteen feet had taken place. Every building in the town, including a stone church, was demolished. And still the expected lava eruption had not commenced.

Within seconds after the great earthquake, a horrifying earth slip occurred in the steep hills above Punaluu. According to one theory, an underground lava stream had encountered an underground water reservoir, causing a vast explosion and converting the soil deposit above it into fluid mud. An avalanche half a mile wide instantly followed. Thundering out of the hills, the sluice of mud carried everything before it, huts, forests, loose boulders.

It spilled over a thousand-foot cliff and in less than five minutes enveloped three miles of the most fertile pasture land in Kau, burying thirty-one men, women, and children under forty feet of debris, engulfing a dozen homes and all the cattle in its path. One rancher alone claimed the loss of a thousand longhorns. Fanning out to the width of three miles, the flow of red sludge drained off into the sea, dyeing the water an eerie bronze from shore to horizon.

The earth convulsions, meantime, had generated a colossal tidal wave. In the usual pattern, the ocean floor was bared clear to the reefs as the water receded. Then the sea rapidly rose for its assault. With a rush and roar the tide swept back in a towering wall of surf, from twenty to more than fifty feet high. It flung itself upon the land to demolish all the low-lying villages along the southwest shore. Punaluu, Ninole, Kawaa, Honuapo, Keauhou were wiped off the map.

In many places the wave rolled inshore a quarter of a mile, casting with it a tangle of uprooted trees, smashed homes, animals, canoes, and refuse; in its backwash it sucked out every movable object. Entire families were lost in the maelstrom. Keauhou was the regional center for the pickers and packers of *pulu,* the soft down gathered from fern trees and exported for mattress and pillow stuffing. Hundreds depended on it for their livelihood. The industry was destroyed, along with a warehouse, presses, boats, landings, and 167 bales of *pulu* ready for shipment.

Natives at Punaluu rushed to higher ground and turned in time to see a colossal wave break over the top of a grove of sixty-foot coconut trees. The bare trunks of two palms were left to mark the site of the village. Altogether the tidal wave accounted for the destruction of over a hundred homes and almost fifty lives.

All this was preliminary to the major eruption. "For ten days," declared Titus Coan, "the earth never ceased rocking like a rocking-horse, and a trembling as if ague-stricken. The quivering was continuous, and a sheet of iron, suspended in the house, never ceased vibrating like a pendulum."

Finally on the night of April 6th, the long-awaited eruption burst forth above Kahuku Ranch, ten miles inland at the 3800-foot level. From a rift in the mountain shot up such showers of ashes and pumice that by morning an area extending twenty-five miles downwind was drifted a foot deep. Accompanied by a series of sharper earthquakes, the rift lengthened from a few rods to three miles, and at nightfall on April 7th four enormous blood-red fountains, fluid as water, were roaring to a height of five hundred and six hundred feet, tossing out twenty-ton boulders like pebbles.

At spectacular moments the four merged into one, forming a single fountain over a mile long. The molten lava showered the thickly wooded surroundings to set off raging forest fires; yet these conflagrations were scarcely noticeable in the general inferno. Quickly the flow channeled itself into the river from two hundred to five hundred feet wide, "tossing, raging and roaring like the rapids of Niagara," surging down steep inclines at a clip of twenty-five miles an hour.

For an hour the raised rim of a five-hundred-foot precipice dammed the stream, building up a reservoir behind it; then, as if on signal, it plunged over in a glaring red cataract half a mile wide and swept on toward the sea. By midnight it reached the shore line and cast itself over the cliff into the ocean in the greatest spectacle yet, throwing up clouds of steam from the boiling waters in its battle with the tide.

For people near South Point it was a night of horror. Those in the path of the advancing stream sometimes managed to escape just in time. Others did not make it. Captain Brown's ranch was overrun. With his wife and four children, still in night clothes, he fled across a ravine to high ground with only minutes to spare and had scarcely reached a safe outlook when he turned to see his home enveloped in flames, his gardens and fertile acres transformed into a fiery lake.

A herd of cattle continued to graze on a knoll as the flow approached. It struck the upper contour of the knoll, divided, and merged again below, leaving the cattle stranded on a narrow island, bound by an impassable river of superheated lava. Caught in exactly the same predicament on a scant half-acre, a plucky Hawaiian family of seven fought the flood for more than a week. Their island lacked sufficient elevation to fend off intruding lava trickles, and they were kept busy night and day digging ditches and mounding up earth dams. They won the battle, and were rescued long after the last of their supply of food and water had given out.

The fire fountains died down during the fourth day, and the excitement was over, though it would take months, even years, for the heaviest deposits of lava to cool. And days after the event, it was discovered that the flow from Kilauea had poured out harmlessly far back in the hills on worthless barren lands. The villain of 1868 was Mauna Loa. Luckily, the outbreak at Kahuku occurred in a thinly populated area; yet it took a toll of thirty-seven lives, destroyed over a hundred homes, and buried some four thousand acres of green pasture, as well as vast tracts of less valuable terrain. "This terrible calamity . . . ," summarized C. F. Gordon Cumming, "changed one of the fairest pasture lands of Hawaii into a region of desolation—the Pompeii of the South Seas."

But Hawaiians, who were used to the flare-ups of Kilauea and Mauna Loa, did not rank it as quite that great a catastrophe. Aside from the coincidental eruption of the two volcanoes and the extreme violence and devastation from the earthquakes, there was nothing about the 1868 upheaval that had not occurred in kind many times before. And after half a century in the Islands, even foreigners had become reconciled to earthquakes, eruptions, and tidal waves as any-day occurrences.

Years might pass before Hawaii would be rocked by another violent convulsion—or it might come tomorrow. Natives were philosophic about the threat. After all, the Big Island was dotted with scores of little half-forgotten Pompeiis, the sites of former villages entombed in coils of solidified lava.

The world was just beginning to be interested in these mid-Pacific phenomena. Only two years before, Mark Twain had facetiously reminded his far-flung public that Vesuvius was a "soup-kettle" compared to Kilauea. The fame of Hawaii's turbulent mountains was spreading. Men on the other side of the globe who were not the least bit interested in Hawaiians, sugar and an alleged "Pacific Paradise" were vitally interested in the big volcanoes.

They were becoming a major attraction, drawing no great number of observers but important observers, a growing invasion of world travelers, professors, mountaineers, naturalists, explorers, men of science. The study of volcanoes was still young and volcanology not yet popularly accepted as a specialized branch of learning. In fact, the study was young enough for Hawaii to be included in the rudimentary probings and even to contribute to mineralogy two technical terms from its ancient vocabulary: *aa* for rough lava, *pahoehoe* for smooth. But first, the marvels of Hawaii's "burning mountains" had to be more firmly established.

So many humbugs were abroad during the nineteenth century, circulating romantic fabrications of the world's wonders, that any skeptic worthy of his caution greeted popular representations of natural phenomena with a degree of incredulity. A reported terrestrial spectacle had to receive the benediction of the learned, a stamp of approval from the professors before it could be considered authentic.

That skepticism was a handicap to Hawaii for decades. Lay observers got there ahead of the scientists. Amateur naturalists wrote home about the incredible wonders of the Islands; they told of violent earth shudderings, of unnatural risings and recessions in the tides, of implausibly gigantic waves that occasionally swept far beyond the shore limits; they described massive lava flows that rolled down mountain sides to congeal into rivers of black rock; they reported stupendous volcanic fireworks that did not conform to the behavior of any known volcano on earth. The accounts were to be taken with a grain of salt until the professors had evaluated them properly, and the professors were slow in putting in an appearance.

Of course, there were natural philosophers of sorts aboard many of the caravels that did the early exploring of the Islands, but they were hampered by the nescience of their age, and their conclusions often were more philosophical than naturalistic.

Captain Cook even sent a team of botanists to the top of Mauna Loa. Unfortunately they did not make it. Rough footing and "impenetrable thickets" turned them back. After tramping over miles of jagged lava, however, they did reach the cautious conclusion that "Hawaii has every appearance in nature to suppose it once to have been a volcano. Its height, magnitude, shape, and perhaps its situation indicate that."

But what bothered them about the volcano theory was the "sharp" peak and its snowcap. That was a complete incongruity, "a new circumstance, and among us not altogether accounted for." John Ledyard, who was a member of the unsuccessful inland expedition, finally gave up fretting over an explanation and tossed it aside: "As a truth and phenomenon in natural philosophy, I leave it to the world."

On their first try, Captain Vancouver's naturalists did little better than the Ledyard detachment. From Kealakekua Bay they climbed to the summit of dormant Hualalai, above Kailua-Kona, located its crater, and pushed on toward Mauna Loa, until the same "impenetrable thickets" the Cook group encountered barred the way.

Archibald Menzies, the most notable British botanist of his day, was the leader of the party, and he refused to yield to the mountain. He took his problems to the local chiefs, who confided that the only practical approach to Mauna Loa was on the opposite side of the Island. Subjected to the pressure of dogged persuasion and smart haggling, the chiefs finally procured guides and supplies, organized a flotilla of canoes, and on February 5, 1794, Menzies set out for the top of the mountain—by sea.

He expected that the assault might take as long as three days. It took eleven. Not until February 16th did the party reach the top, and they almost froze to death en route. Deep snow and temperatures in the twenties were their most serious obstacles.

After beaching the canoes near South Point, they struck out across Kau Desert and struggled up the path of an ancient lava flow, blazing a trail that still bears the name of Menzies. Kilauea was in vigorous eruption at the time, darkening their route with a tormenting cloud of smoke and ashes, but that volcano was not included in the itinerary they had bargained for; so the guides skirted it widely, never hinting to their clientele that they were missing the grandest sight on Hawaii.

The snow line was far down the mountain that February, and as they approached it, the barefoot, scantily clothed natives all but refused to go further. A bitter wind blew off the snow fields, and each night the temperature dropped below freezing. They were without blankets, without firewood, without shelter. The entire company, natives and *haoles*, spent one night huddled compactly together on a flat rock, for the warmth that each could give the other. In the morning the guides rebelled again, declining to stir until the sun dispersed the frost and warning that the cold higher up was so intense "it would certainly kill us and them too."

One by one most of the Hawaiians were permitted to drop out. It was a thin line of stragglers that crossed the snow line on the tenth day of the expedition. No one had guessed that the ascent could be so long and arduous. Their food had given out, except for a few frozen coconuts and a little chocolate. On the last night they sacrificed their walking sticks to make a blaze for warmth.

When at last they reached the top, they wondered if it had been worth all the trouble. There was nothing particularly exciting about the scene. "We found the summit nearly flat for several miles," Menzies noted, "strewed over with huge lumps of loose lava, and here and there deep snow." It was not at all the "sharp peak" that Captain Cook's reconnoiterers had described. But unquestionably it was a volcano. Falteringly they climbed the wall of the immense crater and estimated that its circumference was at least "three miles"; yet the only sign of volcanic activity was a little steam rising from two or three hot springs.

With amazing accuracy, Menzies reckoned the height of the mountain at exactly 13,634 feet, only 46 feet shy of the established altitude. He had climbed Mauna Loa on the assumption that it was Hawaii's highest peak. Even that was a disappointment, for, having arrived there, he made a shrewd guess, without the instruments to prove it, that adjacent Mauna Kea was higher. But after the discomforts he had already endured, he readily abandoned any thought of ascending that too.

Archibald Menzies' field trip added nothing to the prestige of Hawaii. The account of that first ascent of Mauna Loa by white men was not even included in Vancouver's *Voyages,* and did not come to light until geologist Charles H. Hitchcock dug it out of British archives over a century later and had it published in 1909.

Hawaii's strongest claim to the curiosity of scientists, of course, lay in its volcanoes, dead or alive, and thirty more years passed before anyone put on paper the first observations of seething Kilauea, the most frenzied natural phenomenon in all the Pacific Ocean area. And it was not a scientist who made that report, nor one of the New England apostles. The writer was British missionary William Ellis.

On a grand tour of the island of Hawaii in 1823, Ellis kept hearing about the terror of the mountain crater, home of the pagan goddess Pele. By day he could see the smoke rising from the heights, by night the glare in the sky, and periodically day or night he felt the earth tremors emanating from the mountain. His curiosity got the best of him, and with a quartet of fellow missionaries and a following of reluctant natives, he made the ascent from Hilo.

Pele put on a full-dress performance. The entire floor of the crater was active. "A spectacle sublime and even appalling presented itself before us," he wrote. "We stopped and trembled. Astonishment and awe for some minutes rendered us mute, and like statues we stood fixed to the spot, with eyes riveted on the abyss below."

What Ellis saw was a yawning, crescent-shaped gulf, which he estimated to be eight hundred feet deep, two miles long, and a mile wide. The bottom was a surging mass of molten lava, out of which rose over fifty conical islands, half of them simultaneously spewing columns of brilliant flame, billows of dark smoke, or blazing waves of red lava that streamed down the black sides of the cones—all to the accompaniment of a deafening roar, hideous snorts, and thunderous reports.

Still more appalling to him was the scene at night when flames of dazzling white, sulphurous blue, and mineral red danced over the churning, eddying lake of fire, and the fountains played in stunning brilliance against the shadows of the stark perpendicular cliffs. It was "an awful grandeur—terrible and sublime."

No naturalist, poet, or professional journalist ever gave a more lurid and honest description of Kilauea, but anything a missionary wrote was a poor substitute for the sober statement of a recognized scientist. Interpretation of the works of nature by clerics was likely to be colored by scriptural reference; for them nothing could antedate Genesis I, 1. So Ellis' report did not create much of a stir.

A year later, however, an event occurred at Kilauea that stirred

Hawaii itself as no eruption ever had, an event in Hawaiian annals comparable to Liholiho's breaking of the taboos. The high chiefess Kapiolani, one of the most revered women in the kingdom, daughter of a former king of the Hilo district, determined, as a token of her new-found Christian faith, to stage a dramatic defiance of Pele. Many of the other gods had been demoted, but not Pele; she had been worshiped for centuries as the supreme overlord of the volcano world, the deified resident of Kilauea crater, and though others had tried sacrilegiously to dethrone her, none had succeeded. Kapiolani intended to.

With an entourage of eighty jittery Hawaiians, enough witnesses to spread the details of the contest from Kau to Kauai, she descended deep into the crater, which fortunately was in a much calmer mood than the one Ellis had portrayed. "Jehovah is my God," she allegedly cried into the tumultuous void of fire and thunder, so that her audience could not miss a word. "He kindled these fires. If I perish by the anger of Pele, then you may fear the power of Pele; but if I trust in Jehovah, and he shall save me from the wrath of Pele when I break through her taboos, you must fear and serve the Lord Jehovah."

Against the "terrific bellowing and whizzing of the volcanic gases," they sang a gospel hymn and listened to a long Christian prayer, highly prejudicial to Pele. Nothing happened. There was no explosive retaliation, no unusual spitting of flame. Kapiolani was the victress.

Sermonized Hiram Bingham when he heard of the event: "Here is a heroism of a more sublime and immortal character than that which rushes to the battlefield. Here was a philosophy which might put to blush the pride of pagan Athens and Rome." The story spread across America and to England where it later inspired poet laureate Alfred Tennyson to draft the effusive tribute:

> Great, and greater, and greatest of women,
> Island heroine, Kapiolani,
> Clomb the mountain . . .
> And dared the Goddess, and freed the people
> Of Hawaii. . . .

Pele may have been confounded by all the publicity brought to her, to Kapiolani, and to Kilauea, but she was not yet vanquished. The old girl still hung around and down the years continued and continues, to be encountered just before a great eruption, in the form of a sprightly maiden or disheveled hag, on dark roads, in the region of the fiery pits, in the path chosen for a flow of lava; and the *kahunas*, who maintain liaison with her, are still kept busy during periods of volcanic unrest, staking out little areas which she and the lava are entreated not to trespass.

The missionaries made the most of Kapiolani's epochal exploit, and their bulletins brought more expeditions to the crater than ever before. Gradually a few orthodox scientists joined the pilgrimage, though most of them, like Menzies, were botanists and naturalists, rather than mineralogists or geologists.

In June 1825, George Anson Byron and a dozen distinguished Englishmen, who had accompanied the bodies of King Liholiho and Queen Kamamalu from London to Honolulu, moved into the grass shack that had been erected on the edge of the crater for the overnight accommodation of Kapiolani. The famed Scottish botanist James Macrae and British naturalist Andrew Bloxam were among them. It was by far the most eminent group yet attracted to the volcano. And Kilauea put on a good show for them, with towering columns of black smoke, explosive outbursts of flame, red hot stones, and bubbling lava. The celebrities were thrilled.

David Douglas, another great Scottish botanist, appeared in 1834, fresh from his botanical conquest of California and the Northwest, where the Douglas fir was forever to carry his name. Although only 35, he was already one of the world's foremost naturalists, and had been sent to Hawaii by the Royal Horticultural Society of London.

In the course of a few months he classified and sent off hundreds of plants to London, but he was as much a man of the mountains as of the meadows. He was probably the first scientist to reach the top of Mauna Kea, "after immense labor, fatigue, anxiety, and some degree of danger," and the only one ever to consider it an active volcano. "You may pledge my name," he testified elegantly, "for saying that the

GREAT CRATER is on the very summit of Mauna Kea, at present in an active state. One day there, madam, is worth one year of common existence."

In the interest of science, he also climbed Mauna Loa, explored the top, and twice almost lost his life plunging into fissures bridged with snow. He deduced that the crater never overflowed its top but discharged underground and threw out ashes, sand, and gigantic rocks for miles around. He tried to fathom the depth of some of the yawning chasms of the *caldera* and found no measurable termination. "In some places," he propounded, "it is as if the mountain were torn asunder to its very base. . . . Terrible indeed must have been the sight when in a state of action."

Douglas was even more excited about Kilauea. "The sight of the volcano fills the mind with awe—" he marveled, "a vast basin in a state of igneous fusion, throwing out lava in a thousand forms, from tortuous masses like large cables to the finest filamentous thread, some places in large sheets, some in terrible rolled masses, like the breaking up of a large river with ice, of all colors and forms. . . . I assure you that these islands offer rewards to the naturalist above all others. . . . I must return to the volcano, if it is only to look—to look and admire."

But Douglas was never given a chance to return to Kilauea, not even for a look. He died horribly a few months later high on the slope of Mauna Kea, that mountain on which he had declared one day was worth a year of common existence. On July 12, 1834, his mangled body was found at the bottom of a cellar-sized cattle trap, shared by a frenzied wild bull.

Since Douglas, the experienced woodsman, was not one to stumble carelessly into a pitfall, his friends were certain that he had been the victim of foul play, probably from a band of those Botany Bay escapees who used the region as their hideout. The mysterious death became a *cause célèbre* in the Islands, second only to the circumstances of Captain Cook's demise.

Death by violence, however, could not negate what Douglas had done for Hawaii. His was a spontaneous endorsement that left no doubt about the scientist's sentiments. After he had spoken, anyone could be extravagant in his praise of Island wonders.

The admiration by Douglas was shortly echoed by the renowned Polish professor, Count Paul Edmund de Strzelecki, who inspected Kilauea's "mighty engine of nature" and called the sight "unparalleled." "After visiting most of the European and American volcanoes," he deposed, "I found the greatest of them inferior to Kilauea in intensity, grandeur and extent."

Catching the enthusiasm of their learned visitors, Honolulu's business and civic worthies mustered in 1837 to assess for themselves the virtues of their surroundings and to form a museum association that could suitably aggrandize their treasures, the Sandwich Island Institute. Keynoted the presiding officer in his inaugural address: "The natural history of these Islands claims the foremost place in our observation. No country in the world affords greater facilities for making a splendid collection of volcanic specimens." He pictured the archipelago as a veritable storehouse of information for geologists.

The founders of the Institute recognized that all too often residents living closest to a popular attraction were least appreciative of it. They were not going to be accused of that oversight, and were ready three years later to play host to an extraordinary company of visitors.

All the early naturalists of note who came to look at the volcanoes had been European. The Americans waited until 1840 and easily made up for the delay in the ostentation of their equipment and personnel. Not one or two ships, such as other countries had sent, but a squadron of six dropped anchor in Honolulu harbor. Aboard them was a team of the most versatile scientists the United States Navy could assemble for a round-the-world voyage of the Government Exploring Expedition. The distinguished "Commodore" Charles Wilkes was in command.

It was a triumphal entry for the Americans, acclaimed in Honolulu as the most momentous nonpolitical event since the discovery of the Islands. Hawaiians interpreted the visit as a flattering honor; the Islands were being given recognition by an impressive corps of scholars and officers.

The guests stayed on for months, engaged in scholarly research and at the same time thoroughly enjoying themselves, botanists, zoologists, surveyors, mineralogists, artists, sociologists, statisticians, economists. In Honolulu Wilkes set up an enormous tent encampment and tent laboratory on the beach, while the commodore himself was moved into the residence of the premier, as though he were a visiting monarch.

The scholars went about their labors with an energy and purpose that fascinated, mystified, and captivated the natives. They surveyed the coasts and harbors, measured the heights of mountains, penetrated far into valleys and canyons for rare plants, scaled precipices for birds, dove into ocean depths for varicolored fish and coral, and on one notable occasion entertained all Honolulu at a magnificent picnic.

They seemed to appreciate the Islands as they had never before been appreciated by foreigners, and the Hawaiians revered them for it, joined in the searches, got in the way, and volunteered as divers, porters, and boatmen, just for the joy of being in the company of these wonderfully curious men of science.

The crowning exploit of the expedition, of course, was to be the ascent of Kilauea and Mauna Loa on the Big Island. The ships appeared off Hilo at dawn on December 14, 1840, but the reputation of the passengers had preceded them and a watch had been set. Within minutes of the sighting of the squadron, as one young witness related, "the whole village was alive, and every tall tree bore in its topmost branch a copper-colored youth shouting 'Sail-ho!' as loud as he could bawl. As the sun rose, the ship flung out the glorious flag of America, and before noon she was safely anchored in the very center of the harbor. . . . Commodore Wilkes had arrived."

Even in 1840 the United States Navy had developed a propensity for using an extraordinary amount of manpower for accomplishing a mission. Practically every able-bodied man in Hilo was needed for this great expedition, so many porters and attendants, in fact, that a "department of personnel" was created and Dr. Judd brought from Honolulu to supervise it. En route he had raided Lahainaluna for the captains and sergeants he knew Hilo could not supply. While other sizable parties had ascended the mountain with perhaps fifteen or twenty orderlies, the Navy required some five hundred, one third of that number, explained Wilkes, "to carry provisions for the rest."

After days of confused preparation, the procession at last got under way, and the commodore himself described the line of march, stretching out for miles: "It consisted of 200 bearers of burdens, 40 hogs, a bullock and bullock-hunter, 50 bearers of *poi*, 25 with calabashes of different sizes and shapes. . . . Some of the bearers had large and small panels of the portable house on their backs; others frying pans and kettles, and others tents and knapsacks. Then there were a large number of hangers-on in the shape of mothers, wives and children, equalling in number the bearers, all grumbling and complaining of their loads."

Wilkes congratulated himself on not being able to understand the Hawaiian language; so he could ignore the complaints and leave all the arguments for the chairman of the department of personnel to settle. Before the procession had made half a day's advance on the trail, the hogs were scattering in the fern forests; bullocks were giving their captors a mad chase; porters carrying the heavy iron mortar, with which Wilkes hoped to "try some experiments in sound in rarified air," were rebelling; others were laying down their parcels and refusing to budge; and the confusion in general reached such a crisis that Judd was obliged to send back to Hilo for reinforcements. The commodore was thoroughly disappointed with his *kanaka* help and unhesitatingly said so, admitting that he "would prefer to go weakhanded rather than again resort to such aid."

But Wilkes' greatest disappointment was in Kilauea itself. For this state occasion, the temperamental volcano refused to perform and played dead. "I saw nothing before us," he sniffed, "but a huge pit, black, ill-looking and totally different from what I had anticipated. There were no jets of fire, no eruptions of heated stones, no cones, nothing but a depression that in the midst of a vast plain appeared small and insignificant."

The expedition leader, however, was less snobbish about the volcano as soon as proportions and relationships became more apparent;

at length he conceded that the vastness of the crater "transfixes the mind with astonishment, and every instant the impression of grandeur and magnitude increased. To give an idea of its capacity, the city of New York might be placed within it, and when at its bottom would hardly be noticed."

His respect for the volcano loomed still larger a few hours later when it began to act up without warning, and he came close to losing his indispensable personnel director. Dr. Judd had volunteered to descend to the crater floor to collect samples of liquid lava from a rift. He safely reached the bottom and was groping for his specimens in a precarious spot directly under an overhanging ledge. Suddenly a deafening explosion boomed behind him. He turned to see a fiery jet spouting from the center and a river of red lava racing toward him.

His retreat was instantly cut off, and the projecting shelf above him barred the possibility of scaling the wall. He shouted to his native porters above him to come to the rescue, but they had their own peril in mind and were already scrambling to safety. The searing, suffocating heat was upon him when a faithful Hawaiian fought back his panic, returned to the shelf, and reached a hand over the side. The doctor was hauled up just as the molten lava swept under his feet.

Both doctor and rescuer were severely scorched, but not severely enough to discourage Judd from returning to the rapidly filling crater for a souvenir frypan of lava. Along with other mementos of the Wilkes expedition, that souvenir eventually went on display in a show-case of the Smithsonian in Washngton.

The expedition, including the bandaged doctor, continued on to the summit of Mauna Loa, where the mutinous bearers could at last set down their howitzer, their burdens of poi and house panels and go to work constructing a high stone fortress to serve as windbreak for the scientific encampment. The tent village erected in the enclosure was twice leveled by the wind during a three-week battle with the elements, but Wilkes completed his scientific observations and experiments to his satisfaction, the Navy's, and Hawaii's.

Quite apart from any discoveries in the fields of volcanology and natural history, that visit of the United States Navy scored a turning point in 'Island history. As Dr. Henry Lyman, who was in Hilo for all the excitement, explained long afterward: "It may be truthfully said that the coming of the Wilkes expedition marked the beginning of modern life among the native inhabitants of Hilo. For the first time they witnessed civilized action on a large scale. . . . Better still, the natives had a practical exhibition of the fact that white men were not all either missionaries or beach-combers, and that there was, indeed, a vast circle of cosmopolitan interests in which they had hitherto taken no part." What applied to Hilo was about as true for other parts of the Islands.

The effect upon *haoles* and outer civilization was even greater. Wilkes and his team of scholars verified and dignified the superlatives about Island wonders. Most of the world had previously thought of Hawaii as a wretched little ends-of-the-earth kingdom with no possible allurements. The scholars recognized that it had an enchantment and mystery worthy of any traveler's attention.

Gradually over the years visiting geologists pieced together the story of Hawaii's volcanic origins and concluded that the archipelago, slanting across the middle of the Pacific for fifteen hundred miles, from Kure and Midway to the island of Hawaii, was actually one of the world's greatest mountain ranges, built up from the ocean floor by thousands upon thousands of eruptions. The Islands were merely the peaks of the higher elevations in the range.

On either side of the island chain the average depth of the Pacific was 15,000 feet; so even the islands that just broke the surface of the sea were mountains nearly three miles high, and the lofty twins, Mauna Loa and Mauna Kea, were probably the highest and most massive mountains on earth, considering the total elevation from the bases. Mauna Kea rose some 30,000 feet from its base, compared to Mount Everest's 29,141; Mauna Loa's total volume was something like 10,000 cubic miles, compared to a mere 80 cubic miles for massive Mount Shasta.

The mountain-islands had been created progressively from north to south over a period as long as twenty-five million years. So old were the low northern dots that the lava had been entirely eroded away, and all that remained above the surface, on the crests of truncated cones, were the coral, limestone, and sand built up by lime-secreting animals and plants.

Among the larger islands, Niihau and Kauai were the elders by thousands of years, for eruption ceased there first. Famous landmarks like Diamond Head, Punchbowl, and Koko Head on Oahu or magnificent Haleakala on Maui were all ancient volcanoes that long ago blew their tops. But the island of Hawaii was still young, still very much in the growing stage. A brand new outpouring of lava could occur there at any time.

For years Kilauea was considered a sort of appendage of Mauna Loa, a great crater on its side, but that assumption had to be abandoned as it became obvious that there was no correlation in the lava flows of the two. Belatedly Kilauea had to be given status as an independent mountain, a separate volcano virtually embedded in the shoulder of the colossus that overshadowed it.

The elevation of Kilauea was still low enough for underground lava to be forced from its summit, but Mauna Loa had reached such a height that its extrusions worked through weak points on its sides, sometimes in submarine outbursts, sometimes high on its exposed flanks.

From an advantageous lookout on Mauna Kea, Henry Lyman witnessed such a flank eruption at the eight-thousand-foot level on a night in 1852, a fountain of white-hot lava sprouting five hundred feet into the air, forming a river of liquid fire ten miles long. "All along the lower reaches of this mighty stream," he wrote, "the forest was disappearing like straw in a furnace, yet adding apparently nothing to the enormous banner of flame and smoke that floated above the burning island.

"As we gazed and listened, faint sounds reached our ears—the continual, distant susurration, as of locusts devouring a tree; a wonderful composite note that contained the roar of a volcano in action, the wailing of wood-nymphs in agony, and the triumphant laughter of the goddess of fire—all rising and falling together, now dying as if into silence, then swelling again upon the ambient air—a symphony beyond description, infernal. . . . It was easy now to comprehend the process by which the island and its mountains had grown to their present magnitude; for here it was in actual operation before our eyes."

That was one of the flows that took a direct course for Hilo and miraculously halted on the very outskirts of the town. Still more blood-chilling in their terror were the flows that rampaged all the way to the sea to create a primordial convulsion of elements.

Nightly during the spring and summer of 1859 sightseers gathered at Kawaihae for whale-boat excursions down the coast, where a river of lava, some forty miles long and two wide, rolled into the ocean south of Puako. "The red-hot fluid was shooting out in all forms," reported one of the passengers, "bursting out with a great explosion and pouring in dense masses of white heat into the sea that writhed and bellowed like a huge monster in frantic agony. Sometimes a fresh volume of fire would rush from the flow and simultaneously an immense billow would roll onto the shore, and then to see the death grapple of the two!

"With a report like a thunder-clap, they meet in their grim combat and leap high in the air, one in red-hot flakes, the other in clouds of steam, and the vanquishing ocean retires his scalding waters . . . while the fire in triumph pours down a torrent of its liquid heat into the ocean's bed. . . . The water twenty yards from shore was so hot that we could scarcely bear a hand in it. Imagine a hundred iron furnaces all casting at once, and it will give the nearest approximation I can suggest."

For a period of three hundred days that flow continued without interruption, until Mauna Loa had spewed forth more than half a billion cubic yards of molten rock and inundated thirty-three square miles, the most voluminous and protracted eruption on record. The 1868 flood was a brief trickle by comparison.

As Islanders were to discover during the next century, there was no complete refuge from the anger of Pele anywhere around the mighty perimeter of Mauna Loa. When the top of the volcano shuddered, they shuddered with it. The mountain chose its own lava courses down the slopes and forced mere man out of the way; its tremors churned up tidal waves that cast devastating walls of water onto the island littoral, though the worst waves usually originated from earth shocks in other quake-prone regions of the Pacific. Recurrently through the years all the Islands were buffeted by the waves and Hawaii recurrently harassed by the lava outbreaks. The volcanologists could explain them, and even do a little predicting, but control them they could not.

Mauna Loa and Kilauea became the most intimately studied volcanoes in existence, with a corps of experts standing by to analyze every mood and movement in the craters. The fire watchers could point out that over the period of a century Mauna Loa had averaged a major convulsion every three and a half years and spilled out over four billion cubic yards of lava, enough to pave all the principal highways of the world. They were on hand for every showy eruption, virtually taking the pulse of the mountains, reporting their observations hour by hour to the public, and making headlines in San Francisco, New York, Paris, Rome and Tokyo, as well as in Honolulu and Hilo.

Far from taking the reports as *kapus,* tourists and the Island public excitedly thronged to the scene. An eruption of any size was a great show on Hawaii, and a relatively safe one, too. In 1916 spectators began coming by invitation of the federal government, for that was the year the Interior Department was persuaded that one of the most ostentatious natural attractions on earth was being neglected, and took over the mountain summits as the Hawaii National Park.

But soon after Kilauea acquired that status, Pele declined to cooperate; 1924 marked the end of an era for the mountain. For at least a century an enormous plug of semisolid lava had partially blocked the principal gullet of the crater. The plug was dislodged during a series of violent explosions that year, and the displays were never again the same. Occasionally in subsequent years the fire fountains flared up in their old glory, but nothing to count on like their almost perennial performance prior to 1924.

The change in billing, however, did not deter the flow of sightseers to the summit. Even the setting for the flamboyant exhibitions of past decades was a pretentious attraction, and every few years the audience was rewarded with another outburst, such as the display of November 1959, when a lava fountain in Kilauea Iki shot up to the unprecedented height of 1900 feet. But the slightest eruption brought swarms of fire watchers. They came by the carload and busload to watch from the ground, by the planeload to gape from the air.

Volcanoes grew into big show business in Hawaii. For spectators with a little imagination, the turbulent drama of the Big Island unfolded most vividly along the two-hundred-mile highway that circumscribed Mauna Loa, a highway crossing innumerable scars of historic flows, most of them proudly marked and dated. They appeared in almost monotonous succession, 1859 Flow, 1801 Flow, 1850, 1950, 1919, 1926, 1916, 1907, 1868, 1881, 1852, 1955, 1840, 1960, 1880, 1885, 1899, 1843, all memorable years, with more dates to be added, for the show is bound to go on.

On adjacent Maui, Haleakala had not erupted for some two hundred years; yet few volcanologists were taking wagers that it would not come to life again in the next century, the next decade, or next year. They still preferred to classify it as "dormant." Dormant or extinct, the panorama from its summit was one of the stupendous sights of the hemisphere, to the east a crater twenty-one miles in circumference, enclosing a dead, sunken world of ash, cinder cones, and weathered lava that might have been borrowed from the landscape of the moon; to the west, stretching out ten thousand feet below, a fresh green virgin world pasted against a sapphire ocean.

"I felt like the Last Man, neglected in judgment, and left pinnacled in mid-Heaven, a forgotten relic of a vanished world," cried Mark Twain after ruminating for half a day on that upper outpost. "It was the sublimest spectacle I ever witnessed, and I think the memory of it will remain with me always."

Responding to Twain's enthusiasm, Island publicists concluded that their dormant volcano had the most magnificent crater in the world. Far and wide they spread word of its magnitude, until it was accepted as fact in any treatise on Hawaii that Haleakala's sleeping *caldera,* seven and a half miles long by two and a half wide and covering an area of nineteen square miles, was the largest on earth.

Part of the truth was clouded by semantics having to do with "dormancy," part by elastic yardsticks. The tourist folders and glib guides still proclaim the fallacy, though Java's extinct crater, the Idjen plateau, covers eighty-two square miles; Tanganyika's game-filled Ngorongoro Crater, one hundred and fifty; New Mexico's Valley Grande Crater, one hundred and seventy-six; and the paragon of them all, Japan's Aso-san, measures a circumference of over seventy miles; even the "temporarily dormant" stump of Oregon's Mount Mazama, enclosing famed Crater Lake, is a little larger, with a circumference of twenty-six miles and spread of twenty square miles.

But scientists of the age of space discovered uses for the tops of Hawaii's mountains far beyond mere sightseeing and volcanic investigation. They climbed to the crest of Haleakala not because it boasted one of the largest dormant craters on the planet but because it commanded the clearest known outlook into the sky. There on the lip of Haleakala's enormous maw they built a cold concrete acropolis, Science City, a cluster of temples dedicated to the new deity Physics—such complexes as the University of Hawaii's Institute of Geophysics with its solar, airglow and zodiacal light observatories and its Smithsonian satellite tracking station; the University of Michigan's five-million-dollar Astrophysics Observatory; installations supported by the National Aeronautics and Space Administration, Defense Department, National Science Foundation, and National Bureau of Standards.

The prerequisite for citizenship in Science City was a Ph.D. in physics. The residents were all doctors, profoundly concerned with the Van Allen radiation belt, Gengenshine light, Zodiacal light, the "tropical arc," airglow, solar meteorology, and the behavior of orbiting satellites and ballistic missles.

These space explorers had been driven from the Mainland by smoke, smog, frost, the glare of metropolitan illumination at night, the exhausts of industry, traffic, and concentrated population that fouled the atmosphere through which they had to peer. In Hawaii the volcano heads poked above the clouds, and the air was purged by fresh trade winds year in and year out. Here were the ideal windows looking into the heavens. And the windows would be clean at least until tomorrow's eruption smudged them.

HILO HARBOR

XIII

As If Distance and Ocean
Were Shrinking

Fighting head winds and hard luck, battered by gales off the Horn, becalmed for days in the equatorial doldrums of the Atlantic or the Pacific, whalers had often spent half a year beating a passage from the East Coast to Hawaii. Lucky ships, blessed with fair winds and a Spartan skipper, made it in 120 days. The average time was around five months.

From any center of Atlantic commerce, it took about as long to reach Honolulu as any other commonly frequented port in the world. Literally, as well as figuratively, early mariners had fixed the Sandwich Islands "at the ends of the earth," and they remained there. Mileage charts supported the fixation, for the circumference of the globe was set roughly at twenty-four thousand miles, and traveling the eighteen thousand miles from New York to Honolulu via the Horn was like sailing three-quarters of the way around the globe.

There was no way of eliminating many of the miles or much of the tedium in getting there. Regardless of the mode of transport, the slow pace was taken for granted in traveling to all distant destinations during the first half of the nineteenth century. The fleet of windjammers plying the route to isolated Hawaii was the counterpart of the strings of Conestoga wagons crossing the American continent. Hawaii retained its isolation until November 7, 1848.

Early that day the *Sea Witch* rounded Diamond Head, crowded with sail and looking like a white thunderhead drifted in from the horizon. Bank on bank of ballooning, glittering canvas caught the offshore trade winds and seemed to give her the lift of a spectre as she swept abreast of Waikiki and on toward Honolulu harbor.

Nothing quite like the *Sea Witch* had ever before invaded Hawaiian waters; yet anyone who read the newspapers or knew anything about shipping recognized her on sight, the fastest ship afloat, the handsomest vessel sailing out of New York, the marvel of the seas that only a year before had set the world agog by racing from Canton to New York in the unprecedented time of 77 days, so famous that in the very act of adding Honolulu to her ports of call, she inevitably shed a little of her prestige upon the Islands.

On this run she was not out to chalk up any new records, but her coming nevertheless marked the end of an old era in communication and ushered in a new. After November 7, 1848, Hawaii was no longer at the ends of the earth. Wonderful developments in transportation, restyling of hulls and rigging, superior mechanical innovations were bringing the Islands months nearer to the rest of the world.

The *Sea Witch* represented that new class of American ship called the clipper, the Baltimore clipper, distinguished by lofty, raking masts, overhanging bow, long, narrow, graceful lines, full rigging, and acres of canvas, top gallant and royal sails, moonrakers and skysails. In designing it, the Maryland craftsmen had borrowed freely from the lines of the fast French warships, improved on their model, and sent down the ways the swiftest sailing vessel ever constructed. In the *Sea Witch* were embodied the true traits of the clipper; she was the example pre-eminent; and it was she that symbolically introduced the Islands to the new conception of world proximity.

But other notable events were simultaneously helping to relieve Hawaii of its isolation. Mexico's formal cession of California the same year brought the territorial borders of the United States within 2100 miles of the Islands, and the gold rush brought a population rush that much nearer.

Emigrants to the West Coast became very much aware that the nearest likeness of an American community, with Yankee business houses, the charity of a consular agent, medical facilities, and a supply of homely everyday wants like soap, bacon and a good cheap cigar, was not back across the continent but beyond the ocean horizon at Honolulu, an easy sail of a few weeks, rather than a perilous march of months. The whalers and missionaries had established that outpost.

For a few years, long enough to create enduring commercial routes, the Islands became a supply center for the West and a retreat for the malcontents, the ailing, and the drifters whose luck had played out in California. Moreover, a homesick Argonaut was quick to discover that it might be easier to work a passage back East by way of Lahaina or Honolulu than direct from San Francisco.

The gold rush detoured all major Pacific traffic to California, and only the slower freighters continued the Island run; so after that 1848 call of the *Sea Witch*, it was three years before Hawaiians saw another clipper. But 1851 brought the glorious *Flying Cloud*, and in her wake came a veritable parade of sleek three- and four-masters; the *Southern Cross; R.B. Forbes*, 99 days from Boston; *Snow Squall; Invincible; Reindeer*, distinguished by her double topsails; *Staghound; Sea Serpent; Kate Hayes; Pathfinder; N. B. Palmer*. All of them were famous in their day; their comings and goings averaged almost one a month for the whole year 1852, and they raised havoc with the old records. The *N. B. Palmer* made her return run to New York in just 82 days, cutting the preclipper time squarely in half.

While picking up speed, the ships were also increasing in size. The *Southern Cross* registered 950 tons; *Sea Serpent*, 1337; *Staghound*, 1535; *Invincible*, 1726. *Sovereign of the Seas*, which put in at Honolulu on January 15, 1853, topped them all with 2421 tons, loaded 8,000 barrels of whale oil, and 82 days later rode into New York harbor, where her master bragged that he could have easily carried a third more cargo, but had had to leave 3,000 barrels behind to clear the shallow bar guarding Honolulu harbor. Despite the ponderous cargoes, dockside witnesses in Hawaii claimed that those graceful clippers were so fast that after easing out of the harbor and trimming sail, a fair breeze would take them over the horizon in less than two hours.

Discovery of guano on the low-lying islands to the northwest, the tail of the Hawaiian chain between Kauai and Midway, lured larger fleets of fast clippers. There were fortunes in the filthy trade, and it seemed to beckon the prettiest ships with the most poetic names, *Robin Hood, Astoria, White Swallow, Fair Wind, Morning Light, Silver Star.* They, too, made records in rushing their lucrative, foul-smelling cargoes around the Horn.

The completion of the 47-mile railroad across the Isthmus of Panama in 1859 altered the shipping lanes and trimmed six weeks to two months off travel time to Hawaii for those in a hurry. And the completion of the Union Pacific across the United States ten years later cut the time to what appeared to be an irreducible minimum, a month from New York to Honolulu or three weeks with good connections, as if distance and ocean were shrinking before the contrivings of man.

The race from San Francisco to the Islands was on. In 1858 the American bark *Yankee* challenged all comers by reducing the usual sailing time of two weeks or longer to eleven days. *Black Hawk* accepted the challenge and broke the record the following year with nine days, nine hours. In 1861 both *Nor'wester* and *Comet* equalled that mark, and *Fair Wind* astonished the nautical world by making the passage in eight days, 17½ hours, a record that stood for twenty years, until 1881 when the brigantine *William G. Irvin* managed to clip a half-hour off the *Fair Wind's* time on a run from San Francisco to Kahului. Any vessel that could not make the passage in ten days was a tramp.

But while people and goods were being ferried to Hawaii with almost immoral speed, nothing comparable was happening to inter-island transportation. It was incredibly slow, never on schedule, crowded, shockingly unsanitary, tormentingly uncomfortable. On occasion the 250-mile trip from Honolulu to Hilo could take longer than the 2100-mile trip from San Francisco to Honolulu, and for a squeamish passenger every hour of it could be torture.

"There is no such thing as keeping a vessel in elegant condition, when she carries molasses and Kanakas," slurred Mark Twain, noting that the deck of the *"Boomerang"*, on which he traveled, was a solid confusion of "natives of both sexes, with their customary dogs, mats, blankets, pipes, calabashes of poi, fleas, and other luxuries and baggage of minor importance." To convey some notion of the general air of an interisland schooner, he added that as soon as they set sail, "the natives all lay down on the deck as thick as negroes in a slave-pen, and smoked, conversed, and spit on each other and were truly sociable."

Sometimes a small area on the after deck was roped off for "quality folks," and the cabin below was exclusively theirs, but the space reserved on deck was no less crowded than that taken by third-class passengers, and the cabin far too airless and malodorous for civilized occupancy.

The need for comfortable, safe and reasonably punctual service between the islands was great, but it did not materialize. Kings and chiefs had a tendency to grant shipping franchises to favorite relatives, and although Hawaiians were born sailors, they did not make exemplary skippers, supercargoes, and navigators. They built the most seaworthy canoes ever to venture over an ocean horizon, but their attempts at constructing *haole*-style vessels were crude and graceless.

John Young, who once had charge of the shipyards at Kawaihae and organized the first Hawaiian sailing fleet, at best was an improvisator. Better ships were built later at Lahaina and Honolulu; yet they were still clumsy and short-lived.

What was lacking in quality of transportation was made up in quantity. By the late 1830's there were no less than 67 Hawaiian-owned sloops, brigs, schooners, and assorted arks that defied classification sailing between the islands or on longer voyages, but more than half of them were the product of shipyards scattered around the globe from New Zealand to New England, and too many had seen their best days before they passed into the hands of their new masters. Few had a capacity of over fifteen or twenty tons. Foreigners dubbed the Island argosy the "mosquito fleet," before mosquitoes were a common enough pest for natives to appreciate the slight.

As a general rule, the good English names of foreign-built ships were discarded in favor of better Hawaiian ones. The topsail schooner *Post Boy*, for example, was rechristened *Kinoole*; the *Sovereign* became *Ka Moi*; *S. B. Wheeler* was changed to *Akamai*, and *West Point* to *Kalama*.

Though native captains occasionally set out on long voyages to distant Pacific islands, Asia, and the Americas and survived the venture to sail again, most were content with the interisland run, and rarely in maritime history have any seafarers demonstrated a more casual regard for human comfort, safety, and sanitation.

By owners and captains alike, success in a shipping enterprise was judged solely by the quantity of passengers and freight that could be crowded aboard, regardless of weather, crew shortages, and condition of the hull. "I have made a two-day passage on one of the larger of these vessels," avowed a *haole* patron, "when the crowd of sitting natives was so dense that the sailors could pass along the vessel only by walking on the gunwales or the bulwarks."

One excursion on an interisland ferry was enough to cure most *malihinis* of wanderlust. Inevitable nausea was only one affliction; equally distressing were the reek of bilge water, the insufferable heat, the fleas and rodents, the swarms of roaches, the terror of capsizing, the jostling of the natives and, worst of all, the unmitigated tedium. An overnight trip was often gratuitously extended to a week or a fortnight. Ships were blown perilously off course and out of sight of land or becalmed for days within a few miles of shore. Passengers ran out of food, potables, and patience.

"A day or two out, coming from either Maui or Hawaii, could be endured," conceded an Islander, obliged to make frequent visits to Hilo, "but it was on the homeward passage when beating up against the strong trade winds, with all the nauseating effluvia that comes from

the mixture of molasses and sea water, with all the disagreeable ad-
juncts attending a miscellaneous cargo that the trials began . . . decks
crowded with natives in dress and undress, with pigs and poultry,
cattle and horses, so packed together that scarce a place could be
found to spread a mattress."

For scared, seasick passengers the comportment of the captain in
an emergency was seldom reassuring either. He could be as scared and
confused as they, have no compunction about showing it, and in a real
crisis abandon his pride and summon the more responsible white passengers for a vote on what direction to steer. In Hawaiian waters
originated the quip about the baffled skipper who appealed to a distinguished passenger for counsel on what course to pursue and was told
to go back where he started and try again.

Occasionally that happened anyway. After a week or two of aimless drifting, a master might be able to coax his schooner back to
home port where he could restock, discharge a ruined cargo, and set out
once more for the same destination. On the other hand, a coaster
piled up on the reef off Lahaina in the fairest of weather, after an
unusually quick sail from Honolulu, and the only explanation the tipsy
skipper could offer for the debacle was that they had reached Lahaina
"before the nearness to land was discovered."

Native captains were slow to profit from their errors in navigation
or judgment, and even a wreck or two on the record would not neces-
sarily stand in the way of their getting a new ship. Generally they were
inclined to affect a slight haughtiness in bearing and ostentation in
attire. Captain John Hall was a good example. He conferred upon
himself the title of "Admiral" on assuming command of the *Kamehameha III,* outdid the King himself in dashing splendor of getup,
tailored white uniform with yards of gold braid, polished Kamehameha buttons, and betasseled epaulets. When in port, he took advantage of his prestige to promote his wife's profession, and was
rowed grandly in his gig from ship to ship, visiting fellow captains,
with the introduction: "Me Admiral John Hall. *Kamehameha III* my
ship. Me Commander. Suppose you want clothes wash. My wife do it
good."

Though a few of the early interisland schooners stayed afloat, through luck or fair seamanship, for twenty years or longer, most of them had short careers. In laconic phrases, port directors wrote them off one by one when they failed to reappear after a decent interval, rarely hinting of the treacherous waters in which they may have foundered or the inexpert navigation that may have contributed to their doom.

"Never more heard from" was the most common epitaph entered on the records. That was the only notice accorded the *Liholiho*, crack Hilo packet that abandoned her franchise to go off on a guano search, and the *Kamamalu*, lost mysteriously between Hilo and Lahaina with a full cargo and some seventy souls. The toll in ships and lives from such enigmatic disappearances was appalling.

Ships flying the Hawaiian colors foundered almost as rapidly as new ones were commissioned. They ran aground, they burned, they capsized, they were swamped in high seas, and they were wrecked by high winds. The brig *Starling*, loading potatoes off Kalepolepo, Maui, in a "souther" parted her anchors and piled up on shore, a total loss. The schooner *Sally*, taking on *pulu* bales off Kaholakele, Hawaii, met the same fate. A new schooner, anchored off Lahaina for the night, without a soul aboard, simply was not in sight the next morning, and was "never more heard from." *Moi Keiki* went to the rescue of her sister ship *Ka Moi*, which had run ashore at Kaunakakai, and the two wound up side by side in the same grave. The splendid schooner *Emma Rooke*, built in New London, Connecticut, met an ignominious end merely running ashore at Kohala "in fine weather with a light breeze." All the islands were rimmed with wrecks, but the most populous graveyards were along the rocky shores of Kauai.

Even when steamers began to compete with schooners, they did little to improve the reputation of interisland transportation. With a great deal of fanfare and the assurance of a five-year monopoly, the gawky, cumbersome *Constitution* arrived from San Francisco in 1852. Islanders were certain that this steamer would dispel all the discomforts and uncertainties of travel between the islands. A single trip to Lahaina convinced her owners that she was not built to maneuver the tricky channels and reef-bound shores. She returned to Honolulu, where her contract was cancelled, and then headed back for the Golden Gate.

The *S. B. Wheeler,* rechristened the *Akamai,* appeared the following year under the aegis of the Hawaiian Steam Navigation Company. She proved too small and too old. Overloaded with some five hundred passengers and nineteen horses, she sprung a leak in a heavy squall en route to Maui a few months after going into operation and, in an exciting race against time and calamity, barely made port, where she was promptly condemned and sold for junk.

Two weeks after that near disaster, the side-wheeler *Seabird* limped into Honolulu harbor from the Coast to take the *Akamai's* place, as if by prearrangement. The *Seabird,* too, had suffered a close brush with fate in transit. All too optimistically, her owners had calculated she could make the crossing in a week and had provisioned her accordingly. The voyage took twelve days, and she had run out of coal.

Providentially the whaler *Oregon* crossed her path in mid-Pacific and transferred a few tons of blubber to keep the furnaces aglow a while longer. After the blubber was gone, the steerage bunks, furnishings, rails, bulkheads, and miscellaneous cargo fed the boilers. According to a crew member, the ship reached Honolulu "with barely steam enough from the last keg of butter to turn her wheels."

The *Seabird* looked like salvage when she arrived, but she was refurbished and put on the run to Maui and Hawaii. A sister side-wheeler, the *Kalama,* soon took on the Kauai beat. Actually both were nothing but oversized river boats, far too awkward and expensive for interisland service. But despite the high cost, they were kept in operation for more than a year. Then the *Kalama* was blown ashore at Koloa and pronounced a total wreck within a few hours. To avoid a similar fate, the *Seabird* was withdrawn and piloted the rest of the way across the Pacific to resume in China the river service for which she was originally designed.

By that time the Hawaiian Steam Navigation Company was ready to go into coastal transportation seriously, invest in bottoms better suited to Hawaiian oceanography, and secure ship personnel trained to cope with local problems in navigation. At East Boston the company had a sturdy brigantine converted into a screw steamer, renamed her the *Kilauea,* and hired a competent crew to bring her around the Horn. She proved her seaworthiness on the six-month transit, and on January 28, 1860, was given an hilarious welcome in Honolulu.

Wisely the company announced that she was going to be placed on trial for the rest of the year before sailing on regular schedule. She made successful trips to Kauai, to Maui, and to Hawaii, and late in the summer took a huge excursion party to Hilo for a four-day stopover to give her clientele a view of the fiery mountain for which she was named. No one could have conjured up a better publicity stunt. The *Kilauea* immediately topped the popularity list among interisland transports, was always crowded, always heavily laden with freight, and a money-maker. In one quarter she grossed the astonishing sum of $9,499.

Like her sail-rigged competitors, she left many a scar on the reefs and submerged lava flows in her path and had some close calls, but generally was not tied up for repairs more than half the time. During her periods of incapacity, the plucky little steamer *Annie Laurie,* first ship to be constructed at the Honolulu Iron Works, served as stand-in. But she was too small for a profitable substitute, too prone to drag bottom, and eventually went on the rocks at Koloa, leaving her big sister to fend for herself.

On the unlucky thirteenth day of January, 1866, a shrieking gale drove the *Kilauea* over the reef at Kawaihae, where she was impetuously given up for lost. Impounded inside the reef in eight feet of water, she was sold at public auction for $6,100. But a few days later an ingenious salvage crew buoyed her back over the reef, sailed her to Honolulu for repairs, and resold her to the original owners for $16,000.

Repeatedly after that she survived brushes with disaster in storm, fire, collision, shallow water, and tempestuous seas. The *Kilauea* had more lives than a cat, and in 1870 was lauded as a Pacific heroine when she recovered, in a precarious rescue operation, the crew of the wrecked U.S.S. *Saginaw* from Kure Island. After eighteen years of service, she was finally bid off, more or less intact, to the Honolulu Iron Works for $3,700. She has proved "a staunch and excellent seaboat," voiced one of her many eulogists, "having tested her qualities on nearly every reef around the Islands."

The strong constitution of the *Kilauea,* and the dividends she brought in convinced the Inter-Island Steam Navigation Company that coasting under mechanical power was a sound proposition. In 1877 the *Likelike* took her place. Others, with appropriate names like *Lehua, Kinau, Iwalani, Waialeale* and *Pele,* were added, until the company could keep in simultaneous operation a fleet of five and guarantee visits to the outer islands at least once a month and sometimes twice. The days of experimentation had passed. Everyone took for granted that the interisland steamers, serving any little port that could boast of a wharf or offshore lighterage, had come to stay.

By the middle seventies and early eighties, a comparable shift in transportation from the Mainland had occurred, too; clippers were on their way out, and steamship lines, linking Honolulu with any major port in the world, were in. Chanted C. F. Gordon Cumming in 1879, "I see advertisements of Boston Packets, Bremen Packets, Hawaiian Packets, Planter's Packets, Spreckels Line, Merchant Line, New York Line, Liverpool and Glasgow—and last, but greatest, the Pacific Mail Steamship Company. These are represented by five distinct agencies and suggest a condition of commerce by no means insignificant."

Periodically steam-propelled liners and freighters sailed to the principal ports on both sides of the Atlantic, to Portland and Seattle, to Hong Kong, Sydney, Manila, Auckland, and, twice a month, to San Francisco. Honolulu had grown into an indispensable coaling station, and zealous rooters were already trying to picture it as one of the crossroads of the world.

The most voluminous trade was with San Francisco. For years the sailing records made by the clippers between the Islands and the Golden Gate had been treated like sporting statistics. Now these were discarded, and the records chalked up by steamers were the figures to memorize. The *Australia* had made the 2100-mile crossing in the

unbelievable time of six days and sixteen hours; the *City of Sydney*
clipped two hours off that; the *Zealandia* bested the *Sydney* by thirty-
five minutes; then, in July 1883, the new *Mariposa* of the Oceanic
Line topped them all with a mark that stood for years, five days and
twenty hours.

Scarcely noticed among all the traffic was a diminutive and anarch-
ronous sailing schooner of two hundred tons, the *Emma Claudina*,
which made her maiden voyage under new ownership from San Francisco to Hilo late in 1882. *Emma* was not trying to break any records.
She was an ordinary freighter bringing general merchandise to the
Islands and returning to California with a cargo of sugar for Spreckels
Brothers, who had put up most of the capital for the purchase of the
ship. Her commander was a young Swedish immigrant William
Matson, destined to become founder and namesake of the line that
would be Hawaii's major carrier.

Matson was not in a hurry. The week or two saved in transporting
sugar to the Coast by steam was of little consequence to him. Sails were
good enough and fast enough. Over a period of two decades he built
the foundation for his empire slowly and solidly on outmoded vessels.
When the *Emma Claudina* was no longer adequate to carry all the
freight his agents assembled, be purchased more ships like her, the
Lurline, Harvester, Falls of Clyde, Roderick Dhu.

Though William Matson had made a name for himself and his
dependable service long before 1901, the Matson Navigation Company was not even organized until then. And he did not begin changing to steam until the following year, when the *Enterprise* was added
to the fleet as his first coal burner. Fundamentally the success of the
Matson Line was based on rapport between key executives and their
subordinates, rapport and fierce loyalty. "Feed the men well and make
them work," was Matson's gospel in dealing with crews, and the same
principle was extended through the rest of the company organization.

He believed, too, in diversifying his interests, made astute investments in California oil fields, organized the Honolulu Oil Corporation,
persuaded the engineers in the sugar mills to change to oil, and shortly
converted the *Enterprise* into an oil burner, the first such experiment
in the Pacific.

Company headquarters were in San Francisco, and the earthquake and fire of 1906 brought near disaster; practically all of the corporation records were destroyed. Matson responded by purchasing the *Hilonian* that year and a new *Lurline* in 1908 and gradually devoting more space on his ships to passenger service. He saw a future in catering to travelers.

Orthodox shippers were sure that he was making the mistake of his life when he commissioned the *Wilhelmina* with rooms for 140 passengers and an extravagant distribution of twelve baths for their exclusive use. The rash venture was such a success that the *Matsonia* and *Maui*, each with a capacity for ten thousand tons of cargo and two hundred passengers—and still more baths—were added. Moreover, company interests were diversified further by going into the hotel business, so that the passengers he brought to the Islands could count on comfortable accommodations.

Matson died in 1917, as his empire was just starting to boom, but his heirs and his agents Castle and Cooke, who possessed a substantial share of the stock, kept it growing. The big freighters *Manulani* and *Manukai* were purchased in 1920, and more were soon commissioned. A sixteen-story Matson building went up in San Francisco. The Spreckels' Oceanic Line was taken over with its famed ships *Sierra*, *Sonoma* and *Ventura*, serving the South Seas, Australia, and New Zealand.

The *Malolo*, first real luxury liner in the Pacific trade, known as "The Speed Queen of the Pacific," went to sea in 1927 and reduced crossing time between San Francisco and Honolulu to four and a half days. The *Mariposa*, *Monterey*, and the third *Lurline* followed, each costing some eight million dollars. Then, with the purchase of the Los Angeles Steamship Company, great ships like the *City of Honolulu* and the *City of Los Angeles* were added to the fleet. Less than two decades after William Matson's death, forty steamers were flying the Matson burgee, and the company that started in 1882 with a single awkward schooner virtually held a monopoly on surface transportation to Hawaii.

Matson did more than all the other surface shipping concerns combined to make the Islands accessible. He brought Honolulu within less than a week of the Coast and organized tours to the Islands and among the Islands. Residents were thrilled at the sight of multitudes streaming down the gangways. But they had to revise their idea of a multitude when the tourists began coming by air as well as sea.

Before the middle twenties, any thought of flying ordinary visitors to Hawaii was visionary. The first airplane seen by very many Islanders was in December, 1910, seven years after Kitty Hawk, when a daredevil, popularly known as "Bud" Mars, shipped an unwieldy biplane, the *Skylark,* to Honolulu, put it on display at Moanalua Polo Field, and made several brief, hair-raising hops for the entertainment of the public. He drew crowds of spectators before the contraption was declared a menace and grounded.

The next year brought three more exhibitionists, a French barnstormer, Didier Masson, who thrilled Honolulu with three or four real flights over the city; a reckless Chinese adventurer, Tom Gunn, who hitched pontoons to the underside of his biplane and circled over Pearl Harbor; and Clarence Walker, who coaxed a heavily constructed plane aloft from a field outside Hilo, ascended to a breath-taking height of a hundred feet, and dropped from that altitude, demolishing both his flying machine and a stately algarroba that stood in the way.

During the next ten years commercial aviators paid occasional visits to the Islands, and for a price took thrill seekers for rides over their countryside, but sober citizens were inclined to rank flying along with circus acts. They did not see much practical use for it in Hawaii; the land mass was too limited and too rugged, the winds too treacherous, and the islands too far apart. Even after three single-engine seaplanes of the Army Signal Corps started buzzing around Pearl Harbor in March 1917, civilian aviation was not taken seriously.

Then, early in 1919, after World War I had demonstrated the adaptability of planes to a variety of weather patterns and terrain, the conservatives were startled by the announcement that U.S. Army Major Harold M. Clarke, accompanied by his mechanic, had flown all the way from Oahu to Hawaii. To be sure, the major had lost his bearings in dense clouds, had made a forced landing on Mauna Kea, and had been obliged to abandon the plane, but neither pilot nor mechanic were badly injured, and, there was no denying the fact that they had actually covered the one hundred-fifty overwater miles. With better luck, and a stopover on Maui, perhaps flying between the islands was not too scatterbrained an idea after all.

Suddenly there was a complete change of attitude among the detractors. Major Clarke had touched off a revolution. Within a few months army and navy pilots were making routine training flights all over the Islands; civilians were talking about building airports; some two hundred boosters formed a chapter of the National Aeronautics Association; and the legislature jumped on the bandwagon to enact a flying code called "The Uniform Law of Aeronautics."

In 1919 the bumps and boulders were scraped off a few acres on Ford Island in Pearl Harbor, and the resulting stretch of pulverized coral and sand christened Luke Field, after World War ace, Lieutenant Frank Luke, who had shot down eighteen enemy planes in three weeks of combat. Army and navy shared the runway, sometimes competitively, until the Army Signal Corps leveled off Wheeler Field south of Schofield Barracks three years later.

Not to be outdone by the military, the legislature agreed to appropriate the generous sum of forty-five thousand dollars for a civilian airport at Moanalua, halfway between Honolulu and Pearl Harbor, provided the Chamber of Commerce would substantiate its professed interest by raising an additional twenty thousand dollars. That was all the prodding the Chamber needed; with unexpected alacrity a check for the full amount was produced. Meantime, word came from Hilo that a tract of one hundred acres had been set aside for a field there.

Momentum was picking up. "As soon as the Honolulu and Hilo fields are ready for use," augured a respected local prophet, "the Territory will witness the inauguration of an inter-island commercial air service, probably with tri-motored planes similar in general type to the mono-plane used by Commander Byrd in his 1600-mile flight to the North Pole." And when the navy completed the erection of a mooring mast for dirigibles in July 1925, the prophet went out further on the limb to wager that "A few years should witness commercial traffic by dirigible from the mainland and the Orient to Hawaii, in addition to an airplane service among Mark Twain's 'loveliest fleet of islands.' "

To dramatize the urgency for getting some sort of lift in operation between the Mainland and the Islands, late in August 1925 the navy in an impressive gesture ordered to sea most of the Pacific-based fleet. It was to form a veritable bridge of naval craft, spaced not farther than two hundred miles apart, all the way from San Francisco to Honolulu, and over this string of ships, breathing smoke clouds by day and flashing searchlight fingers by night, were to fly the latest thing in far-ranging aircraft, two PN9's, piloted respectively by the crack navy aviators, Commander John Rodgers and Lieutenant A. P. Snody, each with a crew of four.

They took off on the dot of 3 P.M., August 31st. It was the navy's do-or-die bid to beat the army and the aeronauts of the world in the first great transpacific flight. And it was of major importance to Islanders as well, for success or failure of the attempt would determine just how near Hawaii was to the liberation that air travel would bring.

Four hours after take-off, it appeared that the navy had over-extended itself in the quest for glory. Snody's plane developed motor trouble less than three hundred miles from the starting point. He was forced down. The plane, however, was quickly spotted by a destroyer, given a line, and towed safely back to the Coast, only to come to grief in San Francisco Bay.

Rodgers and his crew flew on alone, more than ever conscious of their responsibility in accomplishing the expensive, epoch-making mission. They picked up the beacons on the bridges of ships one by one and sent back reassuring messages: "Feeling fine." "All okay." Following the line of searchlights through the night simplified problems of navigation, and the smoke streamers next morning were almost as easy to spot. Indeed, the flight was going much better than they had dared hope. They were far past the point of no return, and so near to their destination that they were already aglow with anticipation of success. But trouble was in the offing.

"Foul weather ahead," warned both the *Aroostook* and the *Tanager*, last two ships in the long chain. Late in the morning of September 1st, Rodgers bored into that foul weather, only three hundred miles from his goal, to be buffeted and jolted with enough vengeance to make up for all the smooth flying over the first hundreds of miles. Through breaks in the clouds, they could see that the warnings had not been exaggerated. A tempest seemed to be churning the ocean below. Moreover, the fuel supply was dangerously low.

The *Tanager* picked up several garbled and ominous messages about gas shortage, then a clear one: "We haven't gas to last five minutes." A moment later came the frantic call: "We will crack up if we have to land in this rough sea without motive power." There was a long wait before the final terse flash: "Alighted 1:34 P.M." No position was given, no hint of how the plane had taken the shock. Silence followed.

During the morning frequent reports on the progress of the flight had been radioed to Honolulu, and crowds had thronged to the landing area to welcome the five heroes-to-be. Hours before the plane was due, a sea of expectant, upturned faces scanned the skies. When word that the plane had been forced down was circulated, an incredulous, deathly silence swept over the mob. Slowly the assemblage dispersed, as though every individual were a participant in the defeat.

In the next ten days Hawaii served as base for the most extravagant sea search the Pacific had ever known. Owners of every fishing boat, yacht, and ocean-worthy scow in the Islands wanted to join in the hunt. And there was a lot of sea to scour, for no one knew within several hundred square miles where the plane had gone down. Coordinating the search were twenty-three naval vessels and all available scouting planes, which came to a total of six.

Unfortunately there was a great deal of thick weather in early September, and a bewildering number of reports of night flares coming from all points of the compass. Again and again every square mile of ocean between the Islands and about them was combed, without uncovering so much as a trace of the lost plane.

Hope was all but abandoned, and volunteers had long since given up the quest when, late in the afternoon of September 10th, the incredible happened. The Honolulu *Advertiser* received a radio message from Kauai that Rodgers and his crew, all in good spirits though exhausted and half-starved, had just arrived at Nawiliwili in a fuelless plane, towed by a submarine that located them fifteen miles to the northwest. Immediately the destroyer *MacDonough* was dispatched from Pearl Harbor to recover the celebrities and transport them in state to Oahu.

Though Commander Rodgers had not quite reached his destination by air, he still saw the possibility of retaining the flight honors for the navy through the simple expedient of staying physically in his plane until it touched Oahu. Grasping that technicality, he had insisted on remaining with the plane while it was being towed into Nawiliwili, and upon arrival of the *MacDonough,* he contended with equal vehemence that it was his privilege to ride in the cockpit when the PN9 was taken in tow for the voyage to Oahu.

But the captain of the destroyer overruled him, ordered that he travel as a deck passenger, and, as a result, the success or failure of the flight was going to remain a moot point. Rodgers obviously was not too happy about being rescued by the submarine anyway. "We were sailing," he protested later. "We had taken some cloth from the plane, which we made into a sail, whereby we were making two knots an hour, so we knew that sooner or later we would make port, and were about to succeed when somebody came along and found us."

Getting to Oahu *in* his plane was what mattered to Rodgers, and he was deprived of that privilege. But the narrow distinction meant nothing to the throng of lay welcomers in Honolulu. The sirens and fog horns of every warship, tug, and liner in port greeted the quintet early in the evening of September 11th, and those noisemakers were drowned by the cheering thousands that mobbed the Pearl Harbor docks. The heroes were smothered in acclaim and leis. In one banquet after another they were feted like liberators, and in a way they were liberators. Rodgers had proved that air service to Hawaii was feasible; travel to the Islands was no longer restricted to slow surface transportation.

Honolulu flight enthusiasts were no less electrified a year and a half later when bold, black headlines proclaimed that Charles A. Lindbergh had made a solo dash of 3,610 miles across the Atlantic. If a nonstop crossing could be completed so easily from New York to Paris, surely the shorter one from California to Hawaii would be a cinch. The world's greatest pineapple salesman, James D. Dole, shared that view.

The incentive for the Lindbergh feat had been the Orteig prize of twenty-five thousand dollars. When the captain touched down in France on May 21, 1927, to claim the gratuity, the event made such an impression on the president-manager of the Hawaiian Pineapple Company that within four days he announced the Dole awards of thirty-five thousand dollars for the first fliers to cross from the United States to the pineapple fields, twenty-five thousand dollars for the first prize, ten thousand dollars to the runner-up.

Disrespectfully implying that the Rodgers' effort was a failure, Dole haughtily announced: "The flight of Captain Lindbergh is an evidence of the startling progress being made in aeronautics. It seems obvious that a flight from the mainland to Hawaii should be next in order and that definite action to encourage such a flight would be appropriate. . . . It has taken the Lindbergh conquest of the Atlantic to make me realize that Hawaii in particular needs to have the future of aviation brought nearer to the present."

James Dole at the moment was in the midst of an all-out pineapple sales campaign, and, in addition to aviation, he was vitally interested in bringing the future of pineapple consumption nearer the present. In any case, one interest admirably served the other. The wheels of publicity started turning. Rumors were circulated that aviators far and near, commercial and military, amateur and professional, were making plans to enter the Dole Derby, the "Pineapple Derby." Pineapple sales soared, as did excitement over the air tourney.

To eliminate some of the confusion, the local chapter of the National Aeronautics Association was requested to draw up a set of ground rules and regulations for the race. They set twelve o'clock, August 12th, as the hour for take-off, Oakland as starting point.

As if to defy the nonmilitary rule makers and to taunt the navy for its not quite successful try, the army announced that two top-rank airmen, Lieutenants Lester Maitland and A. F. Hegenberger, were on their way from Dayton to San Francisco in a trimotored Fokker, and would fly on to Hawaii as soon as the plane could be serviced and the weather looked auspicious. No, they were not entering the Dole Derby; that was beneath the dignity of the army.

Then another flier, an airmail pilot, Ernest Smith, who was not interested in advertising pineapples either, let it be known that he was readying a plane in San Francisco for a pre-derby try at the honors. To many, these and other announcements reflected a spoilsport attitude toward the great August 12th event, but there was nothing that the Hawaiian Pineapple Company or the National Aeronautics Association could do about it.

The army team jumped the derby date by six weeks, took off from Oakland at 4:40 A.M. on June 28th, and by eight o'clock that evening crowds began pouring onto Oahu's Wheeler Field ready to hail the fliers. Excited welcomers kept coming all night; in fact, there was such a mob of eager rooters for the army that an entire regiment of infantry had to be assigned military police duty to keep them under control and off the runway.

"The sun was climbing into the heavens, and it was whispered about that the fliers were overdue," recalled one of the spectators. "There was much restlessness, and several thousand people began to leave the field.

"Suddenly out of a cloud literally at the back end of the field, came the great Fokker plane. It appeared over Schofield Barracks swooped down towards Wheeler Field, flying low, banked and circled, and a mighty roar went up from the crowd. The first plane in all history had crossed from mainland America to Hawaii."

Maitland and Hegenberger instantly became the new air heroes, and were lavishly honored for almost three weeks, until July 17th when airmail pilot Ernie Smith and his navigator Emory Bronte stole the show and the homage. But theirs was another marginal triumph, like Rodgers'. Throughout the day and night of their flight, they kept in touch with ship and shore radio stations; then at dawn came an SOS—and silence. It was assumed that they had crashed at sea, and preparations for another search were under way when the dramatic report came that they had miraculously arrived on Molokai.

These sensational preliminary flights, of course, were remarkably successful in taking the edge off excitement over the big derby. By August 11th, day before the scheduled take-off, flying to Hawaii was old stuff. Eight entries showed up at Oakland, and they reduced popular interest still further by agreeing unanimously to postpone the contest for four days.

On August 16th four of the big planes got off the ground, and two of them finished next day. The intrepid fliers Auggie Peddar and Jack Frost merely flew off over the Pacific, and, like the crews on vanishing Hawaiian sailing ships of an earlier generation, were "never more heard from." Arthur Goebel copped the twenty-five-thousand-dollar award, and Martin Jensen, as runner-up, claimed the ten thousand dollars. They were duly feted, laureled, and lionized in the Hawaiian manner, but with not quite the spontaneity shown the forerunners. And when it came to choosing the name of a pioneer aeronaut to bestow upon the Honolulu airport, there was little argument; Rodgers was given the distinction.

Undoubtedly the derby "brought the future of aviation nearer the present"—as well as advancing the sale of pineapples—for it sparked a whole series of other transpacific flights, inspired generous legislative support of Island airfield construction, and even promoted attempts to organize interisland plane service.

Four days after the derby, a latecomer from Dallas, Captain William Erwin, took off from Oakland for Honolulu. But he had not proceeded very far from the Coast before a frantic message came through, "We are in a tail spin." For two months the navy combed his route and never came across a vestige of the plane. Hollywood star Richard Grace, eager to share in the glory, had his monoplane shipped to the Islands and, in an aurora of publicity, prepared to fly from Barking Sands, Kauai, to the Mainland. But he was scarcely out of sight of the island when rudder trouble developed and he was forced to return. In landing, the plane cracked up; he was obliged to abandon his hope of being the first to make the eastbound flight, and shipped the wrecked plane back to Los Angeles.

Capitalizing on his newly acquired prestige as Dole Derby runner-up, Martin Jensen soon formed a commercial company for interisland air transportation. The service, however, had hardly started when the plane, affectionately labeled *Malolo,* crashed at Laie, near the Mormon Temple, killing its pilot, a photographer, and two passengers. That one tragedy was enough to terminate the enterprise.

Rather than discouraging other promoters, misfortune and successive failure seemed to stimulate a keener eagerness to climb into Hawaiian skies and to get passengers there, too. A flat strip along Ala Moana Boulevard in Honolulu was turned into Ward Airport, and there a flying school, operated by two former army fliers, thrived for a few years. They maintained a couple of small planes, in spare time running a limited air service to outer islands and supplying Maui with Honolulu newspapers.

From the same runway Lewis Air Tours took up sightseers in open cockpit planes on short, exhilarating hops for extravagant fees. But Ward Airport was too near town, had no room for expansion, and was soon discontinued.

In 1928 the officers of Inter-Island Steam Navigation Company foresightedly pictured the day when local citizens as well as tourists would insist on fast air jumps between the islands, instead of slow, nauseating surface travel. They organized the subsidiary Inter-Island Airways, imported twin-motored Sikorsky amphibians to add to the fleet of ships, and on Armistice Day of 1929 ostentatiously inaugurated the new service. It was efficient, dependable, and safe.

Even Colonel Lindbergh praised the line on a trip to the Islands as technical adviser for the aeronautics branch of the Department of Commerce. The amphibians could carry nine passengers and a crew of two and travel up to 125 miles per hour, bringing any of the islands within two hours of Honolulu. Great day!

The pace for development of air transportation over Hawaiian waters was set by Inter-Island, and it rarely slackened during the next decade. The original Sikorskys were soon replaced by sixteen-passenger planes that could cruise at 185 miles per hour. Airmail service was initiated on October 8, 1934, and passengers flew between the islands as casually as they rode the midget train to Pearl Harbor. The following year brought weekly Pan-American flights from the Mainland, and the dedication of Hickam Field. And early in the fall of 1936 the giant clippers began spanning the Pacific between San Francisco and Canton via Honolulu.

The honors sought by cinema actor Richard Grace in attempting an eastward dash in 1927 had been grabbed seven years later by Amelia Earhart, the first woman to cross the Atlantic in an airplane, the first woman to make that flight solo, the first woman to fly nonstop across the United States, the first women to fly an autogiro, the first woman to receive the Distinguished Flying Cross, the woman who flew for fun, for publicity, and for Beechnut.

In 1937, in a bid to add the distinction of being the first woman to fly around the world, she was on her way back to Honolulu after uneventfully crossing the Atlantic, Africa, India, Australia, and Indonesia to New Guinea. She did not make it, and the noisy Honolulu reception planned for her never came off.

The Wasp-engined Lockheed Electra flown by Amelia Earhart was widely publicized as the "flying laboratory," as though it were unique, but by 1937 all planes flying the Pacific had to be flying laboratories. From the impetus given by advances in plane engineering and navigational equipment, both trans-Pacific and interisland transportation boomed. The Islands actually did become a Pacific crossroads, for military as well as civilian planes.

In November 1940, the Hawaiian Air Force, first such command that had ever been constituted outside the continental limits of the United States, was activated at Fort Shafter, and six months later a mass flight of army bombers, twenty-one B-17's, took off from Hamilton Field in California for Hickam Field on Oahu. Spectacular long-distance flights en masse or single were routine after that.

Altogether the invasion of airplanes transformed the Islands more completely and more quickly than any other intrusive influence since the coming of the first sailing ships. They quickened the pulse of Island life; with the development of jets reduced transit from the Mainland to four or five hours, brought tourists in hordes, converted Waikiki from a quaint vacation resort into a city of plush high-rise apartments, long ago put interisland steamship passenger service out of business, and took the cream off luxury-liner trade from the Coast.

They also created a nostalgia for the good old days when distance was long and the Pacific broad and one could loaf and languish on the high seas in slow-paced contentment.

XIV
Eden, As It Might Have Been

Once the accounts of Cook, Vancouver, and their contemporaries started rolling from the presses, the outpouring of tidings from the Sandwich Islands never let up. Scribes accompanying Pacific exploration parties penned and published an astonishing quantity of information—and misinformation—on Owhyhee, Mowee, Atooi, Wahoo, Whyteete, and Honaroora. Literate mates on merchant vessels, jack-tar scriveners attached to the whaling fleet, officers on reconnoitering men-of-war, and writers who took hitches on windjammers ·contributed to the flow, and the missionaries outdid them all.

The accounts were quaint, contradictory, and endlessly repetitious, but that did not matter; readers reveled in the repetition. Behind all the emphasis on native depravity and indolence, something about the Islands had a universal appeal, gave the imagination a pellet to play with, the eternal balmy climate, the surf, the mountains and the palms, the easy-going "savages," even the innocence of nakedness. It was an

Edenish never-never land for which anyone in the dead of a northern winter could develop a hankering.

Every Island visitor with a flare for authorship felt a compulsive urge to put his observations on paper, and editors, accurately assessing the appetites of their public, begged for more. Newspapers never seemed to tire of repeating anecdotes about pig and poi, leis and luaus, surfing and sugar cane, and the more dignified parlor journals like *Munsey's*, the *Atlantic*, *North American Review*, *Harper's*, *Scribner's*, *Forum*, and *Century* were equally insatiable.

Overland included the Islands in its orbit and welcomed anything on Hawaii. The *Independent* and *Literary Digest* savored newsy tidbits with appropriate editorializing. Argumentative *Forum* managed to give a controversial turn to the simplest exposition on missionaries or sugar production. *Knickerbocker* was not choosy about the subject matter, as long as it had the sophisticated touch, while *New England Magazine* favored stories about Yankee achievements in the Pacific, home boys making good.

No region on earth, unassociated with the main stream of western culture, ever had so much written about it. When time had winnowed some of the aggregate, the pronouncements of Mark Twain, Herman Melville, Jack London, Robert Louis Stevenson, and writers of their rank were what people remembered, but their production was a drop in the verbal bucket compared to the effusions of the free lances.

Reports were pouring onto editorial desks during the blooming of the era of American romanticism, the age of Emerson and Thoreau, of imported Shelley, Keats, and Wordsworth, an age when nothing was more entrancing to either the armchair excursionist or the muscle-bound nature lover than a sunset on an ocean horizon or a moon coming over the mountains. Nature was glorious in the temperate zone; how much more glorious must it be under the spell of the tropics, with blue waters, blankets of bougainvillaea, and the scent of jasmine in the moonlight? The journalists portraying the lore of the Islands took advantage of this national mood; Hawaii's secret was not to be kept.

The reporters meant well, but if they had been slanderers intent on destroying all the aboriginal charm, they could not have been more effective. By writing so exhaustively and engagingly of the lazy, languid life, of the enchanting setting, of the uninhibited natives and their hospitality, they summoned the world, whet its curiosity, eventually converted the Islands into a public playground, and prepared the way for the tourist intrusion and the real estate booms, ignoring the fact that the old Hawaiian charm could not survive in a crowd.

The coming of the journalists was more an infiltration than an invasion. They came and went, and induced others to follow. Few stayed for long. But the result of their reports was total upheaval of the old order; the alluring descriptions they issued wholesale constituted a mass invitation to Hawaii.

It began way back. "I was much struck with the beauty and fertility of the country," glowed Archibald Campbell in 1810 in his *Voyage Round the World*, a little book primarily about the Sandwich Islands that went into edition after edition in both England and the United States, a thriller that could compete with the odyssey of Robinson Crusoe.

Campbell's travelogue could be taken without reservation, for he had no political irons to temper, no personal fortunes to aggrandize. He was an obscure, modest, highly talented young Scotsman, who at the age of thirteen had skipped out on the master weaver to whom he was apprenticed and gone to sea. He had just turned 21 when his ship was wrecked in the Aleutians, and in the midwinter ordeal of trying to reach a Russian fur-trade post, lost both his feet from frostbite.

By sheer grit and good fortune, the cripple survived to reach Honolulu in January 1809, where Kamehameha and the queens adopted him as house guest, put him to work as royal weaver, and soon rewarded him with a considerable estate on Pearl Harbor. Missing feet were no deterrent to his getting about. He so endeared himself to Islanders that they willingly carried him on their shoulders, in canoe, or in a chair anywhere he chose to go. He gathered his information from all classes.

"Many inducements are held out to sailors to remain here," he wrote. "If they conduct themselves with propriety, they rank as chiefs, and are entitled to all the privileges of the order; at all events, they are certain of being maintained by some of the chiefs, who are always anxious to have white people about them. The king has a considerable number in his service, chiefly carpenters, joiners, masons, blacksmiths, and bricklayers; these he rewards liberally with grants of land."

For a footloose British or American adventurer dissatisfied with his lot, what stronger inducement could be offered? No need to worry about connubial felicity either, Campbell counseled; "Their ideas of marriage are very loose; either party may quit the other when they tire or disagree." He pictured a host of eligible mates eager to "strengthen a tie of friendship" with white visitors, handsome, vivacious girls, bedecked in flowers, excellent housekeepers who "pay the utmost attention to cleanliness," and he pictured their habitat as a land of plenty, of incessant play, dancing and laughter, a land as safe for strangers as any civilized nation.

Campbell would have been content to remain on his Pearl Harbor farm permanently and never return to England, but his stubbed legs refused to heal. He lived in agony for thirteen months and reluctantly boarded the first ship bound for the Atlantic, hoping to find a cure. He found relief, but no cure, and the pitiful cripple spent the rest of his life in England and the United States, homesick for the Sandwich Islands and trying to find a way back.

After writing his book, he turned into a wandering minstrel and crawled about city streets grinding music on a barrel organ, pathetically chanting the "metrical history of his adventures" and reciting his aloha for Hawaii to all who would listen. That kind of nostalgia was going to develop into a common ailment among those who had once become enamored of the Islands and been obliged to leave.

No less ecstatic was Francis Allyn Olmsted, a young Yale alumnus who contracted "a chronic debility of the nervous system" from the rigors of academic discipline in the halls of Yale and, as a cure, hurried down the Sound to New London immediately after his graduation in search of a berth on a whaler. Despite his friends' "sage predictions of the wretched life to which he was consigning himself," he boarded the *North America,* set out on a cruise to the Pacific, and never regretted his impetuosity.

He rounded the Horn, visited the usual whalers' haunts of South America and the South Pacific, wrote in *Incidents of a Whaling Voyage* the most graphic and authentic account of the industry that had yet been published, but reserved his most spirited chapters for a description of the Sandwich Islands, where he found "the purity and equable temperature of the atmosphere not surpassed anywhere in the world." In fact, he was enraptured.

Most whalers upon arrival in Honolulu stampeded to the nearest brothel or grog shop. Olmsted, true to his Yale indoctrination, headed for the nearest church, Bethel Seamen's Chapel. He ranked the sermon as "creditable," the congregation as "highly respectable," and the music so impressive that it stirred "emotions of pleasure such as the most studied harmony would have failed to do on ordinary occasions."

With the chords of the melodeon still resounding in his ears, he set out to explore the "flourishing empire" and soon decided that this was just the spot for anyone who wanted to get away from the sophistication, intrigue, and superficiality of modern civilization. He was exultant about the scenery of both Oahu and Hawaii, the wealth reaped from the sea, the productive soil, "delicious melons of several kinds, grapes, figs, pine apples, bananas, plantains, taro, yams, sugar-cane, potatoes, and the common culinary vegetables we have at home."

But the people, their colorful customs, friendliness, and ready response to civilized indoctrination appealed to him most. Their law-abiding nature amazed him. "The supremacy of law upon these islands," he applauded, "has given a perfect security to property, such as is not enjoyed anywhere else in the Pacific; and this is the secret of the commercial prosperity of the Hawaiian Islands, and the appearance of enterprise and affluence exhibited by the foreign residents." Moreover, he attributed all the progress in lawmaking to the missionaries, strong testimony even from a borderline representative of the lawless whaling fleet.

As evidence that progress was being made in letters as well as law, in 1837 a group of young literati in Honolulu decided that the time had come to sponsor an erudite journal, the *Hawaiian Spectator,* on the order of similar regional periodicals published in the States. It would not be limited strictly to local affairs, but speak out as the voice of the cultural center of the Pacific.

"The *Hawaiian Spectator* will occupy an interesting position in the field of Periodical Literature," editorialized the first issue of January, 1838. "The range of its observations will embrace the whole extent of coast that borders the Pacific, . . . a geographical extent nearly equal to one-half the globe. Within these limits may be found . . . all the elements of intellectual and moral greatness that are found in the other hemisphere. . . . That whole region of country cannot fail soon to be the theatre of measures and events, whose consequences upon the world will be as enduring as time. The prospect is full of exciting considerations."

The editors projected an ambitious program for themselves, perhaps too ambitious. Most of the early articles were authored by gospel ministers, but the magazine by no means was an evangelical organ. There were profound analyses of Polynesian sociology, a quaint dissection of Marquesian linguistics, disquisitions on the Oahu Charity School and female education in the Sandwich Islands, descriptive sketches of little-known Pacific islands, an inquiry into the causes of the decrease in Hawaiian population, sections on foreign correspondence, tides, meteorology, and shipping.

It was a fine little quarterly that could readily hold its own with most such journals on the Mainland, but its plan was too far-sighted, the profits visionary, the circulation disappointing. The magazine found its way into many a college library and parsonage, appeared on reading tables of the big shipping companies back east, was warmly received and widely read in the Islands, and through a generous circulation of "exchange" copies, accomplished its purpose in a limited way, but it died for lack of nutrition at the end of two years and left the field open to a number of short-lived successors.

Meantime the Reverend Sheldon Dibble of Lahainaluna set himself to work on a more grandiose literary project than the *Spectator,* writing a definitive history of the Sandwich Islands. His was a perfect setup for the undertaking. Like many a New England college professor of the period, rather than occupying a single teaching chair, he held a whole settee at the mission seminary. He was instructor in Biblical studies, instructor in civil history and in ecclesiastical history, chaplain of the school, and editor of Hawaiian textbooks used in the curriculum.

A majority of his students, of course, were adults, from all corners of the kingdom, the most promising scholars in the realm, and as a research problem for them, he conceived the bright modern idea of putting them to work at collecting authentic raw material for his opus.

Armed with questionnaires prepared by the professor, they radiated out over the archipelago, questioned old men and old women, interviewed converted priests and minstrels whose profession had once been the recital of ancestral annals, investigated abandoned villages and temple sites, catalogued all-but-forgotten customs and traditions, dance routines, and folk tales and turned over to Dibble their findings.

Undoubtedly he possessed as valuable a reservoir of Hawaiiana as was ever assembled, but he was apparently so shocked by the facts of pagan life and so leery of putting it in print for fear that he might serve as agent in perpetuating the customs that when it came to composing his masterwork, he merely generalized on the subject and excluded the details as too appalling to pass on to the civilized world.

"We find that the Hawaiians were sorely oppressed," he apologized, "wretchedly destitute, and exceedingly ignorant; stupid also to all that is lovely, grand and awful in the works of God; low, naked, filthy, vile and sensual; covered with every abomination, stained with blood and black with crime. Idolatry also reigned with all its obscenity, frantic rage and horrid exhibitions of bleeding human sacrifices. . . . The degradation, physical, mental and moral, is so deep that it takes time—it takes years in any good measure to explore it. . . . The longer one lives among the heathen, the more fully does he realize the ignorance, the vileness, and the abominations of the horrible pit in which they are sunk."

With that as an approach, he launched into a prolix chronicle of the wonders accomplished by his fellow missionaries against insuperable odds. The book was a glorification of the Yankee do-gooders, and a thorough deglorification of Hawaii *nei*. The wonderful definitive tome he might have written never reached the printers.

The abortive history, a pretty grim publicity piece for the Sandwich Islanders, was published early in 1843, and was as biased as a volume of exactly the same title by the Reverend Ephraim Eveleth, published twenty years earlier by the American Sunday School Union or the brief historical sketches incorporated in the diaries and travelogues of other missionaries and transients.

But Honolulu's journalistic luminary James Jackson Jarves helped to put native history back into perspective that same year, 1843, by publishing simultaneously in both Boston and London the first really objective secular story of the Islands. It was a professional job, well documented, fresh, and lively, an up-to-the-minute account without any missionary dogmatism. If Jarves had only possessed Dibble's documents, it would have been an epic.

"The peculiar situation of the Hawaiian Islands in the vast North Pacific," readers learned, "is of great importance to commerce, and marks them as a general resting place in that portion of the great highway of the world, and the embryo depot of a vast and flourishing trade . . . being equi-distant from Central America, Mexico, California, and the Northwest Coast on the one side, and the Russian dominions, Japan, China and the Philippine Islands on the other. When a civilized and enterprising population shall have developed the resources of these countries, these islands will bear the same relative importance to them . . . that the West Indies now do to North and South America."

To Jarves' generation even a simple geography lesson like this was an eye opener. Aptly he sorted out the past record, weighed the present, and looked ahead, predicting, through gradual intermingling of races, the emergence of a nation in which "the differences of color, language and influences of the present day will harmonize." English would evolve as the principal language, and Islanders would become "the inn-keepers of the great ocean." Here, indeed, was a prophet with uncanny prescience.

Dibble and Jarves had little in common, but together they seemed to have primed a veritable flux of literature on the Islands: *Glimpses of Hawaii, Recollections of Hawaii, Notes on Hawaii, Life in Hawaii,* further historical interpretations, scientific treatments, diaries, fiction, biography, travel experiences. Many of them were as antithetical as the productions of journalist Jarves and Chaplain Dibble. And the controversy they stirred up promoted interest in Hawaii as could no equivalent in romantic exuberance. For every adverse expose, three advocates stood ready to smother the aspersion in honeyed homage.

Herman Melville found nothing in Honolulu that pleased him and, in an irrelevant appendix to *Typee* in 1846, swung out in all directions at royalty, missionaries, and barbarous natives. To him Kamehameha III was an "imbecile" half-wit; Dr. Judd, "a sanctimonious apothecary-adventurer"; the missionaries in general, "a junta of ignorant and designing Methodist elders . . . ruling with absolute sway over a nation just poised between barbarism and civilization"; and the rule of the land, "the Connecticut Blue Laws," which had confounded "all ideas of right and wrong in the minds of the natives."

He was in Honolulu during Lord Paulet's take-over, and tended to side with the British. When the Union Jack was finally hauled down at the end of the five months of foreign dictatorship, he was appalled by the ensuing celebration. "The spectacle of universal broad-day debauchery which was then exhibited, beggars description," he charged. "The natives of the surrounding islands flocked to Honolulu by hundreds, and the crews of two frigates opportunely let loose, like so many demons to swell the heathenish uproar, gave the crowning flourish to the scene. It was a sort of Polynesian saturnalia. Deeds too atrocious to be mentioned were done at noonday in the open street. . . . The history of those days reveals in their true colors the character of the Sandwich Islanders, and furnishes an eloquent commentary on the results which have flowed from the labors of the missionaries."

As if to refute that allegation, Melville's contemporary, Richard Henry Dana, rushed to the defense of the Hawaiians and contrarily asserted: "In no place in the world that I have visited, are the rules which control vice and regulate amusements so strict, yet so reasonable and so fairly enforced. . . . On the great question of moral influence, the truth is that there has always been, and must ever be in these islands, a peculiar struggle between the influences of good and the influences of evil. . . . I visited among all classes—the foreign merchants, traders and shipmasters, foreign and native officials, and with the natives, from the king and several of the chiefs to the humblest poor, . . . and the conclusion to which I came is that the best men, and those who are best acquainted with the history of things here, hold in high esteem the labors and conduct of the missionaries."

Dana explained that he had just come from the mountains of California and still wore the pistol and money belt he had needed there, but was told that such defenses were unheard of in Hawaii. "I found no hut without its Bible and hymn-book in the native tongue," he concluded, "and the practice of family prayer and grace before meal, though it be no more than a calabash of poi and a few dried fish, and whether at home or on journeys, is as common as in New England a century ago."

Here were two views utterly irreconcilable. Puzzled readers back in the States had to weigh them in terms of the author, and between Melville and Dana, they would probably choose the latter, for he had already established his reputation as a distinguished maritime lawyer in addition to writing *Two Years Before the Mast* and Melville had not yet acquired the following that *Omoo* and *Moby Dick* were to bring him.

Neither lavished many phrases on the beauties of Hawaii. They left that to still another sailor-author, R. T. Macoun, who gushed for fashionable *Knickerbocker Magazine:* "The imagination of the poet, which has pictured to us sunny climes where the blasts of winter are unknown, where the earth is clothed in perennial verdure, and man lives in communion with bountiful nature, without toil, were perhaps never more nearly realized than in the Sandwich Islands."

He pictured a land of perpetual spring where fit and fair natives lived the idyllic existence, with nature supplying all their wants and permitting them to spend their days in pursuit of innocent pleasures, dancing and singing, feasting, sporting in the sea, frolicking in river rapids, free of care and worry.

Island life was epitomized for him in a lush wilderness spot that he stumbled upon north of Hilo, where the cascades of a mountain river plunged over thirty-foot cliffs to create the perfect village playground for old and young. Symbolic of youth, happiness, and innocence were the lithesome maidens who gathered there to display themselves on the sun-baked rocks, to dive from the high cliffs, or hurtle over the falls.

"Whether this performance was caused by a species of savage coquetry, arising from the desire to display their sylph-like forms to best advantage," mused Macoun, "I will not pretend to say, but certainly these island beauties, as free from the incumbrance of dress as was their mother Eve before the fall, appeared to be highly pleased when they attracted particular attention.

"I often passed an hour sitting on the banks witnessing the graceful movements of these Naïads, as they fearlessly sprang into the stream, were swept down over the rocks by the boiling rapids with the speed of a race horse, until arriving at the edge of the cascade they were launched off into the white foam, then plunged into the calm deep basin below, and, still visible, sank down, down through the crystal waters, until suddenly rising again to the surface, they shook the diamond shower from their flowing tresses, swam toward the precipitous rocky walls that shut in the stream on each side, nimbly clambered up the sides, and joyously returned to perform the same feat again."

This indeed was the Hawaii that Mainlanders wanted to hear about. Hang the missionaries! Broadway at its best could not provide Knickerbockers with entertainment like watching nude nymphs gallivanting in all that sylvan beauty. On to Hawaii!

The hospitality was as seductive as were the scenery and the maidens, added Macoun: "Wherever I went, I was greeted with smiling faces, and received the national salutation of 'Aloha' or welcome, and I scarcely ever remember to have passed a house without being invited to enter." But those who wanted to see the real Hawaii and the real Hawaiians would have to hurry, he warned, for within a few years "not more than a vestige of their ancient habits will remain."

It took some doing to square caustic reactions like Melville's with

unreserved adulation of the Macoun type. And the public did not try
very hard. Readers believed what they wanted to believe, accepting
what appealed most to their imagination. Generally it was on the side
of romance.

Editors caught on; writers caught on; and both cooperated in supplying the popular preference. Tirades on the depravity of Hawaiians,
the wickedness of their inhibitions, their sloth, and the lax moral
climate became increasingly unpopular, and the besetting frailties of
the inhabitants, both white and dusky, were gradually turned into
colorful and rather charming attractions.

That was the way Mark Twain saw his "loveliest fleet of islands."
He discovered them in the sixties and in gusts of humor and outbursts of benediction told the world about his find. "The further I
traveled through the town," he reported on landing in Honolulu, "the
better I liked it." And the further he traveled in the Islands the better he
liked all of them.

He had just come from the confusion of gold-happy San Francisco, and the contrast favored Honolulu. "In place of the roughs and
rowdies staring and blackguarding the corners, I saw long-haired,
saddle-colored Sandwich Island maidens on the ground in the shade of
corner houses, gazing indolently at whatever or whoever happened
along; . . . instead of cramped and crowded street-cars, I met dusky
native women sweeping by, free as the wind, on fleet horses and
astride, with gaudy riding sashes, streaming like banners behind them;
instead of the combined stenches of Chinadom and Brannon Street
slaughter-houses, I breathed the balmy fragrance of jasmine, oleander
and the Pride of India; in place of the hurry and bustle and noisy
confusion of San Francisco, I moved in the midst of a summer calm as
tranquil as dawn in the Garden of Eden; in place of the Golden City's
skirting sandhills and the placid bay, I saw on the one side a framework of tall, precipitous mountains close at hand, clad in refreshing
green, and cleft by deep, cool, chasm-like valleys—and in front the
grand sweep of the ocean. . . . When the sun sank down . . . it was
tranced luxury to sit in the perfumed air and forget that there was any

other world but these enchanted islands. It was such ecstacy to dream and dream. . . ."

The man, then better known as Samuel Clemens, also subjected Hawaii to an abrasive ribbing such as only a land blessed with an inordinate display of the picturesque could withstand. He pictured "smoke-dried children clothed in nothing but sunshine"; *kanakas* "with nothing on but a battered stove-pipe hat tilted over the nose, and a very scant breech-clout"; he infested the Islands with scorpions, tarantulas, centipedes "with forty-two legs on a side and every foot hot enough to burn a hole through a rawhide"; cockroaches "with long, quivering antennae and fiery, malignant eyes"; mosquitoes, rats, and pesky cats.

He found enough cats to fill a paragraph: "Tom-cats, Mary Ann cats, long-tailed cats, bob-tailed cats, blind cats, one-eyed cats, wall-eyed cats, cross-eyed cats, striped cats, spotted cats, tame cats, wild cats, singed cats, individual cats, groups of cats, platoons of cats, companies of cats, regiments of cats, armies of cats, multitudes of cats, millions of cats, and all of them sleek, fat, lazy and sound asleep."

While others were glorifying the stately coconut palm, he turned it into an elongated "feather-duster struck by lightning"; he spoofed the delightful habit of young ladies to do their sea bathing in the nude by planting himself on their clothes—"to keep them from being stolen" —and urging the girls to come out because the sea was rising; he dwarfed a "laced and ruffled cataract of limpid water leaping from a sheer precipice fifteen hundred feet high" by alleging that scenery of its kind "finds its staunchest ally in arithmetic rather than spectacular effect."

But despite the joshing, he was enchanted. His way of lauding the Islands was to cut them down to size, accentuate the inconsequential ugliness and the banalities, so that the consequential splendor would stand forth in greater radiance. After having a good bit of fun at the expense of the missionaries, he swallowed his chuckle and cheered for the transformed natives: "The missionaries have clothed them, educated them, broken up the tyrannous authority of their chiefs, and

given them freedom and the right to enjoy whatever their hands and
brains produce, with equal laws for all, and punishment alike. . . .
The benefit conferred upon this people by the missionaries is so promi-
nent, so palpable and so unquestionable, that the frankest compliment
I can pay them, and the best, is simply to point to the condition of the
Sandwich-Islanders of Captain Cook's time and their condition today.
The work speaks for itself."

No experience in Mark Twain's life had so deeply touched him as
his travels in Hawaii. He was not only touched, he was smitten. "No
alien land in all the world has any deep strong charm for me but that
one," he confessed; "no other land could so longingly and beseech-
ingly haunt me sleeping and waking." The haunting never left him.
One unforgettable snatch of scenery that seemed to appeal to him
most enticingly was the panorama of ocean and valley viewed from the
slopes of Maui's sleeping volcano. In a single visit he had become
addicted to Kula and what he called the "healing solitudes of Haleakala," and years later wrote to his friend Charles Warren Stoddard:
"What I have always longed for, was the privilege of living forever
away up on one of those mountains in the Sandwich Islands overlooking the sea."

His "luxurious vagrancy" in Hawaii was actually a newspaper
assignment, and his impressions were first published as letters in the
Sacramento *Union*. But they proved so popular that they were edited
to compose sixteen chapters in *Roughing It* and freely enlarged upon
in coast-to-coast lecture tours. Generally he is credited with being the
star journalist in introducing Hawaii to the American public, a stretch
of fact, for the missionary heralds, the pulpiteers, the Sunday School
teachers, and scores of magazine contributors and authors of books
had already accomplished that.

Roughing It was published in 1872. Two years later Isabella Bird
converted another series of letters, correspondence addressed to her
sister in England, into a plump volume on Hawaii. Miss Bird was
virtually an invalid, but she was not one to let indisposition stand in
the way of adventure. She probed every part of the periphery and

interior of the major islands, on foot, by carriage, in a native chair, but mostly in a Mexican saddle.

She crashed Honolulu society, climbed Kilauea and Mauna Loa, attended missionary services and soirees, inspected plantations, lived in native huts, risked her life repeatedly in crossing rain-swollen rivers, joined a cattle hunt, went bird watching, flower hunting, and fishing, and all but went native. Then in racy, diverting rhetoric she consolidated her experiences into the most glamorous travel book ever written about Hawaii.

Climax followed climax in her chapters, but perhaps her triumph was the penetration of inaccessible Waimanu Valley on the Big Island, a romantic snuggery once the home of two thousand Hawaiians, reduced in 1874 to one hundred and seventeen and long since totally depopulated and rarely visited, except in more recent years by game hunters, Eagle scouts, and Peace Corps trainees encamped in neighboring Waipio. To reach Waimanu, Miss Bird had to descend into Waipio Valley, climb on horseback the zigzags of a narrow path cut into the nearly perpendicular cliff of a three thousand-foot headland, and then make the descent on a treacherous, ten-mile trail that crossed nine deep gulches, a journey considered so perilous that it could be made only on a horse raised in Waimanu and accustomed to the dizzy heights.

She had heard of the silver river that threaded through Waimanu, a river fed by five magnificent cascades, and had a compulsive urge to witness the scene. In ascending the *pali* above Waipio, she and her guide found places where the three-foot cut into the cliff had vanished in the rains. To cross a washout, she was once forced to dismount in a spot so narrow that she looked down into space on one side, while the horse's ribs were chafed by the cliff on the other: "I somehow slid under him, being careful not to turn the saddle, and getting hold of his hind leg, screwed myself round carefully behind him."

The adventuress survived the crossing of that gap by trusting to the horse and clutching his tail for dear life. Here and there the rock footing slanted down as smooth as glass, and at other points the horse had to heave himself up abrupt steps four or five feet high. "My horse went up wisely and nobly," she boasted, "but slipping, jumping, scrambling, and sending stones over the ledge, now and then hanging for a second by his fore feet. The higher we went, the narrower and worse it grew."

Isabella reached Waimanu intact, to discover that even her guide had never been to the cascades; so she changed roles and guided the guide. Since the jungle bordering the silver river was impenetrable, she turned the stream into a bridle path and rode the horse up its course, with the crystal water surging halfway up his belly.

Villagers on the river bank, who had never before seen a white woman, welcomed her like a goddess. She was draped with leis, feted with fruit, fish, pig, chicken, poi, and stared at, smiled at, laughed at. The final stretch of the journey to the cascades had to be made on foot through a thicket of orange and coffee trees in full bloom, clusters of gardenias smothering red hibiscus, banana and coconut groves, all interlaced with millions of rose-crimson *ohia* spikes, "one perfect, rapturous, intoxicating, supreme vision of beauty, . . . a scene on which foreign eyes had never gazed before."

And at last, almost as an anticlimax, she "emerged into broad daylight at the home of the five cascades, which fall from a semicircular precipice into three basins . . . from which it seemed so far to look up to the heavenly blue, and the water falling calmly and unhurriedly, amidst innumerable rainbows, from a height of 3,000 feet."

In thirty "Letters," each spiced with a few hair-raising adventures and mellowed with trim scenic descriptions, Miss Bird told her story, *Six Months Among the Palm Groves, Coral Reefs and Volcanoes of the Sandwich Islands,* and the book proved so popular that it went into half a dozen British and American editions. Compared to ailing Isabella, healthy Sam Clemens was a lethargic rambler.

In writing about the Islands, it became the literary fashion to try out the first draft on the public in a series of articles in a good journal; then, depending on the reception, the material was repackaged for a book. A string of pieces ground out for *Harper's Monthly* by Charles Nordhoff, under the running title "Hawaii-Nei," went into *Northern California, Oregon and the Sandwich Islands;* and Charles Warren

Stoddard's "Lazy Letters from Low Latitudes," dramatizing Hawaiian mountains and lei makers, festivities and fish markets, siestas and seascapes, in *Overland* and other magazines, were reworked for *South-Sea Idyls*.

J. T. Meagher dared to confuse the new popular image of Hawaiians by brushing aside the romanticism and claiming in *Overland* that "the great majority of Hawaiians are not civilized in the strict sense of the word. Their supersititions are yet living; their morality is imaginary; their love of religion superficial; their truth impeachable; and their attachment to the barbarous customs of their primitive days unimpaired." Obviously that was not what the public wanted to hear; so his effusions failed to interest a book publisher.

Robert Louis Stevenson confused things further by siding with the natives at the expense of the *haole* planters and politicians. He arrived in 1889 for a five-month stay, became a boon companion of King Kalakaua, studied Hawaiian with a native teacher, developed a fondness for local music and legends, and set himself up as champion of Polynesian causes in general.

On the Big Island he picked up background for "The Bottle Imp" and "The Isle of Voices" and, as a passing whim, considered purchasing a ranch there. He visited the leper colony on Molokai and for eight days fought back his "horror of the horrible" while playing croquet with leper children, "yarning with old, blind beach-combers in the hospital, sickened with the spectacle of abhorrent suffering, . . . touched to the heart by the sight of lowly and effective virtues among the helpers." But most of his time was spent at a frowsy shack in Waikiki.

Stevenson was too preoccupied with *The Wrong Box*, *The Master of Ballantrae*, and his gleanings from Tahiti and the Marquesas to write much about Hawaii. For him the Islands were already spoiled by commerce and artificial civilization; he was banking on finding a more satisfactory paradise farther to the south. "In vile Honolulu," he scoffed, "there are too many cesspools and beastly *haoles*."

He returned four years later for a shorter visit and found Honolulu even worse. In the interim, the Polynesians had lost out to the plantation-politicians, and a provisional government had taken the place of the monarchy. He had no sympathy for the new regime. "I am a royalist at heart," he reminded interviewers, "with much pity for the Polynesians."

In a furious "Open Letter to the Reverend Dr. Hyde," he defended Father Damien of Molokai's leper colony against an attack by Honolulu's Protestant pastor, Charles M. Hyde: "'Damien was dirty.' He was. Think of the poor lepers annoyed with this dirty comrade! But the clean Dr. Hyde was at his food in a fine house. . . . 'Damien was coarse.' It is very possible. You make us sorry for the lepers who had only a coarse old peasant for their friend and father. But you, who were so refined, why were you not there to cheer them with the lights of culture?"

But later Stevenson expressed remorse at ever penning the "barbarously harsh" reply. "If I did it now," he recanted, "I would defend Damien no less well and give less pain to those who are alive. . . . On the whole it was virtuous to defend Damien, but it was harsh to strike so hard at Dr. Hyde."

Because Stevenson favored Hawaii with two visits, Islanders have ever since chosen to count on him as one of their promoters. He was hardly that, and the contemporary press was very much aware of it. As a parting insult to the presumptuous author, the Honolulu *Pacific Advertiser* cracked in its issue of June 24, 1889: "Robert Louis Stevenson and party leave today by the schooner *Equator* for the Gilbert Islands. . . . It is hoped that Mr. Stevenson will not fall victim to native spears; but in his present state of bodily health, perhaps the temptation to kill him may not be too strong."

The kindest comment he ever made about Hawaii was scribbled in the register of the Sans Souci Hotel at Waikiki, where he was a guest on his second visit: "If anyone desire such old-fashioned things as lovely scenery, quiet, pure air, clear sea water, good food and heavenly sunsets hung out before his eyes over the Pacific and the distant hills of Waianae, I recommend him cordially to the Sans Souci." Immediately recognizing the commercial worth of such an endorsement, the hotel manager had the effrontery to run it as an advertisement for three days in the Honolulu papers.

The celebrated British novelist had barely been dismissed by local gossipers after his first visit, when the celebrated American historian, journalist, editor, and professor, Henry Adams, was in their midst, and, like no one before him, he readily admitted how roundly he had been fooled by the narrators, or how he had fooled himself in inventing his own picture of Oahu: "I conceived of it as a forest-clad cluster of volcanoes, with fringing beaches where natives were always swimming, and I imagined that when I should leave the beach I should be led by steep paths through dense forests to green glades where native girls said *Aloha* and threw garlands round your neck, and where you would find straw huts of unparalleled cleanliness, always on terraces looking over a distant ocean a thousand feet below."

But Adams was a good sport about his delusion. "The reality, though beautiful, is quite different," he admitted. He was fascinated by the natives, whose expressions varied "between the ferocious look of the warriors who worshipped Captain Cook and then killed him, and the melancholy of a generation obliged to be educated by missionaries"; he was rankled by the "ninth-rate samples" of white men that seemed to be drawn to tropical islands; and he found King Kalakaua at least "a more amusing subject" than President Benjamin Harrison. "To be sure, His Majesty is not wise, and he has—or is said to have vices—such as whiskey—and others, but he is the only interesting figure in the government . . . and yesterday he sat up straight and talked of Hawaiian archaeology and arts as though he had been a professor."

Accompanying Adams was the distinguished artist, the "animated prism," John LaFarge. "He has taught me to feel the subtleness and endless variety of charm in the color and light of every hour in the tropical island's day and night," acknowledged the historian. "I get gently intoxicated on the soft violets and strong blues, and the masses of purple and the broad bands of orange and green in the sunsets. . . . The outlines of the great mountains, their reddish purple glow, the infinite variety of greens and the perfectly intemperate shifting blues of the ocean, are a new world to me."

In the end it was LaFarge who turned out to be the better chronicler of the two. The sketches and paintings he made were memorable, but even more memorable were the word descriptions he wrote for *Scribner's Magazine* and for *Reminiscences of the South Seas*. He found color everywhere. By moonlight, the palm trees in front of their Nuuanu house "gradually lit up as if the whole air had been a stage scene seen through the smoothly shining trunks, glistening like dark silver." Approaching Lahaina from the sea at sunset, the backdrop of mountain was "green and peachy gray"; landing at Kaawaloa, "the sea jumped from light aquamarine to the color of a peacock's breast in the shadow"; the sky above Kilauea in early evening was "purple in the yellow of the afterglow and partly covered with the yellowish tone of the hellish vapors."

Adams and LaFarge happened to schedule their visit during a period of relative tranquility, when the setting could be enjoyed without too much political distraction. King Kalakaua died the following year, to be succeeded by Queen Liliuokalani. A provisional government was in the offing, and jounalists for the rest of the century were to have a field day, taking sides on the burning issue of annexation.

In 1894 the Senate Committee on Foreign Affairs resolved that "it is unwise, inexpedient and not in accordance with the character and dignity of the United States to consider further at this time the treaty or project of annexation of the Hawaiian territory to this country." The resolution signaled the kickoff for the pro and con campaigners. To those with affection for the Islands, Hawaii became more enchanting than ever; to those who were nursing grudges against the plantation managers, missionaries, Chinese, Japanese, and ignorant natives, it was an indecent land, a vulgar nation with which an enlightened country like the United States could ill afford to associate.

"The provisional government and 'the missionary element,' now being masters of the situtation," declared the *Nation* cynically, "there is no reason why they should not go on and govern the Islands in their own way, and show the wicked natives what a Christian government is." *Review of Reviews* countered with a glowing panegyric on the virtues of both the natives and their wonderful land: "The chief charm of Hawaii is, after all, in her people."

Though educator Henry S. Townsend was concerned about how readily Islanders would take to "Americanization," he warmly parried slurs leveled at their literacy. "When I first came among the Hawaiian people," he attested, "I was surprised to find the school-children able to put to shame, with their knowledge of Garfield, Grant, Lincoln, Washington, Gladstone, Beaconsfield, Bismarck, 'Unser Fritz,' Nelson and Napoleon, the American school-children with whom I had come in contact. . . . It is as rare an occurrence to find an illiterate adult Hawaiian as it is to find an illiterate adult American in the most favored State of the Union; and such has been the case for a generation. Yet these are the people who must bear the brunt of the malice or ignorance of cartoonists and writers who think it funny to caricature them as ridiculous savages."

When the showdown on annexation finally came in Washington, it was evident that the long line of volunteer journalists had been more effective in establishing the political destiny of Hawaii than all the contemporary Congressmen put together. And once the Islands received territorial status, they stayed on the job.

At last in 1901 there arrived in the Islands a gospel minister who could offer approbation as well as preachment. He was Bishop Henry C. Potter, nationally renowned social reformer and projector of New York's mighty Cathedral of St. John the Divine. What impressed him at once was the "great strength of outline and the boldness of proportion in the mountain ranges—the singularly gracious quality of softness and depth." He suggested that these features of the landscape were typical of the people. "The mountains make them strong and stalwart. . . . Here is something like the original Garden of Eden, as it might have been."

Very few of the later *haole* writers who sang the praises of this Eden were ever admitted to the innermost native circles. They were treated deferentially, warmly entertained, honored, feted, acclaimed, but ultimately accepted with a margin of reserve. Jack London was the exception. For him there was no reserve in their aloha. He became the white beachcomber, fisherman, entertainer and surf rider *par excellence,* swam with the best of the *kanakas,* shared their table, their troubles, and their life, and then drafted his experiences with the conviction of a born-and-bred Hawaiian.

He arrived in Honolulu in 1907 on his *Snark* at the age of 31, stayed for four months, and returned eight years later for a much longer visit. His impressions of Hawaii appeared in *The Cruise of the Snark, The House of Pride, On the Makaloa Mat,* and an assortment of short stories. No one ever wrote more thrillingly of the excitement of surfing, more charmingly of native life, more appreciatively of the tropic setting, and in *Our Hawaii* his wife Charmian filled in the gaps.

London added a new dimension to Hawaii as a Mainlander's haven; he pictured it as one of the world's great sports centers and offered the first popular challenge to athletes of the world to join the natives in a revival of their demanding sports, as participants, not mere spectators.

With few exceptions, all the writers found poetry in the Islands; they wrote *about* the poetry and told everyone it was there in quantity, but they did not write good poetry themselves very often or inspire others to write it. Versifiers composed countless sentimental stanzas and poor ballads, rimed history and folklore, cramped lyrics and a great deal of doggerel, but, despite the wealth of music permeating the Hawaiian scene, it never seemed to bring forth a great poem. Here was the natural home for an epic of the Pacific; yet it did not come. In 1913, two years before his death, Rupert Brooke penned his "Waikiki":

> Warm perfumes like a breath from vine and tree
>   Drift down the darkness. Plangent, hidden from eyes,
>   Somewhere an eukaleli trills and cries
> And stabs with pain the night's brown savagery.
> And dark scents whisper; and dim waves creep to me,
>   Gleam like a woman's hair, stretch out and rise;
>   And new stars burn into the ancient skies,
> Over the murmurous soft Hawaiian sea.

Though would-be critics pointed to those lines as an ultimate in local poetic achievement, they could not stand even as the best of Rupert Brooke. Hawaii still had to find its Emily Dickinson, its Frost, its Jeffers, or its Sandburg.

An endless parade of writers, representing every field from art to zoology, made Hawaii their literary beneficiary. Teams of scholarly anthropologists and sociologists, missionary progeny by the dozens, lauders and snipers of the Big Five, novelists Somerset Maugham, John P. Marquand, and James Michener, essayist-poet Genevieve Taggard, folklorist-poet Padraic Colum, lyricists Don Blanding and Marjorie Sinclair, authoress Armine von Tempski, physician-scholar Peter Buck, historian Ralph S. Kuykendall, economist Theodore Morgan, social historian Lawrence Fuchs are scarcely a cross section; wartime correspondents and postwar scriveners by the score added to the wealth, and movie scenarists contributed in their way.

Whether or not the throng of scribbling invaders intended to be promoters, they were; all had a hand in establishing the popular image of Hawaii with its balmy trade winds, amiable hosts, mountain greenery, palm-latticed moonlight, blue-green waters, and carefree spirit. Then came the latter-day professional promoters and publicists to saccharize the whole overpublicized scene, as though they were the original discoverers of Eden.

PEARL HARBOR

XV

A Second Gibraltar?

It was the genteel James Jackson Jarves, editor, historian, and art connoisseur, not an old campaigner, who first drove home to the American public the military importance of the Sandwich Islands. Ninety-eight years before Pearl Harbor, he predicted that any great power which chose to seize this "Key to the North Pacific" could control half an ocean. "No trade could prosper in the vicinity, or even exist," he maintained, "while a hostile power, possessing an active and powerful marine, should send forth its cruisers to prey upon neighboring commerce. . . . A military colony, once fairly established, might surely put at defiance any means of attack."

Picking up from where Jarves left off, other foreign observers were quick to supplement his conclusions. If Hawaii were the key to the North Pacific, Pearl Harbor was the key to Hawaii. They referred to a broad, landlocked body of water a few miles west of Honolulu, known variously as Wai Momi, Pearl Water, Pearl River, Pearl River Lagoon, Pearl Lochs from the extensive beds of pearl oysters found there. Potentially it was a great port, large enough to offer protected

336

anchorage for all the warships of any major nation in the world, but of little value as it lay, because of an offshore reef and the shallow, bottleneck entrance.

To clear a channel into the harbor was an engineering undertaking far beyond the ingenuity of the Hawaiians or the means of private foreign industry; so Pearl Water, as a roadstead, remained a mariner's dream. Archibald Campbell, whose sixty-acre grant occupied the head of the lagoon, sang its praises, as did the missionaries and the merchants. Even Rufus Anderson, Doctor of Divinity and Foreign Secretary of the American Board of Commissioners for Foreign Missions, a man with no recognizable military longheadedness, seemed astonished that this beautiful body of water was going to waste. "Should the harbor ever be opened. . . ," he conjectured, "it would then greatly exceed that of Honolulu."

Down the years, although political spokesmen for the great powers repeatedly disclaimed interest in acquiring the Islands, they were not always in agreement with military spokesmen. As long as Hawaii remained neutral, unaligned with any western or eastern nation, there was no serious problem, but admirals and the generals foresaw the day when the neutrality might be abjured and Hawaii with its Pearl Harbor become, indeed, the key to Pacific power. Control of the Islands by an enemy would be a disadvantage that any strategist would prefer not to have to cope with.

Yet no nation was quite ready to go all out in an effort to seize the Islands and risk being burdened with the censure and probable retaliation of other interested nations. Possession of the archipelago was pointless without the means to hold and defend it, and that could be very costly. The militarists, however, weren't going to be caught off guard; files of intelligence reports on the geography, the vulnerability and invulnerability of Hawaii accumulated in the military archives of half a dozen national capitals.

The sleuthing of military observers and political opportunists in disguise was no less portentous to the future of the kingdom than the invasions of Yankee planters and hawkers, foreign religious sects, or oriental laborers, but the militarists represented a distinctive class of invader that would eventually alter enormous areas of Island physiognomy, overwhelm metropolitan centers with hordes of transients in white and khaki, add a revolutionary new subsidy to the economy, and turn Oahu into the mightiest island fortress on earth.

Commander S. F. DuPont of the United States Navy had Pearl Harbor in mind when he submitted intelligence to his Washington superiors in 1852, after making a circumspect survey of Oahu. "It is impossible to estimate too highly the value and importance of the Sandwich Islands, whether in a commercial or military point of view," he expostulated, echoing the words of Jarves. "Should circumstances ever place them in our hands, they would prove the most important acquisition we could make in the whole Pacific Ocean, an acquisition intimately connected with our commercial and naval supremacy in those seas; be this as it may, these islands should never be permitted to pass into the possession of any European power."

But whatever enthusiasm DuPont stirred up dissolved in the face of more challenging national conundrums. In fact, War Department interest in Pearl Harbor was shelved until well after the Civil War—until 1873, when Secretary of War W. W. Belknap finally dispatched two of his most trusted generals on "a pleasure excursion" to Oahu, with confidential orders to investigate the harbor and spy out the "defensive capabilities" of the Islands. The agents were given a free hand in their methods of carrying out the assignment and shielded with an advance gossip item that the trip was being made for the health of one of the officers in the hope that he might shake off an obscure malady.

The invalid made a quick recovery under the influence of bracing trade winds and an embracing society, and for two months the generals had a red-letter junket, ostensibly yachting, fishing, surfing, tramping, and partying in the elite social circles of Honolulu. As royal guests they were guided to all the scenic, and strategic, spots on Oahu, from Diamond Head and Punchbowl to the narrow passage out of Pearl Harbor. They developed a peculiar fondness for that area but were such jovial sportsmen and such disarming company that the guides attached no significance to the repeated Pearl Harbor visits.

Perhaps it was only by accident that an editorial appeared in Honolulu's *Pacific Commercial Advertiser* less than a month after their arrival, bemoaning the depressed state of agricultural and commercial affairs in Hawaii, suggesting that the time had come for renegotiating a reciprocity trade agreement with the United States, and rather bluntly advocating that Pearl Harbor be offered to the Americans as an inducement for signing such a treaty.

Once more trade reciprocity, as a cure-all for Island economic ills, became the talk of Honolulu. The War Department envoys could scarcely avoid getting involved in the arguments, and before their mission was completed, they had an opportunity to express a "private" opinion that the *Commercial Advertiser's* proposal might appeal to Washington.

The generals concluded their holiday, set sail for the States, and turned in a report that played up Pearl Harbor, potentially, as one of the most magnificent ports in the hemisphere. To be sure, cutting through the coral at the mouth posed some expensive engineering problems, and dredging would be costly, too, but it was certainly worth the investment; the shores of the bay were an ideal site for docks, repair shops, a coaling depot, and all the necessary facilities for a naval station.

After a monumental quantity of political haggling and hedging, a reciprocity treaty was at last signed in January, 1875, without a reference to Pearl Harbor. To satisfy antiexpansionists in Congress, King Kalakaua agreed instead "not to lease or otherwise dispose of . . . any port, harbor or other territory in his dominion . . . to any other power, state or government," for the duration of the treaty.

That accomplished a temporary purpose, tied Hawaii inescapably into the proper political orbit, and when the treaty came up for renewal twelve years later, the surrender of Pearl Harbor was easily included in the terms. In 1887 the recommendations of the prying generals were finally fulfilled, and the United States was granted, without any attached strings, "exclusive right to enter the harbor of Pearl River . . . to establish and to maintain there a coaling and repair station."

From start to finish, the deal was heavily sugar-coated. If it had not been for the influence of the plantation barons, the broad lagoon might have developed into a world-famed yachting center and tourist capital that could hold its own with Miami, the Riviera, and Waikiki, but without a reliable sugar market, Kalakaua was convinced that the economic future for his kingdom was too bleak to comtemplate. He had suffered through depression after depression, had seen the whaling fleet desert the Islands and other industries abandoned; settlements were disappearing; valley lands were no longer under cultivation; *kiawe* and guava scrub were burying the traces of a former population; he had to agree that sugar growing for years had been "a very disastrous speculation" in which few planters could "do more than keep their heads above water."

Pearl Harbor was ceded to the United States to keep the planters' heads above water. It was the price paid for shipping duty-free sugar to California. The Louisiana planters fought it; the New England merchants, trading in West Indies sugar and rum, fought it; England fought it tooth and nail, knowing all too well that the cession would lead sooner or later to annexation and hoping, too, to protect the Commonwealth markets in Australia, New Zealand, and British Columbia, where over a third of Hawaii's sugar had previously been shipped. And a great many Hawaiians patriotically protested to the last against this cleavage of the kingdom.

Yet once the title to Pearl Harbor had changed hands, the United States displayed remarkable indifference toward the prize acquisition. Nothing was done about it for over a decade. The simple truth was that the navy had no forces to install there, though the admirals did plenty of talking. Looking into the future, one navy alarmist after another appealed for action, stressing the "Yellow Peril" that had been brought on by the importation of Japanese.

"They are inclined to be turbulent," warned Admiral Walker; "they stand together as a solid body; . . . they are a brave people with military instinct, and would fight if aroused to violence." Added Admiral Ammen, "It does not require a prophet to foresee that those islands in the near future will be either American or Japanese." And a mere lieutenant, Lucien Young, who thought the admirals were understating the case, went on record with the declaration that Hawaii was "second in importance to no other single point on the earth's surface. . . . Eliminate Hawaii from the map and there are scarcely any battleships in existence which can operate across the Pacific."

Developing Pearl Harbor and establishing a fleet there were the only answer to the oriental menace, but congressmen could not get nearly as excited as naval officers about that distant body of water. The harbor would undoubtedly have remained untenanted indefinitely if a crisis in the Caribbean had not contributed to the controversy.

At 9:40 P.M. on February 15, 1898, the battleship *Maine* was mysteriously blown up in Havana harbor. The catch-slogan "Remember the Maine" that swept across the American continent had no significance in Hawaii until the United States was at war with Spain two months later and Admiral Dewey was on his way to Manila. Suddenly it was apparent to both the Navy and War Departments that an American base in the middle of the Pacific was desperately needed.

There was no time to blast an entrance into Pearl Harbor; so American troops on the way to the Philippines stormed en masse into Honolulu while their transports were taking on coal. The city had not seen anything quite like it since the heyday of the whalers. Hotel Street did a landslide business. Troopers called for pie, not poi and got it. They rode Honolulu's street cars free, attended a gigantic welcoming picnic, made the most of hastily erected Red Cross booths, sent home thousands of letters on stationery of the Hawaiian government, postage free, praising the glories of Hawaii.

The letters reached the States just in time to help tip the scales in favor of a Congressional vote for annexation. On August 12th the formal transfer of sovereignty took place to make Hawaii a Territory of the United States. And, by coincidence, the Spanish-American War, which had been instrumental in hurrying along the cause of annexation, terminated with an armistice that same day.

To stoic Hawaiians, the swirl of events was almost too much to comprehend. The comings and goings of armies and transports were bewildering. They were not used to all this soldiery. *Kamaainas* could still recall the halcyon years when the standing army of Hawaii was the standing joke of Honolulu, rifle-toting infantry without ammunition, artillery without guns, cavalry without horses, a ragtag army sometimes of fifty recruits, sometimes of five hundred, uniformed in the "castoff regimentals of half a dozen nations" or faded yellow cotton capes in imitation of the golden-feathered cloaks once worn by the king's warriors, an army so totally unreliable that there were also companies of volunteers ready to hold the regulars in check "in case of inadvertence with the rusty rifles." Those days were gone forever; the uniforms were updated, and the standing armies occupying Hawaii in the future would be numbered not by tens, but by tens of thousands.

With almost indecent haste, four days after the formal cession of sovereignty, the first contingent of occupation troops arrived, followed by more the next day. In a clearing back from Waikiki on the edge of Kapiolani Park, these troops of the First New York Volunteer Infantry and the Third Battalion, Second U.S. Volunteer Engineers, established themselves, flippantly naming their bivouac Camp McKinley, after the President of the United States. The park encampment was intended only as a temporary measure, but the Volunteers, and later their relief, remained on the site for years, patiently awaiting construction of a permanent camp.

William Rufus Shafter, the brigadier general who led the American invasion force of some seventeen thousand men from Tampa to Cuba in June 1898 and went on to the conquests of Siboney, El Caney, and San Juan Hill, was still one of the big unmemorialized names on the army roster; so when garrison headquarters were finally laid out west of Honolulu, the stronghold was given his name, Fort Shafter.

But the shabby shacks erected there hardly did credit to a general even of equivocal reputation. None of the makeshift barracks was ready for occupancy until 1907, and for years after that, the crude, haphazard layout was the talk of regulars stationed there, as well as of the local citizenry. To all appearances, the army was given an inauspicious start in Hawaii.

Back in Washington, however, far more auspicious plans were

being drafted for the defense of both Honolulu and Pearl Harbor—
Fort Ruger on Diamond Head, Fort DeRussy at Waikiki, Fort Arm-
strong at the entrance to Honolulu harbor, Forts Kamehameha and
Weaver at Pearl Harbor. And two years after Fort Shafter was first
tenanted, Schofield Barracks, destined eventually to become the largest garrison of the United States, was commissioned high on the
plateau on the dead center of Oahu. Within a few years the island
began to take on the atmosphere of a fortress, and peaceful Hawaiians
were wondering what the fuss was about.

Meantime Wai Momi was being turned into a real harbor. In 1900
Congress was persuaded to appropriate funds to start the dredging of a
channel and to get construction of docks and other installations under
way. The vacationing generals who had made the sleight-of-hand survey more than a quarter of a century earlier had not overestimated the
engineering feat. As Honolulu trembled under the distant dynamite
concussions, it sounded, and sometimes looked, as though the army
engineers were trying to compete with what Colonel Goethals was
doing in Panama.

The first capital ship, *U.S.S. California*, maneuvered through the
channel into the harbor on December 14, 1911, to the accompaniment
of screaming whistles, echoing strains from the Hawaiian band, booming salutes, and stirring salutatory orations. From the *California's*
decks the shores of Pearl Harbor already had the sophisticated look of
a frontier naval base, with an administration building, coaling station,
immense floating crane, sprawling barracks for enlisted men, officers'
quarters, and a gigantic drydock in the making, over eight hundred
feet long and one hundred feet wide.

But a hex had been cast on that drydock. It was the big boggle of
the harbor. Two years of work had gone into it, with amazingly little
to show for the effort and expenditure. Everything went wrong, and
orthodox Hawaiians were so thoroughly convinced that it was being
constructed in defiance of their old deities that they walked off the job
in droves.

Day after day a wizened Hawaiian fisherman in his eighties,
Kupuna Kanakeawe, haunted the site, warning the builders that they

were trespassing, urging them to halt, pleading with them to put their dock somewhere else, assuring them that the labor was at the risk of their lives. "Move away. Move away," he kept entreating until he was a recognized nuisance. "These places are taboo; they belong to Kaaupahau, the shark god."

With genuine tears in his eyes, he implored the men to quit invading the sacred dominion of the god; it was a desecration that could bring nothing but punishment and *pilikia*. Regularly once a week, in generous propitiation for the sins of his people, he came to offer chants and prayers, then dove over the side with a little net of fish and disappeared for minutes. He claimed that he distributed the fish in rock crevasses far down, to feed Kaaupahau and assuage his anger.

For two more years the work went on, interrupted by incessant trouble and tragic accident. It was nearing completion, when, to prove that Kupuna had known all along what he was talking about, the predicted cataclysm came. As if a captive god had put a shoulder to the underside of the massive floor and given a mighty heave, the expanse of concrete erupted in a thunderous explosion. The floor disintegrated; huge timbers splintered like kindling; geysers shot up; workmen barely escaped alive.

It was necessary to begin all over again, pump out the flood of water, clear away the wreckage, and try new engineering methods, a Herculean labor that took another four years. But this time the blessings of a *kahuna* were requisitioned to allay the divine ire of the fish god. "Everything is clear now. Go ahead," advised the priest after reciting suitable incantations and strewing cracker crumbs around the area.

When the water was finally pumped out in preparation for the opening of the dock, sure enough, there on the bottom, directly over the underwater cave that Kapuna Kanakeawe had sworn was the home of his god, stretched the skeleton of a shark fourteen feet, four inches, long.

By the time the ornery god capitulated and allowed the engineers to complete the drydock, Pearl Harbor had developed into a showplace of the Islands. After Waikiki and the Pali, every sightseer had to take in this masterwork of the navy. "This harbor, the finest in the Islands," bubbled a typical feminine tourist, "is a deep lagoon . . . with a shoreline of thirty miles. Algarroba forests cover the shores, and the fertile countryside, in which are rice, sugar and banana plantations, promise abundant supplies for the troops stationed here. . . . As it covers ten square miles, the whole navy of this country could find anchorage there and be in perfect safety. . . . The island of Oahu will soon be a second Gibraltar, we hope."

The Gibraltar look came faster than ardent boosters of reciprocity treaties, Pearl Harbor cession, and annexation had thought possible twenty years earlier, as younger generals and admirals enlarged their views of the strategic importance of the Islands. Ideas of national expansion, wielding the Big Stick, and protective responsibilities to little countries lost their novelty in the two decades after the Spanish-American War. In answer to loose political talk about Japan's interest in Hawaii, President McKinley had once shocked conservative Americans with the blunt remark, "We need Hawaii just as much, and a good deal more, than we need California. It is manifest destiny." No longer was there anything shocking in the doctrine. It had become a national conviction.

Uncle Sam was merely fulfilling his democratic duties in taking defenseless lands into protective custody. Expansion was now politically respectable, and adequate defense of new acquisitions was part and parcel of the national responsibility. Witness Cuba, Panama, Texas, the Philippines, and now Hawaii. There was nothing inconsistent in the show of military might.

The arrival of more troops in Hawaii, more artillery, more warships occurred so gradually, so inexorably, that they all appeared to be part of the routine of Territorial Americanization. Thousands of acres of choice land were quietly appropriated for military use, and the appropriation was accepted by residents as incidental to a predestined plan. In fact, when aviation centers were established at Fort Kamehameha and on Ford Island in 1917, Islanders were flattered to have their shores considered worthy of such newfangled military gear; when Wheeler Field and Hickam came later, they were downright proud.

The Hawaiian Islands, bragged a gratified missionary heir, in applauding the military intrusion, "enable the United States absolutely to command the ocean against an Asiatic or any other power, by making an overseas attack too dangerous to be attempted. No modern war-fleet would dare to get 4,000 miles away from a base of supplies. This great, impregnable oasis of the ocean, moreover, will insure the safety of the important trade routes and will supplement the international value of the Panama Canal."

On April 6, 1917, the United States joined the European conflict against the Huns, and Hawaii cheerfully went to war, too. But the impact of World War I on the Islands was slight. It served more as a justification for all the military personnel and paraphernalia that had already been lodged there. Islanders at least felt secure in their distance from the trenches and in their refuge behind the generous fortifications with which they had been provided.

They contributed magnanimously to organizations like the War Relief Committee and the Red Cross, planted victory gardens, knitted, wound countless surgical dressings, and were exposed to a barrage of poster slogans in shop windows and public places: "Hooverize!", "Grow Your Own Food," "Eat More Bananas." They were given a sense of participation in the war when several German ships that had taken refuge in Honolulu harbor were sabotaged by their crews, when the assets of the old German sugar firm of Hackfeld and Company were taken over by American Factors, and when the splendid Royal Hawaiian Hotel in downtown Honolulu was converted into the Army and Navy Y.M.C.A.

Nearly ten thousand home boys donned uniforms of the National Guard to relieve regular troops stationed in the Islands, but very few of them saw overseas service. The greatest effect of the war was in the disruption of shipping. Islanders had not only the meatless days familiar to the Mainland but occasionally had to get along on short rations of rice, fish, and other staples. And the real pinch came when the bottom dropped out of the infant tourist trade. Everyone from lei makers to travel agents missed those tourist dollars.

Through sharing with Mainlanders a few wartime inconveniences and sacrifices, the average Territorial citizen, by Armistice Day, felt as integral a part of the United States as, say, a Texan. Most of the annexation prejudices had vanished; and the easy-come, easy-go prosperity of the Harding-Coolidge decade resolved the last vestiges of resentment over the acquired national affiliation, except among steadfast old Hawaiian families, who never would cast off their bitterness.

But no one was ever again permitted to forget that the military had come to stay, that the armed forces could claim certain priorities, that civil rights were secondary to military rights. Just before the war, a prominent citizen, William R. Castle, Jr., had observed that "already the military is almost as much in evidence in Honolulu as it is in Gibraltar, and unless the city continues to grow, it seems as though in a few years the civil costume would be the exception rather than the rule."

Honolulu continued to grow, and so did the acquisitive military. During the spring and summer of 1925, Pearl Harbor became the focal point for the grandest-scale maneuvers that had ever been staged by the navy. Practically the entire American fleet, eleven battleships, ten light cruisers, sixty destroyers, eighteen submarines—137 ships in all—manned by forty-five thousand officers and men, swept down upon Oahu.

At the height of the war games, a line of warships extended offshore all the way from Waikiki to Ewa. In the course of a week the forty-five thousand service men thronged ashore, while the army did its playful best to repulse the invasion. Nor were the intruders all in uniform. "There has never been a greater influx of curious and intelligent sightseers in the history of Hawaii," gloated an Island publicist. Backing up the navy were official "referees" and observers from Washington, congressmen by the score, press representatives by the hundred, ordinary rubbernecks by the thousand. Honolulu welcomed them with open houses and open arms. For ten days city life was a continuous round of balls, banquets, receptions, parades, and parties. Just for frills the legislature was obliged to appropriate the extravagant sum of seventy-five thousand dollars. But aside from giving the visitors a preview of Hawaii, the principal product of the games was the

startling discovery that big battle wagons could not maneuver gracefully in the sheltered waters of Pearl Harbor, and few could anchor
there safely at one time. More millions of dollars had to be called for
to enlarge and improve the base.

Meantime miles of shore front and huge tracts of interior land
were taken over on other parts of Oahu. Navy and marine air stations
were established at Kaneohe and at Barber's Point. Militarists had
been nursing the theory that an impregnable Oahu made the whole
island chain impregnable, because of inferior harborage on the other
islands. But with the growing emphasis on air power, that theory
became suspect, and bases, camps, and ranges had to be acquired on
Maui and the Big Island.

William Castle's hunch that civilians were going to be a minority
among an overwhelming uniformed populace had called for a stretch of
imagination in the early twenties, but not in the thirties. As the military build-up grew increasingly conspicuous, peace-minded citizens
were nostalgic for the old days when social prominence was not measured in terms of stripes, gold braid, and scrambled eggs. Alarmists
visualized the Islands' being turned into a colonial outpost of the
United States, a territorial fortress with a military dictatorship, an
insular frontier offering only second-class American citizenship to
civilians. They saw outside authority creeping into all forms of government.

Then in 1931 occurred a social catastrophe that shook the Islands
to their lava foundations. If the Massie case had come off on the
outskirts of a big continental naval base in Boston, Seattle, or Brooklyn, it would have made bold, black headlines in the tabloids for a few
days and been quickly dismissed. But Hawaii was not large enough to
contain such a scandal, and the Territory was not supposed to be
wicked enough to evoke that kind of atrocity.

Bored at a party, Thalia Massie, twenty-year-old wife of navy
Lieutenant Thomas H. Massie, strolled off by herself for a street walk,
and was picked up in a car by five hoodlums, two Hawaiian, two
Japanese, and a Chinese, badly beaten and raped by all five. The long
trial that followed their apprehension ended in a hung jury; while a
second trial was pending, one of the defendants was kidnapped by

Lieutenant Massie, his socially prominent mother-in-law, and two enlisted men; taken to the Massie residence; thrown into a bathtub and
shot. The murderers were captured by police in a wild chase on the
road to Koko Head, where they evidently intended to dispose of the
body.

During the trial, the sordid details had been fed to the press bit by
bit and each detail blown into front-page stories from coast to coast.
The murder made still bigger headlines. "Horror piles on horror and
shock follows shock, as the cables sizzle with details of the revolting
tragedy in 'the Paradise of the Pacific,'" summarized the softspoken
Literary Digest. "The Garden Spot of the World, Mecca of tourists . . .
now gains a new but darker fame as the American press prints thousands of columns and roaring headlines about the tragedy and the
conditions from which it sprang."

President Hoover called a special cabinet meeting to confer on the
situation. The United States Senate was thrown into an uproar. The
navy canceled another scheduled visit to Hawaii. The Attorney General was ordered to make a thorough investigation of Island conditions. The governor was openly accused of being derelict in providing
effective government. In Honolulu a state of semimartial law went into
effect; all sailors were restricted to quarters for fear of race riots. The
American Legion threatened to broadcast a declaration that Honolulu
and Waikiki were unsafe for visitors. While Island publicists were
trying to smooth things over by pleading that the Massie case was an
isolated event and nothing like it had ever happened before, the Commandant of the Fourteenth Naval District crossed wires by alleging
that there had been forty cases of criminal assault in the last eleven
months. Hawaii had never before suffered such humiliation.

Finally in May the murderers, defended by the celebrated Clarence
Darrow, were sentenced to ten years of hard labor in Oahu prison and,
after serving one hour of the sentence, were freed by executive com-
mutation. The national outcry began all over again. Were there two
sets of laws in Hawaii, one for the military and the favored few and
another for the common people? "An insult to human decency and a
blot upon American justice," screamed the Denver *Post*.

The Massie case resisted suppression. *Kamaainas* swore that the navy had been smearing Hawaii in an attempt to obscure the crime of an officer or to get a tighter control on Island government. The last say was left to the Attorney General who had been ordered to make an investigation. He did find ample reason for recommending improvements in law enforcement but no justification for the wild rumors regarding maladministration of justice in the Territory. In any case, the public had lost interest in remedial action by the time his report was issued. It led to a flurry of congressional bills on Hawaii that were never enacted into law, including one which would give the army and navy a voice in a new commission government. To prejudiced Islanders the whole affair was a plot of the military to ruin the effect of superlative advertising brought by pineapples and the publicity bureaus. For ten years the Massie case vied with Diamond Head as the symbol of Hawaii.

It became increasingly evident that much of the congressional and military anxiety over Island affairs fundamentally concerned the imbalance in Caucasian population. Senators seemed to entertain doubts as to how laws that applied to stateside occidentals could be effective in a predominantly oriental community, and the army was conscious of the security problem that would be posed if the United States ever found itself at war with an Asiatic nation. Would the Japanese, for example, serve as a built-in fifth column, should a breach with Tokyo occur?

There was good reason for the concern. In the late thirties, the population chart showed that out of a total of 415,000 Islanders, more than a third, 155,000, were Japanese; pure Hawaiian stock was down to 21,000, with about twice that number of part-Hawaiians; there were 52,000 Filipinos, 29,000 Chinese, some 7000 Koreans, over 30,000 Portuguese, and almost 8000 Puerto Ricans—against 68,000 "other Caucasians," which included, besides families of American ancestry, a considerable representation of fascist and communist countries. Moreover, close to one-fifth of the population was alien, a nightmare for anyone who had to worry about political alignment, military security, possible espionage, and probable sabotage, if a shooting war ever developed.

The tempo of the military build-up rose sharply after 1935. Hickam Field, on a great tidelands area adjacent to Pearl Harbor, was ceremoniously dedicated. In 1936, and again in 1937, the gigantic American fleet paid visits to Hawaii during impressive Pacific maneuvers. In 1939 Honolulu, in cooperation with the army, rehearsed its first blackout, an exercise that brought a touch of alarm into every household.

Pearl Harbor took on new importance on July 20, 1940, when President Franklin D. Roosevelt signed a bill creating a two-ocean navy. During the same year the Honolulu Board of Supervisors began discussions of an Emergency Disaster Plan and set up a Major Disaster Council.

By early 1941, M-Day plans, involving all the doctors, police, and volunteer "society cops" in the Territory, had been widely publicized, and on April 25th, Dr. Robert B. Faus of the new Preparedness Committee and Alfred L. Castle, representing the American Red Cross, issued the stirring statement: "While the United States is not actually at war, and there is no occasion for war hysteria, the international situation is so critical that the civilian population of Honolulu must realize that the time has come *now*—not tomorrow—for intelligent, adequate civilian defense preparedness. No sane person can think otherwise. The Army and Navy are not here to protect the population of Honolulu, their duty is to defend Hawaii as one of the most vital parts of the American Defense system. In case of emergency, the civilian population must be prepared to care for itself."

That reminder, interpreted to mean that it was the business of the army and navy to protect the Islands, not the Islanders, was a startling revelation to most civilians. There was something merciless and cold-blooded about it, as though, after making all manner of concessions to the military, they were going to be deserted and left to fend for themselves.

"Hawaii is in no danger of being starved in war, unless U.S.A. is defeated," an Island journal lugubriously promised. "Interior lines of communication connect Hawaii with the continent and they are as safe for supply as are transcontinental railroads. . . . In 1940 Hawaii produced about 30% of food consumed." Was this supposed to be reassuring?

Together the army and navy, tactically unconcerned about civilian survival, were making their presence ever more conspicuous. Bombings in Europe had convinced the people of Hawaii that their greatest vulnerability to attack would be from the air, and the activation of the Hawaiian Air Force in 1940 added substance to that fear.

Nor was it any token activation, for it consisted of two air-base commands, a bombardment wing of B-10's at Hickam, and a pursuit wing of P-26's at Wheeler. And the delivery of scores of P-36's and P-40's by aircraft carriers could not long be kept a military secret. Then on May 13, 1941, the thunderous arrival of the first mass flight of B-17's direct from California's Hamilton Field had a foreboding significance. There was no mistaking that the army was preparing for both attack and counterattack.

"Japanese May Strike Over Weekend," screamed a banner headline in the Honolulu *Advertiser* on November 30, 1941. That did it. The people of Hawaii were ready for December 7th, and they had reason to be confident that the professional defenders were ready, considering the years of planning and the millions spent to ward off a hypothetical aggressor. But the professionals were not quite convinced that it could happen here, not with all the stored-up fighting power they had at their command, an invincible fleet in Pearl Harbor, arrays of planes on the airfields, ammunition by the thousands of tons, personnel in battle trim. With strength like that, even patrols and radar watch were superfluous, at least on week ends.

The strike came at 7:55 on a Sunday morning. Everyone was off guard, exactly as the enemy had calculated. By mid-morning Pearl Harbor was a flaming devastation, the Pacific fleet was crippled, airfields were a chaos of destruction, and the casualty list numbered over three thousand. The nation had suffered the most staggering, the most humiliating, defeat in its history.

There was valor aplenty in the turmoil of that morning, but the most cool-headed heroes were the civilians. "It was not the civilian population who was confused," Robert Shivers, head of Honolulu's

Federal Bureau of Investigation later testified. He described their contribution as "unequaled in the annals of our country," adding that "Nowhere under the sun could there have been a more intelligent response to the needs of the hour than was given by the population of these islands."

While smoke billowed over Pearl Harbor, the citizens quietly mobilized, took their posts in accordance with M-Day orders, struggled with guards for the privilege of returning to duty at airfields and naval stations, queued up by the thousand to donate blood, avoided panic, and started digging bomb shelters—"scare *pukas.*"

During the previous fall, the legislature had delegated to Governor Joseph B. Poindexter, in the Hawaii Defense Act, more sweeping emergency powers over life and property than any state had ever invested in its chief executive. Three hours after the attack, the governor invoked those powers. But hardly had the proclamation been issued when General Walter C. Short, commander of the army in Hawaii, arrived at the governor's office to request a declaration of martial law, a yielding of all governing authority to the army, and a suspension of the writ of *habeas corpus.* The governor hesitated. The general insisted. "Do you consider it absolutely essential to the defense of these islands?" begged Poindexter. "I do," answered the commanding general.

Later in the afternoon the governor signed a statement that had been prepared by the army months before. It was virtually his abdication: "I do hereby authorize and request the Commanding General, Hawaiian Department, during the present emergency and until the danger of invasion is removed, to exercise all the powers normally exercised by me as Governor; and I do further authorize and request the said Commanding General . . . to exercise the powers normally exercised by judicial officers and employees of this territory. . . ."

The signing of that document was a culmination of sorts to the grip the army had been slowly tightening for forty-three years. The generals and colonels at last had complete control. Hawaii was taken over like a conquered alien land, the greatest military coup in the history of American democracy. And Territorial citizens had to wait four years for the satisfaction of having the action repudiated by the Supreme Court of the United States.

Meantime martial law went into effect. All power, legislative, executive, and judicial, was vested in the military governor. Army personnel moved into the executive offices and court rooms, and civilians were tried in provost courts, where penalties were meted out without reference to the statutes of either the United States or the Territory of Hawaii. Commands of the military governor were issued through general orders, which the local press was directed to publish at its own expense.

Those orders covered the whole range of government affairs from traffic regulation, rent control, curfews, and interisland travel to press censorship, wages, liquor consumption, and garbage collection. Organization of the edicts was without reason or rhyme; a single decree might include regulation of court trials, confinement of dogs, prescribed business hours, carrying of gas masks, and conduct during air raid alerts. And the orders were promulgated, amended, and rescinded with such bewildering rapidity that even law enforcement agents were confused. All of Hawaii, alas, lived under the aegis of the army.

But regardless of the authoritarian rule, everyone, almost everyone, took it in stride. Behind all the grumbling was a self-satisfying comfort in the regimen; it gave people a sense of participation in the war effort, though their employment was far removed from anything related to combat. "You wouldn't know the old place now," was the sentiment most frequently woven into letters sent off to the Coast, and the recipients rarely got more than that general observation, for the details were meticulously scissored out by the censors.

Favorite beaches became a tangle of barbed wire. Fishing sampans and sailing craft were tied up for the duration. Landmarks like the Aloha Tower, pineapple plants, administration buildings, sugar mills, and hotels were presumably shadowed out of existence with mysterious applications of painted camouflage; even the flanks of Diamond Head were tented here and there under acres of chicken-wire shrouds, laced with green cloth, to hide gun emplacements, a disguise that only made "sensitive areas" more conspicuous when adjacent slopes dried into a midsummer yellow.

Tourists disappeared entirely, and their old haunts were converted into rest camps and recreation hangouts for off-duty gobs and G.I.'s. Milling throngs in uniform took over the sidewalks and often the streets; poured into the souvenir shops, shooting galleries, and snack bars; and formed block-long queues wherever there was any entertainment worth lining up for—daytime movies, hip-wiggle shows, bawdy houses. They crowded the restaurants, hotel lobbies, buses, paddy wagons, and police stations.

"The Islands have been turned upside down—revolutionized," summed up a free lance. "It has been a bloodless, social revolution, but it has not only changed the manners and customs of the people, their mental and physical habits, it has altered the very face of Hawaii. . . . Former tourists and business visitors who once arrived in Honolulu and received all the traditional trimmings of a big, boat-day aloha—the off-port greetings, leis, the band, hula girls—would have a difficult time reconciling themselves to the welcome they would receive these days."

That unadvertised wartime Hawaii was predominantly male, a paradise with total nightly blackout and early curfew, bereft of night life, a gasolineless, cars-off-the-street-at-dark paradise, a land of guns and gas masks, I.D. cards and investigators, wailing sirens and roaring planes, Island-wide shortages of potatoes one day and toilet paper the next, no cigarettes today, no toothpaste tomorrow, a land of blood banks, U.S.O., air-raid shelters in every back yard, gun emplacements in the front yard, the shore patrol or military police pacing the walk, a land replenished by convoys that came and went with stealthy irregularity, and always on the horizon a destroyer moving monotonously up and down.

Close to five hundred thousand men in uniform were there at the height of the war, and in 1945 soldiers were arriving at the rate of thirty thousand a month. Over a million men went through Schofield Barracks alone during four years. Most of them despised Hawaii, in particular Oahu, "the Rock," as it was contemptuously known to all.

Thousands based in remote, dusty, wind-blown, muddy encampments never had a chance to see an hibiscus hedge, hear an aloha, or indulge in a dip at Waikiki. Sailors on shore leave moved in packs, and seldom could see much beyond the shoulders of their shipmates. Wolf whistles greeted any human being with youthful bust and skirt. They hated the heat, the Orientals, and the law, and those returning from forward areas hated most of all the piles of apparent plenty that Hawaii seemed to be hoarding, mountainous accumulations of supplies destined for westward shipment; vehicles, canned goods, lumber.

Spotting one of the immense lumber yards that became increasingly conspicuous as the war progressed, a single sailor expressed the sentiments of his fellows in an impassioned outburst: "Why, there's enough lumber stacked on this Rock to crate the god-damned thing and ship it back to the States."

There was little exaggeration in that view of accumulated supplies. Hawaii was the staging area for Pacific attacks, strategic nerve center for army, navy, and marines, training ground for invasion landings, jungle combat, and guerilla tactics, the hub of a Pacific aerial network, home of one of the world's largest ammunition depots, repair yard for seven thousand ships. Navy construction projects in the Pacific, launched from Hawaii, were described after removal of censorship restrictions as "the most stupendous building program ever undertaken in history." Never before had there been such a concentration of military might and material.

Little by little restrictions on civilians were lifted, but not until October 24, 1944, was martial law ended, by Presidential proclamation. Wartime habits, however, had become so firmly fixed, that there was no precipitate swing back to normal, whatever "normal" might be in a changed world. "No one expects to see the Territory ever return exactly to the conditions that prevailed here before the war," was the common conjecture. "The change is not only constant, it is permanent. What the future holds for the Islands, few would hazard to guess."

The generals and admirals would have been the last to hazard a guess in December 1941 that Island-born Japanese would, three years later, be among the most widely eulogized patriots of World War II. The AJA's, Americans of Japanese Ancestry, had been suspect, before, during, and long after the Pearl Harbor attack. Whether or not their loyalty would revert to Japan was a prime enigma of the military government, in fact, the basic excuse for creation of that government.

On the assumption that their loyalty was unreliable, Nisei who belonged to the Hawaiian Territorial Guard were politely placed on inactive status in January 1942. Instead of taking it as an insult, a substantial group, mostly university students, responded by volunteering for any duty the army saw fit to assign them. As "Varsity Victory Volunteers," they were attached to a regiment of engineers and for a year put on trial in both menial and skilled labor. They demonstrated their loyalty beyond any doubt, and when the privilege of enlistment was extended to them, they joined up almost in a body.

The VVV were the nucleus of what eventually became the 100th Infantry Battalion, some 1300 American-Japanese who trained at Camp McCoy, Wisconsin, landed at Anzio in September 1943, and made such a heroic record in the Italian campaign that they were dubbed the "Purple Heart Battalion." Out of the total of 1300, 650 were wounded and 300 killed in less than ten months.

More Nisei volunteers were called for by the War Department, and a new quota for AJA's in Hawaii set at 1500. As if in defiance of the modest quota, 9507 applied for enlistment. The 100th Infantry Battalion was incorporated in the 442nd Regimental Combat Team, including Nisei from both the Mainland and Hawaii. By V-E Day its members had won over 6000 decorations, and military observers declared them to be "probably the most decorated unit in United States military history."

A final analysis of Hawaii's World War II honor roll showed that 80 per cent of those killed and 88 per cent of those wounded were of Japanese ancestry. Moreover, the military had to concede in the end that not a single known act of sabotage had been committed by Japanese in the Territory.

That record was responsible for the greatest change of all in Hawaii's postwar social structure. There had been a tendency before December 7th to treat the Japanese majority as a minority group, to accord them a sort of second-class citizenship. Their war conduct and sacrifices had easily won them first-class status. With pride they could cast off the slight previously imposed upon them and participate freely in all phases of Island life. They did.

In 1941 most of the eight miles of highway between Honolulu and Pearl Harbor were bordered by expansive cane fields that fanned back into the hills. Four years later the cane was gone, and in its place stretched immense housing developments for service personnel and civilian defense employees, storage depots, supply centers, marine camps, army quarters, naval establishments, warehouses, airport facilities, Quonset huts by the hundred, acre upon acre of excess armament. It was grandly symbolic of the military usurpation that occurred everywhere in the Islands.

The grip of the armed forces was yielded reluctantly after the war. Some of the auxiliary flying fields went back into agriculture; thousands of temporary structures were demolished; much of the surplus equipment slowly disappeared, but army, navy, marines, and air force remained as major tenants, with permanent tenure.

During the Korean War the Islands once more became a great staging base for surface transportation as well as the long airlift. Between 1950 and 1954, 42,000 trans-Pacific flights were made, carrying over three-quarters of a million passengers, 71,000 patients, and 124,000 tons of cargo, while a fleet of some 350 passenger, tanker, and cargo vessels plied between Pearl Harbor and Asiatic ports.

Yet the full potential of Hawaii as a coordinated military headquarters was only beginning to be realized. On July 1, 1957, a complete reorganization of Pacific armed forces went into effect under one centralized command, CINCPAC, Commander in Chief, U.S. Pacific Command. It embraced the army, navy, and air force everywhere in the Pacific, the Far East, and Southeast Asia, covering a politically hot and militarily explosive area of eighty-five million square miles, over 40 per cent of the earth's surface.

Working from headquarters at Camp H. M. Smith on Halawa Heights above Pearl Harbor, CINCPAC had a mission of incredible responsibility. In large terms, it called for maintenance of security in the Pacific, the defense of the United States against attack from the Pacific, the direction and control of all U.S. armed forces and armament in the area, comprising a complement of 440,000 men, 400 vessels, 3,500 planes, and countless tons of conventional and nuclear weapons, a command that cost American taxpayers an estimated fifty million dollars a day.

The roll of top-ranking chiefs under the coordinated command on Halawa Heights ran on monotonously, seeming to vie with the power of the Pentagon; Commander in Chief, U. S. Army, Pacific; Commander in Chief, U. S. Pacific Fleet; Commander in Chief, Pacific Air Force; Commanding General, Fleet Marine Force, Pacific; Commanding General, U. S. Army, Hawaii, and 25th Infantry Division; Commander, Hawaiian Sea Frontier and Commandant, 14th Naval District; Commander, Pacific Air Force Bases Command; Commander, Air Material Command, Pacific. And those were only the more luminous of the gold-braided principals.

No superlatives could quite convey the bewildering vastness of military authority concentrated on Oahu. It was the largest single unified military command in the world. From Fort Shafter the Commander in Chief of the U. S. Army, Pacific, directed all the army components from the West Coast to the Far East. From Makalapa Ridge overlooking Pearl Harbor, the Commander in Chief, Pacific Fleet, issued orders to the navy's largest command, 425 ships, 2500 aircraft, and a quarter of a million men. From Hickam Air Force Base, the Commander in Chief, Pacific Air Forces, directed flight operations over two-fifths of the globe.

From a little coaling and repair station, Pearl Harbor had grown in fifty years into a giant complex covering more than ten thousand acres, with installations valued at over a billion and a half dollars. Its shipyard was the largest U.S. industrial organization in the Pacific; its supply center, extending along two and half miles of shore line and carrying stock worth 125 million dollars was the largest merchandising unit in the Islands. And the navy was Hawaii's most munificent paymaster.

The buildup of U.S. troops in South Viet Nam during 1965 once more brought increases in Island command and staff personnel. The Hawaii-based 1st Marine Brigade of 7500 men and the army's 25th

Infantry Division were shipped to Southeast Asia; and the whole Hawaiian military complex was pressed to provide support services for units en route to and from the new war zone. But the military aggregate in the Islands was so vast that early months of the war in Viet Nam caused no major upheaval in the structure and no spectacular rise in operation expenditures. Existing ships, supplies, arms and personnel already on the payroll merely went into action.

Hawaii another Gibraltar? The contrast between that ancient British bastion and the Island stronghold had long since degenerated to metaphor. Gibraltar still retained its title as the world's most impregnable natural fortress, but its whole honeycombed mass could be chucked into a stretch of Hawaiian shore line and never be noticed.

WAIKIKI

XVI

More Tourists Than People

Hawaii was a pretty drowsy holiday resort for avant-garde tourists of the Victorian era. Mark Twain called it "Sunday Land," "paradise for an indolent man," where one could "sun himself all day under the palm trees and be no more troubled by his conscience than a butterfly." Jarves saw it as an asylum for the halt, the ailing and the convalescent, "a retreat for valetudinarians . . . equal to any known place on the globe." People went to the Sandwich Islands to relax and ruminate, to loll and dawdle.

Headquarters for all the composure was the beach at Waikiki, "a hamlet of plain cottages . . . whither the white people go to revel in bathing clothes, mosquitoes and solitude." "It is not a gay watering place," suggested William Root Bliss, who claimed that the nearest thing to excitement he ever found there was the "occasional fall of a cocoanut."

Though the mountain-ocean setting was superb and boarding places like the Seaside and the Sans Souci were considered picturesque by the less critical patrons, both the "hamlet" and its environs fell far short of the idyllic. Bathing was precarious because of the hidden coral; the sand was coarse, rock-strewn, and blanketed to the high-water mark with a tangle of flowering vines. The unpainted, ramshackle cottages, with their conspicuous outhouses, were dependent on a growth of shrubs to hide their ugliness, and interspersed among them were weathered grass shacks and shanties of the natives, their yards littered with derelict canoes, dogs, pigs, and naked children. Even the king's brown retreat with its broad veranda was anything but distinguished.

And the worst of Waikiki was its back yard, acres of swampland given over to taro patches, banana thickets, duck ponds, a poi factory, and a great many piggeries. When the wind was in the wrong direction, the mosquitoes and the smells were intolerable, and *haoles* stayed in town.

Waikiki did not change materially during all the span of years between the 1860's and the 1890's, and when a change finally did take place, it was the military that brought it. The soldiers prompted the first real influx of middle-class tourists, who came in response to the thousands of glowing reports dispatched by veterans of the Spanish-American War; they trailed the garrisons stationed on Oahu after annexation and the engineers and construction crews sent to Pearl Harbor and the forts. Instead of repelling sightseers, the uniforms, the dreadnaughts, and the howitzers added glamor to the scene. People came to take in the martial sideshow, as well as the tropical tranquility.

Too, a great many veterans, after serving short-term Island hitches, were converted into tourists themselves. The environment got into their blood, and once back in New Hampshire or Nebraska, they remembered the trade winds, palms, and hula girls and headed back to Honolulu for a honeymoon. All in all, the men in uniform early in the 1900's were ardent champions of Hawaiian tourism.

But with or without the boost from the warriors, the Islands had long been destined to develop into a tourist mecca. The first explorers hinted of it; the whalers were convinced of it; the missionaries feared it; the merchants conspired for it; and the journalists, with their perennial pitch on verdure-clothed valleys, the invigorating clime, crystal waters, and rollicking natives, prepared the way for it.

In a broad sense, all the early comers were tourists; in the narrower sense, the first occidental to admit that he was a tourist was Britisher William Ellis, who junketed around the Big Island with a trio of other missionaries in 1823, preaching as he went and casing the land for evangelical conquest. "We have ascended its lofty and majestic mountains, entered its dark caverns, crossed its deep ravines, and traversed its immense fields of rugged lava, . . ." Ellis quietly boasted. "We traveled to the south, the east, and the north; twice crossed the interior in different parts; remained a night and a day at the great volcano of Kilauea; visited all the principal settlements, both on the coast and in the interior."

Little escaped their attention. Despite their ministerial frocks, they poked and pried into forbidden places, as well as open, like so many college boys on a gambol. At Honaunau, for example, they found that orders to destroy the ancient idols had not yet been carried out, and the durable "House of Keawe," sacred depository for the bones of departed kings and princes, still stood, guarded by an array of diabolic images and deities. Trespass was strictly prohibited by edict of the king, they were told, but their curiosity was not to be curbed by such admonition.

"By pushing one of the boards across the doorway a little to one side," confessed the missionary, "we looked in and saw many large images, some of wood very much carved, others of red feathers, with widely distended mouths, large rows of sharks' teeth and glaring pearl-shell eyes. We also saw several bundles of human bones, cleaned, carefully tied up . . . together with some rich shawls and other valuable articles."

Ellis set a commendable example by resisting the temptation to appropriate souvenirs from the mausoleum and was content instead to compress his observations into a tour diary that proved to be the most detailed description of primeval Hawaii ever prepared by a *haole*. But his example was not followed by the next group of white tourists to inspect the House of Keawe. A year later Lord Byron and his entourage descended upon Honaunau and, with a nod from the king, virtually cleaned out the repository.

As if they were indulging in a prank, the chaplain of *H.M.S. Blonde*, the Reverend R. Bloxam, gleefully pictured the indignation of the guardian of monuments, as the priceless mementos disappeared before his eyes. "Two immense, though beautifully carved, wooden gods, that stood on each side of the stone altar, were immediately plucked up and sent down to the boats. I succeeded in appropriating to myself two wooden gods, a feathered deity that covered the bones of Keawe, godfather of Kaleiopuu, a beautiful spear, and a few other articles within my reach. . . . Having thus gratified our curiosity, we returned to the ship, laden with the spoils of their heathen temple."

Hawaii's pioneer souvenir collectors had arrived. In fact, natives were so quick to catch on to the "rapacious inclination" of visiting westerners, and so quick to commercialize on it, that within a decade Hawaiians exhausted their stock of ready-made gods and went into the business of modeling "ancient" ones, not for worship, but for sale to gullible tourists. A Philadelphia doctor, W. S. W. Ruschenberger, caught the fakers in the act in 1836, laboriously chipping and carving out works of art, then nicking, weathering, and smashing the creations "to impart an appearance of antiquity—and actually succeeding in the deception."

Hawaiians were marvelously adept at anticipating the wants of their clientele. All during the periods of missionary supremacy, whaling, and exploratory merchandising, they were superior hosts, eagerly catering to visitors in any way they could invent, whether or not there was any money in it. They volunteered their services as porters, boatmen, messengers, cooks, guides, fishermen, entertainers. The warmth of hospitality was one of the encumbrances of Island travel. In the country every family en route wanted to play host. Invitations to pause for a rest, a drink, a meal, a sleeping mat came from all doorways, regardless of the destitution in a household, and a rejection was sure to be taken as an affront. Any native hut was open to a traveler.

When overnight accommodations were accepted, the whole family might move out to make room for the guest and his party, or, more likely, a dozen adults and children, sharing the floor of a single small room, would crowd to one side to provide space for the visitors. If the family had profited from the social indoctrination of the missionaries, a tapa curtain was stretched across one corner of the room to provide minimum privacy, though the reason for this seclusion was far beyond the comprehension of the hosts. What had the foreigners to hide?

Once the curtain was hung, grinning faces intermittently appeared under the curtain, over the top, or in rents. Fits of giggles from the other side clearly indicated that the conduct of the secretive guests was the subject of continued speculation. On one occasion, just as a distinguished couple were disrobing for the night behind their curtain, it was suddenly flung aside. The family merely wanted to know whether the guests were white all over and possessed normal body components, explained the host graciously.

At the home of a chief in Kau a traveler discovered to his bewilderment that he was to share overnight quarters with two adult sisters and a lumbering six-foot hog. He did not mind the sisters, but the hog. . . . It was a harmless, house-broken pet that the girls had adopted when it was a curly-tailed shoat, the chief casually recounted. Joining the dinner circle, the animal was fed from the same calabashes as the rest of the family, much to the displeasure of the guest. And when retirement hour arrived, he was at last relieved of further fear of disturbance from the enormous sow. As it had done since it was a puny pig, the beast grunted to a comfortable position down the center of the sisters' mat; the girls cuddled up on either side and pulled a quilt over the three bodies, leaving the sow's black ears and nose protruding on a pillow between their heads.

For a tourist who really wanted to meet the natives, there was no substitute for living with them. Rough-and-ready John Townsend, who had tramped across the American continent in 1834, lived with the Indians, and then kept going west to investigate the Hawaiian "Indians," made such a favorable impression on his hosts that they organized for him an old-time dance exhibition, in which everyone sang "a strange kind of howling song" and "thumped his calabash most musically."

He was astonished at the "exceeding nicety" of the performance.

"No band of civilized drummers could have kept time more perfectly, nor flourished their sticks with more grace. . . . During the whole time of the singing, the bodies of the performers were not idle: every muscle seemed to have something to do, and was incessantly brought into action by the strange motions, twistings and contortions of the frame."

Except for hardy prowlers like Townsend, however, very few visitors in the nineteenth century, ever deigned to venture very far out of Honolulu, Hilo, or Lahaina without the services of a guide. An escort was essential, not because of any danger of mistreatment, but because there were no roads. The Islands were a network of unmarked trails that could lead a novice hopelessly astray at any fork.

Guides were easy to pick up. For a pittance, or no compensation at all, they would cheerfully agree to lead a trek to a given destination, whether or not they had ever been there. Their natural wanderlust, their natural curiosity, and their eagerness simply to associate with foreigners were incentive enough. Generally they were superb woodsmen, with an uncanny sense of direction, wonderfully adept at piloting their clients across turbulent streams, finding a way over lava flows, and beating through rain forests; they were resourceful, tireless, amiable—and thoroughly unreliable. At a whim, the guide might decide to lay over for a day or two, try to change the destination, or abandon the excursion altogether.

Ordinarily it was safest to hire as pathfinder an experienced runner nominated by the king or a chief. They were not always companionable, attractive, or sanitary, but they were professionals and knew their business. Makoa, who conducted Ellis on his tour, was a good example, "a singular-looking man," who affected a shaved head, a long, knotted goatee and a symbolic representation of goats tattooed over his face, and carried an enormous coconut-leaf fan "to beat away the flies or the boys, when either became too numerous or troublesome."

In one way or another, all professional guides seemed to be freaks or cranks, as if singularity were their badge of office. On Kauai, Jarves turned up the counterpart of Makoa, wearing tattered tapa pantaloons, a red flannel shirt, a necklace of vegetable stalks, and a wreath of flowers on his head; instead of a fan, he carried a castoff iron ramrod.

At intervals he was unquestionably crazy and his conduct "a complete exemplification of savage eccentricity." Yet Jarves praised him as a valuable servant, "perfectly fearless of danger, quick in his movements, careless of fatigue, and an excellent caterer."

No less outlandish was a handsome lad Kaluna, the favorite guide for expeditions out of Hilo, "almost a complete savage, . . . lithe, athletic, and as pliable as if he were an invertebrate animal, capable of unlimited doublings up and contortions, . . . a half-tamed creature out of the woods, . . . thoroughly careless and irreponsible . . . reckless about horses, reckless about himself, without any manners or any obvious sense of right or propriety." And his employers swore by him.

Pioneer tourists put up with a full measure of annoyance from their indispensable guides and with plenty of general discomfort on their journeyings, but by the time they returned to civilization, the recollections of both had usually jelled into humor, and it was the enchantment of the Islands that stuck in their memories. The one ordeal that no tourist ever forgot or attempted to minimize was a voyage between islands.

Hawaiians doted on their vessels as though they were the mascots of the kingdom, but *malihinis* who had traveled the plush coasters and river boats of the eastern seaboard formed their own opinions, as they fought their way aboard a schooner at the Honolulu landings against the crush of natives and their baggage—"men, women, children, dogs, cats, mats, calabashes of poi, coconuts, bananas, dried fish; and every dusky individual of the throng wreathed and garlanded with odorous and brilliant flowers—all talking and laughing."

Every tourist who ever boarded an interisland schooner had his personal tales of travail. Travel-inured Theo. H. Davies warned his friends that the vessels were "not all that stomach could wish" and explained that the quick way to distinguish between a tourist and Island residents on deck was by the little chamber-pot which the *kamaainas* always carried and "held in readiness for the first attack of seasickness."

Francis Olmsted took passage from Honolulu to Kawaihae on the infamous *Clementine,* "one of those vessels rigged in defiance of all symmetry," and imprudently billeted himself in the freshly white-washed cabin below decks. When he came up for air next morning, shrouded like a ghost, he was surrounded by a laughing audience who wanted to know where he had found the flour barrel to sleep in. By daylight he also discovered that his cabin provided the ventilation for the hold, and the horses tethered there accounted for the stable odors that had kept him nauseated during the night.

His return trip was more noxious. Forty wild cattle were loaded aboard at Kawaihae and tied to a framework of spars amidships. Since they monopolized the deck, Olmsted again had to retire to his flour barrel for more sleepless nights, listening to the stamping of terrified animals over his head and the constant thud of their weight as they were thrown to the deck by the violent motion of the ship.

Even when the steamer *Kilauea* was put on the interisland run, she offered little improvement in travel comfort. Regardless of the weather, sensible travelers still slept in the open, sprawled on the deck or hatches and skylights, heaps of natives interspersed with tourists, merchants and ministers. "The residents are very proud of her, and speak lovingly of her," noted Isabella Bird, who had traveled on many ships in many parts of the world and, from her wealth of experience advised disloyally that the ship had no ladies' cabin, was overrun with huge red cockroaches, and had "a shabby, obsolete look about her, like a second-rate coasting collier, or an American tow-boat. She looks ill found, too; I saw two essential pieces of tackle give way as they were hoisting the mainsail."

Miss Bird spread her mat on the transom in company with some of the more polite passengers, and was startled in the morning by a stranger's inquiring whether she realized she was using the head of the governor of Maui as her foot rest.

The informality of ship accommodations carried over to shore hostelry. Periodically there were public houses of sorts in Honolulu, but until the 1860's no establishment that a traveler of character, male or female, would think of tenanting. Tourists of social standing were all entertained in the respectable homes of merchants, plantation managers, royalty, ex-sea captains, or missionaries.

Representatives of these families met every ship that might be bringing passengers and vied with one another for the privilege of serving as host. The parsonages, however, seemed to get the bulk of the *haole* transient trade. That, too, was a tradition transplanted from New England, where village divines were expected to dine and bed down all wayfarers of distinction.

For more than twenty years Hiram Bingham was "mine host" in Honolulu, and missionaries scattered about the Islands fulfilled the same obligations. Not that any of their residences were designed to accommodate the steady flow of guests; every new arrival disrupted the household. The reverend and his wife gave up their bed, and the company moved in; or the children were permitted to occupy the "company room" *pro tempore*, with the standing agreement that they would silently and uncomplainingly withdraw on short notice and spread out somewhere else in the house.

On Kauai the Rices had such an understanding with their young fry, and whenever "tourist people" put in an appearance, all five hurriedly evacuated to a small closet off their parents' room. The Rice youngsters spent a large part of their early life in the confinement of that closet.

At the Lahaina mission it was the same. Since there was no such thing as a schedule for interisland boats, guests ordinarily came unannounced, and might show up at any hour of the day or night. As the Reverend C. S. Stewart sympathetically pictured a typical night arrival of a dozen guests, "Fully aware, from our own experience, of the fatigue and exhaustion attendant on a voyage of two or three days on a crowded schooner, our first object was to secure an opportunity of rest and sleep to our friends. To do this, it became necessary to relinquish our own beds and spread them anew for the females and children, while the gentlemen found couches upon our trunks and the floor; all were soon soundly asleep."

But there was no rest for host and hostess. They spent the rest of the night dressing and cooking half a dozen ducks from their own yard, baking potatoes and taro. Before daybreak Stewart could report that "the whole enclosure was restored to as much order and quietude as if we had been asleep all night."

Guests seldom were aware of the disruption they caused or the strain they put on the family budget. They never quite understood that they were only a small detachment of the parade that moved in and out week after week. Occasionally, however, the long-suffering hosts benefited materially, as with the Lymans at Hilo, when the Scotch botanist David Douglas accepted their hospitality. He more than paid for his bed and board by smuggling armfuls of groceries into the larder, plying the children with little gifts, and flattering the hostess with the present of a gorgeous French muslin dress, an extravagance that no missionary wife could afford.

Away from the ports and missions, along major trails of travel, a few enterprising Hawaiians gradually sensed the need for overnight lodgings and fabricated their conception of good hotels, like Bola-Bola's, to which tourists heading up the rugged Hamakua coast from Hilo were likely to be referred. But anyone with visions of sofas, bright hearths, and a tempting cuisine was due for a shock on arriving there.

As one city-bred patron discovered, it was nothing but a dilapidated frame house, surrounded by a cluster of forlorn grass shacks, and the lobby, a dingy room, fourteen by eighteen feet, *was* the hotel, lounge, dining room, and dormitory combined, already crowded with natives, its dirty floor "littered and piled with mats rolled up, boxes, bamboos, saddles, blankets, lassos, cocoanuts, taro roots, bananas, quilts, pans, calabashes, bundles of hard poi in ti leaves, bones, cats, fowls and clothes." And this was the best establishment on the Hamakua coast.

Most tourists who ventured into the Hawaiian hinterland preferred to take chances on the hospitality of natives who had not yet tried to make a business out of it. That was Charles Nordhoff's choice. He found the common people "as kindly and hospitable as men can be," ready to receive a lodger as if he were conferring them a favor. However, Nordhoff cautioned against ever inquiring about the cost of accommodations when leaving. "The Hawaiian has vague ideas about price. He might tell you five or ten dollars; but if you pay him 75 cents for yourself and your guide, he will be abundantly and thoroughly satisfied." Development of more formal hotel keeping was closely linked with the opening of the West, the gold rush, the opening of rail and shipping lines, and the growth of San Francisco as a city and port.

There was an enormous amount of passenger shuffling in and out of Honolulu, giving the appearance of a steady flux of "tourist people." But the appearance was deceptive; most of the travelers were Hawaiians. In 1861 a British consul took it upon himself to analyze the surging traffic for the first nine months of that year and concluded that "17,717, or nearly one-fourth of the population" had sailed in and out of the harbor between January and September, while only 489 persons had arrived from abroad.

Honolulu, however, was rapidly changing under foreign influences. After a thirty-year absence, Rufus Anderson paid a return visit in 1863, and was astonished at the "garden-like" complexion of the city. "The crooked and filthy lanes of thirty years ago have passed away," he exclaimed, "and so have the huts of dried grass. . . . With no great appearance of wealth, there is an air of civilization in the streets, houses and sidewalks."

During the next decade, as the city continued to grow along with the passenger traffic, it became increasingly evident that the capital demanded more respectable public lodgings than its third-class boarding houses, and when private citizens failed to do anything about it, the government accepted the responsibility and ordered that construction of a spacious hotel be financed from the king's treasury.

The Hawaiian, later known as the Royal Hawaiian, opened its doors in 1872 in the center of Honolulu. It was the first official bid for the tourist trade, cost the staggering sum of $112,000—almost doubling the national debt—and for a time was such an expensive white elephant that it brought the temporary downfall of two cabinet ministers who had been active in promoting it.

Nevertheless, their tourist temple was a triumph, a first-class inn that would have been an ornament to any resort. Deep verandas over-looked a lawn shaded with coconut palms, algarroba and tamarind trees. There were cool courtyards, luxurious rooms, breezy halls, baths, and even a billiard room. Immediately it became Honolulu's social fortress, its club house, exchange, and salon, catering to a clientele as democratic as its staff, for the host was German, the manager American, the steward Hawaiian, the waiters and bellboys Chinese, the outside help Japanese.

Travelers raved about the accommodations, the setting, and the service. "This is the perfection of a hotel," applauded one. "Hospitality seems to take possession of and appropriate one as soon as he enters its never-closed door. . . . One can sit all day on the back verandah, watching the play of light and color on the mountains, and the deep blue green of Nuuanu Valley, where showers, sunshine and rainbows make perpetual variety. The great dining room is delicious. . . . Piles of bananas, guavas, limes and oranges decorate the tables at every meal. . . . I cannot imagine a more fascinating residence."

Even the clientele it drew was approved; American naval officers, planters' families in residence for the season, health seekers from California, whaling captains, tourists from the British Pacific colonies, and "a stream of townspeople always percolating the corridors and verandahs." The charges were right, too, fifteen dollars a week, or three dollars a day, American plan.

With the hotel as a focal point, Honolulu society perked up, and, as soon as he landed, any eligible traveler, with or without introduction, found himself being swept into a round of picnics, veranda parties, court festivities, balls, "sociables," luncheons and dinners on board visiting warships, breakfast parties, swimming parties, riding parties, moonlight sailing parties. Honolulu was blossoming into a real metropolis, "gay, hospitable and restless."

A newly organized Royal Hawaiian Band, under the direction of an imported German master, Captain Henry Berger, was the pride of the city. Distinguished British actors and musicians en route to the colonies stopped off for performances. Periodically there were theatricals, amateur and professional, circuses from the Mainland, minstrel shows, fireworks, horse racing, polo, grand opera, the inevitable Swiss bell ringers, promenade dances, debates, lectures, and, at the less temperate luaus, hula exhibitions. There was something wrong with any tourist who did not have a good time in the midst of all that revelry.

Except for local trimmings, the accent on Hawaiiana, and the wider racial range, it was the same kind of entertainment that would have been found contemporaneously at Saratoga Springs, New Orleans, or Virginia City. But it was seasonal there; in Honolulu the gaiety had no calendar; it continued as a way of life year in and year out. New frills and fashions from the Mainland and Orient added color; trolleys, electricity, and telephones later stepped up the pace, but the general pattern of festivity was set, and it did not change essentially during the next forty years.

Free and unsolicited advertising of this tourist mecca poured from American presses. Samuel Bowles, famed editor of the Springfield, Massachusetts, *Republican*, on a rail trip across the continent to chant the praises of the Union Pacific, added a good word for the Islands: "To us of the East, the Sandwich Islands are a remote foreign kingdom, where our whalers refit and the conversion of whose heathen we dedicated all the sanctified pennies of our childhood, but here in California, they are counted as neighbors. . . . The familiarity with which the Eastern visitor finds "The Islands' spoken of in California, the accounts he receives of their strange scenery, their wonderful volcanoes, their delightful climate—all will strongly invite him to make them a visit."

Charles Warren Stoddard ground out a fancy Victorian brochure for the Oceanic Steamship Company and gratuitously plugged Hawaii: "The tourist who for health or pleasure comes as far west as San Francisco, and omits a visit to the Sandwich Islands, denies himself a rare pleasure. Arrived in Honolulu . . . he is astounded at the grandeur and luxuriance. . . . He is at last in fairy land—the land that poets have sung of, the land the sun loves best."

In 1890 Henry M. Whitney produced one of the first commercial guides, *To Hawaii—the Paradise of the Pacific*, with the big come-on:

"If you are sick or if you are well, it is all the same. In the one case, you can find some place that will build you up; in the other, lovely scenery, pleasant rides and some sights which are the wonder of the world. If you are tired, there is no country in the world that is equal to the Hawaiian Islands for 'laying off.' "

The Islanders did not leave all the tourist baiting to outsiders. Taking a tip from the operations of the land sharks in California, some of the biggest names in Hawaiian business, including Castle and Campbell, Dole and Dillingham, were signed up in 1885 as patrons and promoters of "The Great Land Colonization Scheme," in which 115,750 acres on Oahu were to be sold to statesiders for estates, hideaways, and homesteads. "These lands," promised teasers that were mailed to multitudes of dreamers, "will furnish not only comfortable, but also beautiful, homes for thousands of inhabitants, for it is difficult to conceive of more delightful landscape. . . . It will be the inauguration of a new era in the history of the kingdom."

But the new era did not dawn for that generation of colonization schemers. There was too much competition from the speculators in southern California, where a handier paradise was simultaneously blossoming and the Santa Fe and Southern Pacific railroads were in cahoots, offering transcontinental fares of four and six dollars and dropping off in Los Angeles seekers of "choice residential lots" and "villa sites" at a rate of five hundred a day. Prospective tourists and castle builders found too many distractions elsewhere to take the lure of Hawaiian colonization seriously.

Boom did not hit Honolulu until 1899 and 1900, and it came then as a direct result of of the ballyhoo spread by the hordes of American soldiers who had paused in the Islands en route to the Philippines during the War with Spain. Actually it was not much of a boom, but it looked like one to welcomers who were not yet used to swarms of tourists coming solely to loaf and sightsee. Visitors straggled into Honolulu by the dozen, by scores. The Royal Hawaiian started making money, and in 1900 the manager cockily bragged that he had to turn guests away.

To promoters bewitched by the charm of Hawaii, it was clear as a vision that the real economic future of the Islands was in catering to vacationers. In that faith, a modest Moana Hotel, less than half the size of the establishment completed seventeen years later, was erected on the shores of Waikiki in 1901, and architects commenced drafting plans for the huge and sumptuous Alexander Young Hotel in Honolulu.

For over fifty years the Chamber of Commerce had been directing its efforts primarily to agricultural and industrial promotion. At last that organization climbed on the bandwagon with a cheer for tourism. It joined the Honolulu Merchants' Association in persuading the legislature to appropriate fifteen thousand dollars for an advertising campaign and, as soon as the Young Hotel opened in 1903, helped set up there a central information office for visitors.

A New York advertising agency was retained to place advertisements of Hawaii in Mainland periodicals. Booklets like *Beauty Spots of Hawaii* and *Business in Hawaii* were mailed out in thousands; a quarter of a million copies of a descriptive folder followed. Chamber of Commerce committees started planning floral parades and carnivals, designing posters, and organizing displays for Mainland fairs to attract more tourists.

The most ardent among the promoters was not a *kamaaina*, but a *malihini* from South Carolina, the playwright and journalist Alexander Hume Ford, who had circumnavigated the globe in search of the ideal retreat and something to write about. He chose Hawaii and in 1907 returned there with the intent of letting the world know why.

Like any good publicist, he was aware that he had to establish a symbol in the minds of his perspective clientele. Waikiki was it, a transformed Waikiki, for it was still an untidy fishing village, uncelebrated on the Mainland and lacking much to celebrate. The beach had no color or life. It was deserted even by the surfers, who years before had given up their boards for saddles. There was not so much as a public shelter where one could change into a bathing suit.

The proprietors of the new Moana were on the right track, but they had made only a start. Ford visualized the whole area cleared of the ramshackle cottages, Chinese shanties, and army tents; he pictured the salt marshes drained, the beach cleaned up and lined with handsome homes and hotels. It would make the smartest resort west of the Mediterranean.

The propagandist lived to see his dream come true. With the help of Jack London, he brought back the surfers; he helped organize the Outrigger Canoe Club and started investors thinking about hotels. But he was wise enough to devote most of his energy to stirring action in others and letting them take the credit. "Paradise of the Pacific" and "Playground of the World" were the catch phrases flaunted most frequently by Ford, the Chamber of Commerce, and other Island promoters. Waikiki became the recognized capital of this playground paradise, and the beach house of the Outrigger Canoe Club the center of the play.

It was the surf riding that made Waikiki unique among ocean resorts. "The game has all the excitement of tobogganing, without the effort of dragging the toboggan uphill again," enthused an initiate from the snowbound East. People at last came to Waikiki for sport and fun, as well as contemplation. They came because the rates were moderate, too, $5.00 a day at the Moana for room and meals, or $2.50 at the Seaside, while tourists on a budget could stay in town at the old Royal Hawaiian or the new Alexander Young for $1.00 or $1.50, eat out, and ride the cars to the beach.

In making visits to other islands, it was no longer necessary to put up in grass shacks or a parsonage either. None of the hostelries could compare with the Moana, but for those who did not insist on luxury, there were the Hilo Hotel and the Volcano House on Hawaii; the Maui Grand at Wailuku and later the Pioneer Inn at Lahaina on Maui; the Fairview at Lihue, Deverill's at Hanalei, and Bay View at Waimea on Kauai. Then for one who had stout nerves, a strong constitution, and fifty dollars, a motor car and chauffeur could be hired for a day's sightseeing.

Besides surfing, Hawaii accidentally acquired another symbol that was of inestimable value in spreading the gospel of lighthearted conviviality, the ukulele. Among a group of plantation laborers imported from Madeira in 1879 were three Portuguese who had been instrument makers in the old country. They brought their trade and samples of their handicraft with them, including the viola, the guitar, and the *rajao,* and in spare time modeled new instruments for sale.

Hawaiians were their best customers. The viola soon became known as the taro-patch fiddle; the guitar was ignored at first because it was too large and too expensive; and the *rajao,* most popular of the three, was in such demand that the Madeirans shortly gave up plantation labor to concentrate on mass production of the twangy sound box.

Edward Purvis, a retired army officer turned beachcomber, short, wiry, and hail-fellow-well-met, got hold of a *rajao,* mastered it, and strummed it on the beaches, on the street corners, under the palm trees, always surrounded by a circle of enraptured Hawaiians. Eventually he added hedonistic King Kalakaua to his audience and was promptly adopted as a sort of court minstrel.

The Hawaiians loved him and joined in the songs. He freely transposed some of their *meles* and added them to his repertoire, introduced them to new ditties, and even had King Kalakaua and Princess Liliuokalani composing sentimental lyrics. No gala luau was complete without the bouncing entertainer and the dancing fingers. They nicknamed him "Uku-lele" (jumping flea); the *rajao* was Uku-lele's toy, and shortly the plaything itself became the ukulele.

A fad was born. It swept through the Islands and across the United States, originating the fallacy that Polynesians had been strumming ukuleles on moonlit beaches for centuries. On college campuses and around campfires from coast to coast, the "uke" symbolized Hawaii and spread more fanciful publicity on the Islands than the millions of folders being circulated by the Promotion Committee of the Chamber of Commerce. A repertoire of Hawaiian songs traveled with it. They conjured up pictures of lazy life in the South Seas, of handsome male beachcombers and dazzling brunettes in grass skirts, and they planted in the heart of many a juvenile the idea of one day surrendering to the call of the Islands.

Then in 1893 Joseph Kekuku, a student at the Kamehameha School, gave birth to another fad. He started experimenting with the larger imported Portuguese guitar, using everything from a comb to a jackknife on the strings, holding the back of a steel knife on the strings and rubbing it up and down. Student audiences were delighted; so were Honolulu audiences, and within a few years the whine of a steel guitar was as firmly catalogued among the special sound effects of Hawaii as the roar of the surf on the reefs.

Actually in all this deluge of free musical advertisement that flooded the Mainland there was scarcely a trace of genuine, indigenous Hawaiiana. To western ears the original music of Hawaii was noisy, dissonant, and unmelodic. The natives had seized upon the melody of the gospel hymns taught by the missionaries, on the German lieder later taught by bandmaster Berger, and on the folk songs sung on the plantations by the Portuguese; passionately fond of European and American music, they had adapted it to their own vocal limitations, colored it as they saw fit, and come up with a distinctive art form characterized by invariable feminine phrase endings, yodel-like breaks in songs of considerable range, and a swift gliding from one note to the next.

The resulting product had about the same relationship to original Hawaiian music as Negro spirituals had to African cadence, and most "Hawaiian" songs popularized in sheet music and on Victrola cylinders were tin-pan-alley adaptations of the hodgepodge. But that was of small interest to the uke and guitar artists, and of less concern to the Honolulu promoters of tourism.

By 1919 the labors of the Promotion Committee were paying off so handsomely that it was dignified with the name "Hawaii Tourist Bureau." A branch office was opened in San Francisco, and, between the two, display advertising was being distributed all over the world, along with booklets, stereopticon slides for lectures, pale jumpy movie film, maps, guides, labels, bulletins, posters, form letters, and special hoopla for travel agencies.

"The tourist business in Hawaii has grown phenomenally," declared a bureau spokesman four years later. "Hotels have been built and added to; new stores have sprung up and prospered; public utilities, an exact barometer of the growth of a city, have enlarged their plants; curio shops and local transportation systems have thrived; cottages and bungalows have sprouted like mushrooms throughout the city; new wharves have been built; more ships have been added to the Hawaiian service."

Revolutionary changes were taking place everywhere to make way for the tourists. At last in 1922 Ford's dream of draining the vast, smelly, mosquito-ridden swamp in back of Waikiki began to materialize, as work started on the Ala Wai Canal, a ditch 150 feet wide, 25 feet deep, and two miles long. With all the filling that was called for, it would give Waikiki an additional back yard of 1,400 acres.

But not everyone was happy about the new look that tourist promoters were bringing to Oahu. *Kamaainas* particularly resented the opening of cheap souvenir shops on every other corner in Honolulu and Waikiki and the popularizing of a spurious hula in side-street honky-tonks. Not satisfied with the more creditable symbols of Hawaii, proprietors seemed intent on establishing the hula girl in a suggestive grass skirt as the popular trademark of the Islands.

The grass skirt never was a native Hawaiian dress, screamed the reformers. "The law that aims to protect the public by honesty in advertising should put a stop to this imposition. It is time to call a halt and protest. The money-greed of pandering to a certain element—be it tourist or resident—that clamors for and abets the commercialized hula has brought this shame upon us and is disgracing us abroad."

Even some of the old landmarks were yielding to the new order. During nearly fifty years of service, that architectural pride of Honolulu, the gay, bright, beautiful Royal Hawaiian Hotel had lost some of its glamor, its shaded lawns, and a great deal of its paint. No one grieved very much when it was turned over to the army and navy as a Y.M.C.A. toward the end of World War I. It was a blessing in disguise, for ten years later, on February 1, 1927, a new four-million-dollar Royal Hawaiian came into existence at Waikiki on the site of the razed Seaside, surrounded by an eight-acre palm grove.

The gorgeous pink palace, with four hundred rooms and four hundred baths, private balconies and public terraces, library, shops, theater, resplendent lobbies and dining rooms, was proclaimed "one of the most beautiful hotels in the world," and according to standards of the exuberant twenties, the sobriquet did not exaggerate. The Royal Hawaiian at once became the prototype in Island splendor that no competitor was going to match for a long time.

Ever since the days of Mark Twain's and Dana's visits, Honolulu had been providing small cottages for less affluent tourists. Waikiki borrowed the idea and started erecting rows of airy little bungalows and apartments along the beach, years before motels had been invented on the Mainland. The beach resort grew so fast that by the thirties its whole central area, stretching four blocks back from the shore was dotted with lodgings. Kalakaua Avenue, which cut through it, had blossomed into a promenade of splashy dry-goods shops and tourist traps, and *kamaainas* were avoiding the beach like the plague.

Thanks to the Chamber of Commerce, to Alexander Ford, to the Tourist Bureau—once more renamed the Visitors Bureau—to Matson, Pan American, the ukulele, and the returns in publicity from the swimming prowess of Olympic champion Duke Kahanamoku, tourism with all its flourish and frippery had arrived at Waikiki, and was rapidly spreading to the other islands. So many vacationers were pouring in that an official count was kept, 19,933 in 1933; 24,390 in 1939.

"The European war and unsettled conditions in other parts of the world have turned the tide of tourist travel toward Hawaii," triumphed a Honolulu editor, "with the result that the territory's tourist business is increasing and furnishing hundreds of thousands of dollars in new money." For 1939 the "new money" was estimated at eleven million dollars; it jumped to 16.4 million dollars in 1941, when almost thirty-two thousand visitors were tallied.

But that was the year the "European War" turned into a global war, and the fireworks of December 7th quickly routed the last vacationer who could wangle passage home. The Visitors Bureau closed its doors, and the counting stopped; the Royal Hawaiian was converted into a navy recreation refuge, and officers and defense workers became the principal occupants of all the other hotels, bungalows, and boarding places. "Instead of being a remote lotus land for tourists and the easy way of life," editorialized *Paradise of the Pacific* in 1942, "Hawaii finds herself a center of world-shaping events. . . . The Islands have renounced holiday celebration for the duration."

The renouncement was not total. Hula choruses, lei makers, steel-guitar artists, surf riders, and luau chefs never allowed service men to overlook entirely what the peacetime way of life was like, and long before V-J Day, plans were quietly being laid for a tourist renaissance that would make the old Hawaii look archaic. Between 1941 and 1945 more visitors were exposed to the Islands, perforce, than had seen them in all the years since the voyage of Captain Cook. True, tens of thousands had nothing but loathing for "the Rock," but that still left a few hundred thousand with more than a touch of affection for Hawaii.

They constituted the legion that promoters were counting on. And their optimism proved more than justified. A full year after the end of the war, the chairman of the revived Hawaii Visitors Bureau confessed that "Not by ten thousand tourists does Hawaii 1946 come within range of meeting the demands that traveling America has already placed upon the islands. Nor will another year bring a measure-for-measure equilibrium between requests for hotel and resort accommodations and the facilities which the Hawaiian Islands will be able to offer. But 1947 should raise the curtain on a favorable postwar playground."

And what a playground it turned out to be! The building boom started during the war did not cease in 1945; it merely changed auspices from military to civilian in preparation for an invasion of tourists such as the most incautious visionary had not dreamed of a decade earlier.

They came like a tidal wave. The mere 15,000 that arrived in 1946 before the hotel hosts were ready, swelled to 25,000 the following year, and within a decade after the termination of the war, the total had stretched well over 100,000; by 1962 it reached a fantastic 362,145, and two years later passed the half-million mark. And that figure included only those that the Visitors Bureau could conveniently segregate as actual tourists; the total number of "visitors" was almost twice that, more outlanders coming and going that there were permanent residents, "more tourists than people," as a satirist put it. Statisticians reckoned that they were spending 225 million dollars a year in the Islands, creating a trade in "new money" that topped both sugar and pineapples.

To take care of the onset, old hotels were reconstructed, refurbished, and expanded, and new ones were crowded in alongside them. Complexes, ranging from modest motel quadrangles to skyscrapers, rimmed the popular beaches. Waikiki alone, which could boast of only half a dozen major hotels in 1945, was jammed twenty years later with 150, including row on row of apartment buildings that looked as though they had been transplanted, pool, patio, and roof garden, straight from Miami.

On Maui, Hawaii, and Kauai, shore fronts that had long been scarcely accessible, primitive valleys with remnants of grass shacks, desert areas without water or inhabitants burgeoned into classy resorts. In 1960 cane stretched almost to the beaches on the western shore of Maui; five years later the fields had been completely relandscaped, and a row of plush hotels with an adjacent championship golf course marked the beginnings of the new tourist city of Kaanapali. The nearby town of Lahaina, which had been running down hill since the whaling days, was suffering through a rebirth and being talked up as the future Williamsburg of Hawaii.

Kailua-Kona, which the missionaries once despised for its parched, barren, lava-scarred ugliness, had grown into the lush Riviera of the Big Island. Three miles south of Kawaihae, on desert where cactus and *kiawe* budded with reluctance, emerged the dazzling Mauna Kea Beach Hotel on the edge of a green, palm-planted golf-course oasis. On similar desert land of Oahu Henry Kaiser was laying out a six-thousand-acre planned community that would eventually cost two hundred million dollars. It was a dull month in Hawaii that did not bring the announcement of another five-, ten-, twenty-million-dollar complex about to go up.

To accommodate the visitors who came for a week and stayed for a lifetime, housing developments spread out from Honolulu proper in all directions, blanketed the plains and plateaus, invaded the heights, overflowed into adjacent valleys and covered the hillsides, exploded on reclaimed swamp, desert, and shore lands, edged up to the *kapu* boundaries of forest reserves. Eyries and lowlands that a pauperized native would have spurned for residence only a generation before were snatched up for twenty, thirty, fifty thousand dollars and graced with opulent, glass-fronted ranch houses, while land at Waikiki—what little there was left of it—sold at rates ranging from thirty to sixty dollars a square foot.

There was no end in sight to the *malihini* rush. Each year the Visitors Bureau predicted that a few more tens of thousands would be added to the grand totals compiled the year before, and each year the predictions were exceeded. The head of the bureau umpired a runaway industry, though the welcome to Hawaii had long since become regimented, and the aloha a trifle artificial. It had to be to encompass the throngs.

Back in the infancy of tourism, the promoters had feared that the heterogeneity of races would be the major obstacle to the development of the Islands as a first-class tourist rendezvous, and they had tended toward silence on the question of color. In 1926 a discerning pair of visitors brought the issue into the open by announcing their discovery of "thirty-two distinct races and race combinations" in Hawaii and playing up their findings as the real lure of the Islands.

"Here it would seem that the racial problem has been solved," they reported. "These peoples of many nationalities and of all colors appear to live happily together, a remarkable achievement, bearing witness to the great truth that if we respect our brothers' rights and pay at least some heed to the Golden Rule, this racial problem is not such a difficult one after all."

The promoters picked up the cue as if inspired, turned what they had considered a blight into an attraction, and in news, photographs, and feature stories unveiled Hawaii as the nation's most glamorous showplace of racial affinity. The campaign was a triumph. Through airing the conception of Islanders living in an exemplary community where differences of ancestry, religion, and pigment were disregarded, through hard selling and reiteration, even Nisei, rejected Portuguese, second-generation Filipinos, and fifth-generation Yankees believed it after a while and occasionally practiced the implied preachment. The campaigning did help spread the aloha spirit.

To make sure that there was no lull in the flow of propaganda from Paradise, the Visitors Bureau tantalized Mainland magazine subscribers with full pages of gorgeous color advertisements, brightened the slicks with pageants of gloriously illustrated articles that emphasized the racial harmony, supplied inquiring millions with some two dozen publications free of charge, and on an average day barraged Mainland newspapers with sacks of pleasant news releases, meantime keeping a covetous eye on the Orient for an influx of tourists from that direction.

All things were possible to those with faith in Publicity. Ku, Kane, and Lono were forever dethroned, and another pagan deity, Propaganda, was worshipped in their place. He ministered unto his people providentially. At heart residents of Hawaii had a weakness for the gospel. The people loved their Islands and wanted everyone else to love them. They were determined to share the beauty even at the expense of losing it. The tourists, perhaps, composed the last great invasion, an invasion to end all others. But no one was laying any bets on it.

Epilogue

Of all the waves of *malihinis* that participated in the leavening of Hawaii, unquestionably the Yankee missionaries exerted the most constructive and enduring influence. And remarkable as was their achievement in religious ministration, even more remarkable was their contribution in bringing almost universal literacy to a bookless people. They did not make scholars of the Islanders, but they did establish elemental learning as a major criterion for Hawaiian society. Their plan of democratic education was destined to shape the future of Hawaii in a way that few primeval lands had ever been re-formed.

They transplanted on the Islands that derivative of Puritanism, the New England conscience, a sense of right and duty, a sense of values and of moral obligation, concern for posterity, the urge to inculcate and educate. The transplant took hold and flourished. Schooling became a permanent part of the Island way of life. The cultural level of an entire nation was lifted. And finally the missionaries left an ample deputation of assertive sons, daughters, and votaries to insure that their set of values would be institutionally perpetuated.

By all the standard rules of geography and human conduct, the educational tradition should not have thrived in Hawaii. No similar miracle was ever performed on Trinidad or Tahiti, the Azores or Luzon, Madagascar or Martinique. Was the chemistry of this chain of mid-Pacific islands so different? The sluggish tropical setting was the last place anyone would have chosen to propagate a design for democratic education; the native Hawaiians were too temperamental, too siesta-minded, too addicted to amusement, too saturated in their own pagan culture; and the imported labor groups, who later swelled their ranks, were no better qualified as students.

Yet, against these aggregate handicaps, the idea of education for all flourished. Once the germ was implanted, it spread wondrously. Fundamental learning became a Hawaiian convention, a habit, a social discipline in a region that had been about as undisciplined as any on earth. Nothing quite like it had happened on insular terrain since the days of ancient Greece and Rome.

The grass-shack schoolrooms of the 1820's, '30's and '40's evolved collectively into a more formal public school system under government control, supervised by foreign educators. After 1840 school attendance was compulsory for all Islanders under the age of 14; after 1850 teaching in English gradually replaced Hawaiian until all textbooks, except in remote rural areas, were in English. The shift in language was necessary merely to keep pace with the eagerness of students to acquire information that could not practicably be presented in the native tongue.

In the course of a century after the arrival of the missionaries, educational facilities surpassed those of most American continental frontiers. At Punahou—originally for *haole* children—at Lahainaluna, at Hilo Boarding School, and at a dozen other mission schools scattered about the Islands, the curriculum reached beyond the primary level into college preparatory and occasionally into collegiate subjects. There was an assortment of vocational and manual training institutions, including Kamehameha School, originally started at Honolulu in 1887 to give Hawaiian boys a "Christian industrial education."

The opening of the first public secondary school, Honolulu High, was delayed until 1895, but it was not too significant a delay, considering the fact that 1895 marked the middle of a fifty-year period in which the number of public high schools in the entire United States jumped from a mere forty to an inadequate thirteen thousand.

Through most of the 1800's, Hawaiians or part-Hawaiians constituted a large majority of all public school pupils, but by the 1890's an appreciable number of Chinese, Portuguese, and Japanese children were enrolled, and the schoolyards and classrooms became the meeting ground for all the Island races, except the *haoles,* who continued to favor Congregational Punahou, Catholic St. Louis, or Episcopal St. Albans.

With annexation, however, educational plans for everybody came in a rush. Against frequent tirades from the planters, who balked at footing tax bills for schools that merely educated labor away from the sugar and pineapple fields, institutions of learning sprang up faster than they could be duly authorized and chartered: grammar schools; high schools on other islands; industrial schools; the democratic Mid-Pacific Institute, designed to bring together students of all races in a boarding academy atmosphere; a normal school; Baldwin School at Lahaina with all the fixings from kindergarten to Latin classes and a circulating library; the Damon School for underprivileged Chinese boys; the merger of St. Albans into a superior Iolani; American citizenship evening schools; Y.M.C.A. educational centers; Japanese, Chinese, and Korean language schools; Catholic, Mormon, Episcopal, and Buddhist schools; a College of Agriculture and Mechanic Arts, which was to expand into the College of Hawaii in 1911 and the University of Hawaii in 1920; and an impressive list of additional high and junior high schools perpetuating names like McKinley, Roosevelt, Lincoln, Thomas Jefferson, Robert Louis Stevenson, and Governor Farrington.

There seemed to be no limit in the capacity of the Islanders to absorb education. In terms of contemporaneous developments on the Mainland, there was nothing extraordinary about what was happening in Hawaii, but this could not logically be compared with the Mainland. It was ulterior territory two thousand miles from America.

Yet despite the explosive growth in facilities, the total educational picture was not quite as utopian as was pictured. Year after year, decade after decade, Island visitors professed to be charmed by the sight and sound of a multitude of students from a dozen regions of the earth, reciting and playing together in interracial harmony. But there was less harmony in the formal Hawaiian educational system than some of the casual observers thought they saw. The word "segregation" was never used, but both students and parents were well aware of the predominance of racial groups at different schools, and were even more aware of wide variations in quality of education among "English Standard," "Regular," and private schools. The disparity in the public school organization did not end until after World War II.

After the war the University of Hawaii, too, gradually entered a new period of boom and bloom, growing rapidly in academic stature as well as in numerical enrollment, and it could soon boast of undergraduate colleges in fields ranging from general studies and education to business administration and tropical agriculture, a well-organized graduate school, a junior-college campus at Hilo and another starting at Kahului, adult extension programs on all the islands, and a federally supported Center for Cultural and Technical Exchange between East and West, known as the "East-West Center."

Moreover, it adopted a program of striving for academic excellence in major fields in which it held natural advantages because of the multicultural population and the geophysical location, playing host to a parade of distinguished sociologists, linguists, biomedical researchers, astronomers, engineers, computation specialists, and geophysicists. Although the university had never been ranked among the great institutions of learning, its new role was incxorably leading it to that distinction.

On sustenance from local capital, as well as Mainland sources, Hawaii plunged no less daringly into other ventures in higher education. Besides the university and its subsidiaries, there were half a dozen private or church-supported colleges on Oahu and Maui, most notable of which was the Mormon Church College of Hawaii in Laie. From a start only in 1958 it burgeoned into headquarters for an educational system that reached as far south as Samoa, Tonga, Tahiti, and New Zealand; its Polynesian Cultural Center on Oahu, opened in 1963, was a show window for all Polynesia, a major tourist attraction, and a delightful museum-microcosm of the South Pacific.

As if to exemplify a conviction that classrooms were not the only fountain of stimulation and enlightenment, peripheral educators were constantly coming up with a variety of less formal projects to help educate visitors as well as residents. To be sure, some of the experiments were so disguised in showmanship that it was not always possible to distinguish between instruction and entertainment, but that was the Hawaiian way of doing things.

The double purpose was seen at the Laie Cultural Center; at

Honolulu's Ulu Mau Village, where visitors could catch an intimate and authentic look into Hawaii's past; at Sea Life Park and the Oceanics Institute overlooking Makapuu Point, one of the greatest sea-life shows on earth; at Kilolani Planetarium; at the summit observatories of Haleakala on open-house afternoons; at the Kilauea Museum of Hawaii Volcanoes National Park; at the scholarly Bishop Museum, famed the world over for its extensive Pacific collections; at the Honolulu Academy of Arts; at the Honolulu International Center, reserved primarily for the performing arts; and at a score of local museums scattered throughout the islands. None of them could be disqualified as a purposeful educational agency.

And most effective of all the extra-classroom educational facilities was the State Library System, with major libraries on each of the islands, reading rooms and circulation centers in every populous town, and a bookmobile to serve rural areas. It was a free, public-supported system such as existed in no other state, and the buildings themselves were masterpieces in functional architecture, airy, luminous, busy places, calculated to inspire young and old to take their reading seriously.

Nor was modern industrial education neglected in the plantation towns. Included was every manner of training and investigation from vocational instruction in technical schools to expensive research of the university and the Hawaiian Sugar Planters Association. No one contested the value of these educational investments any more; their results were self-evident. Research and training in twenty postwar years alone had enabled the sugar planters to increase the average yield in cane per acre from some seventy-five tons to more than ninety, and consistently to produce well over a million tons of raw sugar a year.

The same held true with pineapples. As much as one million dollars might be spent on research in a single year, and that expenditure was largely responsible for Hawaii's continuing to provide approximately 50 per cent of the world's supply of canned pineapple products, and 80 per cent of the United States' supply.

Imaginative education, experiment, and investment accounted similarly for such varied and growing Island industries as coffee, macadamia nuts, cattle ranching, a million-dollar orchid business, and another million-dollar perfume business; it accounted, too, for the fact that Hawaii was becoming more and more a manufacturing state, turning out over 150 products from asphalt, bamboo furniture, and chutney to ukuleles, yogurt, and zinc sulphate.

Preparation of an army of recruits to serve the tourist industry was not overlooked either. Whether an enlistee had visions of a future as an advertising magnate, a hotel desk clerk, or a short-order chef, he could find appropriate courses in school or college to give him a start, and before the big new hotels opened their doors to the public, service personnel were customarily put through a free training session or summer school.

Even the shaping of relations between labor and management was essentially an educative process in Hawaii, though edification frequently became confused with brainwashing, and negotiation with cold warfare. An Employers' Council, representing nearly four hundred of the major business firms, was essentially an instructive and research organization in the field of industrial relations, and the predominant labor unions, ILWU, AFL-CIO, and Teamsters, were no less involved in their conception of educational indoctrination.

The effect of the multipurpose pedagogy upon Islanders was usually disappointing to critics from outside. Residents were their own worst enemies in conveying the impression that they were particularly knowledgeable. The devotion to pidgin, the murder of the King's English in the press, on radio, and on TV, the disarming small talk of beachcomber, bar, and cocktail-hour coteries, the anti-intellectual temples to tourism at Waikiki, mongrel speech dialects from the four corners of the earth were anything but the manifestation of an intelligentsia.

The most remarkable evidence of what the educators had achieved was often found well off the tourist trails, in home libraries back in the valleys, in modest, refined Japanese and Chinese family circles; in discussion groups of sober, alert, erudite citizens. Evidence was found in most unlikely personages and places. The unshaven wharfside lounger at Lahaina turned out to be a philosopher in disguise; a Honolulu yardman, a learned bibliophile. And an irrigation ditch attendant riding a mule day after day over his beat high in the Kohala Mountains could put to shame a cloistered sage; to relieve the boredom of his solitary duty, he read while he rode, not the comics or current fiction, but Plutarch, Cervantes, Tolstoi, and Chaucer.

The ordinary Islander was no better informed, no more widely read than the average Mainlander, but the wonder was that in a lazy insular climate he should be concerned at all about his literacy. The tradition of receptivity to education, more than any other single trait, made Hawaii what it is economically and culturally.

The real test of the success of its educational effort came during the 1950's while the Islands were under national and world-wide scrutiny as a candidate for promotion from territorial status to statehood. The racial agglomeration, the physical detachment from the continent, the open exposure to all the political biases of the Pacific were handicaps with which no previous applicant for admission to the Union had been obliged to contend. Ultimately the argument for or against granting membership as the fiftieth state involved an examination of the social order to which the Islanders subscribed, a social order that was inevitably the product of many years of popular tutelage. The Territory never could have passed that examination if the multitude of educational agencies had not accomplished their varied objectives with reasonable éclat.

The Yankee missionary-educators who started it all had long since been lost in the shuffle of other invaders; their influence was no longer immediate. The seed they planted had grown into a monarch tree, but it had been grafted so often, cultivated so erratically, clipped and pruned so freely that only the buried roots and scarred trunk revealed its true origin.

They had dropped the seed in the dawn of a period which western adventurers labeled "the Pacific era." And after the passing of nearly a century and a half, a latter-day generation of zealots were averring, as if it had never been said before, that the world was moving toward another Pacific era, an era in which Hawaii would be the center of a rising tide of intellectual and scientific achievement for a vast area bounded by four continents, the Americas, Asia, and Australia.

Seen as heralds of that new era and status were the procession of scholars being lured to the University of Hawaii; behavioral scientists examining more closely the breached racial barriers; renowned physical scientists superintending important installations like space-tracking stations, the giant telescopes atop Haleakala, and Project Mohole, the stupendous one-hundred-million-dollar-attempt of the National Science Foundation to drill three miles through the earth's crust from ocean platforms near the Island chain. From their eyries above Pearl Harbor generals and admirals were relaying decisions that affected political events of a hemisphere. And some saw portents even in the mass visitations of hundreds of thousands of carefree vacationers.

Hawaii had proven untenable the Kipling homily that "East is East, and West is West, and never the twain shall meet." East and West were meeting amicably in the Islands. Geography had ordained the tryst, and from the meeting place were being exported ideas, along with sugar cane, pineapples, and military orders. To Mainlanders it represented a state that had made exemplary progress in solving its most serious sociological problems, a state that could offer lessons to sister states troubled with racial conflicts, the one American commonwealth that had acquiesced to having a majority of non-Caucasian spokesmen serve as its representatives both in Congress and in its own legislative halls.

Spreading across the United States were elements of the relaxed Hawaiian way of life, with its addiction to sea, surf, and song, the everyday holiday spirit, the colorful, informal garb, the blending of indoors and outdoors. Years of exposure to oriental and Polynesian architecture, landscaping, and decoration had inspired Island builders to translate many of those features into Western structural style and produce distinctive Hawaiian hybrids, which were being freely mirrored on the Mainland.

With Hawaii serving as a mediatory agent, the exchange between East and West worked to the advantage of both. After receiving indoctrination and experience in the Islands, experts or advisers in agriculture, economics, political administration, linguistics, religious education, and scientific fields moved on to the Orient or the South Pacific to share their knowledge. So much faith was being shown in the future of Hawaii that capital was pouring into the Islands from Asia as well as America. Vast expansion in tourist facilities for both Orientals and Mainlanders was the order of the decade, but no one was quite sure that the tourists would ever make a complete conquest of the Islands; a well-schooled people in any locale had a way of pulling off extraordinary surprises.

In all that was occurring on the mid-Pacific archipelago, the original residents, the Hawaiians, were still the catalysts. There were few men and women of great erudition among them. Surviving remnants of their ancient culture were being preserved largely by the museum-minded or the mercenary-minded. Education had transformed their land. Yet they had benefited richly from the infusion. They were esteemed and respected; in the affection of *malihinis* they stood head and shoulders above the other tribes of the earth represented on the Island rolls. There were scores of islands in the equatorial belt almost as alluring as Hawaii, but only one insular group inhabited by Hawaiians. They still were the real hosts. People came to Hawaii because they loved the Hawaiians. Their aloha was everywhere. They no longer owned much of the land; yet it was theirs—and always would be.

Glossary

Hawaiian words used in text

aa—rough lava
alii—chief, royalty
aloha—love, greeting, hello, good-by
auwe—alas! oh! ah!
awa—narcotic drink made from kava root

hala—pandanus or screw pine
hala-kahiki—pineapple
halau—longhouse
hale—house, dwelling
hale noa—common family house without taboo
haole—white person, foreigner
hapahaole—part-white Hawaiian
hau—variety of hibiscus tree
heiau—temple, house, or platform of worship
himeni—hymn
holoku—loose dress with train, patterned after New England "Mother Hubbard"
hoohuli pipi—cattle roundup or drive
hui—partnership, club, corporation
hula—dance or dancer

ili—subdivision of land
imu—pit for cooking, underground oven

kahili—feathered standard symbolic of royalty
kahu—guardian, attendant, nurse
kahuna—professional man, expert, or specialist, such as priest, medical practitioner, teacher, prophet
kamaaina—native, old-timer
kanaka—man, person
kapu—taboo, forbidden, holy; keep out
kauwa—slave, outcast
kiawe—algarroba tree
kihei—cape, shawl
kilu—game played with gourd used as quoit
koa—variety of acacia tree used for making canoes, surfboards, furniture, etc.
kuhina nui—premier, prime minister
kuleana—homesite, small piece of private property

lanai—porch, veranda
lapaau—medical practice
lau hala—pandanus leaf for weaving or thatching
laulima—cooperation, group of people working together
lehua—*ohia* tree or flower

lei—wreath, necklace of flowers, shells, feathers, etc.

luau—feast

luna—overseer, boss

mahele—division, apportionment

mai ahulau—epidemic, pestilence, plague

maika—stone-bowling game

maikai—good, beautiful

makaainana—commoner, the masses, farming class

makahiki—four-month festival period, October to February

makai—toward the sea

malihini—stranger, newcomer, guest

malo—loincloth

maoli—native, indigenous

mauka—toward the mountains

mele—song, chant, poem

muumuu—woman's loose, short-sleeved gown or chemise

nei—this, here

noa—guessing game in which stone is hidden under layers of tapa

ohia—upland tree, used for timber; also mountain apple

okolehao—liquor distilled from ti root

oli—chant

pahoehoe—smooth lava

palani—detested person; brandy; Frenchman

palapala—writing, learning, the Scriptures

pali—cliff, precipice

paniolo—cowboy

pau—woman's skirt, sarong; finished

pili—grass used for thatching

pilikia—trouble, difficulty, tragedy, bother

poi—viscid food staple made from taro root

puhenehene—game played with hidden stone

puka—hole, door, opening

pule—prayer, religion

pulu—downy wool on base of fern tree

ukeke—stringed musical bow

ume—sexual game played by commoners

wahine—woman, girl

waiwai—rich, prosperous

Note on pronunciation: As a rule, every syllable ends with a vowel, and, except in a few vowel combinations, each letter has but one sound.

a is pronounced as in far

e as in fete

i as in machine

o as in joke

u as in rule

ai as in aisle

au or ao as in sauerkraut

ei as in vein

oe as oy in joy

Most words are lightly accented on the next to last syllable.

Quotation Sources

Chapter I. P. 12, System of rulership: David Malo, *Hawaiian Antiquities*, translation by N.B. Emerson (Honolulu: Bishop Museum, 1951), p. 53. Pp. 14-15, Hilo offerings: Isabella L. Bird, *Hawaiian Archipelago or Six Months Among the Palm Groves, Coral Reefs and Volcanoes of the Sandwich Islands* (New York, Putnam, 1894), pp. 180-84.

Chapter II. Pp. 29-30, Cheap market: Charles Clerke, *Log*, January 12, 1778. P. 30, Women: James Cook, *A Voyage to the Pacific Ocean*, Vol. II (London, 1785), pp. 195-96. P. 33, Runner's message: W.D. Alexander, *Brief History of the Hawaiian People* (New York, American Book Company, 1899), p. 107. Pp. 33-34, Reception: John Ledyard, *A Voyage Performed in His Britannic Majesty's Ship Resolution* (Hartford, 1783), pp. 103-05. P. 36, Tempest: *Ibid.*, p. 140. P. 36, Mortification: *Ibid.*, p. 141. P. 38, Orders to give up journals: *Ibid.*, p. 198. P. 41, Winee: John Meares, *Voyages Made in the Years 1788-89* (London, 1791), Extracts, "Hawaiian Historical Society Reprints," p. 36. P. 42, Description of Kamehameha: J.J. Jarves, *History of the Hawaiian or Sandwich Islands* (London, 1873), p. 154. P. 44, Sixty girls: Ebenezer Townsend, Jr., *Voyage of the Neptune Around the World, 1796-99* (New Haven Historical Society, Vol. VI, 1888), "Hawaiian Historical Society Reprints," p. 5. P. 45, On guard: Meares, *op. cit.*, p. 49. P. 46, Olowalu massacre: Jarves, *op. cit.*, pp. 148-50. P. 47, Cargo: Meares, *op. cit.*, pp. 7-8. P. 48, Crowded ship: Peter Corney, *Voyages in the Northern Pacific* (Honolulu: Thrum, 1896), p. 85. P. 48, Rum sale: Townsend, *op. cit.*, p. 13. P. 49, Over fifty haoles: Archibald Campbell, *A Voyage Round the World, 1806-12* (New York, 1819), p. 146. P. 50, King's proclamation: Karl H. Korte, editor, *Brief History of the Forest Reserves of the Island of Maui* (Kahului, 1961), p. 18. P. 54, Happy Hawaiians: Townsend, *op. cit.*

Chapter III. P. 57, Gaylord Coan: Titus Coan, *Life in Hawaii* (New York, 1882), p. 1. P. 60, Watchword: Lucy G. Thurston, *Life and Times* (Ann Arbor, 1882), p. 29. P. 61, Kohala natives: Hiram Bingham, *Residence of Twenty-One Years in the Sandwich Islands* (Hartford, 1848), p. 81. P. 62, Lucy's interview: Thurston, *op. cit.* P. 62, Too much clothing: *Ibid.*, p. 31. Pp. 64-65, Gospel diffusion: Bingham, *op. cit.*, p. 89. P. 66, American Board instructions: *Hawaiian Spectator*, January 1838, p. 36. P. 67, Self-commitment: Bingham, *op. cit.*, pp. 95-96. P. 68, Callers: Thurston, *op. cit.*, pp. 96-98. P. 69, Coan's travels: Coan, *op. cit.*, p. 33. Pp. 70-71, South Point: H.M. Lyman, *Hawaiian Yesterdays* (Chicago, 1906), pp. 160-63. P. 71, Kawaihae assembly: Rufus Anderson, *The Hawaiian Islands* (Boston, 1864), p. 65. P. 72, Kohala lumbering: E.M. Damon, *Father Bond of Kohala* (Honolulu, 1927), pp. 125-29. P. 72, Hilo lumbering: H.M. Lyman, *op. cit.*, p. 66. Pp. 72-73, Missionary lumbering: Bingham, *op. cit.*, pp. 575-76. P. 74, Royal Chapel service: H.M. Lyman, *op. cit.*, p. 45. P. 76, Officer's description: Bingham, *op. cit.*, p. 353-54. P. 79, British criticism: Manley Hopkins, *Hawaii: The Past, Present and Future of Its Island Kingdom* (London, 1862), pp. 384-85. P. 79, Frenchman's query: Bingham, *op. cit.*, p. 557. P. 80, 1800 per cent dividend: Henry T. Cheever, *Life in the Sandwich Islands* (New York, 1851), p. 51. P. 81, Nordhoff's impressions: Charles Nordhoff, *Northern California, Oregon and the Sandwich Islands* (New York, 1874), pp. 22-23. P. 81, Deacon's testimony: Rufus Anderson, *op. cit.*, p. 167.

Chapter IV. P. 82, Howling wilderness: F. T. Bullen, *Cruise of the Cachelot* (New York: Burt, 1927), p. 171. P. 83, Bingham's neighbors: Bingham, *op. cit.*, p. 134. P. 83, Stewart's defense: C. S. Stewart, *Residence in the Sandwich Islands* (Boston, 1839), p. 42. P. 84, Small space: E.L. Doyle, *Makua Laiana* (Honolulu, 1945), pp. 6 and 9. P. 85, Whale hunt: *Ibid.*, pp. 12-13. Pp. 87-88, Busy devils: Cheever, *op. cit.*, p. 65. P. 88, Olmsted's view: F.A. Olmsted, *Incidents of a Whaling Voyage* (New York, 1841), pp. 127-29. P. 89, Sink of iniquity: Chester Lyman, *Around the Horn to the Sandwich Islands and California, 1845-50*, T.J. Teggart, editor (New Haven: Yale, 1924), p. 61. Pp. 89-91, *Daniel* incident: Bingham, *op. cit.*, pp. 273-74. P. 91, Vain efforts: *Ibid.*, pp. 314-15. P. 93, Fines: Honolulu *Friend*, September 1844. P. 94, Hilo influence: Chester Lyman, *op. cit.*, p. 84. P. 94, Receding forests: E.M. Damon, *Koamalu* (Honolulu, 1931), p. 415. Pp. 96-97, Wealth in Honolulu: Theo. H. Davies, *Personal Recollections of Hawaii, 1857-85*, Ms., pp. 2-3. P. 98, Masters and jolly jack-tars: H.M. Lyman, *op. cit.*, pp. 74-75. Pp. 100-01, Wellington mosquitoes: *Ibid.*, p. 202. P. 101, Authors of liquor law: Bingham, *op. cit.*, p. 554. P. 102, Twain on whalemen: Mark Twain, 12th Letter to *Sacramento Union*, June 20, 1866. P. 103, Damon's sermon: as quoted by E.M. Whiting and H.B. Hough, *Whaling Wives* (Boston: Houghton Mifflin, 1953), p. 157.

Chapter V. P. 107, Minister's assertion: as quoted by Antoinette Withington, *The Goldon Cloak* (Honolulu: Star Bulletin, 1953), p. 96. Pp. 107-08, Gordon Cumming's impressions: C.F. Gordon Cumming, *Fire Fountains*, Vol. I. (Edinburgh, 1883), pp. 13, 15, 69-70, 121-22. Pp. 108-09, Vancouver's landing: George Vancouver, *Voyage of Discovery, 1790-95*, Vol. III (London, 1798), p. 165. P. 110, Goodrich's observations: William Ellis, *Narrative of a Tour Through Hawaii* (London, 1827), p. 303. P. 110, Lyon's complaint: Doyle, *op. cit.*, p. 124. P. 113, Poncho: *Ibid.*, p. 102. P. 113, Skeletons: *Ibid.*, p. 47. P. 114; Enemies: *Ibid.*, p. 116. P. 115, Parker's deed: from copy at Mana Museum, Waimea, Hawaii. P. 115, Parker's herds: Parker Ranch archives, Book I, "Journals of Missionaries," Kamuela. P. 116, Waste of beef: Nordhoff, *op. cit.*, pp. 69-70. P. 117, Lee's speech: Parker Ranch archives, Book I. P. 120, Kamehameha's reaction: *Ibid.* Pp. 120-21, Horses in Honolulu: Sereno E. Bishop, *Reminiscences of Old Hawaii* (Honolulu, 1916), p. 60. P. 121, Mrs. Judd's count: Laura Fish Judd, *Honolulu Sketches* (Honolulu, 1928), p. 130. P. 122, Sightseer's description: Bird, *op. cit.*, (London, 1875), pp. 31-32. P. 123, Twain's cheap horses: Mark Twain, *Roughing It* (Hartford, 1872), p. 472. P. 123, Horses in Hilo: L.F. Judd, *op. cit.*, p. 52. P. 123, 1000 horses: Bird, *op. cit.*, pp. 102, 199. P. 123, Agricultural Society report: Parker Ranch archives, Book I. P. 124, No walking: Bird, *op. cit.*, p. 133.

Chapter VI. P. 128, Bingham's alphabet: Bingham, *op. cit.*, pp. 152-55. P. 128, Hopkin's concession: Hopkins, *op. cit.*, pp. 222-23. P. 128, Twain's declaration: *Brooklyn Eagle*. February 8, 1873. P. 130, Petition: J.S. Green, "Female Education in the Sandwich Islands," *Hawaiian Spectator*, January 1838, p. 38. P. 130, Teaching methods: L.F. Judd, *op. cit.*, p. 17. P. 131, Bingham's rebuttal: Bingham, *op. cit.*, p. 215. Pp. 132-33, Waimea and Waipio processions: Doyle, *op. cit.*, pp. 152-54. P. 134, Kailua celebration: Bingham, *op. cit.*, p. 401. P. 134, Untamed children: L.F. Judd, *op. cit.*, p. 17. P. 139, Billet-doux: Cheever, *op.*

cit., pp. 227-28. P. 142, Singing schools: Doyle, *op. cit.,* p. 155. P. 146, Punahou: H.M. Lyman, *op. cit.,* p. 124. Pp. 147-48, Sister's school: Bird, *op. cit.,* pp. 168-69.

Chapter VII. P. 149, Least inviting spot: H.M. Lyman, *op. cit.,* p. 123. P. 151, Southern peddlers: John Bernard, *Retrospections of America* (New York, 1887), p. 42. P. 152, Wyllie's comment: Honolulu *Friend,* July 1, 1844. P. 154, Dispatch: as quoted by R.S. Kuykendall, *Hawaiian Kingdom* (Honolulu: University of Hawaii, 1957), p. 300. P. 156, Reynolds: "Journal," Honolulu *Friend,* May 1844. P. 158, Brinsmade: Hopkins, *op. cit.,* p. 275. Pp. 159-60, Contract: Kuykendall, *op. cit.,* p. 189. P. 162, List of goods: W.A. Simonds, *Kamaaina—A Century in Hawaii* (Honolulu: American Factors, 1949), pp. 18-19. P. 164, Advertisement: Josephine Sullivan, *History of C. Brewer and Company* (Boston, 1926), pp. 114-15. P. 165, Davies' boast: Davies, *op. cit.* P. 168, Native market: Bird, *op. cit.,* (1890), p. 181. P. 169, Hawaiian restaurant: W.S.W. Ruschenberger, *Voyage Round the World* (Philadelphia, 1838), pp. 457-58. P. 169, Illiberal notion: Campbell, *op. cit.,* pp. 97-98. Pp. 169-70, Appeal: Rufus Anderson, *op. cit.,* pp. 76-77.

Chapter VIII. P. 173, Protest: Artemas Bishop, "Inquiry into the Causes of Decline in the Population of the Sandwich Islands," *Hawaiian Spectator,* January 1838, p. 53. P. 173, Malo's cry: David Malo, "On the Decrease of Population on the Hawaiian Islands," *Hawaiian Spectator,* April 1839, p. 125. P. 174, Ellis' comment: Ellis, *op. cit.,* (1917), pp. 119-20. P. 174, Olmsted on death: Olmsted, *op. cit.,* p. 249. P. 175, Interchange of spouses: Sheldon Dibble, *History of the Sandwich Islands* (Lahainaluna, 1843), p. 127. P. 176, Medical review: Alonzo Chapin, "Climate and Diseases of the Sandwich Islands," *Hawain Spectator,* July 1838, pp. 257-58. P. 177, Sodom and Gomorrah: Dibble, *op. cit.,* p. 129. P. 177, Brothel: Malo, *Hawaiian Spectator, op. cit.,* p. 128. P. 177, *Héros* visit: Edmond Le Netral, *Voyage of the Héros,* translation by B.C. Wagner (Los Angeles: Glen Dawson, 1951), p. 53. P. 178, Malo's claim: Malo, *Hawaiian Spectator, op. cit.,* p. 128. P. 178, Ellis' observations: Ellis, *op. cit.,* pp. 243-46. Pp. 178-79, Child burial: Dibble, *op. cit.,* p. 128. P. 179, Abortion: Malo, *Hawaiian Spectator, op. cit.,* pp. 123-24. P. 179, Declamation: Bingham, *op cit.,* p. 486. Pp. 186-87, Pharmaceutical display: S.E. Bishop, *op. cit.,* pp. 16-17. P. 188, Empty streets: H.M. Lyman, *op. cit.,* p. 169. P. 188, Lyon's jottings: Doyle, *op. cit.,* pp. 147-50. Pp. 191-92, Ragsdale: Bird, *op. cit.,* p. 365. P. 192, Kalaupapa: *Ibid.,* p. 370. P. 193, Bliss' observations: William R. Bliss, *Paradise in the Pacific* (New York, 1873), pp. 57-59, 83. P. 194, Testimony: Rufus Anderson: *op. cit.,* p. 67.

Chapter IX. P. 195, Plum pudding: Hopkins, *op. cit.,* p. 313. P. 196, Nordhoff quote: Nordhoff, *op. cit.,* p. 96. Pp. 196-97, Charlton: Hopkins, *op. cit.,* pp. 274, 276. P. 199, French indiscretions: Chester Lyman, *op. cit.,* pp. 154-55. P. 201, Hawaiians in Congress: Cheever, *op. cit.,* pp. 260-61. P. 202, Prince's comment: as quoted by Withington, *op. cit.,* pp. 197-98. P. 202, King's proclamation: *Biographical Sketches of Hawaii's Rulers* (Honolulu: Bishop National Bank, 1956), p. 11. Pp. 204-05, Parliament opening: Bliss, *op. cit.,* pp. 135-36. P. 205, Parliament in action: Mark Twain, *Sacramento Union,* June 20, 1866. P. 206, Richards: Hopkins, *op. cit.,* pp. 241-42. P. 209, Young's statement: as quoted by G.P. Judd, IV, *Hawaii: an Informal History* (New York: Collier, 1961), p. 72. P. 210, Ultimatum: Hopkins, *op. cit.,* p. 246. P. 211, Louis Philippe's persuasion: *Ibid.,* p. 239. P. 211, Premier's rebuff: L.F. Judd, *op. cit.,* p. 64. P. 212, Ultimatum: Hopkins, *op. cit.,* p. 245. P. 214, Paraphrase: *Ibid.,* pp. 250-51. P. 216, Dark days and king's reaction: L.F. Judd, *op. cit.,* pp. 94, 194. P. 218, Celebration: *Ibid.,* pp. 96-97.

Chapter X. Pp. 224-25, Green's assertion: Damon, *Koamalu*, p. 424. P. 228, Kona oranges: Twain, *Roughing It*, p. 502. P. 228, *West Point* wreck: Damon, *Koamalu*, *op. cit.*, p. 215. P. 228, Orange blight: Bird, *op. cit.*, p. 307. P. 229, Greenwell orchard: Greenwell Diary, ms. Pp. 230-31, Lumber: Nordhoff, *op. cit.*, p. 62 and Damon, *Koamalu*, p. 772. P. 232, Kapu's statement: Parker Ranch archives, Book I. P. 235, Waioli mill: Damon, *Koamalu*, p. 330. P. 235, Hilo mill: H.M. Lyman, *op. cit.*, pp. 70-71. P. 236, Excursionist's observations: Bird, *op. cit.*, p. 77. P. 237, Bond's cane: Damon, *Father Bond of Kohala*, p. 182. Pp. 237-38, Makee's garden and promotion: T.G. Thrum, "James Makee," *Thrum's Hawaiian Annual*, 1927, pp. 27-39. P. 238, Hurricane: T.G. Thrum, "Early Ulupalakua Data," *Thrum's Hawaiian Annual*, 1926, pp. 80-87. P. 240, Sand: Bird, *op. cit.*, pp. 222-23.

Chapter XI. Pp. 244-45, Wyllie's appeal: *Reports of the Minister of Foreign Affairs, 1852-62*. P. 248, Worthless laborers: A.C. Alexander, *Koloa Plantation* (Honolulu: Star Bulletin, 1937), p. 21. Pp. 248-49, Bates observations: G.W. Bates, *Sandwich Island Notes* (New York, 1954), p. 126. P. 249, King's demand: *Fundamental Law of Hawaii* (1842), p. 18. P. 252, Kamehameha's plan: as quoted by J.W. Vandercook, *King Cane* (New York: Harper, 1939), p. 55. P. 253, Nordhoff's observations: Nordhoff, *op. cit.*, p. 58.

Chapter XII. P. 267, Cannon ball: Charles F. Hitchcock, *Hawaii and its Volcanoes* (Honolulu, 1911), p. 106. P. 268, Coan's impressions: Cumming, *op. cit.*, pp. 235-36. P. 269, Rocking: *Ibid.*, p. 239. P. 270, Niagara: *Ibid.* P. 271, Calamity: *Ibid.*, p. 242. Pp. 272-73, Cook's and Ledyard's conclusions: Ledyard, *op. cit.*, pp. 112-13, 123. P. 274, Menzies' report: Hitchcock, *op. cit.*, p. 76. P. 275, Ellis' description: Ellis, *op. cit.*, pp. 207-15. P. 276, Kapiolani's defiance and Bingham's sermon: Bingham, *op. cit.*, pp. 255-56. Pp. 277-78, Douglas' expeditions: *Hawaiian Spectator*, April 1858, p. 103 and Hitchcock, *op. cit.*, p. 180. P. 279, Strzelecki's report: *Hawaiian Spectator*, April 1838, pp. 98-101. P. 279, Sandwich Island Institute: *Ibid.*, pp. 27-28. P. 280, Hilo reception: H.M. Lyman, *op. cit.*, p. 51. P. 281, Kilauea expedition: Charles Wilkes, *Narrative of the U.S. Exploring Expedition*, Vol. V. (Philadelphia, 1845), pp. 119-20. P. 283, Effect upon Hilo: H.M. Lyman, *op. cit.*, p. 56. Pp. 284-85, 1852 eruption: *Ibid.*, pp. 229-30. P. 285, 1859 eruption: Davies, *op. cit.*, pp. 21-22. P. 287, Twain's reaction: *Roughing It*, pp. 549-50.

Chapter XIII. P. 293, Boomerang: Twain, *Roughing It*, pp. 498, 500. Pp. 294-95, Condition of coasters: "Early Coasting Reminiscences," *Thrum's Hawaiian Annual*, 1932, pp. 37-39. Pp. 295-96, Marine disasters: "Inter-Island Coastal Service, Past and Present," *Thrum's Hawaiian Annual*, 1932, p. 27ff. P. 296, Lahaina wreck: "Brief History of Steam Coasting Service," *Thrum's Hawaiian Annual*, 1889, p. 75. P. 299, Kilauea eulogist: *Ibid.*, p. 77. P. 299, Advertisement: Cumming, *op. cit.*, p. 24. P. 300, Matson's gospel: G. Hoffman, "Matson Line History," *Paradise of the Pacific*, December, 1932, p. 53. Pp. 303-04, Prediction: "Aviation in Hawaii," *Thrum's Hawaiian Annual*, 1922, pp. 85-86. Pp. 304-06, Rodgers' flight: "Pacific Aviation Pioneers," *Thrum's Hawaiian Annual*, 1926, p. 66. P. 307, Dole Derby: "Dole Derby," *Thrum's Hawaiian Annual*, 1928, p. 27. P. 308, Army flight: *Ibid.* P. 309, Erwin flight: *Ibid.*, p. 29.

Chapter XIV. Pp. 315-16, Campbell's commentary: Campbell, *op. cit.*, pp. 8-9, 116-17, 134, 136, 149. Pp. 316-17, Olmsted's commentary: Olmsted, *op. cit.*, pp. 185, 191, 248, 259-60, 263. P. 319, Dibble's history: Dibble, *op. cit.*, p. 135. P. 320, Jarves' history: Jarves, *op. cit.*, pp. 3, 367, 371. Pp. 321-22, Dana's defense: Rufus Anderson, *op. cit.*, pp. 104-05. Pp. 322-23, Macoun's account:

R.T. Macoun, "A Glimpse of the Sandwich Islands," *Knickerbocker,* November, 1851, pp. 477-88. Pp. 324-26, Twain's comment: *Roughing It,* pp. 176, 178-79, 228, 180-81, 185, 226, 251, 277, 264, 244, 186-88. P. 326, Twain's "Prose Poem": narrated at baseball banquet in New York, 1889, as quoted by W.F. Frear, *Mark Twain and Hawaii* (Chicago: Lakeside Press, 1947), p. 502. P. 326, Twain on Haleakala: Letter to Stoddard, October 26, 1881, as quoted by Frear, *op. cit.,* p. 89. Pp. 327-28, Bird's comments: Bird, *op. cit.,* (New York, 1881), pp. 156-62. P. 329, Meagher comments: J.T. Meagher, "A Hawaiian Feast," *Overland,* May, 1867, pp. 434-37. Pp. 329-30, Stevenson's comments: as quoted by J.W. Ellison, *Tusitala of the South Seas* (New York: Hastings House, 1953), pp. 50, 250; G.P. Judd, *op. cit.,* p. 157; J.C. Furnas, *Voyage to Windward* (New York: Sloane, 1951), pp. 336, 338, 340, 343. P. 331, Adams' impressions: *Letters of Henry Adams, 1858-91,* W.C. Ford, editor (Boston, 1930), Letters to Elizabeth Cameron, August and September 1890. Pp. 332, LaFarge's comments: John LaFarge, "Passages from a Diary in the Pacific—Hawaii," *Scribner's,* May 1901, pp. 537-46. P. 332, Senate resolution: "What to Do with Hawaii," *Nation,* January 18, 1894, p. 42. P. 332, Provisional government: *Ibid.* P. 332, Panegyric: A.W. Gulick, "A Glimpse of Hawaii," *Review of Reviews,* May 1, 1894, pp. 572-76. P. 333, Townsend's remarks: H.S. Townsend, "The People of Hawaii," *Forum,* July 1898, pp. 585-92. P. 333, Potter's comments: H.C. Potter, "Impressions of the Hawaiian Islands," *Century,* September 1901, pp. 762-68. P. 334, Waikiki poem: as quoted by Isabel Anderson, *Spell of the Hawaiian Islands and the Philippines* (New York, 1916), p. 15.

Chapter XV. P. 336, Key to North Pacific: Jarves, *op. cit.,* p. 3. P. 337, Anderson's conjecture: Rufus Anderson, *op. cit.,* p. 207. P. 338, DuPont's survey: S.F. DuPont, *Report on National Defense* (Washington, 1852), pp. 15-16. P. 339, Reciprocity treaty: G.P. Judd, *op. cit.,* p. 96. P. 340, Depression: Bird, *op. cit.,* (1881), pp. 307-08, 77. Pp. 340-41, Admiral's observations: G.W. Browne, *Paradise of the Pacific* (Boston, 1900), p. 147. P. 341, Lieutenant's observations: Lucien Young, *The Real Hawaii* (1899), p. 288. P. 342, Hawaiian army: H.W. Nicholson, *From Sword to Share* (London, 1881), pp. 120-24; Stewart, *op. cit.,* pp. 128-29. Pp. 344-45, Drydock: W.R. Furlong, "Pearl Harbor," *Paradise of the Pacific,* December 1943, pp. 7-8. P. 345, Feminine tourist: Isabel Anderson, *op. cit.,* pp. 24-25. P. 346, Missionary heir: William R. Castle, Jr., *Hawaii, Past and Present* (New York: Dodd, Mead, 1913), pp. 62-63. P. 347, Hawaiian Cibralter: *Ibid.,* p. 62. Pp. 349-50, Massie case: *Literary Digest,* January 23, 1932, p. 3; May 14, 1932, pp. 5-6. P. 351, Stirring statement: "Pearl Harbor Attack Hearings," 79th Congress, 2nd Session, Part 18, pp. 3421-27. Pp. 351-52, Danger of starvation: *Thrum's Hawaiian Annual,* 1940, p. 264. Pp. 352-53, Martial law: J.G. Anthony, *Hawaii Under Army Rule* (Stanford: Stanford University Press, 1955), pp. 5, 8. Pp. 354-55, Changes in Hawaii: LaSalle Gilman, "A Year in Retrospect," *Paradise of the Pacific,* December 1942, p. 4. P. 356, Building program: Anthony, *op. cit.,* p. 3.

Chapter XVI. P. 361, Twain's epithets: *Brooklyn Eagle,* February 8, 1873; letter to the *New York Herald Tribune,* January 6, 1873. P. 361, Jarves view: Jarves, "Sketches of Kauai," *Hawaiian Spectator,* January 1838, p. 66. P. 361, Bliss on Waikiki: Bliss, *op. cit.,* pp. 195-203. P. 363, Ellis' tour: Ellis, *op. cit.,* p. 14. P. 364, Bloxam's rapacity: R. Bloxam, "Visit of the *H.M.S. Blonde* in 1825," *Thrum's Hawaiian Annual,* 1924, pp. 66-82. P. 364, Fake idols: Ruschenberger, *op. cit.,* p. 455. Pp. 365-66, Hula dance: J.K. Townsend, *Narrative of a Journey Across the Rocky Mountains to the Colorado River and a Visit to the Sandwich Islands* (Philadelphia, 1839), pp. 214-15. P. 366, Makoa: Ellis, *op. cit.,* p. 86. P. 367, Jarves' guide: Jarves, "Sketches of Kauai," pp. 77-78. P. 367, Kaluna: Bird, *op. cit.,* pp. 86-87. P. 367, Native baggage: *Ibid.,* p. 28. P. 367,

Davies' advice: Davies, *op. cit.*, p. 17. P. 368, Olmsted's voyage: Olmsted, *op. cit.*, p. 217. P. 368, Kilauea: Bird, *op. cit.*, p. 28-31. Pp. 369-70, Night visitors: Stewart, *op. cit.*, pp. 194-95. P. 370, Bolo-Bola's: Bird, *op. cit.*, pp. 91-93. Pp. 370-71, Nordhoff's entertainment: Nordhoff, *op. cit.*, p. 38. P. 371, Honolulu traffic: Hopkins, *op. cit.*, p. 402. P. 371, Change in Honolulu: Rufus Anderson, *op. cit.*, p. 194. P. 372, Hawaiian Hotel: Bird, *op. cit.*, pp. 23-24. P. 373, Bowles' plug: Samuel Bowles, *The Pacific Railroad—Open* (Boston, 1869), pp. 91-92. P. 373, Stoddard's plug: C.W. Stoddard, *Trip to Hawaii* (San Francisco, 1885). P. 374, Whitney's plug: H.M. Whitney, *Tourist's Guide Through the Hawaiian Islands* (Honolulu, 1890), p. 1. P. 374, Colonization: "Great Land Colonization Scheme," *Daily Bulletin,* October 31, 1885. P. 376, Surfing: Castle, *op. cit.*, pp. 23-24. Pp. 378-79, Growth of tourism: G.T. Armitage, "Capitalizing on Hawaii's Climate," *Thrum's Hawaiian Annual,* 1927, p. 81. P. 379, Hula girls: *Thrum's Hawaiian Annual,* 1923, p. 73. Pp. 380-81, European War: *Thrum's Hawaiian Annual,* 1940, p. 355. Pp. 380-81, Editorial: "The Old Order Changeth," *Paradise of the Pacific,* December 1942, p. 1. P. 381, Chairman's prediction: R.A. Anderson, "Watch for Opening Date," *Paradise of the Pacific,* December 1946, pp. 5-7. P. 383, Racial integration: W.F. Kennedy, "The Lure of Honolulu," *Thrum's Hawaiian Annual,* 1927, p. 63.

Chapter Head Illustrations

Preface. Cook's *Voyages,* Vol. III, *op. cit.,* plate 61. Chapter I. *Voyage Pittoresque, Autour du Monde* (Louis Choris). Chapter II. Cook's *Voyages,* Vol. III, *op. cit.,* (John Cleveley). Chapter III. Bingham, *op. cit.* Chapter IV. Olmsted, *op. cit.* Chapter V. Hopkins, *op. cit.* Chapter VI. Bingham, *op. cit.* Chapter VII. E.T. Perkins, *Na Moto* (New York, 1854). Chapter VIII. Wilkes, *op. cit.,* Vol. IV. Chapter IX. *Report of the Expedition of the Venus,* Gide (Paris, 1840) (G. Masselot). Chapter X. Damon, *Koamalu* (J. May Fraser). Chapter XI. Original drawing by Ernst Reichl. Chapter XII. Bird, *op. cit.* Chapters XIII, XIV, XV. Bingham, *op. cit.* Chapter XVI. Hopkins, *op. cit.*

Index